INSIGHT GUIDE

LAOS & CAMBODIA

Discovery CHANNEL

APA PUBLICATIONS
Part of the Langenscheidt Publishing Group

INSIGHT GUIDE
Laos & Cambodia

ABOUT THIS BOOK

Editorial

Editor
Clare Griffiths
Editorial Director
Brian Bell

Distribution

UK & Ireland
GeoCenter International Ltd
The Viables Centre, Harrow Way
Basingstoke, Hants RG22 4BJ
Fax: (44) 1256-817988

United States
Langenscheidt Publishers, Inc.
46–35 54th Road, Maspeth, NY 11378
Fax: (718) 784-0640

Canada
Prologue Inc.
1650 Lionel Bertrand Blvd., Boisbriand
Québec, Canada J7H 1N7
Tel: (450) 434-0306. Fax: (450) 434-2627

Worldwide
Apa Publications GmbH & Co.
Verlag KG (Singapore branch)
38 Joo Koon Road, Singapore 628990
Tel: (65) 865-1600. Fax: (65) 861-6438

Printing

Insight Print Services (Pte) Ltd
38 Joo Koon Road, Singapore 628990
Tel: (65) 865-1600. Fax: (65) 861-6438

©2000 Apa Publications GmbH & Co.
Verlag KG (Singapore branch)
All Rights Reserved

First Edition 2000

This guidebook combines the interests and enthusiasms of two of the world's best known information providers: Insight Guides, whose titles have set the standard for visual travel guides since 1970, and Discovery Channel, the world's premier source of nonfiction television programming.

The editors of Insight Guides provide both practical advice and general understanding about a destination's history, culture, institutions and people. Discovery Channel and its extensive website, www.discovery.com, help millions of viewers explore their world from the comfort of their own home and also encourage them to explore it first hand.

This first edition of *Insight Guide: Laos & Cambodia* is carefully structured to convey an understanding of the two countries and their culture as well as to guide readers through the sights and activities on offer:

◆ The **Features** section, indicated by a yellow bar at the top of each page, covers the history and culture of Laos and Cambodia in a series of informative essays.

◆ The main **Places** section, with a blue bar, is a complete guide to all the sights and areas worth visiting. Places of special interest are coordinated by number with the maps.

◆ The **Travel Tips** section, with an orange bar, provides a handy point of reference for all information on travel.

EXPLORE YOUR WORLD'
Discovery CHANNEL

its environs and also provided the corresponding Travel Tips information. Dakin works as a freelance writer and consultant to the National Tourism Authority of Laos. CPA staffer **Simon Robson** wrote the chapter on Luang Prabang and the essays on geography. He has travelled widely in Southeast Asia, speaks Thai, Lao and French, and has contributed work to numerous magazines and travel books.

The Travel Tips section and much of the Places section research, especially in Cambodia, was completed by CPA's managing director, **David Henley**. Henley, who has lived in Thailand for 15 years, is a professional photographer and his work has been published widely in the international press. He has contributed to Insight publications on Thailand, Laos, Cambodia, Vietnam and Burma (Myanmar).

The greater part of the Features chapters for Laos and Cambodia, as well as the Cambodia Places section, were written by CPA editor **Andrew Forbes**. Forbes has been involved in Southeast Asian studies for a quarter of a century and has travelled widely throughout the region. He has been published in *The Asian Wall Street Journal*, *Far Eastern Economic Review*, *Jane's Defence Weekly* and *The Guardian*.

In conjunction with CPA, the outstanding photographs for the book were provided by **Bill Wassman, Jim Holmes, Joe Cummings, Oliver Hargreave** and **Steve Davey**.

The book was copyedited and proofread by **Laura Hicks**, and indexed by **Elizabeth Cook**.

As always with a new title, we welcome readers' comments and suggestions for future editions.

The contributors

Insight Guide: Laos & Cambodia was edited by **Clare Griffiths**, who lived and worked in the Southeast Asia region for four years and is now a managing editor with Insight Guides in London. Images for the book were selected by a fellow managing editor, **Tom Le Bas**, another long-time Asia resident now living in London.

The majority of the chapters were commissioned from staff of the CPA News Agency in Chiang Mai, Thailand. CPA also provided most of the superb photographs from its extensive regional slide library.

Much of the Places section covering Laos was written by CPA's **Peter Holmshaw**. A 10-year resident of Chiang Mai, Holmshaw speaks Thai/Lao, Chinese, French, and Arabic. **Brett Dakin**, who lives in Vientiane, wrote the chapters on Vientiane and

Map Legend

— ⋅ —	International Boundary
— — — —	Province Boundary
— • —	National Park/Reserve
— — — —	Ferry Route
✈ ✈	Airport: International/Regional
🚌	Bus Station
■	Parking
●	Tourist Information
✉	Post Office
✝ ✝ ✝	Church/Ruins
✝	Monastery
☾	Mosque
✡	Synagogue
🏰 🏛	Castle/Ruins
∴	Archaeological Site
∩	Cave
⚊	Statue/Monument
★	Place of Interest

The main places of interest in the Places section are coordinated by number with a full-colour map (e.g. ❶), and a symbol at the top of every right-hand page tells you where to find the map.

CONTENTS

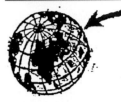

LAOS AND CAMBODIA

Ignored for decades, the two countries are emerging as the most exciting travel destinations in Southeast Asia

Together, Laos and Cambodia form the little-known hinterland of Indochina. In the colonial period they were considered backwaters by the French, who concentrated on exploiting the resources of Vietnam – the third and dominant country in French Indochina, during the long years of warfare that followed independence they were once again considered backwaters, and this view of them continued, though they were hardly forgotten by the military strategists of both sides. Communist Vietnam used the Ho Chi Minh trail through Laos to re-supply its forces in the south, while the United States waged a viciously destructive "Secret War" against the North Vietnamese Army and its Lao allies, the Pathet Lao.

Meanwhile sleepy Cambodia was similarly sucked into the quagmire. Used as a base sanctuary by the Vietnamese Communists, it was secretly – and illegally – carpet-bombed by the US Air Force. The consequences of Communist victory in 1975 were far more terrible for the Cambodians, "liberated" by the auto-genocidal Khmer Rouge, than for the Lao people. Nevertheless, for almost the next two decades, both countries experienced impoverishment and isolation from the outside world.

Nowadays all this is changing fast. Both Laos and Cambodia have opened their doors to the international community and, in particular, to overseas visitors. The governments in both Vientiane and Phnom Penh see tourism and its related industries as a way to increase national development and assure a more prosperous future.

There are other good reasons for linking Laos and Cambodia in a single guidebook. Each carries the scars of the Indochina Wars, and there are areas in both countries that must necessarily still remain off limits until mines and other detritus of past battles have been cleared. Both have a long tradition of Indic culture as well as being culturally related through Theravada Buddhism (*see chapter on Religion in Laos and Cambodia, pages 61–8*) and long years of interaction with neighbouring Thailand. Each is startlingly beautiful, populated by generous and friendly people, and both have benefited from the French culinary tradition – as Cambodia's King Sihanouk once put it: "I am an anti-colonialist, but if one must be colonised it is better to be colonised by gourmets."

Today Laos and Cambodia are free, independent members of ASEAN and stand on the verge of development and prosperity as the 21st century unfolds. There has never been a better time to visit them. ❏

LEFT: Royal Palace Museum, Luang Prabang, Laos.

LAOS

The indigenous culture of Laos, infused with that of its neighbours, has remained unchanged for decades

L aos is an ancient country with a surprisingly sophisticated culture; at the same time, it is simple, easy-going and a great deal of fun to visit. From the 14th century to the 16th century, when the Kingdom of Lan Xang or "One Million Elephants" was at its peak, Laos was one of the most important states in Southeast Asia, and many of the country's religious and cultural traditions date from this period. Subsequently Lan Xang went into decline, and the Lao people found themselves dominated by their more powerful neighbours, most notably Thailand and Vietnam.

Throughout the centuries Laos remained distinctively Lao, however – a society dominated by lowland, wet-rice growing Buddhists closely related to the neighbouring Thai. Yet in the mountains almost 50 percent of the population is still made up of widely varying minority groups, each with its own distinctive and colourful traditions, clothing and world view.

A visit to Laos is, in many ways, a trip back in time. Cultural links with neighbouring Thailand are immediately apparent in the saffron robes of the Buddhist monks, the similarities in temple architecture and the speech of the people – yet Laos is more like the Thailand of 30 years ago. As yet, it has little of the rampant commercialism and vibrant entertainment industry which characterises its neighbour. The waters of the Mekong River which forms the boundary between the two countries may flow past both Lao and Thai banks at the same rate, but the flow of life in the two countries is at two entirely different speeds.

There is another side to Laos, too, which distinguishes the country from Thailand and further enriches an already sophisticated culture, for Laos has benefited from its long association with its other neighbours, at least in terms of architecture and cuisine. Lao food, like Thai, can be delicious, but being able to eat in Chinese and Vietnamese restaurants – the latter are especially numerous – and enjoy excellent coffee, fresh baguettes and croissants and French home cooking are real treats. ❏

PRECEDING PAGES: view from Mount Plu Si, Luang Prabang; ferry across the Mekong River; classroom at a secondary school in southern Laos; Hindu and Buddhist sculptures at Xieng Khuan (Buddha Park) in Vientiane.
LEFT: That Makmo (the Watermelon Stupa) at Wat Wisunalat, Luang Prabang.

Decisive Dates: Laos

THE MISTS OF TIME

3000 BC–AD 1000 Laos and much of the Isaan Plateau is settled by Austro-Tai-speaking peoples, including representatives of the Tai-Kadai and Hmong-Mien subgroups, the ancestors of today's lowland Lao and highland Hmong and Yao.

Populations are not settled, and fixed states have not yet emerged. The basic territorial imperative is southwards, with various peoples and tribes – notably the Tai, Burman and Vietnamese – migrating south into the hills and valleys of

northern Southeast Asia. The Tai peoples, including the Lao, begin to develop a sophisticated wet-rice paddy-based culture. They settle in the valleys and lowlands, leaving the unoccupied hills to later comers.

THE KINGDOM OF A MILLION ELEPHANTS

1200–1300 The Tai peoples acquire sufficient unity to establish nascent states, gradually supplanting the Mon and Khmer peoples.

1353 Fa Ngum founds the Kingdom of Lan Xang, "One Million Elephants", between the Mekong Valley and the Annamite Cordillera, the first clearly discernible Lao state. He becomes king, reigning until 1373; initially almost a vassal of the Khmer

Empire, he develops into a powerful and independent monarch. After marrying a daughter of the Khmer king he conquers Vientiane, Xieng Khuang and finally Luang Prabang, and makes Theravada Buddhism the state religion.

1421–1520 Following the death of Fa Ngum's son and heir, Samsenthai, Lan Xang suffers a hundred years of petty wars and rivalries.

1520 King Phothisarat comes to the throne and reunifies the kingdom, moving the capital to Vientiane to avoid possible attacks by the Siamese, and setting the scene for Lan Xang's greatest years.

1637–94 King Sulinya Vongse presides over the Golden Age of Lan Xang from his capital at Vientiane.

1700 After the death of Sulinya Vongse, Lan Xang begins to break up and be absorbed by its neighbours, including China, Vietnam and Siam.

FRAGMENTATION AND DECLINE

1763–69 Siamese armies conquer northern Laos and temporarily annex Luang Prabang. The Nguyen Dynasty in Vietnam rapidly extends its political control over the middle Mekong region around Vientiane.

1778 The Siamese absorb southern Laos.

1800 The powerful new Chakri Dynasty at Bangkok now controls much of Laos. In 1822 Chao Anuvong of Vientiane attempts to establish Lao independence but is defeated and condemned to death. Siamese armies plunder central Laos; Vientiane is sacked and abandoned.

1885 Laos, as far south as Vientiane, is plundered by bands of Yunnanese Chinese known as Haw in the Haw Wars.

THE COLONIAL INTERLUDE

1893–1907 Unequal colonial treaties forced on Siam lead to French control over all Lao territories east of the Mekong.

1900–39 French colonial policy continues traditional Vietnamese policies east of the Mekong. In Laos, as in Cambodia, Vietnamese settlement is encouraged. Laos remains a colonial backwater, of little economic value.

1939–45 World War II: the Germans conquer France and establish the Vichy regime. The French administration in Indochina backs Vichy and cooperates with Japan. In 1941 Thailand launches an offensive against the weakened French authorities in Laos, taking Sainyabuli and Champasak. The war ends in Laos with a brief

Japanese-inspired declaration of independence, followed by the return of French colonial troops.
1947 Laos becomes a constitutional monarchy, still under French tutelage.
1950 The United States and the United Kingdom recognise Laos as part of the French Union. The pro-communist Pathet Lao rejects this development and forms a government of national resistance with the backing of Ho Chi Minh and the Vietnamese Communists.

LAOS AND THE INDOCHINA WARS

1952 With the support of Hanoi, the Pathet Lao begins a low-scale insurgency in the northeast of the country.
1953 France withdraws, leaving Laos divided between Royalist forces in Vientiane and the leftist Pathet Lao.
1955 Laos is admitted to the United Nations.
1957 Prince Souvanna Phouma leads a coalition government in Vientiane.
1960 Coups and counter-coups rock Vientiane. Pathet Lao insurgency in the north and east of the country increases markedly.
1963 The Communist government of North Vietnam begins extensive use of the Ho Chi Minh Trail in eastern Laos to subvert anti-communist South Vietnam. Covert US military activities begin in Laos.
1973 US troops withdraw from Vietnam, and the CIA "Secret War" in Laos is wound down.
1975 After the Communist victory in Vietnam, the Pathet Lao takes power in December. King Savang Vatthana abdicates. The Lao People's Democratic Republic is established.

THE DEVELOPMENT OF MODERN LAOS

1977 Treaty of friendship and co-operation signed between Laos and Vietnam. Laos tilts towards Comecon and the Soviet bloc. Tension with China and open hostility with Cambodia.
1975–89 Rigid socialist policies introduced; most of the country's intelligentsia and urban middle classes flee. Communist attempts to weaken the popularity of Buddhism do not work. Former King Savang Vatthana and other members of the royal family die in prison camps. Disaffection grows as poverty increases.

LEFT: King Sisavang Vong, installed on the throne by the French in 1946.
RIGHT: patriotic poster painted in the Social Realism style of art, popular in Laos from 1975.

1989–90 Collapse of the Soviet Bloc and general disillusionment with Communist policies lead to economic and political liberalisation.
1992 Death of Lao president and Communist hard-liner Kaysone Phomvihane. Nouhak Phoumsavanh succeeds him.
1992 A slow start is made in restoring individual liberties; Lao émigrés, especially businessmen, are encouraged to return home, and the country begins opening up to tourism.
1994 The "Friendship Bridge" opens across the Mekong, linking Laos and Thailand. Thai cultural and economic influence increases.
1995 Death of "Red Prince" Souphanouvong.

1997 President Nouhak Phoumsavanh makes state visit to Thailand and meets King Bhumibol Adulyadej. Laos is admitted to the Association of Southeast Asian Nations (ASEAN).
1998 Khamtay Siphandone replaces Nouhak Phoumsavanh as president and Sisavath Keobouphanh succeeds Khamtay as prime minister.
1999 Laos continues to move cautiously closer to Thailand as Vietnamese influence gradually diminishes. China exercises considerable influence in the north of the country. Major but controversial hydroelectric schemes are projected and the Japanese Government offers to help the stalled economic reform programme. Declaration of "Visit Laos Year" tourism initiative. ❑

THE KINGDOM OF LAN XANG

The early development of Laos was marked by many internal conflicts. These were not resolved until the 17th-century reign of King Sulinya Vongse

A cademic opinion differs as to the origin of the various Tai-speaking peoples, who include, as well as the Thai, many of the peoples of Laos, including the dominant lowland Lao. It was once fashionable to associate the Tai peoples' move south with the disintegration of the supposed Tai Kingdom of Nan Chao in southern China; other opinions suggest that pressure from Mongol hordes drove them southwards into the fertile ricelands of mainland Southeast Asia. Yet another school of thought – fascinating, though largely discredited – has the Tai moving northwards and inland from an original home in the Pacific.

It is never easy to be precise about the early history of any race: their origins, early movements and way of life are lost in the mists of time. It is now generally accepted, however, that the first Tai peoples lived in southern China, where they had established small statelets, often no larger than a single valley, called *muang*. From around AD 800 these hardy, independent agriculturalists gradually expanded southwards, not in a wave of conquest of already settled land but into hills and valleys as yet unsettled, or only partially, by settled peoples such as the Mon and the Khmer.

Founding two kingdoms

By about 1200 various larger Tai-speaking *muang* were beginning to emerge across a broad belt of land, from the Shan state of Burma (Myanmar) in the west, through the region which is now northern Thailand, to the forest-clad riverine valleys of upper Laos.

The most significant of these "super" *muang* – which can really be classified as kingdoms – were located in the northern part of mainland Southeast Asia. In the east, in an area rather larger than present-day Laos known officially as the Lao People's Democratic Republic – Lao PDR but including most of its territory, the

Kingdom of Lan Xang ("One Million Elephants") – was established in 1353 by King Fa Ngum (1353–73). Further to the west, approximately equivalent to the frontiers of modern northern Thailand, King Mangrai had founded the Kingdom of Lan Na ("One Million Rice Fields") in the late 13th century.

Although it is now considered politically correct to distinguish between the Thai and Lao – especially by the latter, who do not wish to be considered "little brothers" by the Thai – it is by no means certain that such rigid distinctions existed at the founding of Lan Xang. In fact, the first two major Tai *muang* to establish themselves in what are now Laos and north Thailand were destined to be overshadowed by more powerful southern neighbours – Sukhothai, Ayutthaya and eventually Bangkok.

This does not detract from the grandeur of their achievement, however, and although Lan Na eventually became part of Siam (Thailand), the Lao Kingdom of Lan Xang, albeit bruised

LEFT: Lan Xang period Buddha head from Haw Pha Kaew, Vientiane.
RIGHT: illustration of two early indigenous Tai men.

and battered by a series of more powerful neighbours, survives to this day.

Very little is known about the early history of Laos. Indeed, it seems likely that the various Lao *muang* were little more than a series of vassal states of the powerful but declining Khmer Empire further to the south. Boundaries were inevitably less rigid than they are today, and at the height of its power in the 14th century Lan Na included the Lao *muang* of Luang Prabang within its borders. However, times

Fa Ngum and his father were sent to live in exile at Angkor, under the protection of King Jayavarman Paramesvara. Eventually Fa Ngum married one of Jayavarman's daughters, before leading mixed forces of Lao and Khmer northwards to conquer not just Vientiane but also the Phuan region around the Plain of Jars, parts of northeast Thailand, and finally Luang Prabang itself.

Having completed this Chao Fa Ngum felt able to declare himself the first king of Lan Xang, one of the largest kingdoms

LAO BUDDHISM

Fa Ngum made Theravada Buddhism the religion of the new state. The Pha Bang, a golden image of the Buddha from his Khmer neighbours, became the national symbol of the Lao.

changed and, as Lan Na found itself increasingly pressured by the waxing power of Burma (Myanmar), so Lan Xang (Laos) found itself presented with an unexpected opportunity to expand as the Khmer Empire retracted.

Brave new conqueror

In about 1353 a Lao warlord, Chao Fa Ngum, captured the important central Lao town of Vientiane (literally "City of the Moon") with the assistance of 10,000 Khmer troops.

Fa Ngum's early history had been troubled. As a child he had been banished from the court at Luang Prabang because his father, Chao Phi Fa, had seduced one of his own father's wives.

in mainland Southeast Asia, albeit, then as now, a sparsely inhabited one. (It should be noted however, the role played by Khmer mercenary troops in Chao Fa Ngum's empire building – it has been suggested that the first Lao kingdom was in essence a Khmer state.)

Chao Fa Ngum was a conqueror who constantly strove to expand the frontiers of his new state. Within a few years his armies had reached the natural frontier of the Annamite Cordillera, which cuts Laos off from Vietnam to the north and Champa to the south.

Eventually, though, his subjects are said to have grown weary of his endless bid for new territory. In 1373 he was "invited" to retire to the nearby Tai *muang* of Nan, on the frontiers of Lan Na and Lan Xang, where he died peacefully five years later.

Building up a state

Fa Ngum was succeeded by his eldest son, who took the title Phaya Samsenthai ("Lord of Three Hundred Thousand Tai"), a title thought to have derived from a census of adult males living in Lan Xang in 1376. Samsenthai had no hesitation in referring to himself as a Tai lord; only the bitterness and politicking of subsequent centuries would come to mar the relationship between these kindred peoples.

tunately, when he died in 1421 at the age of 60, less competent hands took control. Over the next century no less than 12 rulers succeeded to the throne of Lan Xang. None has left remarkable records or monuments, but at least the kingdom survived – although by the time of the death of King Wisunalat in 1520, Burma (Myanmar), which was already coming to dominate neighbouring Lan Na, was also knocking at the western gateway of Lan Xang.

Rulers and hill people

King Phothisarat, who ascended the throne in 1520, was a different character from his prede-

cessors. Recognising the danger of the advancing Burmese forces, he moved the Lao capital away from Luang Prabang to the less exposed position of Vientiane, on the middle Mekong. He then turned his attentions westwards, subduing Lan Na and placing his son Setthathirat on the throne.

Three years later Setthathirat inherited the throne of Lan Xang, bringing with him the prestigious Pha Kaew (Emerald Buddha). He ordered the building of Wat Pha Kaew to house the new national symbol, and also gave orders for the construction of That Luang, the country's largest and most distinctive *stupa*. Still, apart from these successes, times were

Samsenthai further underscored the ties of blood and culture with the Tai by marrying a Lan Na princess from Chiang Mai and a Siamese princess from Ayutthaya. He then devoted himself to reorganising and strengthening the state administration of Lan Xang, basing it largely on principles already established at Ayutthaya. He built temples and schools, discouraged foreign adventures and devoted himself to building up Lan Xang as a trading nation. In this he was largely successful. Unfor-

LEFT: boat races on the Mekong River.
ABOVE: the Pak Ou caves, discovered it is said, by King Setthathirat in the 16th century.

dangerous; Lan Xang's suppression of all but the broad riverine valleys was tenuous, and many of the hill people were still free, proud men who recognised no lowland authority, whether at Luang Prabang or, more recently, at Vientiane.

In 1571 King Setthathirat disappeared somewhere in the southern mountains on his way back from an expedition to Cambodia. It seems probable that his forces clashed with rebellious highlanders or other mountain people in the wild country east of the Khone Falls, but on the other hand he may have simply fallen into a ravine. The death of Setthathirat began another

quently triumphed over both Buddhist morality and customary law. Accordingly, on assuming the throne at Vientiane, Sulinya Vongse moved fast to secure his position. Aged just 25, he represented the strongest faction at court, and was able to exile one brother to Vietnam and to force another to enter the Buddhist *sangha*. Two cousins who might perhaps have raised rival claims to the throne died soon after. This fortuitous series of events created stability at court, and set Sulinya Vongse on course for his marathon rule.

Comparatively speaking, a good deal is known about Sulinya Vongse's Laos, largely as

downwards cycle for Lan Xang. For 60 years no leader of merit emerged, and this led to long periods of internecine strife and intervention by the forces of Burma.

Only in 1637 did a Lao king worthy of the name once more ascend the throne. His name was Sulinya Vongse, and his 57-year rule – the longest of any Lao monarch – is generally considered the Golden Age of the kingdom.

The Golden Age

There is no doubt that Sulinya Vongse was a wise ruler. The bane of Lao (and Thai) politics had long been that there was no absolute rule of primogeniture, and personal ambition fre-

EARLY TRADING

Gerrit van Wuysthoff waxes lyrical – as does Leria – about the cultural refinements of the Lao capital. But the young Dutchman's eyes were in reality looking elsewhere, as he sought trading opportunities and the fabled "wealth of the Indies". In this context he reports caravans of Yunnanese Haw entering the country from the north, trade by ox across the Annamite Cordillera with Vietnam, and an extensive trade involving pack buffaloes with Ayutthaya and the Chaophraya Valley. Although trade was slow, difficult and potentially dangerous, it was beginning to attract merchants from as far afield as Malaysia, India, Persia and even the Arab World.

a result of the peaceful conditions and relative prosperity that distinguished it. Spared the long years of warfare with Burma and courtly struggles with Ayutthaya, the king was able to spend lavishly on temples and Buddhist endowments and on generally embellishing the capital. As a consequence Vientiane acquired a reputation as a centre of Buddhist learning, attracting novices and devotees from as far afield as Burma, Cambodia and northern Siam.

Foreign visitors

Another invaluable source of information about Sulinya Vongse's capital is the extensive diaries and mission reports of western visitors, who sought to take advantage of the peaceful conditions for once prevailing on the Middle Mekong. Most of the visiting businessmen were Dutch Protestants. A steady flow of Portuguese Catholic missionaries also provides written accounts of the area.

The historian Martin Stuart-Fox has found from these sources that the art and architecture of Vientiane was inspired not only (although mainly) by that of Ayutthaya but also by that of northern Thailand, Cambodia and Burma. Sculpture, he tells us, was highly developed, with both seated and standing 17th century Buddha images showing Siamese stylistic influences yet remaining characteristically Lao. While temples were constructed in brick and stucco, with elaborately sloping, curved and overlapping roofs of gold tiles, secular buildings, excluding the royal palace, were mostly of wood on a brick base.

Both sacred and secular structures were lavishly decorated, and the effect created by the coloured tiles, painted stucco and carved and gilded panels and pillars greatly impressed European visitors.

Perhaps the most interesting contemporary account of Lan Xang at this time comes from Giovanni-Maria Leria, an Italian Jesuit missionary, whose *Relation nouvelle et curieuse du Royaume de Lao* was published in French in 1640. Leria describes Sulinya Vongse's palace, to which he had frequent access, in the following terms: "The royal palace, of which the structure and symmetry are admirable, can

be seen from afar. Truly it is of a prodigious extent, and so large that one would take it for a town, both with respect to its situation and the infinite number of people who live there. The apartment of the king, which is adorned with a superb and magnificent gateway, and a quantity of fine rooms together with a great hall, are all made of incorruptible timber and adorned outside and in with excellent bas reliefs, so delicately gilded that they seem to be plated with gold rather than covered with gold leaf."

Another more personal view of King Sulinya Vongse as a young man is afforded by Gerrit van Wuysthoff, a merchant in the employ of

the Dutch East India Company. Van Wuysthoff travelled to Vientiane from the Cambodian capital at Lovek, reaching the Lao capital on 3 November 1641. After a warm welcome he followed a royal procession, led by the king, from the royal palace to the grounds of That Luang, the most important Buddhist edifice in the city. He reported: "The king is a young man, about 23 years old. Before him marched about 300 soldiers with spears and guns; behind him elephants carried armed men, followed by some groups of musicians. They were followed in turn by 200 soldiers and by 16 elephants carrying the king's five wives (and their ladies in waiting)." ❑

LEFT: an early print of That Luang in Vientiane, the most important national monument in Laos.
RIGHT: a modern image of That Luang.

THE DOMINANCE OF SIAM

After the golden reign of King Sulinya Vongse came to an end,
the kingdom of Lan Xang plunged into a period of fragmentation and decline

King Sulinya Vongse (1637–94) was an absolute monarch who appears to have ruled justly and wisely, despite his remoteness from his people. Certainly his lengthy reign ensured that Laos enjoyed peace and prosperity for most of the 17th century. Nevertheless, two unfortunate developments

combined to weaken Lan Xang; one of these can be blamed on the king, while the other was effectively beyond his control.

Adultery and isolation

Sulinya Vongse may have had many wives, but he only had one son – Chao Rachabut. This royal heir was essential to the continuity of Sulinya Vongse's line, but when Chao Rachabut was found guilty of adultery with the wife of a palace servant the irascible andunbending old king ordered his son's execution. Unfortunately for Lan Xang, this command was carried through despite numerous appeals by palace officials.

The second adverse development was the growing power and influence of coastal states such as Burma (Myanmar), Vietnam and, above all, Siam (Thailand). Laos remained an isolated inland entity, wishing and indeed eager to trade with the advancing western powers but increasingly cut off by its more powerful neighbours, who effectively limited Vientiane's access to foreign trade. The inevitable results were poverty and backwardness.

King Sulinya Vongse eventually died in 1694, leaving two young heirs presumptive, the children of the son he had executed. In an all-too-familiar pattern, no regency was established; the throne was usurped by a powerful minister, who was in turn overthrown six months later. After more than half a century of peace and stability, Lan Xang was fast descending into factionalism and chaos.

Powerful neighbours

On this occasion, however, things were worse than usual. To the east Vietnam had expanded hugely in terms of both power and territory, and the city of Hue, capital of the powerful Nguyen Lords, was shortly destined to become the new capital, replacing Hanoi. To the west and south an even more formidable rival had developed in Ayutthaya – Siam was even being treated on equal diplomatic terms with the court of Versailles. To the north, albeit more remote from the Mekong Valley towns of Luang Prabang and Vientiane, lay the Chinese Empire.

In these circumstances, factionalism at the Lao court was a very bad idea. For instance, if one faction seized power with tacit Siamese support, its rivals would turn to Vietnam for backing. Both Siam and Vietnam encouraged these manoeuvrings. Siam eyed all Lao territories west of the Mekong and considered itself the rightful ruler of Luang Prabang and Vientiane, while Vietnam coveted the Xieng Khuang region of the Plain of Jars, to which it gave a Vietnamese name, Tranh Ninh, to justify its attentions. To use an antiquated but entirely appropriate Thai phrase, Laos without Sulinya

Vongse had become "a bird with two heads" – a weak power paying tribute to two masters, while trying to play one off against the other.

This was a bad time for Laos: the ordinary people mired in poverty, the court divided by petty squabbles, and Siam and Vietnam competing for land, people and tax. An interesting way of assessing tax from this period is as follows: if people lived in stilt houses, ate sticky rice with their fingers and decorated their temples with images of *naga* (like the Siamese), then they were obliged to pay tax to the representatives of Ayutthaya; if, on the other hand, they lived at ground level, ate long-grain rice

former Lan Xang into three petty fiefdoms, centred on Luang Prabang in the north, Vientiane in the centre and Champasak in the south. Meanwhile the Lao Phuan inhabitants of Xiang Khuang continued to be effectively dominated by the Vietnamese. By contrast, in the far north, the various *panna* (small states) of Sipsongpanna, territory far removed from even Luang Prabang, paid tribute to China; the question of their partial incorporation into modern Laos would not arise until the advent of French colonialism at the end of the 19th century.

Laos was, however, saved briefly from the growing weight of Siamese power as Ayutthaya

with chopsticks and decorated their temples with dragons (like the Vietnamese), they had to pay tax to the representatives of Hue. This was a complex if logical statement of the age-old fault line between the Indic and Sinitic traditions along which Laos lies.

Overall, and for obvious geographical reasons, it was the Siamese who tended to be the more powerful of the two overlords. By the beginning of the 18th century Ayutthaya had intervened in the politics of Laos to divide the

---

LEFT: portrait of a Luang Prabang king.
ABOVE: an early painting of Wat Mai Suwannaphumaham at Luang Prabang.

SINGING FOR CONTROL

A popular Viet song of the 18th century illustrated the country's desire for Laos:

Laos encompasses mountains and jungles
The petty prince of Luang Prabang was conniving with Siam ...
The isolated barbarian chief of Xieng Khuang was disturbed
And offered as tribute [to Vietnam] his seven districts ...
The sympathies of Khammuan, Sam Neua and Savannakhet
Gradually surrender to the influence of our country.

itself came under attack from Burma (Myanmar). All across the kingdom, from Nakhon Sri Thammarat and Phuket in the south, to Chiang Mai and even Luang Prabang in the north, the conquering armies of Hsinbyushin took their toll. This time it was the turn of Ayutthaya to suffer destruction. On 7 April 1767 the great Siamese capital fell to the Burmese forces, and thousands of Siamese, including most of the royal family, were carried off to Burma.

Siamese control

Unfortunately for Laos, the Siamese made a truly remarkable recovery. Between about 1775 and 1800 King Taksin and then King Rama I established a Siamese hegemony throughout Siam and Laos as well as the greater part of Cambodia. The Burmese had to fall back on their own devices, and the Vietnamese, at least temporarily, were emasculated. Siamese armies occupied both Vientiane and Champasak in 1779, and a few months later King Surinyavong of Luang Prabang opened the gates of the city to the advancing Siamese. Nor was it just historical Laos that fell so completely under Siamese hegemony – the various Lao-speaking *muang* of the northeast, which now make up the Thai region of Isaan, were brought

STEALING THE PEOPLE

A significant part of the logistics of and motivation for pre-modern warfare in mainland Southeast Asia rested on the acquisition of people rather than territories. This concept, alien to the Europeans, is based on the effect of warfare on a defeated nation. If Siamese armies penetrated into the traditional territory of Lan Xang – as they often did – they were more likely to withdraw with spoils, including much of the population, than to establish permanent bases. Lao prisoners were, in fact, very much in demand. They were seen as a brother people, obedient, and good farmers. This added to the weakness of Lan Xang, plunging it deeper into despair.

fully under Siamese rule for the first time. Henceforth cities such as Si Saket, Ubon Ratchathani, Surin, Roi Et, Mukdahan, Nong Khai and Udon Thani became definitively Siamese, and not Lao, in their political fealty.

Yet, badly defeated though Laos had been, worse was to come. By the beginning of the 19th century three separate Lao kingdoms continued to exist, albeit much curtailed. Separate Lao kings ruled, always under Siamese suzerainty, at Luang Prabang, Champasak and Vientiane. Of these, the first two had lost much of their territory, particularly on the west bank of the Mekong. Vientiane, by contrast, remained a substantial territory. Its major dependencies included Xieng Khuang, Nakhon Phanom, Udon Thani and Mukdahan, the last three extending over much of the Khorat Plateau. Vientiane retained political aspirations, too. The last representative of the once great kingdom of Lan Xang did not intend to go quietly.

Vientiane revolt

The first signs of Vientiane's ambitions occurred in 1792. King Nanthasen reinforced his suzerainty over Xieng Khuang by seizing the Phuan prince and putting him under house arrest in Vientiane. He was only released on promising to pay an annual tribute to Vientiane similar to that already paid to Vietnam. Shortly thereafter Nanthasen's forces surrounded Luang Prabang, eventually taking the town by guile.

Next, in 1796, word reached Bangkok of a plot between Nanthasen and the governor of Nakhon Phanom to throw off Siamese rule. King Rama I, a forceful and active man, moved immediately to curtail the activities of Nanthasen, who was clearly emerging as a potentially rebellious subject. Nanthasen and the governor of Nakhon Phanom were both arrested and escorted to Bangkok. According to some reports, Nanthasen was investigated and found guilty of plotting treason; other reports suggest that he died before he could be put on trial.

In any event, Bangkok thought – mistakenly – that the Vientiane problem had been nipped in the bud, and appointed two new rulers to govern the troublesome province. Rama's choice fell on two of Nanthasen's younger brothers – Inthavong to reign as first king and Anuvong to reign as *uparat*, or second king, in the Siamese fashion – but he soon found that his decision had been unwise.

Inthavong's reign was uneventful and discreet. He did what he could to re-establish Vientiane's sway over Xieng Khuang, but without unduly alarming the Siamese. When he died, in 1804, he was succeeded as a matter of course by his brother, Anuvong. Like both his predecessors, Chao Anuvong was well known at the Siamese court, and apparently both liked and trusted by Rama I and Rama II. For the first 20 years of his reign Anuvong seems to have had no serious problems with Bangkok. He

began his reign in the expected way, by constructing a new palace as well as numerous monasteries, restoring That Luang and generally observing Lao and Buddhist customs. On the other hand – a possible sign of future ambition – he was quick to recognise Gia Long, the first Nguyen emperor at Hue, by sending tribute.

Things changed in 1825, however, when Anuvong, together with the other Lao princes, travelled to Bangkok to witness the funeral ceremonies for Rama II, who had died a year earlier. Relations between Anuvong and Rama III seem to have been poor from the start. Anuvong is said to have felt slighted because Rama III treated

King Manthathurat of Luang Prabang with more respect than the ruler of Vientiane. Rama III also refused to allow a group of Lao exiles who had been forcibly resettled near Saraburi to return to their homes in Vientiane. Anuvong also resented the Siamese King's widespread use of Lao unpaid labour.

War with Siam

Whatever really happened, Anuvong appears to have returned to Vientiane a changed man, determined to throw off Bangkok's authority and re-establish the glories of the former Lao kingdom. He lost no time erecting new defensive works, and called a general council of

LEFT: group portrait of Lao, executed by Louis Delaporte in the mid-18th century.
RIGHT: a wat mural of water carriers.

senior Lao leaders to plan his revolt. It appears that Anuvong felt that Bangkok's power was in decline and the time was right for action. Alas, from a Lao point of view, he was quite wrong. One ally who might have helped him, Vietnam, was not kept fully informed of his plans; another potential ally, Burma, was preoccupied with war with Britain. Not even Luang Prabang could be counted on. The Lao states remained disunited to the end.

Anuvong's plan was to send four armies across the Khorat Plateau to seize Khorat (also known as Nakhon Ratchasima), Ubon Ratchathani and Suvannaphum. He would then

gather up the entire population and take everyone back to Vientiane, leaving an unpopulated wilderness between Bangkok and himself. Perhaps he believed that, should this plan work, undecided *muang* such as Luang Prabang and even Chiang Mai would join his cause.

The campaign began in December 1826, but from the beginning it was apparent that the Siamese were both more numerous and better armed. Despite initial successes – Khorat was seized, as well as numerous smaller towns – the offensive became bogged down, and the Siamese began a swift-moving counterattack.

A story from this time, much loved by the people of Khorat, involves a woman called Khunying Mo, the wife of the deputy governor of that city. The story recounts how the local population was rounded up by Anuvong's men and sent north towards Vientiane. During the march the male prisoners were kept in close captivity, but the women were instructed to act as menials, serving the Lao soldiers their meals and generally "attending to their needs at night". This was to prove the undoing of the Lao army. One of the captive women was Mo, and she arranged with her fellow women captives to encourage the soldiers in drunken revelry. When the festivities were at their height she slipped away and released the male prisoners, who made short work of their drunken foes. Two thousand of the invaders were reportedly slain, beginning a Lao retreat towards Vientiane that soon became a rout. In honour of her bravery Mo was raised to the rank of *khunying* (princess), and to this day the people of Khorat revere her as their local heroine.

The defeat of Anuvong

Anuvong, meanwhile, had fled back across the Mekong but, realising there would be no security in Vientiane from the Siamese armies, he left with his family to seek asylum in Vietnam. Within five days Vientiane was in Siamese hands. Palaces and other buildings were burned and Buddha images were carried off, although monasteries were, by and large, left untouched. Some months later Anuvong returned from Vietnam, apparently in the hope of restoring the status quo, but he was betrayed to the Siamese by Chao Noi, the ruler of Xieng Khuang, whom he had held for four years under house arrest in Vientiane. He was then taken to Bangkok, where he was condemned to death.

With the death of Anuvong the dream of a renewed Lan Xang ended, and a new stamp was put on Siamese-Lao relations which has lasted to the present day, although things now seem to be improving. Siam inherited dominance over the Tai-speaking world, Laos was relegated to an impoverished and greatly reduced state, and much bitterness was generated. It is not without reason that the present-day government of the Lao PDR refers to the war of 1827 as Chao Anuvong's War for Independence, but the official Thai view remains that Anuvong was a rebel troublemaker. ❏

LEFT: the ruins of Wat Pha Keo, Vientiane.

The Red Prince

Souphanouvong, a member of the royal house of Luang Prabang, revolutionary nationalist and founding member of the Lao Communist movement, was born in 1912, one of 23 children sired by the Luang Prabang viceroy, or second king, Boun Khong. As a son of Boun Khong, by his eleventh wife, Souphanouvong automatically acquired the status of a royal prince at birth, as had his elder brothers Phetsarath and Souvanna Phouma, born to the viceroy's first wife, and Souvannarath, born to his ninth wife.

All four sons would go on to play important roles in the government of independent Laos, though public attention focused largely on the political rivalry between two of the half-brothers, Souvanna Phouma and Souphanouvong. The former served as prime minister of the Royal Lao Government on six separate occasions between independence in 1953 and the Communist seizure of power in 1975, whilst the left-leaning Souphanouvong took to the jungle in pursuit of the revolutionary goals which earned him the sobriquet "the Red Prince".

As a young man in Luang Prabang, Souphanouvong studied under French teachers before being enrolled in the Lycée Albert Sarraut in Hanoi – the beginning of a relationship with Vietnam which would last a lifetime. He showed a natural aptitude for languages, becoming fluent in French, Vietnamese and English. After studying in France he returned to Indochina where he married a Vietnamese girl and became involved in the anti-colonial movement, being wounded in fighting with the French at Tha Khaek, on the Mekong, in 1946.

In 1953 the French laid the foundations of the Royal Lao Government which would function under a succession of conservative prime ministers including two of Souphanouvong's royal half-brothers, Souvannarath (1947–48) and Souvanna Phouma (1951–54).

Meanwhile, in 1949, under the guidance of his Vietnamese mentor Ho Chi Minh, Souphanouvong set up the Lao People's Liberation Army, later to become known as the Pathet Lao, in a remote part of Sam Neua Province. By 1951 Pathet Lao forces were controlling one-third of Laos, and the Communist base area in the impregnable limestone caves of Sam Neua and Phongsali was already secured. Souphanouvong had chosen his path, and

with one exception – when he entered a short-lived government of national union headed by his half-brother Souvannaphouma – he remained in opposition, directing the Pathet Lao from Sam Neua and Hanoi.

Souphanouvong did not enter Vientiane again until 1974, by which time the Communist victory throughout Indochina was assured. For 18 months, until the establishment of the Lao PDR in December 1975, Souphanouvong served as head of the National Political Consultative Council. His return to the Lao capital was greeted with great enthusiasm – the Red Prince had retained his popularity through almost 30 years of armed struggle.

Souphanouvong was appointed President of the Lao PDR, a post he retained until the Fourth Party Congress in 1986, when he retired because of ill health. In 1983, on his way to a meeting of the Non-Aligned Movement in Zimbabwe, he had suffered a stroke. His plane landed in the then Soviet Union, where he spent nearly a year in intensive care before returning to Laos. From this time on he made few public appearances. His last official appearance was at the Fifth Party Congress in March 1991, though he continued to see people at his Vientiane home. He died in Vientiane on 9 January 1995. Until the end he remained popular with ordinary Lao people, who referred to their Red Prince as "uncle president". ❏

RIGHT: portrait of Souphanouvong "the Red Prince".

COLONIALISM AND INDEPENDENCE

Intricate power struggles between foreign powers during the early part of the 20th century eventually led to the formation of the Lao PDR in 1975

In the half-century after their conquest of Vientiane the Siamese continued to expand their influence over the Tai and Lao *muang*, from Sipsongpanna in Yunnan to the remote Hua Phan region of Laos, and even to Sipsongchuthai, which today constitutes the westernmost part of North Vietnam. For their part the Vietnamese responded by occupying Xiang Khuang, executing Chao Noi for allegedly betraying Chao Anuvong to the Siamese (*see page 30*), and incorporating the region into Vietnam as the prefecture of Tranh Ninh, under direct Vietnamese rule. As a consequence of the Siamese-Vietnamese struggle for the spoils of the former Lan Xang, the Lao territories east of the Mekong River suffered serious depopulation through forced resettlement in Siam. Xiang Khuang eventually emerged as a joint tributary statelet, though for many years Vietnam continued to hold the upper hand.

The French arrive

And there it might have ended, with Laos effectively partitioned between Siam (Thailand) and Vietnam, but for the arrival of the French in Indochina. The process of colonisation began in 1858 when the French seized the Vietnamese port of Da Nang, which was to become their major naval base in the region.

In 1862 France occupied most of southern Vietnam; by 1863 protectorate status had been imposed on Cambodia, and in 1867 Siam was obliged to accept the new status quo in exchange for the former Cambodian provinces of Battambang and Siem Reap. It was the era of high imperialism and mercantile adventure, and with control of the Lower Mekong France now sought a "river route" to China – a route which led through the very heart of Lan Xang.

A solitary French explorer, Henri Mouhot, had penetrated Laos from Siam as far as Luang Prabang, where he died in 1861. In 1863 a

young Frenchman, Francis Garnier, proposed the idea of a voyage up the Mekong, and in 1865 official approval came from Paris. The expedition, led by Doudart de Lagrée and accompanied by Garnier, set out from Saigon on 5 June 1866. It returned just over two years later, having sailed up the Mekong, marched through Yunnan and sailed down the Yangtze to Shanghai. From a commercial point of view the mission was a complete failure – the "river route" to China was completely blocked by the great Khone Falls on the Lao-Cambodian border – but Garnier did bring back to Europe the first detailed information on Laos since the 17th century, which he published in 1873 in an extraordinary two-volume publication, complete with paintings and engravings, entitled *Voyage d'Exploration en Indochine*.

This remarkable work makes clear the extent of the devastation which 50 years of war had wrought on Laos. Vientiane, in particular, lay mainly in ruins, semi-deserted by its population,

---

LEFT: mural depicting Lao wearing traditional clothing and dancing with Socialist construction in background.
RIGHT: old colonial-style homes in Luang Prabang.

with many buildings overgrown by jungle. In the interests of French imperialism, however, Garnier emphasised the desirability of the region, based on potential mineral and agricultural wealth rather than the disproved possibility of riverine trade. The French, almost without knowing it, were taking a Vietnamese perspective on Indochina.

> ### NATIONAL SYMBOL
>
> Vientiane's symbol of nationhood, the gilded spire of That Luang, was thrown to the ground in a frenzied search for gold by the Haw invaders.

The Haw Wars

However, a further three decades were to pass before the French inherited the Vietnamese will. In Vietnam the "Black Flags" emerged as an anti-French force, and so enjoyed some rather dubious political legitimacy. In Laos, by contrast, the "Red Flags", "Yellow Flags" and "Striped Flags" were bandits pure and simple. With years of fighting experience behind them they swept aside local Lao and Vietnamese forces, easily reaching as far south as Tha Khaek. Luang Prabang was threatened, Vietnamese forces were driven from Xiang Khuang, and most seriously, from a Siamese perspective,

"forward imperative" in Laos as well as Cambodia. In the meantime Laos would have to endure a terrible period of invasion and looting known as "the Haw Wars".

"Haw" is a generic name given by the Tai-speaking peoples to the Chinese of Yunnan and southern China. In the mid-19th century this region was torn apart by the Taiping and Yunnan Muslim Rebellions. As the Qing Empire slowly struggled to reassert itself, defeated rebels fleeing Qing reprisals crossed the borders into Laos and North Vietnam in ever increasing numbers. Armed, ruthless, with nothing to lose, they banded together in so-called "Flag Gangs" which looted and killed at

Vientiane was taken. Everywhere Buddhist temples were sacked.

For Bangkok this situation was intolerable, but defeating the Haw was not going to prove easy. Between 1875 and 1887 Siam's King Chulalongkorn was obliged to order three military expeditions against the Chinese marauders. The first, in 1875, succeeded in expelling the Haw from Vientiane, but failed to achieve its primary objective of defeating them because the Haw pulled back and waited for the Siamese to withdraw, refusing, guerrilla-style, to fight in open battle. Eight years later, faced with a renewed Haw threat to Luang Prabang, the Siamese mounted a second expedition. This was accompanied by James McCarthy, a British surveyor in Siamese government employ, who subsequently described the expedition as "ill-conceived, inadequately planned and ultimately unsuccessful".

The Siamese defence

In 1886, angered by the continuing failure of his forces to dislodge the Haw and alarmed by French advances in Indochina, King Chulalongkorn ordered a third, more ambitious expedition to the region. On this occasion the objective was not merely to defeat the Haw but also to annex to Siam all regions formerly

invaded Tonkin in 1883. Muang Thaeng (better known today by its Vietnamese name, Dien Bien Phu) was taken, and three princes of the Sipsongchuthai ruling family were seized and sent to Luang Prabang as hostages in a bid to ensure the submission of their brother, the White Tai chieftain Kham Hum.

This was the high point of Siam's control in the region. Had Chulalongkorn's bold move succeeded, not only Laos but also a sizeable portion of North Vietnam might have been incorporated within Siam. Kham Hum, however, chose not to submit and, allied with Haw bands, advanced on Luang Prabang, which had

subject to Luang Prabang, together with as much of Sipsongchuthai as possible. This time the Siamese army, together with troops levied from the Lao, succeeded in dispersing the Haw. Chulalongkorn's first territorial objective, Xiang Khuang, was seized, and its rulers were escorted to Bangkok to prevent their appealing to Hue – or, even worse, France – for assistance. Next the Siamese turned their attention to Sipsongchuthai, threatened from the east by a major French expeditionary force which had

LEFT: anti-French colonial painting in the Lao Revolutionary Museum, Vientiane.
ABOVE: French colonialists in Luang Prabang.

been left largely undefended. On 7 June 1887 the Lao royal capital was seized and sacked; the elderly ruler, King Unkham, barely escaped with his life. As luck would have it, he was accompanied by the French vice-consul, Auguste Pavie, from whom he requested formal protection. Six years later, in 1893, this appeal would be used as legal justification for the French annexation of Laos, resulting in Siam's permanent loss of control over the region.

Land of the lotus-eaters

Through a succession of treaties essentially forced on Bangkok by Paris between 1893 and 1907, Siam gradually relinquished control of all territories east of the Mekong, the islands in the great river, and the territories of Sainyabuli and part of Champasak on the west bank. The French Indochinese administration united all former Lao principalities within a single colonial territory which they called "Laos". The word was, in fact, a misnomer which has stuck, since in the Lao language both country and people were and remain simply "Lao".

In 1900 France chose Vientiane as the administrative capital of this newly created entity, and began the establishment of a simple colonial administration. By 1904 a mere 75 French officials were administering the whole of Laos, and

by 1940 no more than 600 French citizens were resident there. Most administrative officials under the new regime were Vietnamese.

In fact, the brief French presence in Laos may be seen as a fleeting interruption of the social and political relationship between the Lao and the Vietnamese, with France representing traditional Vietnamese interests. Initially there were plans for a railway from Da Nang to Tha Khaek, and for extensive Vietnamese migration to farm the under-populated lands of the eastern Mekong Valley. Had these come to fruition, Laos might eventually have become entirely absorbed within Vietnam. But the railway was not built, and the many Vietnamese who settled in Laos chose to do so not as farmers but as city-dwellers: members of the civil service, jewellers, tailors, hairdressers, restaurateurs and so on. By 1945, as a result of this immigration, Viet Kieu (migrant Vietnamese) communities dominated all the major Lao towns except Luang Prabang, accounting for more than 50 percent of the inhabitants of the capital, Vientiane, and as much as 85 percent of the second city, Tha Kaek.

Back in France (as well as in Saigon) Laos would become famous as a land of lotus-eaters, the easiest and reputedly the most dissolute posting east of Suez. But the fact is that at no time did Laos account for more than one per cent of the exports of French Indochina, and by far the most important part of this was opium, which France made a state monopoly.

The lowland Lao mostly accepted the status quo, though they chafed under the pressure of rising Viet immigration, French taxation and French-imposed *corvée* (unpaid labour). What nationalist opposition there was to French rule came mainly from the highlanders and the Vietnamese of the cities, although the concern of the latter was almost exclusively for their homeland, of which they saw both Laos and Cambodia as future appendages. Only a few lowlanders paid any attention to the rise of Vietnamese nationalism, and these were almost exclusively children of the Lao élite studying in Hanoi or Saigon. Communist ideals, similarly, took no root in Laos, Marxists being limited to Viet Kieu followers of Ho Chi Minh who were constantly harassed by French security police. The Indochinese Communist Party was formed, under Vietnamese auspices, but only one ethnic Lao is known to have joined before World War II.

Japan intervenes

The period of "lotus-eating" came to an abrupt end in 1940 with the German defeat of the French in World War II, the establishment of the collaborationist Vichy regime in France, and increasing Japanese interference in Indochina, where the colonial administration supported Vichy.

In 1941, under the military ruler Phibun Songkhram, Thai forces fought a series of battles with French Indochinese troops for control of the Lao territories of Champasak and Sainyabuli on the west bank of the Mekong. Though the struggle was indecisive on land (the

within months Japan had surrendered, and the first French paratroopers had landed in southern Laos.

Free Lao Movement

The French were opposed by Prince Phetsarath, the wartime prime minister, and by the small Lao Issara ("Free Lao") underground movement which had grown up in protest against both French and Japanese rule. For six months, from October 1945 to April 1946, a Lao Issara government, backed by the Viet Minh government of Ho Chi Minh, attempted to set up a functioning administration. A small defence

Thais suffered defeat at sea), Japan intervened and imposed an armistice. As a result of this agreement France ceded all Lao west bank territories to Thailand. The French, though humiliated, were to retain nominal power in Indochina for a further four years, but on 9 March 1945 the Japanese, sensing defeat by the Allied forces, staged a coup against the Vichy administration and forced the pro-French Lao monarch, King Sisavang Vong, to declare independence. Despite this confidence,

LEFT: Lao prince on his way to the temple (*circa* 1910).
ABOVE: the Pathet Lao leadership.

force was set up under Phetsarath's half-brother, Prince Souphanouvong (who later became famous as "the Red Prince"), and negotiations were entered into with the French, but to no avail. In March 1946 French forces moved north. Lao Issara forces, supported by resident Viet Kieu, attempted to make a stand at Tha Khaek but were roundly defeated.

Although Laos was back in French hands by the end of May, within months the restored colonial authority indicated a willingness to concede autonomy. This offer caused the Lao Issara to become hopelessly split. One faction, led by Prince Phetsarath, set up a government in exile in Bangkok; a second faction, led by

Prince Souphanouvong, favoured an alliance with Ho Chi Minh and the Vietnamese Communists; while a third faction, led by Prince Souvanna Phouma, another half-brother, favoured a deal with the French. As a consequence, France proceeded without Lao Issara co-operation, and in 1949 recognised Laos as an "Independent Associate State" of the French Union. This unilateral move caused the break-up of the Lao Issara movement, but one year later Prince Souphanouvong announced the formation of the Neo Lao Issara, or "Free Lao Front" – a pro-Communist organisation later known as the Pathet Lao, or "Land of the Lao".

France, being fully caught up In its punishing war of attrition with the Viet Minh, continued largely to ignore Laos. As a consequence, in 1953, with the decisive battle of Dien Bien Phu looming, Laos was granted full sovereignty and independence as a constitutional monarchy known as the Kingdom of Laos. After the French withdrawal from Indochina in 1954 the United States, anxious to counter rising Communist influence in Laos, began to fill the coffers of the Royal Lao Government in Vientiane. During the same period the Pathet Lao established secure bases in the northeastern provinces of Hua Phan and Phongsali, within easy

Independence and Communism

Souphanouvong was joined in this revolutionary endeavour by the veteran Lao Communists Kaysone Phomvihane and Nouhak Phoumsavanh, and given the full backing of the Viet Minh authorities in Hanoi. The consequence would be some 25 years of armed struggle, during which Laos would become inextricably bound up with the war in Vietnam (*see page 59*), culminating in the establishment of the Lao People's Democratic Republic (Lao PDR) in 1975. For the moment, however, the Pathet Lao remained a tiny force, with their Viet Minh allies doing most of the fighting against France on Lao soil.

supply distance of Hanoi. There followed years of complex political and military manoeuvring, with a Royalist-Pathet Lao coalition in 1957–60, followed by a series of Neutralist and Royalist coups and counter-coups until 1964. From this time on the Pathet Lao refused to participate in any negotiations, believing correctly that it would eventually seize power through military means.

Between 1964 and 1973 the Pathet Lao areas of Laos suffered massive bombing by the United States (*see page 59*) but nevertheless continued inexorably to expand. In 1973, when the US eventually negotiated its way out of direct military involvement in Vietnam, a cease-

ceasefire was negotiated in Laos. This time the Pathet Lao was clearly the dominant party. In 1975 first Phnom Penh then Saigon, fell to the Communists. The writing was on the wall in Vientiane, and a mass exodus of Royalist ministers and generals across the Mekong to Thailand began. The subsequent takeover was bloodless, with the Lao PDR formally established on 2 December 1975.

For the next five years Communist policy was extremely harsh, particularly by the usually relaxed standards of the Lao people. Buddhism was curtailed, links with Thailand were practically cut, and a vicious campaign was mounted against the Hmong minority, many of whom had refused to accept the Lao PDR and lay down their arms. Tens of thousands of people were arrested and sent for "re-education" to camps known as *samana* in the remote northeast. These arrests covered all levels of society, from the prostitutes and pickpockets of Vientiane through small businessmen and landholders to members of the former ruling élite. In 1977 King Savang Vatthana, who had abdicated, joined this group, together with his family; they reportedly died of malnutrition in a remote part of Hua Phan.

New thinking

By 1979 these policies had aroused fierce resentment among the Lao peasantry, the traditional power base of the Pathet Lao. It was also becoming painfully apparent that Communist economic policies were failing to deliver positive results as Laos slumped far behind its rich Thai neighbour. This resulted in perhaps as many as 400,000 people (about 12 percent of the population) taking the relatively easy option of crossing the Mekong to Thailand, where many simply blended in with their fellow ethnic Lao. Laos was losing many of its brightest and best-qualified citizens.

As a result, younger, less hard-line party members, together with non-party members, increased pressure on the old, pro-Vietnamese leadership of the Lao PDR – particularly since Communist economic policies in Vietnam were

---

FAR LEFT: portrait of Lenin on a children's book cover.
LEFT: Nouhak Phoumsavanh (president 1991–97).
ABOVE: King Savang Vatthana, who reigned 1959–76.

> ### RISE OF COMMUNISM
>
> At the time of the 1957 coalition the Communists controlled a mere two of the country's 13 provinces; by 1973 this equation had been almost precisely reversed.

manifestly failing too. In 1989 this led to the introduction of *jintanakan mai*, or "New Thinking", an economic and political liberalisation which in some ways closely paralleled the process of *perestroika* in the former Soviet Union, and went beyond the supposedly parallel process of *doi moi* in Vietnam. During the 1990s this process continued, particularly after the death of the Lao PDR president and the Communist hardliner Kaysone Phomvihane in 1992. Restrictions on individual liberties were slowly lifted, Lao

émigrés (especially businessmen) were encouraged to return home, and the country was gradually opened to tourism. Relations with Thailand have improved dramatically, symbolised by the opening of the "Friendship Bridge" in 1994 and the official visit of President Nouhak Phoumsavanh to Thailand in 1995, when he held a formal meeting with the Thai king. As a direct result of these reforms, the Lao PDR joined ASEAN in 1997.

Today the process of reform is so far advanced that it would be all but impossible to turn the clock back – not that many of the Lao people, enjoying peace and an improved standard of living, would wish to do so. ❑

MOUNTAINS AND RIVERS

Laos is a mountainous land, cut through and bounded by the mighty

Mekong River, and home to many rare and endangered species

Set firmly within tropical Southeast Asia between latitudes 14°N and 23°N, the Lao People's Democratic Republic, as it has been known officially since 1975, covers just over 235,000 sq. km (90700 sq. miles). It shares borders with China and Burma (Myanmar) in the north and northwest, Thailand in the west, Cambodia in the south and Vietnam in the east. The familiarity of the alliterative cliché "landlocked Laos" perhaps disguises the significance of the republic's geographical insularity. It is the only country in Southeast Asia, an area traditionally heavily involved in maritime trade, which doesn't have a coastline. What Laos does have in abundance is mountains and rivers. Over 90 percent of the country lies more than 180 metres (585 ft) above sea level, and around 70 percent comprises mountains and plateaus.

The northern region is more mountainous than the south, and is characterised by rugged mountain ranges cut through by narrow river valleys. Most of these rivers eventually flow into the Mekong (Mae Nam Khong in Lao), which forms Laos' border with Burma (Myanmar) before sweeping inland towards Luang Prabang and then swinging south to Vientiane to form much of the country's southern border with Thailand. Rivers in the far east drain through Vietnam into the Gulf of Tonkin and the South China Sea.

Mountains and plateaus

The country's highest mountains are found in Xieng Khuang province in the central northwest. The landscape is typified by jagged limestone peaks, often severely eroded to form serrated ridges and ranges. Many of the mountains exceed 2,000 metres (6,500 ft) in height, the highest being Phu Bia which reaches 2,820 metres (9,165 ft). Behind that peak is the extensive Xieng Khuang Plateau, the largest such

PRECEDING PAGES: the scenic surroundings of Vang Vieng, renowned for its karst topography.
LEFT: Taat Lo, Bolaven Plateau.
RIGHT: dense forest in Nam Tha Province.

feature in the country, which is principally rolling grasslands rather than a flat plain. Prehistoric stone jar-shaped vessels dot some of the plateau, lending it its popular name, the Plain of Jars (*see page 128*). Most of southern Laos is at a lower elevation than the north, except for the Annamite Cordillera, the principal mountain range, which runs northwest to southeast for half the length of the country, forming much of its border with Vietnam. The cordillera is the watershed between the Mekong and the South China Sea, and extends some 1,100 km (688 miles).

Geologically the range is a complex mix of rock formations. Ancient lava flows have formed several notable plateaus within central and southern Laos: the Khammuan Plateau, in the cordillera's central stretch, is an area of karst peaks, steep valleys and grottoes. Further south the Bolaven Plateau extends for 10,000 sq. km (3,860 sq. miles), although its average elevation is only just over 1,000 metres (3250 ft).

The mighty Mekong

The mountainous terrain of Laos makes much of the country relatively inaccessible and unsuitable for high yield or commercial agriculture. It is no surprise, then, that the country's main population centres are found in the Mekong Valley, and particularly, with the exception of the former royal capital Luang Prabang, in the southerly lowland flood plains. The two biggest cities, the capital Vientiane (pop. 135,000) and Savannakhet (pop. 125,000), which are also the administrative centres of the country's most populous provinces, sit on the banks of the Mekong River.

The Mekong begins its journey 4,350 km (2,720 miles) from the sea, high up on the Tibetan Plateau, before passing through China for half its length. It next forms the Lao border with first Burma (Myanmar) and then Thailand, traverses the Lao interior, turns south, and again marks the Lao–Thai border from Chiang Khan (in Thailand) to just northwest of Pakse, where it once more heads inland before passing into and through Cambodia and Vietnam and finally reaching the South China Sea. It is difficult to overestimate the importance of the Mekong to the Lao people and their country. In addition to depositing fertile alluvial silt in the soils of its flood plain, the Mekong is a major artery of trade and travel and a source of fish, a food beloved of the Lao. The transport infrastructure in Laos is patchy at best, and the river remains a practical means of moving goods and people effectively and efficiently.

The central stretch of the Mekong, from Luang Prabang to slightly north of the Khemmarat rapids in Savannakhet Province, remains navigable all year round, but, despite the fact that the river swells to widths of almost 15 km (9 miles) in the south (around the Si Phan Don area), the upper stretches beyond Luang Prabang can be treacherous and shallow in the dry months, impassable to ships. There has been talk of blasting these areas to afford the river year-round navigability and increase its potential as an international trade route, but there is opposition to such schemes.

Blasting is only one of a number of Mekong projects that have been discussed, most revolving around damming the river to provide irrigation and hydro-electric power. One major dam,

A TROUBLED ECONOMY

Laos remains one of the world's poorer countries, its economy heavily propped up by extensive foreign aid, which currently accounts for 40–50 percent of the annual budget. Important exports include wood, wood products and electricity. Laos is rich in minerals; tin and gypsum are the most important, but copper, gold, iron and zinc also exist. As yet these natural resources remain largely untapped, although several companies are engaged in oil exploration. Secondary manufacturing industry is slowly developing, with some clothing now being exported, but investment is needed in education to increase the skills of the workforce before more sophisticated manufacturing

concerns move in. Some basic products are already produced in local factories, helping to keep imports low.

The best hopes for economic growth lie in the many hydro-electric projects under discussion – despite the environmental concerns surrounding them. Thai, American, French and Australian as well as Lao companies are already pouring money into these developments, secure in the knowledge that the regional market for electricity, particularly in neighbouring Thailand and Vietnam, will continue to grow rapidly. A possible by-product of hydro-electric projects is the fish which can be farmed in the new lakes, for which there would be a ready market.

on the Nam Ngum River was constructed in 1975, flooding an area of 250 sq. km (96 sq. miles) and forming the Ang Nam Ngum Reservoir 90 km (56 miles) north of Vientiane. A hydro-electric power station here generates much of Vientiane's power, and the excess is sold to Thailand. Entrepreneurs are keen to repeat this set-up, but environmentalists worry about both the long-term effects of damming and the logging concessions that are invariably part of such ventures. Thai and Lao firms are involved in underwater logging at Ang Nam Ngum; elsewhere, holders of concessions are operating before dams have been constructed.

provinces of Vientiane and Savannakhet get more rainfall than the north-central provinces of Xieng Khuang and Luang Prabang but substantially less than the southern areas of the Annamite Cordillera.

The great majority of the Lao people live and work in the rural areas. Traditionally the lowland river valleys are inhabited by those who are ethnically Lao – about 50 percent of the population – and they are involved in subsistence wet-rice cultivation, which still accounts for most of the use of valley land. The higher areas are inhabited by other ethnic groups, the members of which grow dry rice as well as

Cultivation and climate

The climate revolves around the annual monsoon cycle, which produces three distinct seasons. The southwest monsoon arrives between May and July and continues until November, bringing most of the year's rainfall. From November to March Laos is dry and relatively cool, catching breezes from the tail end of the northeast monsoon; from March to May temperatures are higher, with little rain. The low-lying Mekong Valley is much warmer and more humid than the more mountainous areas. The

LEFT: dusk falls on the Mekong River.
ABOVE: rice harvesting.

practising slash-and-burn agriculture, and hunting and gathering. Agriculture, albeit at subsistence level, occupies most of the population, although less than 10 percent of the land is suitable for cultivating. Apart from rice, crops include tobacco, wheat, corn, soybeans, fruits, nuts and vegetables in the lowlands, and tobacco, tea, coffee, maize and, of greatest economic importance, opium in the hills.

Ecology

Timber is an important source of revenue, although at great cost to the environment. Areas which 30 years ago were covered in forest, for example the Bolaven Plateau in the far south, today have but a few trees left after irresponsible logging. Efforts have been made to curb the deforestation, including setting up 17 National Biodiversity Conservation Areas (NBCAS), covering just over 10 percent of the land area, but logging continues. Even within the NBCAS concessions are granted, and elsewhere the military runs its own concerns, in breach of all agreements and laws. The revenues are too high for laws to have much effect.

Despite such justifiable worries about logging in various parts of the country, Laos still has one of the most unspoilt ecologies in Southeast Asia. Much of the country is covered with monsoon

forests – unlike rainforests these are characterised by deciduous trees which shed their leaves in dry weather to prevent water loss. The highest canopy of the forests consists of tall thin dipterocarps, often reaching 30 metres (100 ft). Below them are the valuable hardwood trees, including teak and rosewood, and finally, at the lowest level, are smaller trees and grasses. Along river valleys bamboos are particularly prolific.

A few regions have slightly different forest cover, including evergreen and tropical pine. On the plateaus of the Annamite Cordillera, forests give way to savanna. The pristine forests and grasslands of Laos support a diverse array of fauna, some of which have been hunted to

extinction in neighbouring countries while others are found across Southeast Asia. Among endemic mammals are the lesser panda, concolor gibbon and giant barking deer. Several rhinoceroses are reportedly living on the Bolaven Plateau, and elsewhere in the south there have been sightings of kouprey, a rare cattle species.

Quite a few endangered and threatened species of mammal and bird are found in Laos, and many more are increasingly becoming rare. Among endangered species are the Asiatic black bear, the Malayan sun bear, the Asiatic jackal, leopards and tigers, several kinds of deer and cattle, and the freshwater Irawaddy dolphin which can sometimes be seen in the Mekong around the Si Phan Don area in southern Laos.

Several years ago scientists discovered a "new" mammal in the Annamites, the spindle-horn (*nyang* in Lao), a creature described in ancient Chinese writings. There are still a few hundred wild elephants in the forests of Laos, and over a thousand more used for logging and transport. Non-mammalian species include snakes, of which six are venomous (two types of cobra, three of viper, and the banded krait), and many birds, indigenous and migratory.

Prospects for the future

With few controls on hunting, trapping and exporting endangered species, and little public awareness of the value of maintaining biodiversity and the problems involved in species extinction, conservation measures seem unlikely. Laos has been slow to ratify the Convention on International Trade in Endangered Species (CITES), although how much difference this would make is questionable.

Several international companies, Non-Governmental Organisations (NGOs) and local government offices are working on upgrading the road network throughout the country in an attempt to provide a more workable infrastructure for economic development and tourism, and there has also been some economic regionalisation. But increasingly, with improved communications, investors will be looking to develop southern towns, especially those on the Thai border and the cross-country routes to neighbouring Vietnam. ❏

LEFT: forests are being replaced by cash crops such as coffee.
RIGHT: the dok champa is the national flower of Laos.

THE ETHNIC MIX

The population of Laos is a broad ethnic mix, product of an uneasy history,
but past hostilities have given way to mutual co-operation

With fewer than 5 million inhabitants, Laos has one of the lowest population densities in Asia – just over 20 people per sq. km (9 per sq. mile). Outside a handful of relatively large towns in the Mekong Valley, most Lao – around 85 percent – live in rural areas and lead agricultural lives.

In fact, only around 50 percent of the country's population is ethnically Lao, the rest being divided between numerous tribal groups; the methods of classification for these are varied and frequently in disagreement. The ethnic Lao are the traditional inhabitants of the lowland river valleys, typically involved in subsistence wet-rice cultivation, which accounts for most use of valley land. Other ethnic groups tend to live at higher altitudes, practising slash-and-burn agriculture, growing dry rice where appropriate, and hunting and gathering.

Ethnic diversity

By any standards the country is ethnically diverse. The (approximately) half the total population who are ethnic Lao, known locally as Lao Lum, are closely related to the Lao-speaking inhabitants of neighbouring northeast Thailand and, slightly more distantly, to the Thai themselves. These are the people of the Mekong Valley lowlands who predominate in the provinces of Luang Prabang, Vientiane, Tha Kaek, Savannakhet and Pakse, and who have traditionally controlled Lao government and society.

The distinction between Lao and Thai is rather indistinct and something of a new (and politically motivated) phenomenon. Certainly the two groups are part of the same family, something both sides will happily accept – yet the Lao can be irritated by the rather arrogant and frequently stated Thai contention that the Lao are their "little brothers". Of the remaining half of the population, an estimated 20 percent

comprise Lao Tai groups such as the Tai Dam (Black Tai), Tai Daeng (Red Tai) and Tai Khao (White Tai), all ethnic Tai sub-groups. All these groups are closely related to the Lao Lum, but they live higher up in the hills and cultivate dry rice, as opposed to the irrigated rice-paddy culture of the lowland Mekong Valley.

Next there are the Lao Theung, or "approaching the top of the mountain Lao", a loose affiliation of mostly Mon-Khmer people who live halfway up the mountains and are generally animists rather than Buddhists. Formerly known to the ruling Lao Lum by the pejorative term *kha*, or slave, this group constitutes a further 15–20 percent of the population, and makes up by far the most economically disadvantaged section of Lao society.

Finally, on the distant mountaintops live – as might be expected – the Lao Sung, or "High Lao", people whose communities are at altitudes of more than 1,000 metres (3,200 ft) above sea level. Representatives of this group

---

PRECEDING PAGES: early morning mist.
LEFT: Hmong mother and baby.
RIGHT: Akha woman at Muang Sing market.

are also to be found in northern Thailand, north-western Vietnam and southern China, and include Hmong and Mien, together with smaller numbers of Akha, Lisu and Lahu.

This unusual way of classifying the inhabitants of Laos by altitude is both arbitrary and rather unsatisfactory. Nevertheless it has become the established Lao government system, with the additional simplification that Lao Lum and Lao Tai are assimilated for demographic purposes.

In official terms the Lao Lum and Lao Tai constitute 60 percent of the population, the Lao Theung a further 34 percent of the population, and the Lao Sung the remainder. Given the still considerable numbers of Vietnamese and Chinese in the country, however, these figures must be considered applicable only to the "indigenous Lao people". Currently the three major groups, Lao Sung, Lum and Theung, are depicted from left to right on the back of the Lao PDR 1,000 kip bank note.

Laos is also home to sizeable and very significant ethnic Vietnamese (Viet Kieu) and ethnic Chinese (Hua Chiao) communities. Both groups are largely urban based and tend to be involved in commerce. The Vietnamese, in particular, settled in Laos during colonial times,

THE MUSLIMS OF LAOS

Chinese Muslims from Yunnan, known as Chin Haw, once carried on much of the traditional trade in the mountains of Laos. These pioneering caravanners drove their mule trains south to Luang Prabang and beyond. In the late 19th century Haw Wars (*see page 34*) outlaw bands of Haw sacked Vientiane, where they tore the spire off That Luang in search of buried gold. Some Haw Muslims still live in the mountains, where they act as middlemen in the trade between lowlanders and hill people. There is also a small South Asian Muslim community in Vientiane, centred on the Jama' Masjid behind the central Nam Phu fountain. Signs inside the mosque are written in five languages –

Tamil, Urdu, Arabic, Lao and English. The unexpected presence of South Indian Tamil script is a reminder that, in crossing the Mekong, the traveller has traversed not just one of the great rivers of Asia but also one of the great cultural divides of the old European empires. For Jama' Masjid, like the surrounding city and indeed Laos itself, was once part of French Indochina. The unexpected Tamil influence derives from Pondicherry, France's former Tamil toehold on the Indian mainland. Most of Vientiane's South Asian Muslims are businessmen, involved in the manufacturing of textiles, or various branches of import-export, or serving their community, as butchers and restaurateurs.

and were employed by the French authorities as teachers and civil servants and at lower levels of administration.

The ethnic Vietnamese

Relations between Lao and Viet have not always run smoothly. In terms of their traditions the two peoples live on opposite sides of the great cultural fault line that divides mainland Southeast Asia into Indic and Sinitic zones. In geographical terms, too, they are largely divided by the mountainous Annamite Cordillera, which separates the two countries along the ridges of a shared 1,950-km (1,220-

widely divergent Brahmin and Mandarin world views – but they have also been sharpened by practical realities. To begin with, and most importantly, there are a great many more Vietnamese than there are Lao, making the former of necessity an expansionist people.

Fortunately for the Lao, their homeland is protected by the jagged mountains of the Annamite Cordillera, so they have escaped the full weight of Vietnamese expansion.

Instead, the territorial imperative of the Viets has been channelled south, to the former kingdom of Champa, the Mekong Delta and Cambodia. For this reason anti-Vietnamese

mile) border. A number of folk aphorisms exist which supposedly sum up the ethnocentric views which the two peoples have of each other. "Lao and Viet, Cat and Dog" is an old Lao proverb which indicates the difficulties of mutual coexistence, while another old saying claims: "The Viets plant the rice, the Khmers watch them planting, but the Lao listen to the rice grow."

Traditional antagonisms between Lao and Viet may, indeed, be rooted in their disparate cultural godfathers, India and China, and the

LEFT: Akha woman smoking a pipe.
ABOVE: girls of the Hmong ethnic group.

feeling is much stronger in Cambodia than in Laos. Still, an inherent suspicion of their serious, hardworking and disturbingly numerous Viet neighbours runs deep in the psyche of most Lao.

There is no doubt that this suspicion hardened into near certainty with the advent of the French imperialists at the end of the 19th century. The French conquered Indochina from east to west, and almost from the moment of their arrival looked on Laos and Cambodia – then both owing a loose joint allegiance to Bangkok and to Hue – from a Vietnamese perspective. A example of this viewpoint may be found in the writings of the French explorer

Louis de Carné, who travelled through the thinly-populated lands of Laos and Cambodia in 1872 and noted that: "At the sight of a naturally fertile soil, only half-inhabited and half-cultivated... one cannot help thinking of the Vietnamese."

Colonial administration

The French did, of course, think of the Vietnamese when they thought about controlling the area. They were less interested in them as rice farmers to settle the land – though in neighbouring Cambodia they facilitated the settlement of more than 200,000 rice farmers – than

DIVISIVE EDUCATION

Because public services were predominantly staffed by Vietnamese, it was inevitable that the children of Vietnamese immigrants took up many of the available places in secondary education. For example, in the whole of the 1930s only 52 ethnic Lao completed their education at the Lycée Pavie in Vientiane, as against 96 ethnic Vietnamese. Even in 1945 two-thirds of primary and assistant schoolteachers in Laos were Vietnamese. How did the Lao feel about this? Virginia Thompson, a contemporary American observer, commented: "The contempt of the industrious and formalistic [Vietnamese] for the carefree Lao is only matched by the latter's impotent hatred."

as professionals to staff the lower and middle ranks of the Lao bureaucracy. This was partly because the Vietnamese were ambitious and hungry for work, and had long perceived where their destiny lay: in expansion into the relatively empty lands to the west.

But nationalist aspirations apart, cultural considerations militated in favour of the Vietnamese as the French established a colonial bureaucracy in Laos. The Vietnamese, with their long-established Sinitic traditions, were natural bureaucrats, while the Lao – in common with their Indicised Thai brethren to the west and the Cambodians to the south – most decidedly were not.

This totally different approach to life was noticed by Sir John Crawfurd, British ambassador to the courts of Bangkok and Hue in 1821–22. He observed that any action of the slightest importance in public affairs in Vietnam was accompanied by an appropriate written record, whereas in Siam (as Thailand was then called) it was difficult to persuade any government official to write anything at all on any subject.

By contrast with Laos, an efficient postal service existed in pre-colonial Vietnam, with organisational rules and a fairly complex priority system for messages worked out in advance. The Vietnamese administration took regular censuses, right down to village level, maintained landholding records and enforced a systematic military *corvée* (an obligation to provide military service). Above all, there was an efficient official civil service, with advancement within the organisation based on merit and not on influence. In short, for the French in their newly acquired Lao colony, the Vietnamese were a bureaucratic godsend.

During the half century which elapsed between France's acquisition of Laos in 1893 and the subjugation of Indochina by the Japanese, the French actively encouraged the migration of Vietnamese to Laos. These immigrants, who totalled more than 50,000 people by the outbreak of World War II, included technicians, artisans, lower-ranking officials, schoolteachers, doctors, dentists and other professionals. By 1939 the public services of Laos were all largely staffed by Vietnamese, and the urban population, too, was predominantly Viet Kieu. When Laos eventually achieved independence from France, in 1953, the traditional ethnic balance of the country had changed almost beyond recognition. Viet Kieu – migrant Vietnamese settlers – made up 7 percent of the total population, and ethnic Chinese (primarily from Fujian and Guangdong) a further 2–3 percent. In urban terms the contrast was startling: between them the two non-indigenous peoples completely dominated urban Laos, constituting 57 percent of the population of Vientiane (Vietnamese 53 percent, Chinese 4 percent, Lao 42 percent), 89 percent of that of Tha Kaek (Vietnamese 85 percent, Chinese 4 percent, Lao 10 percent) and 85 percent of that of Pakse (Vietnamese 62 percent, Chinese 23 percent, Lao 14 percent).

The language of the cities was Vietnamese or French, and for many years the Lao were even prevented from establishing a vernacular newspaper in case it generated feelings of discontent among its readership.

During the Indochina Wars which followed France's withdrawal, much of the hostility of the Royal Lao Government and the general urban populace towards the Vietnamese stemmed from this colonial experience. It is therefore not surprising that the Viet Kieu population of the Lao Mekong Valley cities came under pressure either to return home to Vietnam, or to cross the river to Thailand where considerable numbers, particularly Roman Catholic Christians, settled in towns such as Sri Chiang Mai and Nakhon Phanom.

By contrast the Chinese, who were involved almost exclusively in trade and had eschewed government service under the French, were generally accepted by the Lao.

Origins of the PDR

Meanwhile, in the mountain fastnesses of Sam Neua and Phongsali, opponents of the Royal Lao regime – dissident Lao, who enjoyed strong links with Vietnam – set up the Lao Issara, or Free Lao, which subsequently became known as the Pathet Lao.

The top leadership – Kaysone Phomvihane, Nouhak Phoumsavanh, the "Red Prince" Souphanouvong and others who were to become founders of the Lao People's Democratic

Republic – were all educated in Vietnam or married to Viets, and spoke fluent Vietnamese. Kaysone himself, who went on to become first president of the Lao PDR (and remained so until his death in 1992), was half Vietnamese.

Given the special links between the Pathet Lao leadership and the Viet Minh, strengthened by 30 years of mutually supportive armed struggle, it was widely expected that, following the Pathet Lao victory and the establishment of the Lao PDR in 1975, Vietnamese migration to Laos would resume in a big way. Such was not the case, however.

After 1975 the relationship between the Lao

PDR and the Socialist Republic of Vietnam was marked more by continuing military co-operation, and the presence in Laos of Vietnamese advisers and specialists at all levels, than by the return of Viet Kieu settlers.

For example, at the height of the Sino-Vietnamese hostilities of the early 1980s, following China's "lesson" to Vietnam, between 50,000 and 80,000 Vietnamese troops were moved into northern Laos to deter further Chinese attack.

Yet as tension declined, both to facilitate improved Sino-Viet relations and in consideration of Lao national feelings, these troop levels were reduced, and by mid-1988 they were as

LEFT: a game of boules (*pétanque*), a legacy of French colonialism.
RIGHT: relations between Laos and Vietnam have not always been harmonious.

low as 15,000. This is not, of course, to deny that some migration – or re-migration – of Vietnamese people to Laos took place during Kaysone Phomvihane's presidency, although it seems to have been more casual than was originally planned.

Nevertheless it is interesting to note that in 1990 – two years before the death of President Kaysone, but at a time when both Thai and Western influence were markedly on the increase in the Lao PDR – a census of Vientiane found 15,000

COSY WITH VIETNAM

The "special relationship" between the governments of Laos and Vietnam was described by the Lao as "closer than the lips and the teeth" and by the Viets as "deeper than the Mekong River".

The ethnic Chinese

Trapped by the arbitrary dictates of geography between larger and more powerful neighbours, Laos has enjoyed little control over its political and economic destiny since the final collapse of Lan Xang, the "Kingdom of One Million Elephants", at the end of the 15th century (*see page 26*). In the elegant language of the old Siamese court, it was "a bird with two heads" – that is, a state obliged to pay tribute to two masters at the same time. Those two powers were

Vietnamese living illegally in the capital. Most of them were promptly deported back to Vietnam. Today a small but flourishing Viet Kieu element survives in Vientiane, although it is rapidly being outnumbered by incoming Thai entrepreneurs and returning Chinese businesspeople.

The hostility of the Lao to the Vietnamese on an ethnic basis has perhaps dulled over the years, yet the failure of Vietnam's socialist economic system has inevitably affected Lao thinking; Thailand, whose economy far outperforms Vietnam's, is now generally regarded as a better model for economic (although not social) development for the Lao PDR.

Siam (Thailand) and Vietnam, rivals who have competed for power and influence in the Middle Mekong Valley for almost a thousand years.

This equation only changed in 1893, with the coming of the French. Using a combination of diplomacy and force, France pushed the Siamese claims to land in Laos back as far as the Mekong River – in some cases even beyond – and fixed the boundaries of the Indochinese countries where they still are today. Equally important, although often overlooked, was the fact that the French expanded the northern frontiers of Laos into regions traditionally controlled by China. In 1896 the French annexed into Laos two southern portions of the Tai Lu principality of Sipsongpanna – literally "the 12,000 rice paddies" – from the Chinese. On a map of Laos the areas in question, Muang Ou (northern Phongsali Province) and Muang Sing (Luang Nam Tha Province), appear as two northern lobes, projecting deep into China's Yunnan Province. The Chinese never forgave or forgot this territorial loss. With this annexation Laos gained a third, and powerful, regional overlord: for almost 100 years China – Imperial, Nationalist and Communist – has done all it can to project and maintain its authority in northwestern Laos. Today, as Thai influence waxes in the centre and south of the

resented by most Lu, as well as by the Chinese authorities. For the next three decades, torn apart by foreign invasion and civil war, China was in no position to pursue border claims in distant Laos. But in 1940, when metropolitan France succumbed to German attack, and Japan subsequently assumed *de facto* primacy in French Indochina (*see page 37*), China was quick to take advantage of French weakness in the region.

In September 1945, following Japan's surrender at the end of World War II, Nationalist troops owing allegiance to Chiang Kai-shek crossed into Laos and advanced as far south as

country and that of Vietnam wanes, northern Laos is emerging as an economic and political fiefdom of China.

At the time of its dismemberment by the French the Tai Lu principality of Sipsongpanna was already strongly influenced by Chinese culture. About two-thirds of the Lu aristocracy were literate in Chinese, and their highly centralised court bureaucracy was based on Confucian principles; as a result the division of Sipsongpanna, and the annexation of Muang Ou and Muang Sing, was deeply

LEFT: body building contest in Vientiane.
ABOVE: playing a game of checkers with bottle tops.

Vientiane, where they rounded up the defeated Japanese. It took the returning French more than a year to persuade the Chinese to leave, and by the time the last KMT detachments withdrew into Yunnan, at the end of 1946, China's claim to special status in north-western Laos had been graphically restated.

Mao takes charge

Predictably, the Communist seizure of power in 1949 made no difference to China's proprietary attitude towards northern Laos; indeed, if anything, Mao's forward policy in the region was firmer than that of the defeated Nationalists had been. From the beginning the Chinese

Communist authorities supported the Viet Minh, and later the Pathet Lao, in their struggle against French colonialism.

After the French defeat at Dien Bien Phu in 1954, and the establishment of an independent Laos, China maintained its special interests in the far north-west, arming and supplying leftist opponents of the Royal Lao Government in Vientiane. This policy reached its zenith during the 1960s and early 1970s.

Following the fall of Saigon in April 1975, and the establishment of Communist rule over Laos in December of the same year, the new Lao authorities did their best to keep on good

terms with both Hanoi and Beijing. Vietnam was undoubtedly the dominant power in Indochina, but China was invited to stay on and to continue road building and other developmental aid in the northwest of the country as far south as Luang Prabang. The Chinese stayed until 1978 when the Laos government was forced to take sides, and they finally asked the Chinese to withdraw.

Return to the status quo

When the mutual hostilities of the early 1980s came to an end in the middle of the decade (*see box*), movement across the Sino-Lao border became increasingly free, and Chinese consumer goods once again became widely available in the northern provinces.

Since that time Beijing has hardly looked back, and today China's political and economic influence over its traditional "fiefdom" in northwestern Laos is once again paramount. The country remains poor, of course, and the contrast between China's Tai Lu autonomous region of Xishuangbanna (as Sipsongpanna is now known) and the Tai Lu principalities detached by the French in 1896 is marked. It is immediately noticeable on the frontier at Ban Boteng: Lao buildings are little more than wooden shacks, while on the Chinese side new concrete buildings sprouting radio aerials form the customs post.

China's comeback

In time, no doubt, the people of northwestern Laos will benefit substantially from the political and economic developments. Certainly standards of living are already rising for the residents of Luang Nam Tha and Bokeo, strategically located between the fast-expanding economies of China and Thailand, as they begin to feel the benefits of free trade. In economic terms the area is rapidly becoming more closely tied to China than it has been at any time since the French annexation in 1896.

In political terms, it seems highly unlikely that Vientiane, preoccupied with the spectre of Thai influence spreading through central Laos, is in a position to do much about limiting Beijing's growing authority in the industrialised north of the country. After a hiatus of more than 100 years, China's primacy in northwestern Laos seems to be on the way back. ❏

ENMITY IN THE EIGHTIES

During the early 1980s relations between Laos and China reached an all-time low. The Lao Communist leader Kaysone Phomvihane publicly accused Beijing of "dark and extremely cruel schemes against Laos", and Beijing responded with a warning that "criminal Vietnamese schemes to intensify their control over Laos will only invite stronger opposition from the Lao people". Many ethnic Han Chinese residents fled Laos during this period, and were eventually resettled on Hainan Island. By the mid-1980s, however, as the hot war between Vietnam and China gradually cooled down, Laos wasted little time in discreetly re-establishing amicable relations with Beijing.

LEFT: elderly man in Phongsali.

The Secret War

For more than 10 years, between 1963 and 1973, Laos was the hidden arena for a "Secret War" that most of the world knew little or nothing about. Under the Geneva Accord of 1962 Laos was officially recognised as a neutral state in which no foreign military personnel might be stationed, but in practice this was ignored by all sides. The greatest violator of Lao neutrality was North Vietnam. The Communists had used northeastern Laos as a springboard for attacks on the French during the First Indochina War and never subsequently withdrew. By 1970 an entire North Vietnamese division – the 316th – was deployed in Laos, fielding a total of more than 75,000 troops. Eastern Laos, too, was criss-crossed with a network of hidden tracks comprising the notorious "Ho Chi Minh Trail" for resupplying Communist units in Cambodia and South Vietnam.

Communist China, too, maintained an area of special interest in the far northwest of Laos, arming and supplying leftist opponents of the Royal Lao Government in Vientiane, not least to offset the predominance of Vietnamese influence over their Pathet Lao allies. This policy reached its zenith during the 1960s and early 1970s, when the People's Liberation Army (PLA) built a network of roads throughout Phongsali and Luang Nam Tha, reaching as far south as Pakbeng on the northern bank of the Mekong in Udomxai Province. This road-building programme owed its origins to an agreement reached between Chou En-lai and the Lao premier Prince Souvanna Phouma at Beijing in January 1962. By the mid-1960s, however, Vientiane could only watch helplessly as the Chinese, without consultation, built roads at whim throughout the far northwest. At the height of the programme as many as 10,000 labourers toiled under the protection of Chinese armed sentries and PLA anti-aircraft units. The Chinese Consulate at Phongsali became the control centre for this emerging fiefdom, which by 1971 was protected against air attack by numerous sophisticated fire-control radar stations.

Meanwhile the USA was equally active. Although it was legally prohibited from intervening in support of the Royalist forces, US "technicians" appeared in Laos as early as 1959 when they began training the Royal Lao Army and building up a Hmong Hill

Tribe army under the leadership of Vang Pao. By 1962 this US-armed secret army had reached a strength of around 10,000, centred on Vang Pao's headquarters at Long Tien in the Plain of Jars. So secret was this US involvement that the name Laos was never used in official communications – the country was known simply as "The Other Theatre", and Long Tien as "Alternate".

Meanwhile, as Laos was torn apart by civil war, involving Vietnamese, Chinese and US-backed forces, the USA resorted increasingly to air power in an attempt to defeat the leftist forces. By 1973 nearly 600,000 sorties had been flown over Laos, dropping an average of one planeload of bombs

every eight minutes, 24 hours a day, for nine years. By the end of the war in 1973, almost two million tonnes of bombs had been dropped on this tiny land-locked country – about half a tonne of explosives for every person in Laos.

And yet it was to no avail. The Hmong Secret Army and Royal Lao forces were consistently out-manoeuvred by the North Vietnamese and their Pathet Lao surrogates. The single most expensive covert paramilitary operation ever conducted by the USA ended in failure with the Communist takeover of Vientiane in December 1975. And yet, despite the bombing, bloodshed and years of brutality on both sides, the US Embassy was shut for just one day! ❑

RIGHT: sitting on a bomb dropped by a US B-52.

RELIGION IN LAOS AND CAMBODIA

Both countries have a strong spiritual base. Buddhism is the major religion, but a significant number of people adhere to other faiths

The dominant religion in both Laos and Cambodia is Buddhism – its followers account for around 65 percent of the population of Laos and 90 percent of the population of Cambodia, although other religions – Islam, Christianity and spirit cults – also flourish. As in Thailand, Burma (Myanmar) and Sri Lanka, the Buddhists are followers of the Theravada system, or "Way of the Elders". In contrast, the Buddhism practised in neighbouring Vietnam, as in China, Korea and Japan (and among the Vietnamese population of Laos), is Mahayana.

Buddhism in Laos and Cambodia

Buddhism is thought to have been introduced to Luang Prabang in the late 13th or early 14th century. The first ruler of the Lao Kingdom of Lan Xang, Fa Ngum, declared Buddhism the state religion, but it took centuries for the faith to spread throughout the lowland Lao inhabitants of the region – indeed to this day spirit cults remain widespread.

While the Communist government made some effort to circumscribe or eliminate Buddhism in the first years after its seizure of power in 1975, all such attempts met with the overt hostility of most Lao people and were soon abandoned. Today the lowland Lao – that is, mainly, the people of the Mekong and other major river valleys – are overwhelmingly Buddhist and generally quite devout.

Buddhism gradually spread throughout Cambodia from the 10th century onwards, receiving a significant boost during the reign of the Buddhist monarch Jayavarman VII (1181–1219). In time it replaced Hinduism as the state religion – although some residual respect for Vishnu and Shiva may still be met. Buddhism, like other religions, suffered badly under the Khmer Rouge, but in Cambodia today it is making a major comeback.

LEFT: Buddhist prayer flags.
RIGHT: Buddha statue in Xieng Khuan (Buddha Park) in Vientiane.

The nature of Buddhism

Theravada Buddhism emphasises personal salvation rather than the way of the *bodhisattva* associated with Mahayana teachings (*see page 64*) – that is, the temporary renunciation of personal salvation in order to help humanity achieve enlightenment.

The goal of the Theravadin is to become an *arhat* or "worthy one" – considered to be one who has travelled the Noble Eightfold Path and, having eliminated the "ten fetters" or erroneous mental conceptions, attained Nirvana.

The ultimate goal of the *arhat* is Nirvana ("self-extinction"). In essence this means an end to corporeal existence and the endless cycle of rebirth. Not many people seriously aspire to become an *arhat* or achieve extinction in this life – that is usually seen as many lifetimes away. Instead, most Theravada Buddhists aim to achieve a better rebirth, which can be done by accruing good *karma* and minimising bad *karma*: in short, by being and doing good.

Spirit cults

Although frowned upon by both the Theravada Buddhist establishment and the Communist government of the Lao PDR, spirit cults have many adherents throughout Laos and remain the dominant non-Buddhist belief system in the country. Essentially, most Lao believe in the existence of spirits or *phii*. These are often locality spirits associated with, for example, trees, rocks, waterfalls, and other natural elements or phenomena.

Spirits should be treated with proper caution and respect. Sometimes they need appeasing. Of special importance are the 32 *khwan* or guardian spirits necessary for good health and mental equilibrium. A common Lao spirit practice is the *basi* eremony which ensures that the 32 *khwan* are all present in a person's body. Belief in spirits is very prevalent among the upland peoples of Laos, notably the Black Tai, while animism and shamanism play central roles in the rites and religious beliefs of the Hmong, Akha and Mien minorities.

The spirit world is also very real to the people of Cambodia. Spirit houses are frequently found in Khmer homes, and tutelary spirits of good, bad and indifferent character are widely believed in and revered across the country. Ani-

mism in Cambodia is generally limited to upland minority peoples – Khmer Loeu – such as the Kuy, Mnong, Brao and Jarai of northeastern Mondulkiri and Ratanakiri, and the Pear and Saoch of the southwestern Cardamom and Elephant Mountains.

Christianity

Christianity, introduced to Indochina by the French, never made much headway among the Buddhist Lao or Khmers. In Laos, Vietnamese converts to Christianity migrated to the large cities, and because of this Christianity in Laos is more closely associated with Vietnamese expatriates than with Europeans or indigenous

RULES FOR A GOOD REBIRTH

Simple ways of achieving a good rebirth are: not taking life, refraining from alcohol, gambling and sexual promiscuity, keeping calm, not getting angry and honouring elderly people. Merit can be gained by giving donations to temples and monks, perhaps by regilding a *stupa* or donating a handful of rice to an itinerant monk.

Above all, honour and respect should be paid to the *tri-ratana*, or "Three Jewels": the Buddha, *sangha* (order of monks) and *dhamma* (sacred teachings). Most men will join the *sangha* and become monks at least once in their lives. Women may also be ordained as nuns, but this decision is often delayed until childraising is complete.

Lao. The former French Roman Catholic cathedral still stands in Vientiane, but these days it is attended by relatively few worshippers.

In Cambodia, too, it was the Vietnamese who were far more open to new religions, and several million became Catholic, so here, too, Christianity is more associated with *Viet Kieu* – expatriate Vietnamese – than with Europeans or Khmers. This is probably why the Khmer Rouge went to the trouble of completely destroying Phnom Penh Cathedral, so that not one brick remained. Today Christian missionaries are once more openly preaching the Gospel, but indigenous Christians – including Vietnamese residents of Cambodia – are unlikely to constitute more than 1 to 2 percent of the population.

Vietnamese and Chinese religions

As has already been mentioned, the ethnic Vietnamese who constitute a significant minority in Laos are mostly Mahayana Buddhists. There are two practising *chua* or Vietnamese temples in Vientiane. The larger of these, Chua Ban Long, is located in a small Vietnamese enclave to the west of Khun Boulom Road and is well worth a visit.

With about a million people, the ethnic Vietnamese constitute the largest ethnic minority in Cambodia, and most are Buddhists. But while Cambodian Buddhists are Theravadins, the Buddhism practised by the Vietnamese, as in Laos, is Mahayana – a distinction which reinforces already deep cultural and social differences between the Khmer and Viet peoples.

But the Vietnamese minority, made up of a wide cross-section of Viet society, includes representatives of all Vietnamese religious persuasions: as well as Buddhists, Confucians and Christians there are followers of such exclusively Vietnamese faiths as Cao Dai and Hoa Hao Buddhism. The Holy See of the Cao Dai is in the Vietnamese province of Tay Ninh, close to the Cambodian frontier, and this extraordinary syncretic religion – which counts Victor Hugo, Laozi and Jesus among its saints – has in some cases bridged the wide Viet–Khmer divide to win Khmer converts.

The Chinese population of Laos are mostly urban dwellers, and their temples are readily visible in the towns. They practise a mixture of Confucianism, Taoism, Mahayana Buddhism and ancestor worship.

Islam

There are almost no ethnic Lao Muslims, but the country does have a small Muslim minority made up of South Asian migrants of Punjabi and Tamil origin. More recently Cham Muslim refugees from Cambodia, victims of the Khmer Rouge reign of terror, have settled in Laos, while small numbers of Muslim Yunnanese or Chin Haw may be found in the north of the

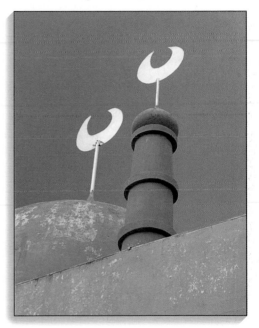

country. There are two mosques in Vientiane; one – the Jama' Masjid – is very central, close to Fountain Circle.

Perhaps surprisingly, Islam is Cambodia's second religion. Nearly all Cambodia's Muslims are ethnic Chams – at around 500,000 people they are the country's largest minority after the Vietnamese. Originally refugees from 18th-century Vietnam, the Chams practise a rather lax form of Sunni Islam: fasting one day a week during the month of Ramadan, abstaining from pork but often drinking alcohol.

Since the time of the Khmer Rouge, when Islam suffered particularly severely, aid in the form of money, assistance in building new

LEFT: the Vietnamese cemetery, Vientiane.
RIGHT: the minaret and dome of the Vientiane Jama' Masjid.

mosques, and the provision of books and educational help from Malaysia and the Middle East is gradually resulting in the establishment of a more orthodox Sunni Muslim tradition.

Mahayana and Theravada

The religious face of both Laos and Cambodia most immediately apparent to the visitor is Theravada Buddhist. Saffron- and orange-robed monks, white-robed nuns, richly ornamented temples with characteristic *chao-fa* eaves reaching to the heavens, alms bowls, *chedis* and *naga* serpents all epitomise the essence of Theravada Buddhism – closely paralleling the Theravada

influx only occurred after the French takeover of Indochina at the end of the 19th century (*see page 54*). The French colonialists employed Vietnamese as petty officials and in professional positions such as school teaching.

As a result, Viet people migrated to Laos in tens of thousands, transforming the demographic base of the country and establishing a series of Vietnamese-dominated towns along the Mekong River from Vientiane to Pakse. Their impact was, and still is, even more noticeable in Cambodia.

What is it that makes Chinese and Vietnamese Buddhism so distinctive, and so easily

establishments in Thailand, Burma (Myanmar) and Sri Lanka.

Yet not far from the surface, in the dragon-ornamented temples of Vientiane's Chinatown, or behind a shopfront in Phnom Penh or Battambang, a parallel Buddhist tradition, the Mahayana, also exists. This is best seen in the Chinese and Vietnamese temples, where the Mahayana Buddhist traditions of Central Asia merge and mingle with Chinese Confucianism, Taoism and the archaic spirit worship that is indigenous to the civilisations of mainland Southeast Asia. Chinese and Vietnamese have been travelling to and settling in Laos and Cambodia from time immemorial, but a sizeable

differentiated from the Lao and Cambodian variants of the Middle Path? The main difference is that the Buddhism of both China and Vietnam belongs to the tradition of the "Greater Vehicle", or Mahayana. This distinguishes it from the Theravada, or "Way of the Elders", variant of Buddhism (described on *page 61*), so called because of its great antiquity – Theravada has existed for around 2,400 years, or as long as Buddhism itself. The Mahayana, by contrast, is regarded as a relative newcomer, having developed in South India a mere 1,900 years ago.

Despite Buddhism's division into two sects, its central tenets are common to both – specifically, the principles contained in the Four Noble Truths and the Eightfold Path, the laws of *karma* and the goal of Nirvana. The differences lie in issues of emphasis and interpretation. Whereas the Theravadin strives to become a worthy one, an *arhat*, ready to attain Nirvana, the Mahayanist ideal is that of the *bodhisattva* – one who is perfected in the necessary virtues of generosity, morality, patience, vigour, concentration and wisdom, but elects voluntarily to stay in this world and help others, rather than entering directly into Nirvana.

Mahayanists consider that Gautama, "the Enlightened", is not a unique deity but just one

is to distinguish it from the Theravada Buddhism practised by ethnic Cambodians in the Mekong delta, known as Tieu Thua or Nam Tong, which translates as "from the south", or from India. The main form of Mahayana practised by Vietnamese is called Thien, or Zen – although the Pure Land school, or Dao Trang, is also widespread, particularly among southern inhabitants.

Ancestor worship, known in Vietnamese as *hieu*, or the ritual expression of filial piety, is also very important and widely practised, alongside other belief systems. Yet even this truly heterogeneous mixture of beliefs is not

of many manifestations of the Buddha. They believe that there are countless Buddhas and Bodhisattvas, "as numberless as the universes to which they minister".

Together with an equally large number of Taoist divinities, these have combined to form a pantheon of deities and demi-gods whose aid and advice can be sought on any issue through invocations and offerings.

To the Vietnamese, Mahayana Buddhism is known as Dai Thua or Bac Tong, literally meaning "from the north", or from China. This

LEFT: outdoor prayer.
ABOVE: offerings of monks' robes and incense.

THE TRIPLE RELIGION

For ethnic Chinese and Vietnamese believers the "Great Vehicle" of Mahayana Buddhism is closely associated with Khong Giao, or Confucianism, an ethical system which originated in China and was based on the teachings of the great moral philosopher Confucius (551–479 BC).

Similarly linked is Taoism, or Lao Giao, founded in China during the sixth century BC by Laozi as a system of speculative philosophy centring on the concept of man's oneness with the universe. As the basic tenets of the three teachings are not in conflict they have practically fused, and are known as Tam Giao, or the Triple Religion.

enough to satisfy the spiritual needs of the eclectic Vietnamese. It may be that the Triple Religion, as it stands, is just too Chinese for Viet tastes. After all, Vietnam's long relationship with the Middle Kingdom has been essentially a love–hate relationship, with greater emphasis on the latter emotion. The Vietnamese, Sinicised though their civilisation may be, are still a Southeast Asian people, so locality spirits, too, must be appeased.

Buddhism in DK

Traditionally Cambodia was considered "the most Buddhist country in Southeast Asia". To

several months as a novice at Wat Botum Vaddei, a monastery near the Royal Palace in Phnom Penh. Buddhism provided a spiritual explanation for existence, a moral code for living and a retreat from mundane concerns when this proved necessary or desirable. Disgraced politicians, or those who had fallen from power, often took refuge in the saffron robe.

All this changed with astonishing swiftness after the Khmer Rouge seized power. In the new society that Democratic Kampuchea (DK) was building there was no room for any spiritual or moral authority other than that of the party. Angkar – the organisation – would

be a Khmer meant being a Buddhist. The three jewels – the Buddha, *sangha*, *dhamma* – were everywhere honoured, if not always followed, and the national religion was omnipresent. From the smallest upcountry village to the heart of Phnom Penh the country was studded with Theravada Buddhist temples and *stupas*. Everywhere, too, were spirit houses – those less orthodox but enduringly popular ancillary manifestations of Southeast Asian Buddhism.

Before the Khmer Rouge seizure of power in 1975, Cambodia had almost 3,000 registered temples, and most Khmer men became monks for at least some part of their lives. For example, in the mid-1930s the young Pol Pot spent

brook no rival in its bid to establish total control over the hearts and minds of the Cambodian people, and this alone would have been enough to seal the fate of Buddhism in Democratic Kampuchea.

Yet apart from the issue of control there were ideological reasons for the Khmer Rouge leadership's determination to stamp out Buddhism. The driving force behind intellectuals in the DK leadership – people like Pol Pot and Ieng Sary – was nothing less than the complete transfor-

ABOVE: children selling incense sticks at Wat Phu, Champasak.
RIGHT: group of monks with begging bowls.

mation of Cambodian society. This goal was to be achieved by blending elements of China's Cultural Revolution with North Korea's *Juche,* or "self reliance", but taking both processes further, and from an exclusively Khmer base.

Pol Pot and his comrades scorned ideas of a simple "great leap forward" and transitional stages to building socialism. Democratic Kampuchea would achieve Communism in a single bound, and that bound would be a "super great leap forward", trebling agricultural production at a stroke.

How could monks possibly fit into such a society? Monks were wandering mendicants, begging for their food and thus permitting others to improve their *karma* through the act of giving. They were prohibited by *dhamma* from working in the fields in case they harmed any living creature – even an insect – which might be crushed underfoot.

Worse still, from a Khmer Rouge viewpoint, monks preached the transience of mundane objectives (such as tripling the harvest, for example), and held the achievement of *nirvana,* or self-extinction, as the ultimate purpose of existence.

Clearly these aims and objectives were at a variance with those of DK intellectuals like Pol

POL POT AND THE PARASITES

Pol Pot wished to build a controlled, collectivised society based primarily on agriculture, in which everyone worked. As monks were forbidden to work in the fields, they were parasites. "The monks are bloodsuckers, they oppress the people, they are imperialists," it was claimed. "Begging for charity... maintains the workers in a downtrodden condition." The people were forbidden to support the *sangha*: "It is forbidden to give anything to those shaven-arses, it would be pure waste"; and, more chillingly: "If any worker secretly takes rice to the monks, we shall set him to planting cabbages. If the cabbages are not fully grown in three days, he will dig his own grave."

Pot and military commanders like Ta Mok. To the Khmer Rouge, monks were nothing more than worthless parasites who – rather like townspeople, only more so – lived free of cost, depending on the labour of the peasantry, contributing nothing to society other than a negative, non-productive superstition. Quite simply, they had to go. And go they did.

Monks in the killing fields

From 1975 – even earlier in those areas that had been under Khmer Rouge control during the civil war – Buddhism was proscribed: it was not merely discouraged, or simply prohibited, but physically expunged. Temples were closed (and sometimes torn down) while resident monks were ordered to take off their robes, don black peasant garb and go to work in the fields. Those who refused were unceremoniously killed.

Khmer Rouge propaganda and slogans from this period provide a telling record of DK attitudes towards Buddhism and the Buddhist establishment. Pol Pot wished to establish a militarised, fiercely nationalistic state, which would be capable of taking back the Mekong Delta from Vietnam and the Khmer-speaking border regions of Surin and Buriram from the Thais. Buddhism abhorred violence, therefore, according to the Khmer Rouge: "The Buddhist

religion is the cause of our country's weakness." During a little more than three years of DK rule, between April 1975 and December 1978 – the terrible time called the "zero years" – the Khmer Rouge set out to disestablish Buddhism completely. Worship, prayer, meditation and religious festivals were forbidden. All Buddha figures, scriptures and other holy objects and relics were desecrated by fire or water, or simply smashed to pieces.

Pali, the theological language of Theravada

ABOVE: placing offerings on the way to the summit of Phu Si.
RIGHT: worshippers at Wat Paeng, Vientiane.

Buddhism, was proscribed. Most temples were turned into storehouses or factories; some were destroyed, others still were converted into prisons and execution centres. Only symbols of past Khmer greatness, such as Angkor Wat, were actively preserved, although many temple buildings in Phnom Penh and the other main cities survived the DK period in varying states of disrepair.

At the same time the brotherhood of monks was forcibly disbanded and almost completely destroyed. The most prominent, most senior and most popular monks, including the abbots of many temples, were simply taken outside and killed – on occasion the DK cadres responsible for such executions would display the saffron robes of the murdered monk on nearby trees for the people to see. Monks who agreed to abandon their robes were forced, against all their principles, to marry. Angkar needed a growing population to fight the hated Vietnamese, so celibacy ran counter to the interests of the revolution.

Slaughter of the Buddhists

Before the Khmer Rouge seizure of power Cambodia supported an estimated 60,000 Buddhist monks. After 44 months of DK rule, in January 1979, fewer than 1,000 remained alive to return to their former monasteries. The rest had died – many murdered outright by the Khmer Rouge, but still more as a result of brutality, starvation and disease.

Only at Wat Ko, the birthplace of Nuon Chea, Pol Pot's shadowy right-hand man and DK's "Brother No 2", was a monastery permitted to remain open. Here four monks – almost certainly the only functioning monks left in the whole of Democratic Kampuchea – received alms from Nuon Chea's mother on an almost daily basis. She disapproved of DK anti-clericalism, and clearly wasn't taking any notice of her doting son.

With the destruction of the DK regime and the expulsion of the Khmer Rouge from Phnom Penh in 1978, a concerted and increasingly successful attempt was made by the new Cambodian authorities to restore the national culture. At the forefront of this movement has been the return of organised religion. Monasteries have been re-opened, prohibitions on making offerings and holding festivals have been lifted, and Cambodian Buddhism is rapidly recovering from the Khmer Rouge onslaught. ❑

THE IMPACT OF SOCIAL REALISM

Lao culture, like that of neighbouring Cambodia, suffered under the Communists.

But traditional art forms have survived and are re-emerging into daily life

The traditional art and culture of Laos are closely related to those of neighbouring Thailand, and especially to those of Thailand's Lao-speaking northeastern provinces. The very close relationship between Lao and Thai culture is immediately apparent to anyone crossing the Mekong River between the two countries. Between 1975 and about 1990, however, a strange phenomenon occurred. Tiny, sleepy, Buddhist Laos became a Communist country, closely influenced by its traditional rival Vietnam and the distant, very different Soviet Union. Since the collapse of the Soviet bloc everything is fast returning to normal, with traditional art forms coming back into vogue and Thai cultural influence resuming its former dominance.

For all that, 15 years of rigid Communist domination and isolation behind the "bamboo curtain" have made a real and fascinating difference to Laos which is unlikely to disappear completely for quite a few years to come. Some of the most interesting aspects of contemporary Lao cultural arts are directly related to the brief period of Communist ascendancy; they are examined here, together with more usual and traditional subjects such as dance, literature and music.

Finally, in fairness to the rulers of the Lao People's Democratic Republic (PDR), it must be said that, while the impact of their Communist beliefs on traditional Lao society produced some very strange hybrid "art and culture", their regime stands in marked and benevolent contrast to that of the Khmer Rouge in neighbouring Democratic Kampuchea (Cambodia), which produced nothing of cultural value whatsoever (*see page 198*).

Literature

The most popular and enduring epic in Lao literature is the *Pha Lak Pha Lam*, the Lao version of the Hindu *Ramayana* (*see page 223*). This classic is thought to have come to Laos about 1,000 years ago when the southern part of the country was dominated by the Hindu Khmer Empire. Also derived from Indian tradition are the *jataka*, the stories of the life cycle of the Buddha, called *saa-tok* in Lao. Traditionally, religious texts and other literature were written by hand on palm leafs.

Music and dance

Traditional Lao music is much less complex than that of Vietnam and Cambodia. When sung it is always memorised, and improvisation is popular. The main Lao instrument is the flute-like *khene* which is made of bamboo. There are two types of orchestra, the *seb gnai* which uses large drums and wind instruments to play religious music, and the *seb noi* which employs *khene*, flutes called *khuy*, a two-stringed instrument called the *so*, and the *nang-nat*, which is a form of xylophone. To this is generally added the music of the *khong vong*, a semi-circular instrument made from cane which carries 16 cymbals around its periphery.

LEFT: retaining the traditional dance through practice.
RIGHT: the *khui*, a traditional flute made from bamboo.

Modern popular Lao music is often based on *khene* music. However, most Lao living in the Mekong Valley tend to tune in to Thai radio stations and watch Thai TV programmes, and in Thailand's Isaan provinces the influence of Thai popular music culture is predictably great.

Lamvong, the Lao equivalent of Thai *ramwong* dancing, is extremely popular. At its best this is performed by graceful female dancers who use their arms and hands to relate stories from the *Ramayana* and other epics. In general, though, *lamvong* may be performed by anyone of either sex at times of happiness, spontaneous parties and festivals.

Architecture

Laos is blessed with a surprisingly rich range of temple styles. The most famous temple in the country is That Luang in Vientiane – effectively the symbol of Lao nationhood (*see page 75*). Most traditional Lao architecture relates directly to Theravada Buddhism, and especially to the country's many *wat*, or temples.

Most typically, a Lao *wat* complex will consist of several structures including a *sim*, or building where *phra* – that is, monks – are ordained; a *haw tai*, or library; *kuti*, or monks' dwelling places; *that*, or stupas; and generally a *haw kawng*, or drum tower.

FOLK THEATRE

Maw lam khuu is a traditional music drama during which a man courts a woman by love songs. The songs involve question and answer "dialogues". By contrast *maw lam dio* is a popular form of folk theatre at present quite often used as a propaganda vehicle for government doctrines, but in the past – and, increasingly, again today – it was used to teach or promote religious concepts. It is always performed by a single person. *Maw lam luang* is a popular and more lighthearted form of Lao musical drama, while *maw lam chot* is a form of folk theatre where two performers of the same sex will either discuss or argue about a particular subject.

The classic temple style of Vientiane differs from that of the north. The *sim* is generally narrower and higher than in the north of the country, and is often distinguished by an elaborately carved wooden screen over the front entrance porch. Figures in such carvings may represent the Buddha or be mythical figures such as the *garuda* (a fierce half-bird, half-human creature who serves as Vishnu's mount) or the *kinnari* (a female creature with a human upper torso but the wings and legs of a bird). The main part of the *sim* is generally made of brick and stucco. Roofs are high-peaked and culminate in characteristic *jao faa* or upward-sweeping hooks.

Luang Prabang temples differ quite markedly in style from those of Vientiane. In historical terms this is logical enough – Vientiane and central Laos have been architecturally influenced by central Thailand, while the north of the country shares cultural and artistic links with the ancient northern Tai Kingdom of Lan Na, now the region around Chiang Mai.

The temples of Luang Prabang are lower and broader than those of Vientiane, with sweeping, multi-tiered roofs. Wat Xieng Thong is probably the best example of the Luang Prabang architectural style anywhere in the country (*see page 116*).

adding to the richness of the architectural heritage of the northern capital – Wat Sop on Thanon Xieng Thong is the best such example.

Contemporary Lao socialist art

With Social Realism established as the sole legitimate art form in both the Soviet Union and Communist China, it followed naturally that the genre was introduced throughout Vietnam following the Communist victory in 1975. The Lao Communists, always strongly influenced by their Vietnamese "elder brothers", had long applied Social Realist standards in their northeastern base in the provinces of Hua Phan

There was once a third Lao temple style, that of the ancient Phuan Kingdom centred on the Plain of Jars. This style – known as Xieng Khuang after the old Phuan capital – resembled the Luang Prabang temple style but with single rather than tiered roofs. Unfortunately the unrestrained bombing of the Plain of Jars during the Vietnam War resulted in the total destruction of all Xieng Khuang temples in their native Phuan region. Fortunately, however, a few still survive in Luang Prabang,

LEFT: Lao dancers performing the *Pha Lak Lha Lam*, the Lao version of the Hindu *Ramayana*.
ABOVE: mural in Social Realism style.

and Phongsali. Following the establishment of the Lao PDR in December 1975 the highly formalised style was extended to the rest of the country as a matter of course – as usual, brooking no rivalry.

In easy-going non-industrialised Buddhist Laos the results of this policy seemed particularly incongruous. Images of heroic peasants shooting down marauding US planes with AK47 assault rifles alternated with images of massively muscled Lao "shock workers" building steel mills for the socialist society. Other unlikely images included, for example, Lao hill tribes demonstrating their unshakeable solidarity with Cuban forces in Angola.

In Eastern Europe and the Soviet Union, following the collapse of Communist power, Social Realism was abandoned almost overnight as people celebrated their new-found cultural freedom. Some countries of the former Soviet Bloc even established museums to house especially lurid examples of totalitarian kitsch. In cautious Laos, by contrast, change has been rather more gradual.

Today militant images celebrating the anti-imperialist struggle have all but disappeared – except from the walls of the People's Museum of the Lao Army, which is, in any case, generally closed to visitors. By contrast, hoardings celebrating the more pacific side of Communist aspirations – mass inoculation campaigns, the construction of heavy industry, and the "bumper harvest" – still exist. A recent and telling change has been the introduction of two previously uncelebrated elements of Lao society: the monk and the businessman. In downtown Vientiane these formerly shunned figures have now joined those stalwarts of Lao Social Realism, the peasant, the soldier and the worker, in hoardings celebrating the achievements of the government. In the Lao PDR the writing is, literally, on the wall – Buddhism and private enterprise are both back in style.   ❑

TEXTILES AND JEWELLERY

Weaving is an ancient and honoured craft throughout Laos, especially among the lowland ethnic Lao. Both silk and cotton fabrics are woven, generally as a cottage craft beneath the stilt houses of villagers by the banks of the Mekong River and along its tributary valleys. Generally patterns comprise repeated geometric shapes, or feature animals and flowers. The most common item manufactured is the traditional *phaa nung*, or tube-skirt, which forms part of the Lao female national dress. Weaving is also practised among upland peoples such as the Hmong and the Mien, and among the Mon-Khmer minorities of the southern uplands.

Gold, jewellery and silverware are all manufactured to a high standard in Laos and are for sale, notably, at Vientiane's *talaat sao* (morning market). The highest standards of craftsmanship are attained by the Lao silversmiths, whose intricate belts complete the traditional costume of Lao women. Fine handbags and other decorative items are also manufactured, as well as equally fine rings, bracelets, necklaces and various vessels. Lao silverware is closely related to that of Chiang Mai; this probably dates from the time when the two independent kingdoms of Lan Na and Lan Xang were neighbours, and their respective courts exchanged cultural gifts and skilled artisans.

That Luang

Pha That Luang, the "Great Sacred Stupa" of Vientiane, is the most important religious edifice in Laos. It also has great spiritual significance for the Lao people, having been considered the symbol of Lao independence and sovereignty ever since it was buillt in the mid-16th century – at that time it was the most distinctive *stupa* of the kingdom of Lan Xang Setthathirat. It is a strange and exotic structure, combining the features of a Buddhist temple with the mundane requirements of a fortress.

According to legend, That Luang was first established in the year 236 of the Buddhist Era, corresponding to 307 BC, when five Lao monks who had been studying in India returned home bearing the breastbone of the Buddha. The five pilgrims persuaded Phaya Chanthaburi Pasithisak, then Lord of Vientiane, to build a *stupa* over the sacred relic "for those who wished to pray and worship". The original structure is said to have been tumulus-shaped and made of stone, with four "flanks", each 10 metres (33 ft) wide, 4 metres (13 ft) thick, and 9 metres (30 ft) high. It is commonly believed that this, the earliest *stupa* at That Luang, is enclosed within the present structure.

The second historic establishment of Pha That Luang was undertaken by King Setthathirat the Great, who consolidated the move of the Lao capital from Luang Prabang to Vientiane begun by his father, King Phothisarat (*see page 23*). Construction of the great *stupa* began in 1566, on the site of the former Khmer temple, and in subsequent years four smaller temples were built at the cardinal points around the central *that.*

In 1641, about 70 years after the completion of Pha That Luang, Vientiane was visited by a representative of the Dutch East India Company, Gerrit-Van Wuysthoff. He was greatly impressed by That Luang, which he described as "an enormous pyramid, the top of which is covered with gold leaf weighing about a thousand pounds". His admiration is especially noteworthy bearing in mind that Wuysthoff was a Protestant businessman who was more interested in making money than in the mores of the Lao.

LEFT: traditional Lao textiles.
RIGHT: the central *stupa* of Pha That Luang, supported by a bowl-shaped base said to represent India's first Buddhist *stupa* at Sanchi.

A less friendly account, penned by the Italian Gian Filippo de Marini and published in French in 1664, purports to see heathen licentiousness at every street corner in Vientiane. Even so, when the author is confronted with That Luang, his style becomes unusually lyrical; he notes that the great central tower "is surrounded by leaves of fine gold, suspended so that they strike against each other in the smallest and most gentle wind, making a harmony so soft and so agreeable that one could easily believe one were listening to a musical concert".

Today the great edifice still retains a very fortress-like appearance. It is surrounded by a high-

walled cloister which is pierced by tiny windows, and access is by way of finely gilded red-lacquer doors which add to the impression of a medieval keep. The narrow, pointed lesser *stupas* surround the main *that.* Close up, the sacred character of the structure is unmistakable because of the abundant religious imagery. *Naga* serpents – those characteristic insignia of Theravada Buddhism – compete for space with gilded figurines of the Buddha and stylised lotus flowers.

Seated on top of a white plinth some 80 metres (260 ft) from the main entrance is a statue of King Setthathirat. Across his knees he holds a long curving sword which is guarding That Luang, the heart of the Lao nation.　❑

SOCIAL REALISM: A REAL-LIFE FANTASY

Laos, the "last frontier" of the Cold War, is an unlikely setting for the imperial twilight of an essentially European art form

The heroic style of Social Realism is rooted in the artistic traditions of late 19th-century Russia. During the 1870s a group of Russian painters known as the Peredvizhniki rejected Classicism for a new type of art that would "serve the common man". After the Bolshevik seizure of power in 1917, revolutionary art emphasised idealised notions such as the withering away of the state and the law. Following the death of Lenin, Stalin ordered a shift away from such fanciful doctrines towards a more conservative model. Under the culture of Stalinism the acceptable face of art was to be traditional in form, aimed at the masses, laudatory of the Party and generally optimistic.

SOCIAL REALISM IN LAOS

Standards first set in the 1930s by Stalin were generally accepted across the Socialist world, from Hanoi to Havana and from Pyongyang to Phnom Penh. From 1975 the government of the Lao PDR has adhered closely to the style. Today, however, the artistic world of Laos is in flux, and Social Realism is having its swansong. Images of heroic struggle are disappearing, whilst Buddhism, businessmen and traditional dance are on the way back. For the present, however, even these new images retain a strong Social Realist influence.

▷ HARD-HAT
A happy, well-fed and clearly well-educated worker brandishes a calliper, not a machine gun, in a modern mural.

▷ BUILDING THE FUTURE
A young schoolgirl gets a lift home in a *samlor*, in the background can be seen a mural celebrating the reconstruction of the Lao capital.

△ DIGGING DEEP
A sturdy peasant breaks the soil in a revolutionary fruit orchard in a painting which aims to increase agricultural production by inspiring rural workers.

△ STAND TOGETHER
This statue celebrates the solidarity between the military and the common people which brought victory over the USA.

▷ HAVE YOUR SAY
Encouraging minority nationalities in Laos to use their right to vote – even though there's only one party to vote for!

KING SISAVANG VONG

Vientiane's monument to Sisavang Vong, king of Laos between 1904 and 1959, husband of 12 wives and father of 24 children, is an artistic enigma. After all, Laos is a Communist country, and statues of past monarchs do not usually survive Marxist revolutions. One explanation may be that the statue was presented by the Soviet Union, which would also explain the portrayal of a traditional monarch in Social Realist style. Another explanation might simply be that this is Laos. Perhaps it is worth remembering that the first Lao revolutionaries in 1945, precursors of the Pathet Lao and of the present government of the Lao PDR, called their nascent nationalist movement Lao pen Lao, or "Laos is Lao". How right they were!

△ **NEW THINKING**
The old-style socialist triumvirate of worker, peasant and soldier is joined by the less traditional figures of monks and businessmen.

▷ **OLD AND NEW**
In this calculated balance of old and new traditions and values, a Lao man and woman dance the traditional *ramvong* in a Social Realist style.

LAO FOOD

The cuisine is similar to that of Thailand and has grown in popularity,

though the country dishes of raw meat may not appeal to all

Lao cuisine, although distinctively and unmistakably "Lao", is by no means confined to Laos. Just across the Mekong River in Northeast Thailand there are perhaps six times as many ethnic Lao as there are in Laos itself, while the number of Lao-speaking inhabitants of Thailand's broad northeast (known as Isaan) flocking to Bangkok means that there are now far more ethnic Lao in the Thai capital than in any other city, Vientiane included. As a consequence Lao cuisine has gained in fame and popularity, being enjoyed throughout Thailand and even having a chain of fast-food restaurants developed to serve it called "Isaan Classic" (unfortunately but amusingly mistransliterated in the English signs that hang outside as "Isn't Classic").

Staple diet

Lao cuisine, like that of neighbouring Southeast Asian countries, revolves around rice. This isn't the long-grain rice that Viets, Central Thai and most Westerners are used to eating, however, but *khao niaw*, or glutinous "sticky rice", deftly rolled into a neat, small ball and eaten with the hand. In Vientiane, as indeed in all other large towns, long-grain rice, or *khao jao*, is readily available, but *khao niaw* remains the basic staple of the Lao people and is the single most distinctive feature of Lao cuisine. Along with it there is another vital ingredient, *paa daek,* a highly pungent fermented fish paste. On the back verandah of virtually every Lao peasant's house you will find an earthenware jar of *pa daek*.

Sticky rice, then, forms the central theme of virtually every Lao meal. It is generally accompanied by a selection of dips, parboiled vegetables, salads, soups and various curried meat or fish dishes. The sticky rice is usually served in a simple but attractive woven bamboo container called a *tip khao*. It's considered bad luck not to replace the lid on top of the *tip khao*

LEFT: keeping the vegetables fresh.
RIGHT: transplanting rice.

at the end of the meal. When Lao go off to work in the fields or elsewhere you will often see hanging at their sides small woven baskets in which they carry supplies of sticky rice and perhaps small amounts of fish or meats which will serve as their mid-day meals. While sticky rice is eaten by hand, long-grain rice is always eaten

with a spoon and fork. Chopsticks are reserved for Chinese-style noodle dishes or for use in Chinese and Vietnamese restaurants.

Lao food is quite similar to Thai food – and indeed identical to much of the food eaten in Thailand's ethnically Lao northeast. Dishes are generally cooked with fresh ingredients that include vegetables, poultry (chicken, duck), pork, beef and water buffalo. Fish and prawns are readily available but are nearly always freshwater, since Laos is a landlocked country relatively far from the sea. Mutton and goat are not eaten except by the country's small South Asian Muslim population, nearly all of whom live in Vientiane. Upcountry, particularly in the north, jungle foods and game are popular – besides wild boar and deer this includes such unlikely animals as pangolin, monitor lizard, civet, wild dog and field rat.

Popular dishes

Popular Lao dishes include *tam som* – really the equivalent of Thai *som tam* – a spicy salad made of sliced green papaya mixed with chilli peppers, garlic, tomatoes, ground peanuts, field crab, lime juice and fish sauce. This is often eaten with sticky rice and *ping kai* (grilled

chicken). Another standby is *laap*, a spicy dish of minced meat, poultry or fish mixed with lime juice, garlic, chilli pepper, onion and mint. Meats and inner parts used in *laap* are finely chopped and spiced with onion, chillies and other herbs such as mint. Lao *laap* is generally cooked, unlike *laap dip* in northern Thailand, but can be raw. If you are concerned about this ask for *laap suk* (cooked *laap*). Many rural Lao prefer *laap seua,* or "tiger *laap*", which is raw chopped meat. Visitors will usually be served cooked *laap*, especially in restaurants.

Other popular Lao dishes include *tom khaa kai* (chicken soup with galingal and coconut milk); *kaeng jeut* (mild soup with minced pork

> ### SOUP STARTER
>
> Soup is considered a necessary part of any Lao meal. Visitors should look out for *kaeng no may,* fresh bamboo shoot soup, and *kaeng het bot,* made with a variety of fresh mushrooms.

and bitter gourd), and *khao laat kaeng*, or curry, served on a bed of *khao jao* long-grain rice – all virtually identical to Thai dishes of the same name served on the other side of the Mekong. Then there is rice vermicelli, or *klao poun.* This is served cold with a variety of raw chopped vegetables, on top of which is placed coconut milk sauce flavoured with meat and chillies. This is considered an auspicious dish at weddings and other celebrations, and is usually a favourite with foreigners. A popular regional dish is *or lam* from Luang Prabang. Lemon grass, dried buffalo meat and skin, chillies and eggplant along with *pa daek* are slowly stewed together, then eaten with crisp-fried pork skin and sweet basil.

For breakfast or a snack Vietnamese *pho* (noodle soup) is extremely popular, as are *yaw jeun* or deep-fried spring rolls. For a variant try *yaw dip* or fresh spring rolls. Vietnamese food is good and plentiful, especially in Vientiane and the larger cities. The same is true of Chinese food, which is generally Cantonese or Hokkienese, though some Yunnanese food is sold in Vientiane. Other popular cuisines available include Thai – just about everywhere – Italian and French (especially in Vientiane and Luang Prabang), and South Asian (only in Vientiane). Laos is an excellent place for breakfast, chiefly because of the French colonial legacy. French bread or *khao jii* is freshly baked each day and served with pâté, fried eggs and omelette. Good coffee is also available; you can start the day with coffee and croissants in the major urban centres, though upcountry the croissants may have to be replaced with *pah thawng ko* or deep-fried Chinese dough sticks.

Country cuisine

Travelling upcountry away from the "big cities"is a rather different experience, and not necessarily to every visitor's liking. Upcountry Lao cuisine is very definitely an acquired taste. Raw meat is common, served with a salad of chopped jungle leaves and herbs, usually washed down with fiery homemade rice whisky. The Australian writer Grant Evans speculates that this preference for raw meat tells us a good deal about Lao society and culture; for example, that most Lao still live near to forests where hunting and gathering of food remains a way of life. When a deer is shot it is carried back to the village; there the whole animal is prepared for *laap*, to be eaten at once, as there are no refrigerators in these areas, and so the family's friends and neighbours come to join in the feasting and drinking. Evans adds that Lao cooked food, even its haute cuisine, differs from Thai food because of the availability of ingredients from the "wild" forest.

Haute cuisine

The *haute cuisine* once served at the royal court of Luang Prabang is world away from the

both the master chef at the royal palace in Luang Prabang and also the Royal Master of Ceremonies. Davidson describes him as a "sort of Lao Leonardo da Vinci… at a court of many and beautiful ceremonies, a physician, architect, choreographer, sculptor, painter and poet". Phia Sing died in 1967; he had been ill for some time and, knowing that his days were numbered, devoted his last years to compiling a detailed account of his experiences as a royal chef, listing 114 recipes in all.

At the time of Phia Sing's death these recipes were collected in two handwritten notebooks in French, but they have since been painstakingly

"peasant food" described above, and it has long been absent from most Lao dining tables. As Laos increases in prosperity, and as tourist demand rises, this distinguished form of cooking is likely to return. Fortunately its secrets have been kept alive in a book published in Lao and English called *Traditional Recipes of Laos*. The author, Chaleunsilp Phia Sing, was born at Luang Prabang in 1898.

According to Alan Davidson, a former British Ambassador to Laos, Phia Sing was

LEFT: dishes made from insects are common in Laos – it is best to eat them without looking.
ABOVE: fried chicken, southern Laos.

translated and annotated. The published work (*see page 335*) concludes: "*Traditional Recipes of Laos* is and will remain a book of unique interest for cooks and scholars. Virtually nothing has been published in the past about Lao foods and cookery, distinctive and fascinating though these are. The recipes are preceded by full information about Lao eating habits, utensils and ingredients. This information is illuminated by 100 drawings, all by Lao artists. Almost all the recipes can be used by anyone with access to Chinese and oriental grocery stores." Clearly this is a book that will be appreciated by any lover of Lao food, as well as being a potential goldmine for the Lao tourist industry.

Fruit and drinks

There is plenty of fruit in Laos, although – as with food in general – the range and quality is much better in the Mekong Valley than upcountry and in the hills. In the appropriate seasons, and especially towards the end of the hot season in May, markets overflow with a wide variety of exotic fruits including mango, papaya, coconut, rambutan, durian, custard apple, guava, mangosteen, starfruit, pineapple, watermelon, jackfruit and bananas.

It is always advisable to drink bottled water in Laos. The traveller should also beware of ice of dubious origin, particularly upcountry or at

street stalls. Soft drinks like cola and lemonade manufactured by internationally known companies are available everywhere, as is canned and bottled beer. International beers to look for are Carlsberg, Heineken, Tiger and Singha; various Chinese beers are available in the north of the country, but the real treat to look out for is the excellent and cheap local product, Beer Lao, which comes both bottled and draught. Imported wine – a reminder of Laos' colonial past – is available in major towns, as (sometimes) is Stolychnaya vodka.

Caution should be exercised with fresh fruit juices and sugar-cane juice, but cartons and cans of fruit juice, milk and drinking yoghurt

are available in supermarkets in Vientiane and Luang Prabang.

Good coffee and tea are generally available throughout the country. Chinese tea is often served free as an accompaniment to meals or with the thick strong Lao coffee.

A Lao recipe

The following example of a popular dish can be made at home:

Lao Chicken Curry
Ingredients to serve four people:

> 1 x 1.5 kg (3 lb) roasting chicken
> 1½ teaspons salt
> 2 cloves garlic, crushed
> 1 tablespoon oil
> 2 medium onions, finely chopped
> 250 g (8 oz) minced meat
> ½ teaspoon salt
> ½ teaspoon ground black pepper
> 1 fresh red chilli, finely chopped
> 1 tablespoon chopped fresh coriander leaf
> coriander powder to taste (a pinch)
> cumin to taste (a pinch)
> ½ cup uncooked rice
> 1 cup thick coconut milk
> 2 cups thin coconut milk

Wash and dry chicken well, then rub it inside and out with salt and half the crushed garlic. Heat oil in frying pan, fry remaining garlic and half the onions with the chopped chicken meat. Season with salt, pepper and chilli. When meat has been fried well add powdered coriander, rice and thick coconut milk. Bring to simmering point, then reduce heat. Chop the remaining onion finely. Put the oil in a saucepan large enough to hold the amount of liquid. Add onion and fry gently for 5 minutes, stirring frequently. Add coriander and cumin and continue to stir for a few minutes. Add thin coconut milk and the mix from the frying pan, together with salt and pepper, then cover saucepan, turn heat very low and allow to cook for 10 minutes, lifting lid and stirring two or three times. Add hot water and bring to the boil. Simmer for 5 minutes. Serve immediately, sprinkled with chopped coriander leaves. ❏

LEFT: watermelon makes a juicy snack.
RIGHT: spice market stalls.

LAOS: PLACES

*A detailed guide to the entire country, with principal sites
clearly cross-referenced by number to the maps*

L aos is often described as a "tiny, land-locked country". True, the population of around 5 million is not large, especially set against that of nearby China and Vietnam, but at 236,800 sq.km (91,430 sq. miles) Laos is almost exactly the same size as the United Kingdom, and has far more spectacular rivers and mountain ranges for the visitor to explore.

The outstanding destination in Laos must be the ancient royal capital of Luang Prabang, set amid beautiful scenery on a bend of the mighty Mekong River. This jewel of a city, now a World Heritage Site, is the most perfectly preserved traditional capital in Southeast Asia. It is difficult to exaggerate the tranquillity of the atmosphere and the exquisite distinction of the architecture in this place. Then there is the modern capital, Vientiane: like Cambodia's capital, Phnom Penh, a hybrid, French-influenced city which contrives to combine the best of both Lao and French architectural traditions.

Winding through the country from north to south, the Mekong River serves as a source of nutrition in the form of fish and provides irrigation for the surrounding rice paddies. It is also a major commercial highway, linking Luang Prabang with Vientiane and the cities of the south – Tha Kaek, Savannakhet and Champasak. Just a few kilometres from the latter are the outstanding remains of Wat Phu, a magnificent Angkor-period Khmer temple set in a spectacular mountain setting. Finally, just before you leave Laos and enter the neighbouring state of Cambodia, the waters of the Mekong spill over the mighty Khone Falls, a series of cataracts carrying the largest volume of water per second in the world – almost twice that of Niagara. ❏

PRECEDING PAGES: Hmong women making and selling traditional textiles; along the banks of the Mekong River, Vientiane.
LEFT: men and working elephant, Luang Prabang.

Laos

Vinh Bac Bo
(Gulf of Tonkin)

Vinh
Dien Chau

C H I N A

V I E T N A M

B U R M A
(MYANMAR)

L A O S

B o k e o

Phu Den Din

Phongsali

Phou Sam Sao

Luang Nam Tha

Udomxai

Sayphu Luang

Xieng Khuang

Hua Phan

Vientiane

Sainyabuli

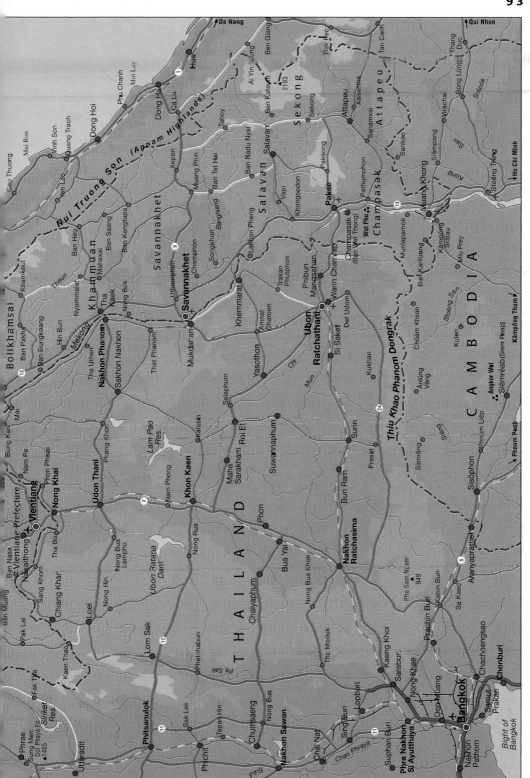

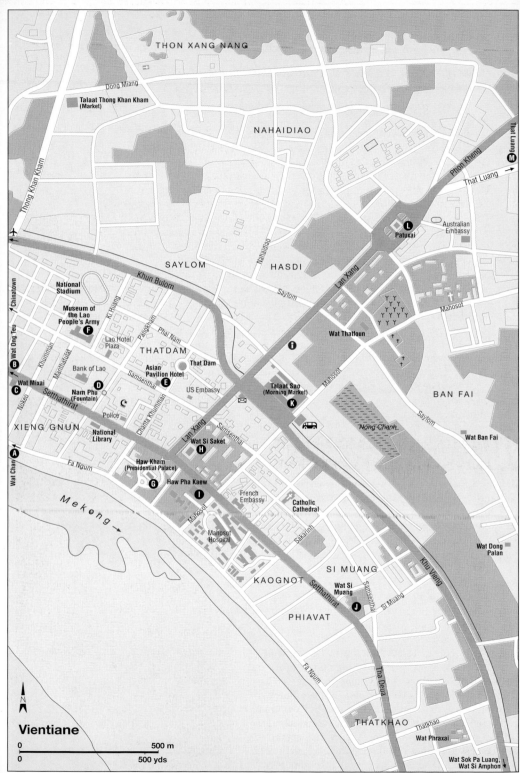

THON XANG NANG

Dong Miang

Talaat Thong Khan Kham
(Market)

NAHAIDIAO

That Luang

Phon Kheng

That Luang

M

SAYLOM

HASDI

Patuxai **L**

Australian
Embassy

Chinatown

Khun Bulom

Lan Xang

Mahosot

National
Stadium

Museum of
the Lao
People's Army **F**

Ki Kuang

Pangkham

Phai Nam

Saylom

Wat Thatfoun

Lao Hotel
Plaza

THATDAM

Manthatulat

Khunman

Bank of Lao

Samsenthai

Asian
Pavilion Hotel **E**

That Dam

t

Wat Ong Teu

B

Wat Mixai

C

D

Nam Phu
(Fountain)

Chanta Khunman

US Embassy

Talaat Sao
(Morning Market) **K**

BAN FAI

Setthathirat

Police

Lan Xang

Samsenthai

Wat Ban Fai

XIENG GNUN

National
Library

Wat Si Saket **H**

Nong Chanh

Fa Ngum

Haw Kham
(Presidential Palace) **G**

Haw Pha Kaew

I

French
Embassy

Catholic
Cathedral

Wat Dong
Palan

Wat Chan

A

Nokeo

Mahosot

Mekong →

Mahosot Hospital

Sakarinh

SI MUANG

Khu Vieng

KAOGNOT

Setthathirat

Wat Si
Muang

Samsenthai

Si Muang

J

PHIAVAT

Fa Ngum

Tha Deua

N

Vientiane

THATKHAO

Thatkhao

Wat Phraxai

0   500 m
0   500 yds

Wat Sok Pa Luang,
Wat Si Amphon ↓

VIENTIANE

The crescent-shaped city is lethargic in comparison with other frenetic Asian capitals and its air of decaying grandeur adds to this relaxed charm

Map on page 94

"**V**ientiane is exceptional, but inconvenient," wrote Paul Theroux in 1975. "The brothels are cleaner than the hotels, marijuana is cheaper than pipe tobacco, and opium easier to find than a cold glass of beer." Though much has changed in Laos since Theroux's romp through Southeast Asia – under the influence of 25 years of Communist rule – Vientiane still retains a bit of its old frontier-town spirit: a city where almost anything goes, but not quite everything works. Until quite recently Vieng Chan (the name "Vientiane" is a French romanised invention) was a city under siege, controlled at various times over the centuries by the Vietnamese, the Siamese, the Burmese and the Khmers – and, more recently, the French and the Americans.

A positive result of all this outside intervention is that the city is now a compelling melange of Lao, Thai, Chinese, Vietnamese, French, American and even Soviet influences in architecture, cuisine and culture. The capital is home to about 10 percent of the country's population but a far larger share of its wealth. As a result of rapid modernisation in recent years, Vientiane today is a far cry from the time immediately after the Second Indochina War, when the author Norman Lewis found that light bulbs only worked occasionally – and never at night. Today not only is electricity reliable but there is also access to the Internet. The streets are crowded with expensive four-wheel-drive vehicles hurtling off to air-conditioned offices, villas and nightclubs.

PRECEDING PAGES: looking west from Phu Si in Luang Prabang. **BELOW:** French architecture in Vientiane.

Downtown Vientiane

Vientiane owed its early prosperity to its founding on the fertile alluvial plains on the banks of the Mekong River – as good a place as any to begin your exploration of the city. Named for the founder of the Kingdom of Lan Xang, **Fa Ngum Road** is a pleasant riverfront boulevard that runs right along the Mekong at the southern edge of the town. Head for the path on top of a newly reinforced dyke – actually the site of the old town wall, built as a line of defence against invading armies and overflowing waters – for a pleasant walk with a view across the river to Thailand. A few outdoor cafés have appeared along the riverfront serving papaya salad, fruit shakes and beer.

A few small streets run through the neighbourhoods between Fa Ngum Road and **Setthathirat Road**, named after the king who consolidated the move of the capital of Lan Xang from Luang Prabang to Vientiane in 1560. **Chao Anou Road** is a reminder of Chao Anuvong, the ruler of the Kingdom of Vientiane from 1805 until 1828. In 1826 Anuvong launched an ill-fated attack on neighbouring Siam which prompted a fierce response that resulted in the obliteration of the city in 1828. The Siamese resettled large numbers

The sim (the place where new monks are ordained) of Wat Mixai is surrounded by a verandah in a style typical of Vientiane temple architecture.

BELOW: rush hour in Vientiane.

of Vientiane residents to Northeastern Thailand (even today there are more ethnic Lao living in Thailand than in Laos), and captured Anuvong, bringing him to Bangkok, where he was condemned to death.

This area of the town is dotted with temples that have been rebuilt after their destruction in the 1828 Siamese invasion. The *sim* of **Wat Chan Ⓐ** (open daily), located at the intersection of Chao Anou and Fa Ngum roads, houses a large bronze seated Buddha that survived the destruction, in addition to a series of beautifully carved wooden panels. **Wat Ong Teu Ⓑ** (open daily), on Setthathirat Road between Chao Anou and François Nginn roads, is named after the large 16th-century "Heavy Buddha" found at the rear of the *sim*. Home to the Buddhist Institute, a school for monks who come from around the country to study here, Wat Ong Teu is one of the most important religious centres in Laos. **Wat Mixai Ⓒ** (open daily), east of Wat Ong Teu on Setthathirat Road, is built in the Bangkok style with a surrounding verandah. Two guardian giants stand at attention outside the heavy gates, and there is a lively elementary school in the grounds. East of Chao Anou Road is **François Nginn Road**, named after a member of the 1885–93 Indochina exploratory mission led by France's Auguste Pavie. Born to Cambodian parents in Phnom Penh in 1856, Nginn studied at the Ecole Coloniale in Paris and took the name François after becoming a naturalised French citizen in 1906. After working as a secretary, guide and interpreter for Pavie – who eventually awarded him the cross of the French Legion of Honour – Nginn entered the colonial government in Laos as an administrative and commercial officer. He then retired to Vientiane and died here in 1916.

Continuing east on Setthathirat Road you will see the former Lao American Center, once a haven for the promotion of American culture in the 1970s, now

the main office of the Lao KPL news agency. Just ahead is **Nam Phu** , the central fountain at the heart of Vientiane's downtown area, built in the late 1960s on the site of an old roofed market. Across the street from Nam Phu, and lined with a row of beautiful frangipani trees (*dok champa*, Laos' national flower), is the **National Library** (open Mon–Fri 8–12am; 1–4pm; Sat 8.30–11.30am; 1–4pm), originally built by the French as a police headquarters. Just off the fountain to the East is the **Jama' Masjid Mosque**, where Muslim worshippers gather daily to hear prayer calls in Arabic, Tamil, Lao and English.

Map on page 94

Lao and Chinese commerce

North of Nam Phu is **Samsenthai Road**, the main route through Vientiane's prosperous commercial district. Just a few years ago this area was a ghost town: most of the shops were shut, as the government had yet to initiate economic reform or to open up Vientiane to foreign influences. Things have changed a good deal since then, and the imposing Thai-owned **Lao Hotel Plaza** is a monument to the city's recent economic growth. The nearby **Asian Pavilion Hotel** , known before 1975 as the Hotel Constellation, was popular with the press corps during the Second Indochina War; journalists sat out the 1960 Battle of Vientiane in the lobby while, outside, 500 people died during the fighting that followed a coup by the Neutralist general Kong Le.

The Constellation's owner, a colonel in the Royal Lao Army, was sent to a re-education camp by the Pathet Lao and the hotel was confiscated in 1975. On his release in 1988 the government returned the hotel and helped him to reopen it as the Vieng Vilay in 1989. It was renovated and renamed again in 1991.

Just northeast of the Asian Pavilion, off Samsenthai Road, is **That Dam**, or

BELOW: the fountain of Nam Phu.

The chest expander used by Kaysone Phomvihane is exhibited in the Museum of the Lao People's Army.

BELOW: the Presidential Palace.

the Black Stupa, which dates to the early Lan Xang period. According to local legend, That Dam is home to a seven-headed dragon that came to life and protected Vientiane residents during the 1828 Siamese invasion. Nearby is the sprawling **American Embassy** complex, once the largest in the world; the embassy remained open even at the height of the Indochina wars and during the Communist takeover in Vientiane.

West on Samsenthai Road, adjacent to the **National Stadium**, is the **Museum of the Lao People's Army** ❻ (open Mon–Fri 8am–1pm and 2–4pm, Sat 8–11.30am; times may vary). Built in 1925, this elegant structure was once the French governor's residence, and was used by the Lao government as an administrative building before being converted into a museum in 1985. The permanent exhibition provides a selective history of Laos' struggle for independence, leaving out major details like the heavy Vietnamese involvement in the "revolution". But it is filled with interesting artefacts from the war, particularly weapons, clothing and supplies of key revolutionary figures.

Continuing west on Samsenthai you will enter Vientiane's **Chinatown** district, home to the city's ethnic Chinese population and one of the capital's most vibrant areas. Filled with Chinese and Vietnamese restaurants, cafés and ice-cream shops, Chinatown also has three grand old cinemas. Unfortunately these "Salles de Spectacles" have been closed for years due to falling business.

North of Chinatown is **Thong Khan Kham Market**, one of the best places in the town to buy traditional Lao baskets and pottery. Laos' **National Circus**, built by the Soviet Union at the height of the Cold War, is located nearby. The national circus troupe offers occasional performances, but even Vientiane residents find it hard to discover when they actually occur.

Map on page 94

Royal and Buddhist headquarters

Heading east from Nam Phu on Setthathirat Road, past a series of restored French colonial villas, you soon arrive at the **Presidential Palace** (Haw Kham) Ⓖ, originally built as the French colonial governor's residence. The French took control of Laos in 1893 and administered the territory directly through the *resident superieur* in Vientiane. After independence King Sisavang Vong and, later, his son Sisavang Vatthana used the palace as a residence when visiting Vientiane from the royal seat in Luang Prabang. It is now used for hosting foreign guests of the Lao government and for meetings of the presidential cabinet – the president himself does not live here.

Just east on Setthathirat Road, and across the street from the Presidential Palace, is **Wat Si Saket** Ⓗ (open daily), built in 1818 by Chao Anuvong. A vassal of the Siamese, he designed the temple in early Bangkok style; perhaps this is why it was left relatively untouched when the Siamese destroyed the city in 1828. Wat Si Saket is probably the oldest original temple in Vientiane – all the others were either constructed after this one or were rebuilt after the invasion.

The interior walls of the cloister surrounding the central *sim* of Wat Si Saket are filled with small niches containing more than 2,000 miniature silver and ceramic Buddha images, most of them made in Vientiane between the 16th and 19th centuries. On the western side of the cloister is a pile of broken and melted-down images, relics of the 1828 war. Behind the *sim* is a long wooden trough resembling a *naga*, or river-snake spirit, used during the Lao New Year celebrations to pour cleansing water over the temple's Buddha images. To the left of the *sim* is a raised Burmese-style structure that was once a library containing Buddhist scriptures, which are now housed in Bangkok. Today Wat Si Saket is home to the head of the Lao *sangha*, the Buddhist order of monks.

Haw Pha Kaew Ⓘ, the former royal temple of the Lao monarchy, sits just across the street from Wat Si Saket. King Setthathirat built Haw Pha Kaew in 1565 to house the Emerald Buddha which he brought with him to Laos after his father, King Phothisarat, died and Setthathirat moved from Lan Na (Northern Thailand) to Vientiane to rule over the Lan Xang kingdom. During the Siamese invasion of 1779, Vientiane was completely looted, and a host of sacred images was carried off to Bangkok along with members of the Lao royal family; today the Emerald Buddha sits in Bangkok's own Wat Phra Kaeo. The temple was rebuilt under Siamese patronage, only to be destroyed again during the invasion of 1828.

The current structure is the result of a 1937–40 restoration under the supervision of Prince Souvanna Phouma, a Paris-educated engineer and, later, prime minister of an independent Laos. While Haw Pha Keo is no longer used as a temple, busloads of Thai tourists often worship here. The museum (open Tues–Sun 8–11.30am and 2–4.30pm) contains a gilded throne, Khmer Buddhist stelae, and bronze frog drums of the royal family. The two main doors contain the only remnants of the original temple: sculptured wooden panels with images of the Buddha in nature. The garden, a peaceful retreat from the dust and heat of

BELOW: a Buddha statue in Wat Si Saket.

Vientiane, contains a small jar from the Plain of Jars in Xieng Khuang Province. The area surrounding Wat Si Saket and Haw Pha Kaew was once the administrative centre of French colonial rule, and in this neighbourhood are the spectacular **French Embassy** and residential complex, the Roman Catholic **Cathedral**, built by the French in 1928 and still offering daily services, and a number of administrative and residential buildings. For the capital of a colony that ran at a financial loss – the French made up for Laos with profits from operations in Cambodia and Vietnam – Vientiane experienced a fair amount of construction under French rule.

The lucky temple

Wat Si Muang ❶ (open daily), one of the most active temples in Vientiane, is located to the east of the French Embassy on Setthathirat Road. After the temple site was selected in 1563 by a group of King Setthathirat's advisers, a large hole was dug to receive the *lak muang*, or city pillar, which contains the city's protective deity. Legend has it that, on the day the temple was dedicated, the *lak muang* was suspended over the hole with ropes as the authorities waited for a volunteer to jump in. A pregnant woman (or a virgin, depending on whom you ask) finally did, and the ropes were severed, the woman's sacrifice bringing good luck to the new capital. The *sim* was constructed around the *lak muang*, which is wrapped in sacred cloth. Wat Si Muang was destroyed by the Siamese in 1828, of course, and reconstructed in 1915.

The temple is filled with Buddha images, at least one of which dates from before the 1828 invasion; partially damaged, it sits on a pillow in front and to the left of the main altar. Worshippers believe that the image has the power to grant

The museum at Haw Pha Kaew houses some excellent examples of the three Buddhist sculpture types common in Laos: "calling for rain", with hands straight at the sides; "offering protection", with palms stretched out in front; and "contemplating the tree of enlightenment", with hands crossed at the wrist in front.

BELOW: Vientiane's gilded city pillar.

wishes and answer important questions about the future. The platters of fruit and flowers scattered throughout the *sim* are evidence of the popularity of this belief (offerings are brought to the temple when a wish is granted), as are the votive flowers, candles and other offerings sold at the small market across the street.

Just east of Wat Si Muang is a small public park surrounding a statue of **King Sisavang Vong**, a pre-war gift from the Soviet Union. In his outstretched hand the King holds a palm-leaf manuscript of the country's first legal code. The statue's identifying plaque was removed after the 1975 communist victory.

Shopping with a view

Heading northeast from the Presidential Palace is **Lan Xang Avenue** ("Avenue de France" under the French), which runs past the **Talaat Sao** (Morning Market) . The market, open daily from 6am to 6pm, is a maze of individually owned stalls selling everything from antique textiles and carvings to household appliances. At the centre is the **Vientiane Department Store**, which offers goods from Thailand, China and Vietnam. At the morning market you will probably see stalls selling tickets for the immensely popular National Lottery, which is a central preoccupation of Vientiane residents, many of whom will consult monks or nuns before choosing a lucky number.

Lan Xang Avenue ends at a traffic circle resembling the Etoile in Paris, at the centre of which stands **Patuxai** , Vientiane's own Arc de Triomphe. Patuxai (Victory Gate) was completed in 1969 in memory of the Lao killed in wars before the Communist revolution. It is also known as the "vertical runway", as the project was finished with cement paid for by the Americans and intended to be used for the construction of a new airport in Vientiane. Despite the French

> **Map on page 94**

Jumbos or tuk-tuks are a good way to get about town, but fix the fare before you start your journey.

BELOW: the view towards the Presidential Palace from the Patuxai.

Map on page 94

inspiration, uniquely Lao elements are evident: Buddhist imagery is present in the Lao-style mouldings, and the frescoes under the arches represent scenes from the *Ramayana*. Climb the winding staircase to the top of the monument for a panoramic view of the city.

That Luang – symbol of Laos

Northeast of Patuxai is the shining **That Luang**  (open Tues–Sun 8–11.30am and 2–4.30pm), or Great Stupa, the symbol of the Lao nation and the most important monument in the country. According to legend, the breastbone of the Buddha was placed on this site by Indian missionaries in the 4th century BC. King Setthathirat began the construction of That Luang in 1566. Its official name is Lokachoulamani, or "monument of the world", and the multilevel *stupa* represents the different stages in Buddhist enlightenment: the lowest level represents the material world; the second, the world of appearances; the highest, the world of nothingness. A surrounding cloister contains examples of both classic Lao and Khmer sculpture. The cloister's tiny windows were added by Chao Anuvong as a defence against attack; they were of little use during the Siamese, Burmese and Chinese invasions of the 18th and 19th centuries, which left That Luang in ruins. Serious restoration work didn't begin until the French initiated a project in 1931, completed four years later.

That Luang originally faced east, with its back to Vientiane (Buddhism divides the world between East, the sphere of illumination, and West, the sphere of ignorance), but the restoration authorities failed to respect this orientation. The surface of the 45-meter (146-ft) -high *stupa* was regilded in 1995, the 20th anniversary of the founding of the Lao People's Democratic Republic. Of the four temples that King Setthathirat originally had built to surround That Luang, only two remain: **Wat That Luang Neua** to the north and **Wat That Luang Tai** to the south, both are open daily.

Further north of That Luang is the **National Assembly** building, and beyond, on Phon Kheng Road, the **Unknown Soldiers Memorial**. This white *stupa*-like monument is dedicated to Pathet Lao soldiers who died during the Second Indochina War.

Phon Kheng Road takes you northeast from Patuxai to the **Kaysone Phomvihane Memorial and Museum** (open daily except Mon 8–11.30am and 2–4.30pm; entrance fee), at Km 6, opened in 1995 on the 75th anniversary of the late president's birth. The museum is located within the former USIAD/CIA compound, which was taken over by the Communist leadership in 1975. The first part of the museum is an exhibition surrounding a bust of Kaysone, one of 150 such statues donated by the North Korean government and now found in provincial capitals around the country. The exhibits detail Kaysone's childhood in Savannakhet Province, his role in the Communist revolution, and his leadership of Lao PDR from 1975 until his death in 1992. Certainly the most interesting portion of the museum is the tour of Kaysone's private living quarters, a small house among series of identical structures inside the compound, reminiscent of postwar suburban America. ❑

BELOW: the Patuxai. **RIGHT:** young street vendors.

Map on page 105

VIENTIANE ENVIRONS

Travelling out of the capital into the surrounding districts and suburbs provides a vista of rural life and a glimpse of the countryside beyond

Most visitors to Laos end up staying in **Vientiane ❶** for only a few days, and it is the rare tourist indeed who takes the time to explore the area around the city. This is unfortunate, as there is a great deal to see in the districts surrounding the capital; you don't have to go far from the city centre to find beautiful natural areas and simple village life. Most of the attractions surrounding Vientiane lie along a loop just north of the capital; we will follow Route 13 northwards as far as Ang Nam Ngum, and then return to Vientiane in a southerly direction via Route 10. The final section of this chapter highlights attractions in the Vientiane suburbs which include the government National Ethnic Cultural Park and the Xieng Khuan (Buddha Park).

North of Vientiane

About 25 km (16 miles) north of Vientiane, just off Route 13, lies the **Nam Tok Tat Son ❷** waterfall and picnic area. Created more than 20 years ago by a dam, the "waterfall" is really a series of modest rapids. A recreational area with restaurants, picnic facilities and caged animals surrounds the falls. Walk away from the rest area for about 200 metres (220 yards) and you'll find a peaceful rock upon which sits a simple altar with primitive Buddhist statues; the shaded spot overlooks the surrounding forest.

BELOW: Talaat Lak Haa-sip Sawng.

More rewarding is the area near an incomplete temple, **Wat Lansoun**, 2 km (1 mile) beyond Nam Tok That Son at the end of the barely navigable dirt road. Too isolated to have resident monks, the temple sits upon a hill among aging Buddha images and caves. Some of the imposing rock formations are marked by Buddhist stele inscriptions. The panoramic view of the valley below is one of the most breathtaking in central Laos.

Continuing along Route 13 at Km 52 we come to the **Talaat Lak Haa-sip Sawng** (Km 52 Market), a large daily market specialising in wild foods and minority handicrafts, frequented by Hmong and other local ethnic minorities.

Just off Route 13, 65 km (40 miles) north of Vientiane, lies **Vang Sang ❸**, or "Elephant Palace", a Mon sanctuary featuring 10 sculptures of the Buddha on cliffs. The site dates as far back as the 11th century, and may have been a stopover for Buddhist worshippers heading north from Mon-Khmer city-states in today's southern Laos. The name refers to an elephant graveyard that was once found nearby. Another small cluster of images can be found about 20 km (13 miles) away from the main site.

To reach the reservoir we turn off Route 13 at the roadside town of Phon Hong and head east to **Thalat**, a town where the central market, much to the chagrin of environmental organisations working in Vientiane, sells animals such as deer, rats and assorted forest insects, in addition to some less common species for local consumption.

Ang Nam Ngum ❹, about 90 km (55 miles) from Vientiane, is a large artificial lake created in 1972 when the Nam Ngum was dammed and the entire area flooded. The dam remains the country's pride, generating enough electricity both for Vientiane and for export to Thailand. When the lake was created, 250 sq. km (100 sq. miles) of forest were completely submerged, and several logging companies are now using hydraulic underwater saws to extract the high-quality teak trees. The lake is filled with hundreds of small islands, to which prostitutes and criminals from Vientiane were sent for several years following the Communist takeover in 1975. Two islands – one for women and the other for men – are still used as prisons to this day.

An easily arranged boat cruise from the main pier in Nakeunon will allow you to explore the abandoned islands and to view the beautiful scenery. Waterfront restaurants offer tasty lunches featuring fresh fish from the lake: grilled fish, fish *laap*, fish soup – all the dishes are excellent. Overnight stays at Ang Nam Ngum are also possible.

The hotel on **Don Dok Khon Kham** island, said to be owned by the wife of the late Lao revolutionary Kaysone Phomvihane, is a 10-minute ride from the waterfront and offers limited running water and electricity. A much older guesthouse, without power or running water, sits on **Don Santiphap** island. Towards the dam on the lakeside you will find a series of bungalows once used by the Japanese engineers who helped to design and build the dam; they are open to tourists, and have hot water and air conditioning.

The art of fishing with Chinese-style nets on the Mekong River.

BELOW:
logging trucks.

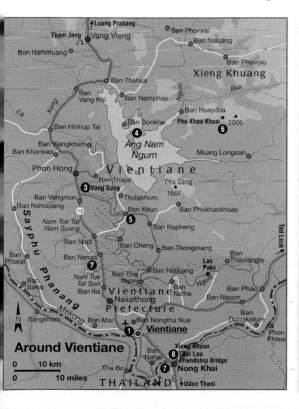

Around Vientiane

0   10 km

0   10 miles

An Indochinese tiger surveys his domain from the water.

South of Vientiane

Heading back southwards to Vientiane from the dam on Route 10, you will soon come to the ancient city of **Viengkham**. The area is not well marked, but with some help from the locals you should be able to find this famous historical and religious site. When King Fa Ngum set about creating the unified Kingdom of Lan Xang in the mid-14th century he had to conquer a number of small fiefdoms along his victorious route from Cambodia to Northern Laos. One such town was Viengkham, surrounded by a thick forest of bamboo as a defence against attack. Legend has it that Fa Ngum ordered his soldiers to shoot gold-plated arrows into the trees; not realising that they were not solid gold, the villagers cut down the trees in order to reach the arrows, and the invading army easily swept in. Fa Ngum and his soldiers launched their attack from the **Wat Viengkeo** temple complex, around which they built a deep moat. Today the view from the edge of the moat across the surrounding countryside is fabulous, and the remains of a small structure built to house the sacred Prabang image – which Fa Ngum carried from Cambodia to the royal city of Luang Prabang – can still be seen on the temple grounds.

After Viengkham you come to **Ban Keun ❺**, a bustling town on the banks of the Nam Ngum. The remaining French colonial buildings and riverfront scenery are worth a short stroll. Just beyond Ban Keun on Route 10, about 60 km (40 miles) from Vientiane, lies the **Thulakhom Inter Zoo** (open 8am–4.30pm daily; entrance fee), a large complex of animals kept in surprisingly humane conditions. The zoo, also known as the Vientiane Zoological Gardens, is still being constructed but the number of species is gradually increasing. At present animals range from the usual deer and ducks to the more exotic tigers, sun bears, a

Map on page 105

white elephant, and even emus and camels. Built by a Vientiane-based Thai businessman, the zoo offers good landscaping and a simple restaurant. A botanical garden and an aquarium is planned to be completed by 2001. The zoo is a popular weekend destination for families from Vientiane and it is a good idea to visit the zoo during the week if you want to avoid the crowds.

The entrance to the **Dansavanh Nam Ngum Resort** lies just ahead, a left-hand turn off Route 10. Built by Malaysian developers, this $200 million casino and lakeside resort on Ang Nam Ngum is supposed eventually to offer hang-gliding, powerboat cruises, an "island floating shopping network", an insect museum, a golf course, a disco – even a "wildlife island" featuring imported kangaroos. These days, however, all you will find at the site is a tasteless concrete nightmare housing a hotel, restaurant and casino. Gambling is available 24 hours a day; in addition to 70 slot machines, 27 gaming tables offer roulette, baccarat and blackjack. All gambling is in Thai baht, as 70 percent of the customers are from Thailand; the rest are mostly Chinese and Vietnamese. Lao citizens are forbidden by law to gamble.

Continuing on Route 10, 65 km (45 miles) north of Vientiane is the beautiful **Nong Bo** lake at Ban Sivilay village. Nong Bo is a seasonally flooded wetland, home to a great variety of birds – including the Chinese pond heron, black crowned night heron, common kingfisher, cattle egret and little egret. In the late dry season more than 1,200 whistling teal roost in the wetland. The lake is used by the nearby villagers for commercial fish breeding; fish are released annually during the wet season, and then from mid-February to late April they are caught and sold to nearby communities and in Vientiane. Nong Bo is a good example of a community-managed ecosystem, and the villagers work to main-

BELOW: fishing in the Mekong River.

A novice monk has his head shaved before ordination.

tain an ecological balance: regular guards ensure that birds are not killed and fish are not poached. Income from fish is evenly distributed in the village, which now has more than 225 shareholding householders.

At the moment there are no tourist facilities at Nong Bo, but the Lao government has plans, dependent on outside funding, to improve transportation to the lake and to develop the area as an eco-tourism site. The plans involve building a bird-watching hall, a guard facility and a parking area. If it is done properly (and that's a big "if") Nong Bo could be an excellent place for ecological research and education, and could also prove to be a way of providing financial benefits to villagers while conserving the local environment.

Further along Route 10 is the turning for **Phu Khao Khuai** (Water Buffalo Mountain) ❻, a pine-forested plateau surrounded by 2,000-metre (6,500-ft) peaks. One of the country's National Biodiversity Conservation Areas (NBCA), the 2,000-sq. km (770-sq. mile) Phu Khao Khuai is said to be full of local wildlife, including elephants, black bears, tigers and clouded leopards. Seventeen NBCAs, totalling 24,600 sq. km (9,500 sq. miles), or about 10 percent of the country, were designated by the Lao government in 1993. While this marked a positive step forward for environmental protection in Laos, corruption, lax enforcement and inadequate planning and management have plagued the NBCA initiative. Inside Phu Khao Khuai there is a pleasant picnic area by the Nam Ngum from which you can take short nature walks, and a telecommunications centre on the top of the mountain provides a good view of Vientiane and the surrounding districts. In the years following the Communist victory in 1975, foreigners were not allowed into this area as it contained a military base – the old airstrip is still visible today. Phu Khao Khuai offers a cool retreat from the heat

Map
on page
105

of Vientiane during the hot season; at other times of the year it can be cold and misty so it is a good idea to bring extra clothing with you for the evenings. Visitor facilities are lacking so it is also advisable to bring food with you if you are planning or _____ on Route 10, you will cross a small toll bridge at th_____ bridge are a number of float-ing restaura_____ m Ngum flow past as you eat some of the_____ a.

One of t_____ Vientiane is the **Houei Nyang** forest rese_____ miles) from the centre of the city. The f_____ the Swedish government, and offers an_____ e Kha nature trail. The nature walk last_____ numbered points of interest described_____ large animals in Houei Nyang, but rather_____ eer, porcupines and wild cats. A variety o_____ asily be seen (and heard). The reserve i_____ vers – the forest has experienced consider_____ ther human involvement over the years, ar_____ od look at the stages in the devel-opment

East

Locate_____ miles) from Vientiane, **Lao Pako** (tel: 22_____ ecological resort built using local materi_____ by an Austro-German couple, the resort_____ e rooms with private bathrooms; a

BELOW: the Thai-Lao Friendship Bridge.

Map on page 105

seven-bed dormitory with shared bathroom; separate bungalows, each with a two-bedded room and bathroom; and a verandah for sleeping under the stars (mosquito nets are available). Lao Pako also offers a bar and restaurant serving overpriced Lao food although there are barbecues on the weekends. Expatriates in Vientiane head to Lao Pako mostly to relax, but possible activities include village visits, trekking, river rafting, swimming, boating, volleyball and badminton.

Vientiane suburbs

If you are only in Vientiane for a short while, it is still possible make afternoon or day trips just outside the city to other attractions. South of the city centre, Tha Deua Road runs along the Mekong River and leads to the **National Ethnic Cultural Park** (open daily 8am–6pm; entrance fee), at Km 18, which is managed by the National Tourism Authority of the Lao PDR. Built in 1994, the park features mock houses in the style of the Lao Loum, Lao Theung and Lao Soung ethnic groups. The concrete structures are not at all authentic, but the place gives you some idea of the way in which the current government is attempting to combine the diverse ethnic groups of Laos into a unified Lao PDR. It is not surprising that the park also includes a small zoo (with a few very depressed specimens) and life-size replicas of dinosaurs. The riverside restaurants along the Mekong are the main attraction for Vientiane families, who often spend a day here at weekends.

BELOW: statue at Xieng Khuan.
RIGHT:
Buddha figure at Xieng Khuan.

Beyond the National Ethnic Cultural Park, still on Tha Deua Road, is the **Thai-Lao Friendship Bridge ❼**, built in 1994 at a cost of about US$30 million; it was funded by the Australian government. The Friendship (Mittaphap) Bridge, 1,240 metres (¾-mile) long, connects Nong Khai in Thailand to Vientiane, and is symbolic of the recent opening of Laos to outside influences. One day the bridge might even carry a railway line connecting the two countries; a joint venture for a railway that would reach as far as Luang Prabang was established in 1998, but realisation of this project still seems a long way off.

Still further along Tha Deua Road, about 25 km (16 miles) southeast of the city centre, is the odd yet attractive **Xieng Khuan ❽**, or Buddha Park (open daily 8am–6pm; entrance fee), which features a collection of Buddhist and Hindu sculptures built in 1958. The park was constructed by Bunleua Sulitat, a priest-shaman who merged Hindu and Buddhist traditions to develop quite a following in Laos and Northeastern Thailand; he left Vientiane in 1975 and moved across the river to Nong Khai, where he built a second Buddha Park. The oversized concrete statues – images of Shiva, Vishnu, Buddha and even a few secular Lao figures – give the place an air of fantasy which is emphasised by the massive pumpkin-shaped structure that dominates the park. This has three levels, representing hell, earth and heaven; the level of disrepair is such that the interior looks like the aftermath of a war, but there is a good view from the very top which is reached by a spiral staircase. Xieng Khuan is now a popular public park, complete with riverfront food stalls and the whole place makes an enjoyable half-day out of town. ❑

LUANG PRABANG

Maps:
City: 114
Area: 119

*The temples and culture of Luang Prabang, capital of Laos
and seat of the monarchy until the 16th century, have been so
well preserved that the city is now a World Heritage Site*

For centuries before the city was founded, the area of **Luang Prabang ❶** played host to various Thai-Lao principalities in the valleys of the Mekong, Khan, Ou and Xuang rivers. It was in 1353, though, that King Fa Ngum (1353–73) consolidated the first Lao Kingdom, Lan Xang (One Million Elephants), on the site of present-day Luang Prabang. At the time the city was known as Xawa, possibly a local form of Java, but it was renamed Meuang Xieng Thong (Gold City District) in 1357. A little later, Fa Ngum received from the Khmer sovereign the gift of a Sinhalese Buddha image called Pha Bang, from which the city's modern name derives.

In 1545 King Phothisarat (1520–48) moved the capital of Lan Xang to Vientiane, but Luang Prabang remained the royal heart of the kingdom. After the collapse of Lan Xang in 1694 an independent kingdom was established in Luang Prabang, which co-existed with kingdoms based in Vientiane and Champasak further south. Kings ruled Luang Prabang until the monarchy was officially dissolved by the Pathet Lao in 1975, though they were at various times forced to pay tribute to the Siamese, the Vietnamese and most recently the French. The last king and queen were imprisoned in a cave in the northeast of the country, where it is thought they perished some time in the 1980s – though an official statement on this has never been issued.

Luang Prabang's royal legacy, though a story of decline, combines with its splendid natural setting at the confluence of the Mekong and the Nam Khan to create one of the most intriguing and magical cities in Asia. The city is crowded with fine old temples, and dominated by the 100-metre (330-ft) -high rocky outcrop Phu Si. In December 1995, Luang Prabang was added to UNESCO's World Heritage List.

LEFT: Wat Xieng Thong. **BELOW:** the Royal Palace Museum.

In the city

In the centre of the city, between Phu Si and the Mekong, is the **Royal Palace Museum** (Haw Kham) **Ⓐ** (Thanon Phothisalat, open Mon–Fri 8.30–10.30am), which offers an insight into the history of the region. The Palace was constructed from 1904 as the residence of King Sisavang Vong, and is a pleasing mix of classical Lao and French styles, cruciform in layout and mounted on a multitiered platform. In a room at the front of the building is the museum's prize piece, the famed Pha Bang Buddha image. The 83-cm (32-inch) -tall image, in the attitude of Abhayamudra, or "dispelling fear", is almost pure gold and weighs between 43 and 54 kg (95–120 lbs), according to different sources. Legend says that the image originated in Ceylon in the 1st century AD; it was presented to the Khmers, who gave it to Fa Ngum. The image was twice seized by the Siamese (in 1779 and 1827) before

Lavish detail on the façade of the Royal Palace Museum.

finally being restored to Laos in 1867 by the Siamese King Mongkut. In the same room are several beautifully embroidered silk screens and engraved elephant tusks. The rest of the museum houses a fairly substantial collection of regalia, portraits, diplomatic gifts and art treasures. Particularly interesting are the many varied friezes, murals and mosaics throughout the building.

Across, to the west of the Royal Palace, is **Wat Mai Suwannaphumaham B** (Thanon Phothisalat; open Mon–Fri 8.30–10.30am). Dating from the early 19th century, this temple was once the residence of the Sangkhalat, the supreme patriarch of Buddhism in Laos. The *sim* is wooden, with a five-tiered roof in classic Luang Prabang style. The main attraction is the gilded walls of the front verandah, the designs of which recount scenes from the *Ramayana* and the Buddha's penultimate incarnation. For the first half of the 20th century the Pha Bang was housed here, and it is still put on display here during the Lao New Year celebrations. Within the compounds are two longboats, kept in their own shelter, which play their part in the celebrations at New Year.

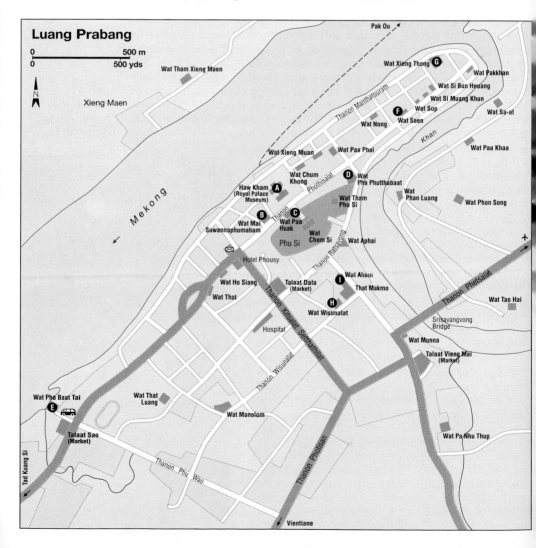

Luang Prabang

0 — 500 m
0 — 500 yds

N

Pak Ou

Wat Tham Xieng Maen

Xieng Maen

Wat Xieng Thong **G**

Wat Pakkhan

Wat Si Bun Heuang

Wat Si Muang Khun

Thanon Manthatourath

F Wat Sop

Wat Saen

Wat Sa-at

Wat Nong

Khan

Wat Xieng Muan

Wat Paa Phai

Wat Paa Khaa

Wat Chum Khong

Phothisalat

D Wat Pha Phutthabaat

Haw Kham (Royal Palace Museum) **A**

Wat Tham Phu Si

Wat Phan Luang

Wat Phon Song

Mekong

Thanon

B Wat Mai Suwannaphumaham

C Wat Paa Huak

Wat Chom Si

Wat Aphai

Phu Si

Thanon Ratsavong

Hotel Phousy

Wat Aham **I**

Wat Ho Siang

Talaat Dala (Market)

That Makmo

Wat That

H

Wat Wisunalat

Thanon Phetsalat

Wat Tao Hai

Thanon Kitsalat Sethathirat

Hospital

Srisavangvong Bridge

Wat Munna

Thanon Wisunalat

Talaat Vieng Mai (Market)

Wat Pha Baat Tai **E**

Wat That Luang

Wat Manolom

Thanon Photisan

Wat Pa Nhu Thup

Tad Kuang Si

Talaat Sao (Market)

Thanon Phu Wao

Vientiane

On the other side of Thanon Phothisalat rises Mount Phu Si, a sheer rock with wooded sides. At its foot is the derelict **Wat Paa Huak** Ⓒ, which despite its abandonment contains very well preserved 19th-century murals showing Mekong scenes. From this temple 328 steps wind up Phu Si to **Wat Chom Si** on the summit, which has an impressive gilded *stupa* in classical Lao form. The summit also offers fine views of Luang Prabang and the mountains.

The path continues down the other side of Phu Si past an anti-aircraft gun to **Wat Tham Phu Si**, a cave shrine housing a Buddha image of wide girth, in the style known locally as *Pha Kachai*. Close by the main road is **Wat Pha Phutthabaat** Ⓓ, a temple containing a 3-metre (10-ft) -long Buddha footprint and originally constructed in the late 14th century. There is another Buddha footprint temple, **Wat Pha Baat Tai** Ⓔ, behind the *talaat sao* – the fresh produce morning market in the southern part of the town; this one more modern and decidedly garish, showing distinct Vietnamese Buddhist influence. It is a fine place to watch the Mekong flow by, though.

Heading north along Thanon Phothisalat from the foot of Phu Si towards the confluence of the Nam Khan and the Mekong you pass a string of glittering temples, interspersed with evocative colonial buildings. **Wat Paa Phai** (Bamboo Forest Temple) on the left is noteworthy for its 100-year-old fresco and carved wooden façade depicting secular Lao scenes. Further along the street, also on the left, is **Wat Saen** Ⓕ (One Hundred Thousand Temple; open daily), whose name refers to the value of the donation with which it was constructed. This temple is different in style from most others in Luang Prabang, and the trained eye will immediately identify it as heavily Thai influenced. The *sim* was originally constructed in 1718 but was restored twice in the 20th century.

 Map on page 114

BELOW: family posing on top of Mount Phu Si.

Mosaic detail in the Red Chapel of Wat Xieng Thong.

BELOW: Wat Xieng Thong during a new year festival.

City of temples

Close to the tip of the peninsula, on the banks of the Mekong, reminding the visitor of the importance of river transport in Laos, is Luang Prabang's most renowned temple, **Wat Xieng Thong** (Golden City Monastery) **G** (Thanon Phothisalat; open Mon–Fri 8.30–10.30am; entrance fee). This temple, which epitomises in its low sweeping roofs the classic Luang Prabang style of temple architecture, was built in 1560 by King Setthathirat (1548–71) and was patronised by the monarchy right up until 1975. Inside the *sim* the eight thick supporting pillars, richly stencilled in gold, guide the eye to the serene golden Buddha images at the rear, and upwards to the roof which is covered in *dhamma* wheels. On the outside of the *sim*, at the back, is an elaborate mosaic of the Tree of Life set against a deep red background. Throughout, the combination of splendid gold and deep red give this temple a captivatingly regal atmosphere.

Adjacent to the *sim* is a smaller building, dubbed by the French "*La Chapelle Rouge*", the Red Chapel, containing a unique reclining Buddha figure. What makes the image so unusual is the Lao proportions, especially the robe curling outwards at the ankles, and the graceful position of the hand supporting the head. This figure was displayed at the Paris exhibition in 1931, but happily returned to Luang Prabang in 1964 after several decades in Vientiane. The Red Chapel itself is exquisitely decorated. On the outside of the rear wall is a mosaic showing rural Lao village life, executed in the 1950s in celebration of two-and-a- half millennia since the Buddha's attainment of Nirvana. Also in the Xieng Thong compound are various monks' quarters, reliquary *stupas* and a boat shelter. Close to the east gate is a building housing the royal funeral carriage.

Another temple of note – one cannot get away from the fact that Luang Pra-

bang is primarily a city of temples – is **Wat Wisunalat** (Wat Vixoun) (Thanon Phothisalat; open Mon–Fri 8.30–10.30am; entrance fee). Built by King Wisunalat (1501–20) between 1512 and 1513, this is the oldest temple in the city still in use. The *sim*, rebuilt in 1898 under the inspiration of the original wooden structure which was destroyed by fire in 1887, is unique in style, with a front roof sloping down over the terrace. Sketches by Louis Delaporte of the original building exist from the 1860s, and confirm what a later visitor wrote: "[Vat] Visunalat is shaped like a boat, the same shape that Orientals give to their coffins. The wooden walls are sculpted with extreme refinement and delicacy." Though the wood has gone, the builders who performed the restoration attempted to capture the shapes of the original wood in the stucco work. Inside is an impressive collection of Buddhist sculpture.

In the temple grounds is That Pathum, or Lotus Stupa, which is affectionately referred to as That Makmo, or Watermelon Stupa, and which is just as distinctive as the temple itself. The *stupa* is over 30 metres (100 ft) high, and was constructed in 1503–4, at which time it was filled with small, precious Buddha images. Many of these were stolen by Chin Haw marauders from Yunnan in the 19th century – the rest are now safely on display in the Royal Palace Museum.

Next to Wat Wisunalat is the peaceful **Wat Aham** ●, formerly – before Wat Mai took the honour – the residence of the supreme patriarch of Buddhism in Laos. The temple's red façade combines with striking green *yak* temple guardians and mildewed *stupas* to provide an atmosphere of extreme tranquillity. The temple rarely has many visitors, other than those quietly making offerings at an important shrine at the base of the two large old pipal trees. In fact, Luang Prabang's notable temples are far more numerous than those indicated

Map on page 114

BELOW: shop front.

Ancient traditional patterns are incorporated into contemporary weavings.

BELOW:
Buddha images in the Pak Ou caves.

here. A few kilometres to the southeast of the city is a forest retreat, **Wat Paa Phon Phao ❷**, with a three-floor pagoda complete with an external terrace near the top which affords excellent views of the surrounding countryside. The *chedi* is a popular destination for locals and visitors alike.

Across the river from the centre of the city, in Xieng Maen District, are no fewer than four more temples set in beautiful surroundings, one of which, **Wat Tham Xieng Maen ❸**, is situated in a 100-metre (330-ft) -deep cave. This is generally kept locked, but the keys are held at nearby Wat Long Khun, the former retreat of kings awaiting their coronation. A small donation is requested for having the cave temple opened. Boats transport people across to this side of the river from behind the Royal Palace.

Outside town

A short distance to the east of the city, about 4 km (2½ miles) beyond the airport, is the Tai Lü village of **Ban Phanom ❹**, renowned as a silk- and cotton-weaving village. At weekends a small market is set up for those interested in seeing the full range of fabrics produced. However, villagers are willing – sometimes too willing – to show off their goods at any time. All weaving is done by hand at traditional looms, a fascinating process to watch. In the vicinity, a few kilometres along the river, is the tomb of Henri Mouhot, the French explorer who took the credit for "discovering" Angkor Wat in 1860. He died of malaria in Luang Prabang in 1861, though his tomb was not discovered until 1990.

A two-hour (by long-tail boat), 25-km (15-mile) journey up river from Luang Prabang is the confluence of the Mekong and the Nam Ou. Opposite the mouth of the Nam Ou, in the side of a limestone cliff, are the **Pak Ou caves ❺** (open daily; entrance fee). Legend maintains that King Setthathirat discovered these two caves in the 16th century, and they have been venerated ever since. Both caves are full of Buddha images, some of venerable age. The lower of the two caves, Tham Ting, is easily accessible from the river. The upper cave, Tham Phum, is reached by a staircase, and is considerably deeper, requiring a torch for full exploration. There is a pleasant shelter between the two caves, an ideal spot for a picnic lunch.

On the way to Pak Ou, boats will stop by request at **Ban Xang Hai ❻** (Jar-Maker village), named after the village's former main industry. Jars still abound, but they are made elsewhere, and the village devotes itself to producing *lao-lao*, the local moonshine rice-wine. Archaeologists digging around the village have unearthed jars dating back more than 2,000 years. Opposite, at Ban Thin Hong, close to Pak Ou village, recent excavations have uncovered even earlier artifacts – tools, pottery and fabrics – around 8,000 years old. As yet the site hasn't been developed as a tourist attraction, but it may well be in the near future.

There are several waterfalls in the vicinity of Luang Prabang which can make for attractive half-day or day excursions, perhaps combined with stops in some of the very rural villages along the way. About 30 km (20 miles) south of the town are the multitiered Kuang Si falls, replete with interesting limestone formations and crystal-clear pools. Food vendors keep most of the local visitors at the lower level of the falls, which can be very crowded during holidays. Up a trail to the left of the lower cascade is a second fall with a pool which makes for good swimming and is generally quieter. The trail continues to the top of the falls, though after rain it can be hazardously slippy.

Taat Sae ❼, also south of town, are closer to the city, and hence more crowded at weekends, though often deserted in the week. The falls here have more pools and shorter drops. They can be reached by boat from the delightful village of Ban Aen on the Nam Khan.

Festivals in Luang Prabang

Because of Luang Prabang's long status as the chief royal city of Laos – a status surpassing that of the less princely cities of Vientiane and Champasak – the location is particularly richly associated with festivals and special rites. While it is true that many of these were either circumscribed or banned outright during the earlier and more hard-line years of the Communist government, everything is now changing, and Luang Prabang's festivals are gradually on their way back. This is both a result of the city's elevation to the status of a UNESCO World Heritage Site, and because the Lao authorities are keenly aware of the potential appeal such traditions can bring to the expanding tourist market. Besides, it is a simple fact that the Lao people delight in festivals and festivities.

The **Festival of the Twelfth Lunar Month**, once celebrated each October full moon, was probably the oldest of the city's festivals. It marked the end of the rainy season and, by extension, the end of the rice-planting season. The rites of the festival originally invoked the deities of the soil and of the water to renew

Map on page 119

BELOW:
the multi-tiered Kuang Si Falls.

Around Luang Prabang

0 — 5 km
0 — 5 miles

N

Pak Ou ❺
Pak Ou
Nam Bak
Ban Xang Hai ❻

Luang Prabang

Ban Som
Ban Pakxuang
Xuang
Mekong
Ban Longlan

Wat Tham Xieng Maen ❸
Ban Paklung
Khan
Luang Prabang ❶
Wat Paa Phon Phao ❷
Ban Huayse Nua
❹
Ban Xat
Ban Phanom
Ban Kokngiu
13
Tad Kuang Si
1341
Taat Sae ❼
Vientiane
Xieng Ngeun

for another year the agricultural cycle on which the prosperity of the kingdom depended. In times long past the festival was celebrated in a very grand manner, as the king's boatmen, clad in red jackets and scarlet hats with yellow borders, rowed the royal barges to a group of rocks at the confluence of the Mekong and the Nam Khan. Here they placed elaborate floral arrangements together with candles "the length of the king's forearm". These were lit, and prayers were offered beseeching the sacred *naga* river-snake spirits to protect the kingdom and its people during the coming year.

As Buddhism became the dominant religious tradition of Lan Xang the emphasis on the *naga* declined (without ever fully disappearing, however), and the central focus of the festival was transferred to Wat That Luang, the Monastery of the Great Stupa (*see page 102*). The entire community took part in the festivities – king, royal family, supreme patriarch and accompanying monks, as well as masked dancers representing Pu No and Na No, the *devata luang* or royal guardian deities of the kingdom.

Nowadays, of course, there's no king to take part in such festivals, but the *sangha* is as important as ever, and the shaggy masked costumes used by dancers representing Pu No and Pu Na have survived the revolution. In times past a highlight of the festival was the firing of large bamboo rockets called *bang fai* from huge scaffolds that were erected by That Luang.

The **Festival of the Fifth Lunar Month**, celebrated each April full moon, revolved around a symbol of the Lao kingdom, the Buddha image, Pha Bang, from which Luang Prabang takes its name. This marked the beginning of the agricultural year when days lengthen and rains begin to fall. Like the Festival of the Twelfth Month, it was celebrated by the entire community. In times past,

BELOW: the royal guardian deities of Luang Prabang.

celebrations lasted for around three weeks as the entire population of the city indulged in an apparently endless round of ceremonies, rituals, games and processions. According to one description: "The sound of gongs, bells, drums and tambourines deafened the ears, while the entire city paraded through streets newly adorned with streamers of coloured paper bearing the signs of the zodiac." The king's elephants, gaily caparisoned, were out in force, driven by *mahouts* drawn from the tribal minorities.

Today remnants of the old festivities exist and, indeed, are likely to continue making a comeback – though with more than a touch of the 21st century to them, and without the traditional monarch. The Fifth Month Festival is celebrated with great vigour all over Laos, but most extensively at Luang Prabang. Boat races are held on the nearby Mekong River, and much water is thrown and poured over the celebrants. The Festival of the Twelfth Month is, for the present, only celebrated at Vientiane – the site of the central government – and without much pomp or ceremony. Laos is a country currently rediscovering its past, however, and it can only be a matter of time before this, too, is re-established at Luang Prabang, albeit in an appropriately modern form.

Map on page 119

Entrant in the Luang Prabang new year beauty contest.

Luang Prabang as a World Heritage Site

Owing to its relative isolation, and because the French colonial administration moved the Lao capital to Vientiane, old Luang Prabang survives in a remarkable state of preservation down to the present day. Even during the long years of civil war it remained unscathed, and the main threat to the ancient royal city at the start of the 1990s – when Laos reopened to the outside world – seemed to be urban development. Accordingly, the matter was brought to the attention of the United Nations, and an investigation was launched. In its resultant report UNESCO declared Luang Prabang to be "the best preserved city in Southeast Asia", and in December 1995 the city was added to the Register of World Heritage Programme. This development, which entitles the city to receive funds from the United Nations for restoration and preservation, should assure Luang Prabang's future.

UNESCO's brief in Luang Prabang is to conserve the city's present atmosphere and to preserve its architectural heritage, both Lao and French, as well as its traditions and cultural festivals. In 1998 two French architects and five Lao architects were stationed in Luang Prabang working full time for UNESCO to bring about these aims. So far they have identified almost 700 historic buildings or other structures in the city – an astonishing number for so small a place – all of which are being registered, classified, described and, where possible or necessary, given official legal protection. UNESCO's programme also calls for careful consideration of all new construction work in the city – in other words, there will be no high-rise buildings or other development detrimental to the city's cultural environment. So far the policy seems to be working rather well, and it seems increasingly certain that the attractions of historic Luang Prabang will be preserved for the enjoyment of future generations of Lao and visitors alike. ❑

BELOW:
World Heritage procession.

FRANCE ON THE MIDDLE MEKONG

During France's presence in Laos, Vientiane emerged as a Franco-Buddhist enclave, and the French lifestyle influenced the Lao urban élite

One of the most pleasant surprises awaiting the visitor to Vientiane is the French cultural influence surviving in the city. It is a pleasure to enjoy a breakfast of croissants and café-au-lait. Lunch may well comprise freshly-baked baguettes and pâté accompanied by a carafe of wine. In the evening, excellent French cuisine is available at upmarket restaurants despite the years of socialist austerity.

This agreeable ambience aside, Vientiane's most notable memorial to the French influence must be its architecture. There are numerous small residences, and not a few mansions, built in the style of the former colonial power. Many of these may be found in the older part of the town, along the riverside appropriately designated Quai Fa Ngum. Here, as by the shaded boulevards in the vicinity of That Dam and along Lan Xang Avenue, the "Champs Élysées" of Vientiane, may be found fine examples of colonial French architecture, complete with shutters and red-tiled roofs, which would not be out of place in Dijon or Toulouse. Many of these former private residences are in stages of advanced decay, and some are clearly beyond saving. Others, however, have been painstakingly restored — and as the authorities come to realise the potential value to tourism of this unique architectural legacy, not to mention the inherent charm of the Lao capital, preservation rather than demolition is becoming the order of the day.

▷ FRENCH ON THE MENU
English is fast replacing French as the second language of Laos, but signs in French are still common, as the menu opposite and post box above shows.

△ BAG A BAGUETTE
Delicious, freshly baked sticks of French bread are for sale all over Laos, but stocks often run out by lunchtime. Eat with a lavish serving of pâté.

▷ FRENCH RULES
One of the less attractive aspects of French colonialism: Lao *corvée* (unpaid) workers labour at road construction.

△ FORMER GLORY

This former colonial mansion In Luang Prabang Is one of many buildings from this period that have been restored (it is now a restaurant).

▽ COLONIAL ELEGANCE

The façade of the National Library in Vientiane, which has recently been restored. It was originally built in the French colonial era as a police station.

THE FACE OF FRANCE IN LAOS

Born in France in 1847, Auguste Pavie was a French explorer and diplomat who almost single-handedly brought Laos under French control. Pavie had a gift for languages and learned to speak Vietnamese, Khmer, Thai and Lao. In 1886, he became the first French vice-consul in Luang Prabang, the Lao capital. During the next five years he travelled throughout northern Laos, and gained the friendship of local rulers for France, frustrating Bangkok's attempts to bring the region fully under Siamese control. Arguing that the Lao states had been vassals of Vietnam and that France had succeeded to Vietnam's rights in Laos, Pavie justified regional military movements, provoking a crisis that resulted in Laos becoming a French protectorate in 1893.

▷ LE PETIT DÉJEUNER

Watch the world go by and start the day the French way with coffee and croissants at a Vientiane pavement café.

NORTHEASTERN LAOS

Map
on pages
126–7

*One of the most mysterious sights in Laos, the ancient Plain of Jars,
brings tourists to the northeast of the country, as does more recent
history in the Pathet Lao's military caves of the 1970s*

Vientiane

The northeastern Lao provinces of Xieng Khuang and Hua Phan owe much of their history and character to their proximity to Laos' eastern neighbour, Vietnam; indeed, both of these provinces have existed more often as independent statelets, or vassal states, of Vietnam than as part of a Lao political entity. In recent times, although they were distinctly part of the kingdom of Laos, it was chiefly their proximity to Vietnam that led to the area's unfortunate distinction of being the target of saturation bombing during the Vietnam War. The Pathet Lao forces chose the area as their headquarters for its close strategic position to its North Vietnamese allies. This attracted the attention of the Americans, who pounded the region from their B-52s, obliterating thousands of towns and villages and forcing the population, both military and civilian, to make their homes in the region's mercifully plentiful caves. It should be noted that the North Vietnamese also took part in the destruction, attacking areas under control of the Royalist forces with heavy artillery.

Although the scars of war remain, northeastern Laos has made a remarkable recovery, and has much to offer the visitor. The local people have put the past behind them and bear no ill will to foreigners. Fascinating and as yet not fully explained archaeological sites, rugged mountainous terrain, raging rivers, a temperate climate and a plethora of ethnic minorities make this region well worth a visit.

LEFT: pedal power.
BELOW: bomb cases from the war are scattered throughout the region.

Exploring the northeast

The following pages take the reader from Phonsavan, the capital of Xieng Khuang, to Sam Neua, the capital of Hua Phan. An important consideration is how to get as far as Xieng Khuang in the first place.

Travel by land requires you first to get to Nong Khiaw in the north of Luang Prabang Province. From here you travel east via Route 1 until it ends at Route 6 in the village of Nam Noen. Route 6 runs south to Muang Kham, where Route 7 doubles back west to reach Xieng Khuang. This complicated and circuitous route (which requires a change of bus in Nam Noen, if you are using public transport) takes no less than 12 hours, on difficult roads. If travelling on to Sam Neua you need to allow a further 12 hours.

Another route, prominently signposted and shown on maps (as Route 7), is a turn-off from the main Vientiane to Luang Prabang road just north of Kasi, which leads to Xieng Khuang via Muang Sui. This trip takes two days and passes through the Saisombun Special Zone ("special zone" being the name given by the government to areas still not secure from guerrilla/bandit activity). As a consequence of this, the route is a foolhardy and unadvised option until the security situation improves.

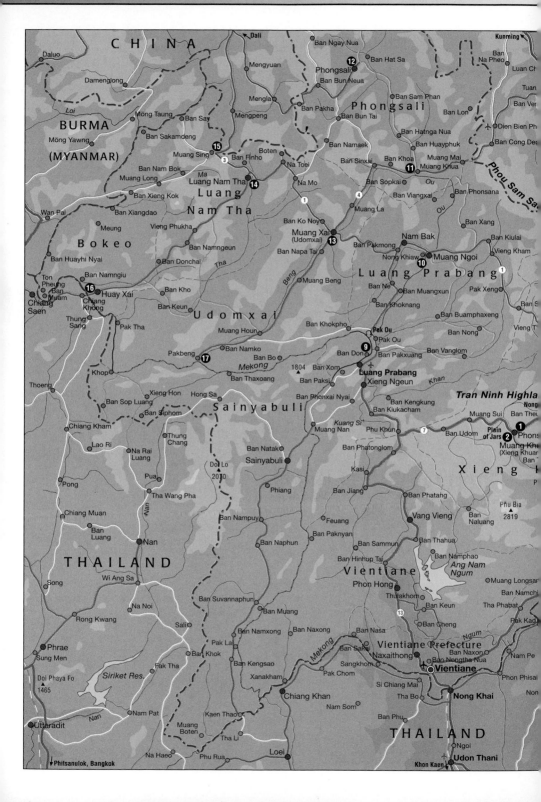

By far the best way is to fly from Vientiane to Xieng Khuang, travel by land from there to Hua Phan Province, enjoying the various sights en route, and return to Vientiane by air. For the hardy, and those not wishing to double back to Vientiane, fly into Sam Neua, travel by land to Xieng Khuang, and then continue west towards Nong Khiaw by land. From Nong Khiaw one can reach Luang Prabang, Udomxai also known as Muang Xai, and Phongsali.

Xieng Khuang Province

Xieng Khuang Province, with a population of over 200,000, had often been something of a battleground even before the Vietnam War period. This was possibly due to its strategic location equidistant between the Lao and Vietnamese capital cities, or to its agriculturally fertile temperate plain. Only briefly was it subdued into the Lao kingdom of Lan Xang (*see page 22*), and at other times it was ruled by both Siamese and Vietnamese. Indeed, during the 1830s Vietnam annexed it, and the local inhabitants were forced to dress and behave according to Vietnamese custom. Home to a proud and independent people, the attempts of the Xieng Khuang Province to exist as an independent state have usually been thwarted by its more powerful neighbours.

The present-day provincial capital, **Phonsavan ❶**, was established after the former capital, located to the southeast, was obliterated during the Vietnam War (it has now been re-built and re-named Muang Khun). A rapidly expanding population (now exceeding 60,000) and its proximity to some of the Plain of Jars sites give this small town the amenities required for visitors as a base for exploring the region. The best hotel in Phonsavan, Auberge de Plaine des Jarres, offers pleasant cabins, complete with fireplaces which can be welcome on chilly evenings. The Auberge, as well as another reasonable hotel, the Maly Hotel, can arrange trips to the Plain of Jars and other sites of interest in the area. Both are located outside the town centre, leaving the traveller either isolated or tranquil, depending on your perspective. In the town centre a large **market** offers tribal handicrafts as well as the standard range of goods that sustain the local people. Other handicraft shops on the main street of Phonsavan offer interesting local textiles and silver wares.

The Plain of Jars

The **Plain of Jars** ❷ is doubtlessly Xieng Khuang's major attraction. Huge stone jar-shaped vessels are spread, in no apparent pattern, over a dozen major locations in the vicinity of Phonsavan. Locals speak of other sites they have discovered on hunting and gathering forays. But the eternal questions remain: what exactly are these ancient megaliths? Who constructed them? When did they build them and why?

A French archaeologist, Madeleine Colani, undertook the most comprehensive study of the jars in the 1930s. Colani spent three years in the region, travelling by elephant. Her work, *Megalithes du Haut-Laos*, a two-volume study published in Paris in 1935, details the history of both the jars and the upright stone pillars found in Hua Phan Province (*see page 132*). Colani conclusively linked the two sets of monuments to a single civilisation which flourished in the area between 300 BC and AD 300. Colani postulated that both the jars and what she called the "menhirs" of Hua Phan were funerary monuments.

The jars of Xieng Khuang average about 1.5 metres (4.8 ft) in both diameter and height, although some are considerably larger. The largest weighs an estimated 15 tonnes. Most were carved from the local sandstone where they now lie, although some show evidence of having been dragged to higher ground. The fact that the jars were carved using iron implements, whereas the menhirs

BELOW:
the Plain of Jars.

Map on pages 126–7

were only fashioned from stone cutting tools, allows us to date the civilisation. Colani proved her hypothesis that the jars were funerary monuments by recovering charred human bone fragments from them, and she also discovered what appears to be a central crematorium at the village of Ban Ang on the Xieng Khuang plateau. The round discs which are now scattered in the vicinity of the jars are not lids, as one might logically suppose, but were placed, decorative side down, over ritual objects such as stone axes.

Other artefacts found in and around the jars included beads from China, bronze figurines from Vietnam and ornaments associated with Tai culture. This allows us to conclude that the civilisation that produced these monuments was highly developed and had trading links throughout the region. Colani herself drew no conclusions as to the origins of the civilisation, but more recent researchers have attempted to trace them alternatively to the Cham of Vietnam or to some of the Lao Theung groups which now inhabit Attapeu Province in southeastern Laos (*see page 167*). No researcher has yet offered a convincing explanation for the civilisation's demise.

An interesting postscript to Colani's research leaves the door open to continued speculation: although her work was illustrated with photographs taken in situ, the artifacts which she collected have mysteriously disappeared. Without such "proof" some later researchers have discounted Colani's work, and claimed that the jars were used for either rice storage or wine fermentation. Further research has been made difficult by both the heavy bombing of the area during the Vietnam War, and the presence of unexploded ordnance (UXO) there. It is entirely possible that the creators of these monuments have taken their secrets with them forever.

Three major sites are easily accessible from Xieng Khuang, and have been cleared of UXO, although it's always best to stay on the main paths. Site 1 or **Thong Hai Tin** (Stone Jar Plain) is located 15 km (9 miles) southwest of Phonsavan. This site has the biggest collection of jars, numbering over 250, and also the largest jar, which according to local lore is the victory cup of the Lao king Khun Jeuam, who liberated the local people from an oppressive ruler. On nearby hillsides you will notice odd bottle-shaped excavations; the locals use these as bird traps. Although the site is impressive, the presence of a nearby Lao air force base and some buildings erected for the visit of Thailand's crown prince a few years back detract from the overall atmosphere. Another jar site, known locally as **Hai Hin Phu Salato**, or Site 2, is located 25 km (16 miles) south of Phonsavan. Here about 100 jars are spread across two adjacent hillsides. The view from the top is worth the short climb.

The most attractive site is another 10 km (6 miles) south from Site 2, and is called **Hai Hin Laat Khai** or Site 3. Here about 150 jars are located on top of a small hill from which one can enjoy great views not only of the surrounding plains, but also of the prosperous farming community of Ban Sieng Dee, set on an adjacent hillside. This Lao village, another 2-km (1-mile) walk from the jar site, has a small Buddhist temple and visitors are welcome. If you plan to visit

The origin of the huge jars on the Plain of Jars remains a subject of debate among archaeologists.

BELOW: a woman of the Yao ethnic minority.

Truck-buses transport people and goods around the region.

only Site 1, a jumbo (motorised trishaw) chartered in Phonsavan will do the job nicely, but for visiting all three sites more solid transport, for example a jeep, is recommended. Any of the hotels or travel agencies in Xieng Khuang can make the necessary arrangements. Hmong villages are located in the vicinity of Phonsavan and can be included in the itinerary.

Time permitting, you could also visit old Xieng Khuang, now known as **Muang Khun** ❸, located 30 km (18 miles) southeast of Phonsavan, or about 10 km (6 miles) beyond Site 3. This town was once a royal capital, the centre of the Phuan kingdom. This period ended when Vietnamese invaders abducted the king, Chao Noi Muang Phuan. The town was heavily bombed during the war and its once beautiful temples have been left in a ruined state. The palace of the French legation, though badly damaged by 1960s bombings, still stands. The authorities' decision to relocate the provincial capital, and leave the destruction visible, makes Muang Khun a memorable but painful place to visit.

A different itinerary would be to visit the jar sites in one day, and the following day travel north and east via Route 7 towards the market town of Nong Haet. This comparatively well-built road continues on to the border with Vietnam, although at present only Lao and Vietnamese nationals are permitted to cross. En route you could visit a variety of local attractions, each of which, in its own way, offers an insight into the history and everyday life of the Xieng Khuang region.

Mineral springs and caves

About 25 km (15 miles) east of Phonsavan the Nam Ngum begins its journey south to the Ang Nam Ngum (*see page 45*). Known as **Nong Pet**, this tranquil spring makes a pleasant picnic or swimming spot. A few kilometres further, on

Map on pages 126–7

the south side of Route 7, you arrive at **Baw Noi**, a **hot mineral spring**, also a pleasant spot for a dip, especially when the weather is cool. Another 5 km (3 miles) along Route 7, you reach the turn-off for **Baw Yai ❹**, another mineral spring, larger than Baw Noi, which has now been developed as a resort, with bungalows and bathing facilities. The resort was originally open only to the party élite, but with the shift in political climate in Laos it has now been opened to the public. A nominal entry fee is charged.

At **Muang Kham,** 50 km (30 miles) and a two-hour drive from Phonsavan, the road forks. The left fork becomes Route 6, heading towards Hua Phan, and the right remains Route 7, leading to Nong Haet and the Vietnamese border. Muang Kham is no more than a crossroads trading village, but there are guides who will take you to nearby **jar sites** or on to **Tham Piu ❺**, a cave a few kilometres northeast of Muang Kham. Tham Piu is another Vietnam War-related site, where in 1969 a single rocket fired from a Royalist (or American, depending on the version you choose) aircraft caused the death of hundreds of people who had taken refuge in the cave. Controversy still exists about whether these were Lao locals or, in fact, Vietnamese who had set up a makeshift hospital in the cave.

For those who might wish to avoid another reminder of the region's troubled past it is still worth making the trip to Tham Piu to enjoy the beautiful scenery and the tribal villages in the vicinity. Another cave, **Tham Piu Song,** which was spared the bombing, can also be visited. Although the caves are only a few kilometres from the main Route 7 a guide is recommended, as the trails are not clearly marked and, as always in this area, the risks posed by UXO are real. Guides can best be hired in Phonsavan, where you can arrange an itinerary to include a visit to the mineral springs as well as the caves and a minority village.

BELOW: children supervising a grazing buffalo.

The dangerous search for unexplored ordnance (UXO – land mines, cluster bombs and mortar shells) still continues.

BELOW: returning from the maize fields.

Hua Phan Province

Lying northeast of Xieng Khuang Province, Hua Phan Province shares a similar history. It has, for the past several hundred years, been alternately a vassal state of Vietnam, known as Ai Lao, owing to its position close to Hanoi, or an independent kingdom. Even more distant than Xieng Khuang from the traditional Lao capitals of Luang Prabang and Vientiane, it was in fact only incorporated into the Lao polity during the French colonial period.

Hua Phan currently has a population of approximately 250,000 people. More mountainous than Xieng Khuang, it is home to over 20 ethnic minorities, who are mainly Tai speaking. The weather in the province can become quite cold, especially for those accustomed to the adjacent tropical regions.

To reach Hua Phan from Xieng Khuang Province, travel northeast to Muang Kham via Route 7, bear left onto Route 6, and continue to Nam Noen, which is about a four-hour trip in total. Past Nam Noen the road ceases to be paved, and starts to climb through beautiful mountain scenery with many tribal villages in evidence. About 20 km (12 miles) beyond Nam Noen is the village of Hua Muang, where, unless you already have a guide, it is possible to obtain directions to **Suan Hin** ❻, literally meaning "Stone Garden" in Lao. This site is an earlier manifestation of the civilisation that built the jars of Xieng Khuang. Here, rather than jars, one sees several groupings of upright stone pillars, ranging in height from 1–3 metres (3–10 ft).

Adjacent to the pillars are small underground chambers, believed to be burial crypts. This site was also researched in the 1930s by the French archaeologist Madeleine Colani (*see page 128*). It was inhabited before the Plain of Jars, as witnessed by the fact that only stone and not iron cutting tools were used to produce

Map on pages 126–7

these pillars, which Colani called "menhirs". The site calls to mind a miniature Stonehenge, and Colani also hypothesised the existence of a sun cult among these prehistoric inhabitants of the region.

The menhirs of Suan Hin are several kilometres off the main Route 6, but are now accessible by vehicle. An American government opium suppression project built a road to some nearby Hmong villages, hoping to give the inhabitants access to local markets with the produce they were to grow instead of opium. Unfortunately, the road passes dangerously close to the main grouping of stelae, and this has caused some to collapse. Local villagers have carted the smaller ones away to use as tables. Nonetheless, the menhirs of Suan Hin are an impressive and mysterious sight, spread over several adjacent hillsides. Constructed of stone containing silica-like chips, they sparkle in the afternoon sun.

Sam Neua ❼, the capital of Hua Phan Province, is 45 km (28 miles) northeast of the Suan Hin site. Its setting in a verdant valley at an altitude of 1,200 metres (3,900 ft) is more attractive than the town itself, although Sam Neua's **market** is thriving as the largest in the region, and is a good spot to observe the many ethnic minorities, including Hmong, Tai Daeng and Tai Lü, who come here for supplies. Sam Neua's famous handwoven textiles, as well as handmade silver jewellery, are sold in some of the small shops and market stalls. Cutlery made from downed aeroplanes can also be found.

Although Sam Neua is one of the least visited towns in the country, basic accommodation is available in the town. Two kilometres (1 mile) from Sam Neua's market is Wat Pho Xai, a tiny monastery with only five monks in residence. A 1979 independence monument, mounted on a red star, is situated on a hill on the outskirts of town, with views over Sam Neua.

LEFT: identifying types of UXO.
BELOW: the market at Sam Neua.

Map on pages 126–7

Pathet Lao district

The heart of Hua Phan's significance is the district of **Vieng Xai** ❽ (a recent appellation meaning "City of Victory"). It is here that the Pathet Lao leadership established its headquarters during the 20-year struggle for supremacy in the Second Indochina War. The area was chosen for its proximity to Vietnam and also for the abundance of caves which afforded shelter from American bombs.

The authorities have an ambivalent attitude towards allowing foreigners to visit these sites. On one hand, they are proud of their tenacious struggle and resourcefulness in surviving in these conditions; on the other hand, they still consider the area to be a high security military zone. An explanation for their reticence to allow visitors free access to the area is no doubt the legacy of "*samana*".

After the Pathet Lao victory in 1975 thousands of Lao were sent to camps for lengthy "re-education" under extremely harsh conditions, including isolation, forced labour and political indoctrination. Many did not survive. The camps that held the higher officials (including the Lao royal family and former ministers) were located in Vieng Xai and nearby Sop Hao. Most camps were closed by 1989, but there is still a belief that at least one camp still exists, although this has never been confirmed officially.

The caves of the Pathet Lao leaders, of which there are estimated to be about 100, are most likely to be accessible to the visitor. They are within walking distance of Vieng Xai, which is about 30 km (19 miles) east of Sam Neua. Located in an impressively narrow limestone valley, the caves are treated as a serious historical monument to their struggle by the military "guides" who must accompany all visitors. The first cave, which one must visit to register, pay a nominal fee and be assigned a guide/guard, is **Tham Thaan Souphanouvong** (open daily). This was the home and office of the famous "Red Prince", a member of the Lao royal family who sided with the revolutionaries. Befitting his royal background, this cave is well appointed with wooden walls and floors dividing it into different working areas. A comfortable house was constructed for the Red Prince outside the mouth of the cave after the 1973 Paris accords brought an end to the American bombing.

Tham Thaan Kaysone was the cave residence and headquarters of the Pathet Lao supremo and first President of the Lao People's Democratic Republic, Kaysone Phomvihane. Larger and more office-like than the Red Prince's cave, it extends down to a depth of around 150 metres (490 ft), including a meeting room and library, and has an exit at the back which leads to an outdoor meeting area and a kitchen. An attractive house lies in front of the cave. One of the deepest caves, **Tham Xieng Muang**, was used as a temporary military hospital.

Of the many caves in the Vieng Xai area, it is thought that about 12 were used for various purposes during the war, but only three are regularly open to the public. Entry to the others is subject to the mood of the army personnel in charge. The precipitous terrain, natural beauty, and historical significance all add to a powerful atmosphere. ❑

BELOW: the landscape of Vieng Xai.
RIGHT: taking aim with a sling shot.

NORTHWESTERN LAOS

Map on page 126–7

The northwestern areas of Laos are where the borders of China, Thailand and Burma converge, so the towns and villages give a fascinating insight into numerous ethnic minorities

L aos' wild and mountainous northwest shares frontiers with Thailand, China and Burma (Myanmar), and it has therefore been, throughout history, a natural path of migration, generally towards the south, for a wide variety of peoples. Many, intentionally or otherwise, ended their peregrination in this region, giving this section of the country some of Laos' greatest ethnic diversity. The cultural and ethnic ancestors of the Lao people, the Tai, originated just north of the region in the area of China's Yunnan province known as Sipsong-panna (Xishuangbanna in Chinese, but in fact a Tai word meaning "12 administrative districts"). The greatest of the Lao kingdoms, Lan Xang, traces its origins to the early *meung* (city-states) which originated here (*see page 21*).

In addition to the Tai, northwestern Laos is home to a large number of colourful Tibeto-Burmese peoples, such as the Yao, Hmong and Akha. The Lao government now collectively refers to these groups as Lao Sung or "High Lao", a reference to the mountaintops that they have historically chosen to inhabit. In Luang Nam Tha Province these "ethnic minorities" are in fact a majority, outnumbering the ethnic Lao by two to one.

Malefactors and opium

Being a frontier region is not without dangers, and some considerable strife has characterised the area's history. The depredations of the Haw, "Overland Chinese" freebooters, accompanied by Vietnamese mercenaries and French deserters who terrorised Laos at the end of the 19th century, were particularly brutal here. More recently the area has become known as part of the infamous "Golden Triangle", where an ever-changing parade of malefactors of various nationalities has chosen to profit from one of the local people's traditional crops, opium. Although it was spared the heavy American bombing which devastated northeastern Laos during the 1970s, the northwest was heavily involved in the strife, largely because the Hmong, supported by the American CIA, resisted the Communist Pathet Lao forces which had major bases in Luang Nam Tha Province. Air America, the CIA airline, based many "training forces" here, and once again the lure of opium as a source of financing military activities raised its ugly head.

Toward the end of the "American War", as the Second Indochina War is known in Laos, the northwest was "liberated", and the Chinese allies built a network of paved roads connecting Mengla in China with Udomxai, Nong Khiaw on the Nam Ou and Pakbeng on the Mekong River. Although the worse for wear after 20 years, these roads still provide the major land thoroughfares of the region. With the gradual re-open-

LEFT: Tai Lü girl at Muang Sing market. **BELOW:** scored poppies at a Hmong village.

A small cargo boat hoisted onto stilts and used as a home.

ing of Chinese borders in recent years, road-building soldiers have been replaced by a variety of traders and skilled labourers from the nearby provinces of China. Sometimes trading only in Laos, sometimes en route to and from Thailand, they add another interesting dimension to this multifaceted cultural environment. This ethnic pot pourri, combined with the mountainous geography and possibility of river travel, make this region well worth the sometimes arduous travel conditions.

Along the Nam Ou

Indeed it is travel by river, not only the mighty Mekong but also such tributaries as the Nam Ou, which offers the visitor a truly Lao experience. Ironically, as roads are improving, riverboats are becoming a less cost-effective way for the Lao to travel, so the future of river trips is uncertain and they should be enjoyed while they still exist. Since for most villages the river is the focus of many daily activities, social and domestic, travel on a riverboat will provide glimpses of Lao rural life that you simply cannot get from road travel.

The Nam Ou is a major tributary of the Mekong, which flows south from the mountains of China's Yunnan province through the Lao provinces of Phongsali and Luang Prabang, finally flowing into the Mekong 20 km (12 miles) upstream from Luang Prabang. It is possible to travel along the Ou by boat from its confluence with the Mekong to within a few kilometres of the mountaintop town of Phongsali (*see page 141*).

BELOW: scenery at the confluence of the Nam Ou and the Mekong near Luang Prabang.

The journey begins at **Ban Don ❾**, a small village on the Mekong some 10 km (6 miles) north of Luang Prabang, to which the local authorities have wisely exiled the noisy high-powered speedboats which ply the Mekong and the

Ou. The boats use a gimbal-mounted engine from which protrudes a long shaft attached to a propeller. These light 5-metre (16-ft) -long craft can reach speeds of 80 kmph (50 mph) on the Mekong, but travelling up the smaller Ou they go more slowly.

At Ban Don one can negotiate directly with the boatmen for a charter as far as Nong Khiaw or points further north. Since the completion of the road from Luang Prabang to Pakmong the locals have understandably chosen to forego the boat trip in favour of the faster and cheaper buses, so for this section of the river you will need to charter a boat. Rates vary according to water level and demand, but US$40 will certainly secure the charter of a worthy craft. These boats can take up to six passengers, so sharing a boat makes the cost quite reasonable. It should be noted that river travel on the Ou can become impossible during the dry season (late March to June), when water levels fall.

The trip to Nong Khiaw passes through splendid mountainous scenery, with villages around every bend in the river. Soon after embarking at the confluence of the Ou and the Mekong, you reach the Pak Ou caves. If you charter a boat be sure to ask the boatman to make brief stops at one of the picturesque villages en route.

You will soon arrive in **Nong Khiaw ⑩**, a large village which seems to owe its existence to a bridge that crosses the river here. Across the river lies another, more attractive settlement, Muang Ngoi. The bridge is an important link in the Chinese-built Route 1, which travels from Luang Nam Tha Province in the west to Xieng Khuang Province in the east, so if you choose not to travel further north on the Ou it is possible to secure public transport either towards Udomxai in the west (about four hours by bus) or to Xieng Khuang (10 hours) and Sam Neua (another 12 hours) in the east. Only basic accommodation is

Map on page 126–7

BELOW: looking out from a boat on the Nam Ou.

available in Nong Khiaw. Boat travel from Nong Khiaw is still the most effective way to reach Muang Khua, and so a wider variety of craft ply the river, catering to locals making intermediate stops at villages totally unreachable by road. In addition to the ubiquitous speedboats, a slower variety of riverboat leaves Nong Khiaw for Muang Khua on a regular basis. What these craft forfeit in speed they gain in comfort. Unlike the speedboats they have covered cabins which give shelter from the sun.

The trip to Muang Khua takes four hours and, because of constant local demand for the service, prices are reasonable. The boat ride also offers a glimpse into the life of the people who have dwelt for centuries along the banks of the Ou. If you have chartered your own riverboat you should ask to stop in some of these villages. Although contact with the outside world is limited, to say the least, the fertile land and river sustain the local inhabitants with abundant food and building supplies. The people, though not prosperous in a western sense, are certainly contented. Visitors are welcomed.

Muang Khua to Phongsali

The village of **Muang Khua** ⓫ is, like Nong Khiaw, located next to a bridge that crosses the Ou. Road access is on Route 4, an unsurfaced monstrosity that runs from Udomxai in the west (six hours) and goes east to the Vietnamese border near Dien Bien Phu. The road was built by the Vietnamese and Chinese in the late 1970s, and appears to have had no maintenance since then. Unfortunately (given the historical significance of Dien Bien Phu, the site of a battle that doomed the French presence in Indochina) it is not possible to cross the border into Vietnam here. Muang Khua offers more accommodation than Nong Khiaw,

BELOW: the village of Muang Khua.
RIGHT: barber at Phongsali.

Map on page 126–7

which is fortunate, since if you are coming from Luang Prabang this will be as much travel as can be accomplished in a day. Muang Khua itself is a tranquil but friendly town, with many people from the local ethnic minorities visiting the town for trade or transport.

Proceeding upriver from Muang Khua, your next destination is **Hat Sa**. Again there is a choice between a powerful speedboat and a placid "slow boat", as the Lao name translates. The trip takes two hours by speedboat, six hours by slow boat. This section of the river is even more spectacular than the Nong Khiaw to Muang Khua sections, with thick primary forest cover and a never-ending parade of pristine villages. The mountains looming in the distance are of substantial elevations. The air is cool regardless of the time of year, and particularly pleasant after the often torrid plains. The village of Hat Sa is the northern terminus of river traffic on the Ou, although little but its remoteness and the variety of ethnic groups who visit it distinguish the place.

From here one can board a jeep or similar 4-wheel-drive vehicle to travel the remaining 20-km (12-mile) climb to Phongsali. The fact that this short passage requires two hours indicates the condition of the road. Built by the French, it has been nicknamed "Route Buffalo" by the locals, with the clear inference that at times it could only be traversed by such a beast of burden.

Phongsali ⓬ (population 25,000), the capital of the eponymous province, is located along the lower slopes of Phu Fa (Sky Mountain). Its 1,400-metre (4,550-ft) elevation guarantees a year-round temperate climate. Possibly as a result of its strategic location, sandwiched between China and Vietnam, the French took an interest in the area and established a garrison. A few traces of French architecture remain, but it is being quickly overshadowed by the utili-

Large ear pendants are worn by women from Phongsali.

BELOW: watching a communal video screen at Phongsali.

Many of the roads in northwesten Laos are still dirt tracks, but with foreign investment paved roads are beginning to be built.

tarian Chinese style of construction that characterises most towns near to the frontier of Laos' Immense neighbour. The French wrested Phongsali from Chinese control by a treaty in 1895. Prior to this time it was affiliated with the Tai Lü statelet of Sipsongpanna, and nominally under Chinese control. The province of Phongsali is ethnically one of the most diverse in Laos. In addition to the well-known Hmong, Akha and Yao there are several branches of Tai tribal groups, Vietnamese and Chinese, both long-term and recent immigrants. The Lao government, with its penchant for "unity in diversity", lists 22 ethnic groups, although anthropologists would doubtlessly dispute this number. Phongsali's market is a good place to see the great variety of peoples who call the province home. The Sky Mountain hotel offers reasonable accommodation.

Udomxai to Muang Sing

From Phongsali, you have the option of continuing southwest on a recently built but still unpaved road towards Udomxai. After a steep descent, eventually the new road joins Route 4 which stretches from Udomxai to the Vietnamese border. The travel time is 10 hours, and the scenery is not as spectacular as that previously seen along the Nam Ou. Possibly adding insult to injury, the provincial capital of **Udomxai** ⓭ (also known as Muang Xai) has seen better days.

In the 1970s the town was the centre of Chinese support for the Pathet Lao forces in northern Laos. The former Chinese Consulate now houses a hotel of low standard. As payment for their road-building efforts, the Chinese were given carte blanche to log the Udomxai valley, and the resultant deforestation makes for a somewhat dusty and bleak environment. Udomxai still has a strong Chinese influence, but it is now more commercial than political. In the centre of the

BELOW: farm near Muang Sing.

town, across the street from the best hotel, the Chinese-run Sing Thong Hotel, a **Kaysone Monument** is located in the middle of a debris-strewn field. As a backdrop the government has constructed a large *stupa* or *that* on a hilltop southeast of the town. Udomxai's saving grace is its lively market, also near the Sing Thong Hotel. If time permits, a walk through the back streets behind the market can also give a more favourable impression. It is a good place to rest and recover, but more attractive venues lie ahead.

Travelling west towards Luang Nam Tha along Route 1 (another Chinese-built road still in acceptable condition), you again enter some spectacular mountain scenery, although some sections have been heavily deforested, both by logging and the slash-and-burn agricultural techniques used by local farmers. The area is home to large populations of Lao Sung, mainly Akha, Hmong and Yao. At the village of **Na Toei**, about 90 km (60 miles) or three to four hours from Udomxai, the road branches, and the right-hand branch leads to **Boten**, the Lao village at the Chinese border. With a Chinese visa (obtainable in Vientiane) you can legally cross into China's Yunnan Province, although this should not be done with the intention of re-entering Laos unless you are ready to make the 800-km (500-mile) trip to Kunming, the provincial capital, to obtain another Lao visa.

It is probably better to bear left at Na Toei and within an hour find yourself in the pleasant town of **Luang Nam Tha ⑭**. During the "American War" (*circa* 1955–75), this area witnessed fierce fighting between the Pathet Lao forces and the CIA-backed tribal (largely Hmong) guerrillas, and after the war the devastated town was relocated about 7 km (4 miles) north of its former site. It now boasts wide avenues (usually empty of traffic) and a pleasant location on the Nam Tha. Wander down to the footbridge east of the town's main road at sunrise. The **morning market**, just south of the "bus station" (in fact a large vacant field), is full of local products and people. A handicrafts shop, Paseutsin Shop, one block north and east of the Kaysone Memorial, offers interesting local textiles and woven bamboo. About 2 km (1 mile) outside the town, on the road to Muang Sing, a European Union-funded project, the **Luang Nam Tha Handicrafts Centre**, helps villagers get their handmade products to the market.

The former site of Luang Nam Tha, south of the "new town", is still home to a large market, a Buddhist temple, the airport and a boat landing. As the road south to Huay Xai is greatly improved (once an insecure track, now a safe but rough eight-hour ride), the boat traffic on the Nam Tha is diminishing. A good way to enjoy the scenery would be to negotiate a two-hour round-trip cruise. This is possible only after the summer monsoon rains have raised the waters to a navigable level.

Muang Sing

Continuing northwest, now on Route 3, a 60-km (37-mile) two-hour trip leads through steep mountains and along raging rivers to the town of **Muang Sing ⑮**. Located on a fertile plain surrounded by mountains and irrigated by the waters of the Nam Yuan and Nam Ma, this town of 25,000 is a centre of Tai Lü culture and has a rich history. Muang Sing has existed as a

BELOW: stalls at Muang Sing's annual festival.

Banners suspended from the ceiling of a Tai Lü temple.

BELOW: monks with begging bowls at Muang Sing.

small but important urban centre for hundreds of years as a result of its strategic location and agricultural wealth. At times it was under the rule of various Northern Siamese principalities. The British, and later the French, laid claim to it, the latter building a garrison which still exists today.

The predominant Lü people are a branch of the Tai ethno-linguistic family (which also includes lowland Lao, a few of the mountain-dwelling tribes, the people of northern Thailand and the Shan of Burma (Myanmar). The Tai Lü are those who inhabit the southern part of China's Yunnan province, which lies 10 km (6 miles) from Muang Sing. Being closest to the source of the culture, they are arguably the most ethnically and culturally homogeneous of the many sub-groups of Tai outside their ancestral homeland.

Their society is matrilineal: the women have strong influence in family decision-making, and are keen upholders of the group's traditions. A people known for their grace and physical beauty, they are Buddhists but also have a rich oral tradition of various mythical heroes and spirits. Among these tales one of is how they were taught to build their distinctive sloping roofed, stilted houses by a divine swan, and they still refer to their traditional style of dwellings as *heuan hong* ("swan houses").

A Tai Lü-style Buddhist temple, **Wat Luang Baan Xieng Jai**, located just west of the town's main street, near the river, shows the characteristic small windows and red lacquered pillars which typify Tai Lü temple architecture. In the centre of town, behind yet another Kaysone memorial, you can see the **former French garrison**, which is now a Lao army base, and a colourful market is located across the main street from the memorial. If you go south for about 1 km (half a mile), another Buddhist temple, **Wat Nam Kaew Luang**, is

housed in an agreeable tree-filled compound. In addition to the Tai Lü, Muang Sing is also home to a large population of Yao, Akha and Lanten tribal peoples whose villages are located in the hills outside the valley. Local guides can arrange trekking tours to these areas. Otherwise the newly opened Adima Guesthouse, located 8 km (5 miles) north of Muang Sing, near the Akha and Yao villages, allows the visitor to make more casual day trips to the villages. At present the Lao government "strongly discourages" visitors from staying overnight in tribal villages.

Muang Sing is also noted for its **annual festival**, called Bun That Muang Sing. The festival's date varies according to the lunar calendar, but it is always towards the end of October or beginning of November, at the full moon. The festival occurs at a Buddhist *stupa* or *that* on a hill south of town. Since it is nominally a Buddhist religious rite, the presentation of incense and candles at the *stupa* and the offering of alms to the monks who converge on the site for this event are central to the festival, but it is also an important social and commercial gathering. The crowds dance to live bands in the evenings, with tasty snacks for the children and home-distilled spirits for the adults adding to the fun. Although not Buddhists, the local hill tribe population would not dream of missing the fun, and attend in full regalia. Muang Sing is also an excellent venue for participating in the festivities associated with Lao New Year in April, or the rocket festivals that call for rain during the dry season.

It would be unfair to discuss Muang Sing without mentioning something that will certainly confront any visitor: the use of opium. Muang Sing has historically been a centre of poppy production; during their period of rule the French sanctioned and monopolised the trade. Traditionally used as a medicine and by the

Map on page 126–7

 TIP

The Tai Lü villages surrounding Muang Sing are interesting, and bicycles for hire in restaurants and guesthouses are an ideal way to explore. Just head north towards the village of Udomsin and take any side road that looks promising.

BELOW: snooker game by the river.

elderly, opium is now openly proffered to foreign tourists on the streets of Muang Sing by emaciated local addicts, who use the profits from sales at inflated prices to finance their habits. Opium is *not* legal in Laos. The government does not appreciate Muang Sing's reputation, and unpleasant encounters between the police and foreigners using opium have been reported.

Although the Chinese border is only a few kilometres north of Muang Sing, only Lao and Chinese nationals are permitted to cross. From Muang Sing it is possible to double back to Luang Nam Tha and reach Huay Xai by road, but a much more interesting route is via **Xieng Kok**, a small village on the Mekong 75 km (47 miles) west of Muang Sing. The road has recently been improved, and the trip takes two to three hours, passing through beautiful scenery along the Nam Ma. Across the Mekong from Xieng Kok is Burma (Myanmar), although only Lao and Burmese nationals are permitted to cross. With little to detain you in Xieng Kok (there is a guesthouse should necessity require), you can board a speedboat for the four-hour trip down river to Huay Xai. All boats stop at **Ban Muam**, which could be considered the centre of the Golden Triangle since the borders of Laos, Burma and Thailand converge here. Truck-buses leave Muang Sing early in the morning, so it's possible to reach Huay Xai the same day, although, as with all travel in Laos, be prepared for surprises.

Huay Xai and the Mekong River

Huay Xai ⑯, the Lao town across the Mekong from Chiang Khong in Thailand, has become a popular entry point for visitors wishing to cross from Thailand. Although it is not possible to get a Lao visa on arrival in Huay Xai, as you can in Vientiane and Luang Prabang, guesthouses and travel agents

BELOW: the market at Muang Sing.

can secure one, usually within a few hours, for around 2,000 Thai *baht* (US$50). Alternatively, you can apply for a visa from any Lao embassy or consulate abroad. Huay Xai is the capital of Bokeo Province. Since becoming a legal port of entry it has experienced a mini-boom, with new hotels, shops and even some palatial private homes in evidence. Indeed, a plan for a bridge (currently there is only a car ferry) and further upgrading of the Huay Xai-Luang Nam Tha road have been bruited about. This infrastructure would allow efficient vehicular travel from China to Bangkok and vice versa. Predictably the Thais and Chinese have been most enthusiastic about the plan, with the Lao wanting to assess fully the impact such a scheme would have on their country. However the economic downturn of 1997 put this plan back on the shelf, for now.

Huay Xai is a pleasant little town built on the small hills that descend to the banks of the Mekong. A Buddhist temple, **Wat Jom Khao Manilat**, can be reached by a long staircase with serpentine *naga* balustrades. Built in the late 19th century, the temple affords good views of Huay Xai and the river below. Nearby, **Fort Carnot**, built by the French, is visible from the outside, but is off limits to visitors since it is now a Lao military installation. Travel agents in Huay Xai offer trips to the nearby **sapphire mine** (the province's name, Bokeo, means "gem mine" in Lao), but the site is not particularly attractive, and the uninitiated who purchase the stones on offer will not be getting a bargain.

From Huay Xai there are several forms of river transport. The ubiquitous speedboats leave from about 2 km (1 mile) south of town. These six-passenger craft can reach Luang Prabang in six to seven hours, or the town of Pakbeng in about half that time. Helmets and life jackets are supplied and obligatory by Lao law. Even so, not everyone enjoys the speedboat trip down the Mekong. The vast

Map on page 126–7

A plane from the Lao Aviation fleet. The airline's new logo features a swan-tail flower, a traditional national motif.

BELOW: cooling off in the Mekong River.

Long-tail boats whizz up and down the Mekong River.

BELOW: walking along a street in Pakbeng.
RIGHT: monk at Wat Sin Jong Jaeng.

expanses of smooth water, unlike the Nam Ou that reaches north from Luang Prabang, allow the speedboat jockeys to propel their light but powerful craft at high speeds: exhilarating or nerve-racking, depending on your perspective. Seven hours of this would rattle even the most steel-nerved, so consider breaking the trip up with a night in Pakbeng. Fares fluctuate according to season and demand, but a charter to Luang Prabang could cost around 5,000 Thai *baht* (US$140), or half of that to Pakbeng, for six passengers.

A more placid alternative to the speedboats is the 20-person passenger ferries. Called *heua saa* (slow boats) by the Lao, they live up to their name. Reaching Luang Prabang requires spending two nights en route, at Pakbeng and another village further downriver, arriving at Luang Prabang around noon on the third day. The boats leave in the early mornings from a terminal just north of the Lao immigration checkpoint in Huay Xai. Be sure to bring your own food and water. Accommodation is available in Pakbeng, but bring your own sleeping gear if you plan to travel all the way to Luang Prabang by slow boat. Prices for the ferries are low.

A final travel alternative has recently appeared which will appeal to those wishing to make this trip in style. A French-managed company, Mekongland, based in Bangkok, now offers a comfortable cruise on a luxurious modern vessel, the *Pak Ou*, with onboard refreshments and washrooms. The *Pak Ou* leaves Huay Xai twice a week, stopping to visit scenic spots on the way to Pakbeng where passengers spend the night in the company's private resort, the Luangsay Lodge, located just outside the town. It then sets out the following morning to reach Luang Prabang in the afternoon. The price per person is currently around US$200, including all meals.

Imaginative travellers often choose a mixture of passenger ferry and speedboat travel by breaking the trip in Pakbeng. For example, you can take the ferry as far as this rustic riverside village and spend a night or two before continuing by speedboat. Whichever way you travel, the rewards are the same. Mountains on both sides border this stretch of the Mekong, and the forest cover is often pristine. It is not uncommon to see elephants bathing in the shallows on the Lao side of the river.

Pakbeng to Luang Prabang

Pakbeng ❼ is a pleasant small town at the confluence of the Mekong and Beng rivers (Pakbeng means "mouth of the Beng"). Built on steep slopes, it has several adequate guesthouses and restaurants, and many hill-tribe villagers visit its market. An interesting Buddhist temple, **Wat Sin Jong Jaeng**, just north of the town, has an exterior mural of the *sim* depicting moustached Caucasian visitors. For those not wishing to continue downriver to Luang Prabang, the road north from Pakbeng, Route 2, leads to Udomxai (120 km/75 miles). The trip takes six to eight hours as the road is poor. In some spots logging has decimated the forests.

One recommendation is to continue on to Luang Prabang, the historic northern capital. If travelling by passenger ferry or the *Pak Ou* you will arrive at the old city. Those travelling by speedboat will be deposited at Ban Don, where jumbos complete the journey. ❑

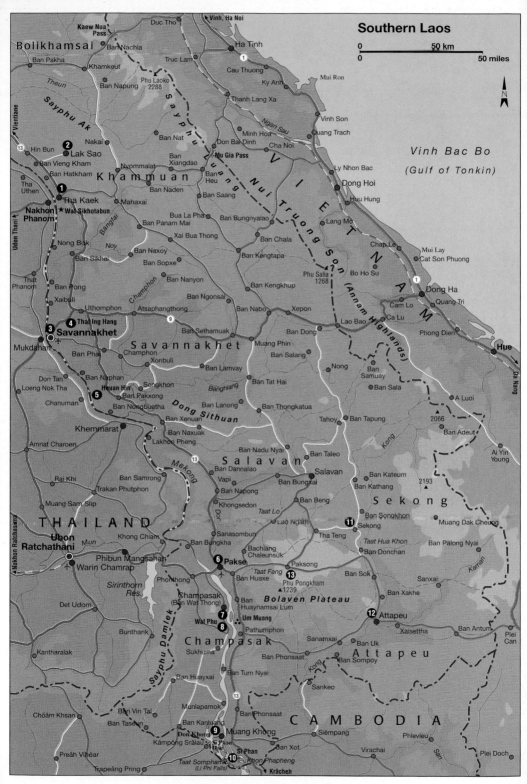

Southern Laos

0   50 km
0   50 miles

N

Vinh Bac Bo
(Gulf of Tonkin)

Bolikhamsai

Kaew Nua Pass
Duc Tho
Vinh, Ha Noi
Ha Tinh
Ban Nachia
Ban Pakha
Khamkeut
Truc Lam
Cau Thuong
Ky Anh
Mui Ron
Phu Laoko 2288
Ban Napung
Theun
Sayphu Ak
Nakai
Minh Hoa
Don Bai Dinh
Cha Noi
Thanh Lang Xa
Ngan Sau
Vinh Son
Quang Trach
Ban Nat
Vientiane
Hin Bun
Lak Sao
Ban Vieng Kham
Ban Hatkham
Mu Gia Pass
Ban Xiangdao
Ban Heu
Ly Nhon Bac
Dong Hoi
Tha Uthen
Tha Kaek
Khammuan
Ban Naden
Ban Saang
Huu Hung
Nakhon Phanom
Wat Sikhotabun
Mahaxai
Ban Bungnyalao
Lang Mo
Bua La Pha
Ban Panam Mai
Xai Bua Thong
Ban Chala
Chap Le
Mui Lay
Cat Son Phuong
Bangfai
Nong Bok
Ban Naxoy
Ban Sopxe
Ban Kengtapa
Bo Ho Su
Ban Sikhai
Phu Salia 1268
That Phanom
Ban Pong
Ban Nanyon
Ban Kengkhup
Cam Lo
Dong Ha
Quang Tri
Xaibuli
Champhon
Noy
Ban Ngonsai
Xepon
Ca Lu
Lao Bao
Uthomphon
Atsaphangthong
Ban Nabo
Phong Dien
Thai Ing Hang
Ban Sethamuak
Ban Dong
Savannakhet
Muang Phin
Hue
Mukdahan
Savannakhet
Ban Phai
Champhon
Xonbuli
Ban Salang
Nong
Ban Samuay
Ban Sala
Don Tan
Ban Naphan
Songkhon
Ban Lamvay
Ban Tat Hai
Loeng Nok Tha
Heuan Hin
Ban Pakxong
Banghiang
A Luoi
Chanuman
Ban Nongbuatha
Ban Lanong
Ban Thongkatua
2066
Ban Adeut
Ban Xenuan
Dong Sithuan
Tahoy
Ban Tapung
Khemmarat
Ban Naxuak
Lakhon Pheng
Ai Yin Young
Amnat Charoen
Ban Nadu Nyai
Ban Taleo
Salavan
Rai Khi
Ban Dannalao
Ban Kateum
Ban Kathang
2193
Mekong
Vapi
Ban Bungxai
Salavan
Sekong
Trakan Phutphon
Ban Samrong
Ban Napong
Ban Beng
THAILAND
Muang Sam Slip
Khongsedon
Taat Lo
Ban Songkhon
Muang Dak Cheung
Ubon Ratchathani
Khong Chiam
Sanasombun
Lao Ngam
Sekong
Ban Palong Nyai
Mun
Dor
Tha Teng
Taat Hua Khon
Ban Donchan
Khong Chiam
Ban Bungkha
Bachiang Chaleunsuk
Paksong
Ban Sok
Kaman
Phonthong
Pakse
Taat Fang
Ban Xakhe
Det Udom
Sirinthorn Res.
Ban Huaxe
Phu Pongkham 1239
Sanxai
Champasak (Ben Wat Thong)
Bolaven Plateau
Ban Huaynamsai Lum
Ban
Wat Phu
Um Muang
Attapeu
Buntharik
Pathumphon
Sanamxai
Xaisettha
Plei Can
Kantharalak
Sukhuma
Champasak
Ban Uk
Attapeu
Ban Antum
Ban Phonsaat
Ban Sompoy
Ban Huayxai
Ban Tum Nyai
Kong
Chốăm Khsan
Ban Vin Tai
Sankeo
Munlapamok
Ban Phonsaat
CAMBODIA
Ban Taseun
Ban Kanlaang
Don Khong
Muang Khong
Siempang
Phlevleu
Plei Doch
Preăh Vihéar
Kâmpóng Srâlau
Si Phan Don
Ban Xot
Virachai
San
Trapeăng Pring
Taat Somphamit (Li Phi Falls)
Si Phan Don
Khon Phapheng
Krâcheh

MEKONG VALLEY

The great Mekong River is ideal for travelling by passenger ferry to visit the three provincial capitals in the area, with their rural atmospheres, temples and historical buildings

Map on page 150

Located in three adjacent provinces south of Vientiane on the Mekong are three cities that for many epitomise the Lao way of life. **Tha Kaek**, **Savannakhet** and **Pakse** are all provincial capitals of, respectively, Khammuan, Savannakhet and Champasak provinces, but this description is somewhat misleading. All of these three cities, although significant both culturally and historically, exude a decidedly small-town atmosphere which defines their real interest for the visitor. The air is clear, the river wide, and fresh breezes blow through the trees.

Tha Kaek and environs

Tha Kaek ❶ is Lao for "guests landing": a reference to the foreigners who arrived from Nakhon Phanom in Thailand, which is directly across the Mekong. This pleasant town, located 350 km (220 miles) south of Vientiane via Route 13, still greets its foreign visitors as its name suggests. Although shortly after the revolution it was renamed Muang Khammuan, the name Tha Kaek appearing to have sounded insufficiently nationalistic to the current regime, the only place one sees this appellation used is on government maps.

Historians have concluded that the site where the Nam Don flows into the Mekong, just south of the city, was settled by the Funan and Chen La Khmer kingdoms around the 5th century AD and was known as Sri Gotabura. The current site was chosen by the French, and building began in 1910. Nothing remains of Tha Kaek's distant past save a few pottery shards in the unimpressive Khammuan Museum, but the French era is still evident, not only in architecture but in the central *place de ville* and fountain. Tha Kaek currently has a population of around 40,000.

The most atmospheric section of Tha Kaek is the tree-lined esplanade along the river, from the fountain to the ferry landing. The fountain is located at the west end of the central city square. Directly west of the fountain is a now abandoned colonial-era **customs house**, from which stairs lead to the river; an old French iron-hulled gunboat lies beached at the bottom of them. As you go north along riverside Setthathirat Road, a few tables shaded by large trees are good for either just a rest or a cold drink, which can be called for from the small noodle shops opposite. Further north a **boat restaurant**, serving fresh fish dishes, is berthed on the Mekong. You remove your shoes and sit cross-legged at low tables in separate dining enclosures. Another 200 metres (650 ft) north, on the right side of the street, lies **Wat Nabo**, a bustling tree-filled temple which also houses a school. Adjacent to Wat Nabo, the **Souksomboon Hotel** is definitely worth a

BELOW: street scene with French architecture at Tha Kaek.

Woman using a traditional tool to remove rice husks.

BELOW: Tham Aen.

visit, even if its attached disco might deter some from staying there. It was built in the 1930s in an unusual blend of Art Deco and neo-rococo styles. Further north is the **ferry landing** to Nakhon Phanom; passenger ferries leave throughout the day, car ferries once a week. Given the condition of the road between Vientiane and Tha Kaek, arriving via ferry from Thailand might be worth considering, depending on your itinerary. Although improvements are ongoing, the bus ride from Vientiane to Tha Kaek still takes between seven and nine hours.

Wat Sikhotabun is known more as a picnic site than an active Buddhist temple. Located on the river, about 6 km (4 miles) south of Tha Kaek, the complex includes an impressive *stupa*, a worship hall and Buddha images. The *stupa* was built during the reign of King Setthathirat, the Lao monarch who ruled in the mid-16th century. The name of the temple is the Lao spelling of Sri Gotabura, the 5th-century Khmer settlement, and local lore relates that the site has been sacred since antiquity. The *stupa* has been restored several times, and that fact, coupled with the absence of monks, makes this destination more scenic than cultural.

Other side trips worth making from Tha Kaek are to the various **limestone caves** about 10 km (6 miles) east of the town on the unpaved Route 12. They are all located down side roads without signposts, so engaging the services of a local jumbo (motorised trishaw) driver to serve as a guide is necessary. The most popular cave, **Tham Aen** (*tham* is Lao for cave), unfortunately suffers from multicoloured fluorescent lights installed to enhance the atmosphere. More attractive caves closer to the town are **Tham Xiangliab**, through which a stream flows, and **Tham Pha Ban Tham**, where locals come to venerate a Buddha image.

Northeast of Tha Kaek, about 30 km (18 miles) on Route 13 and another 20 km (12 miles) east on Route 8, the new town of **Lak Sao ❷** is now much in the limelight. The headquarters of the military-controlled Mountainous Areas Development Company (MADC), the town which had a population of 24 in 1984 is now home to more than 20,000 people, a hospital, an airstrip and a radio station. The government is now promoting Lak Sao as a tourist destination, emphasising the attractive limestone karst formations along Route 8, the forest cover and the tribal villages. A road has been constructed to link Lak Sao with Vietnam, and border crossings are permitted. There is some dissent, however, regarding all the development. The MADC is heavily involved in logging, notably on the Nakai Plateau, which will be flooded if the Nam Thuen II dam project proceeds. Minorities are being removed from their highland village homes and resettled in "model villages" where, in return, they are given access to schooling, medical care and clean water.

The Lao Tourism Authority encourages tourists to visit these villages, where handicrafts are sold and cultural performances arranged. Eco-tourism and development, says the MADC. Plundering of natural and human resources, reply the dissenters. Responsible visitors will decide for themselves.

Savannakhet

The city of **Savannakhet ❸**, also known (again, only officially) as Muang Khanthabuli, is the second largest urban centre in Laos. With a population of 140,000 it

trails Vientiane by about 20 percent. Savannakhet, however, although not without interest, lacks the small town charm of Tha Kaek, and does not approach the cosmopolitan status of Vientiane. The 80-km (50-mile) stretch of Route 13 between Tha Kaek and Savannakhet takes two to three hours; this should improve, as substantial roadworks are under way. Located across the Mekong from the Thai city of Mukdahan, Savannakhet is a major transit point for trade between Thailand and Vietnam. Indeed, a bridge is planned to cross the Mekong at this point, and major construction work is taking place along Route 9, which runs from Savannakhet to the Vietnamese port of Da Nang. When completed this road will provide an important link for landlocked Laos.

As in Tha Kaek, the most appealing part of the city is the street running parallel to the river, Tha He Road. Towards the northern end of this road, **Wat Sainyaphum**, an active temple complex, houses a school building constructed in an interesting mixture of French colonial and Buddhist architectural styles, a *sim* (ordination hall) with fantastic stucco bas reliefs of camels and rhinoceros on the exterior walls, and French tiled floors. The gate of the temple facing south is an exceptionally well executed example of Theravada Buddhist temple architecture. A large drum tower and many trees add to the atmosphere of this temple, the oldest (founded 1896) and largest in Savannakhet.

Across the street from the temple, on the river embankment, more arcane deities are worshipped at a **spirit temple** called San Jao Suttano. Many and varied spirits, derived mainly from Chinese folk traditions, are venerated here, and notable among them is Kuan Yin, the Goddess of Mercy. An elderly man serves as intermediary for those coming to make requests from the spirits. The raised pavilion is small, but rich with incense smoke and mystical imagery.

Map on page 150

BELOW: a game of football by the Mekong.

Slightly south of this shrine a **night food market** offers a variety of Lao dishes as well as the ubiquitous Beer Lao at open-air tables. Across from the market, housed in a colonial era villa, the Mekong Hotel and Nightclub offers raucous live music and taxi dancers, catering mainly to visiting Vietnamese businessmen.

A few hundred metres south along the river the **passenger ferry terminal** is a hive of activity, well worth a visit even if you have no intention of crossing the river to Thailand. Porters, wearing brightly coloured uniforms to show that they are official, scramble up and down the precarious embankment carrying the many varieties of cargo that the passengers are transporting. The lively scene can be viewed from the comfort of an air-conditioned restaurant in the modern terminal building.

Turning away from the river at the passenger ferry terminal, onto Si Muang Road, you pass through the old commercial town centre, where the colonial ambience still prevails. A few hundred metres further in this direction, **St Teresa's Catholic Church** attends to the spiritual needs of Savannakhet's mainly Vietnamese Christian community.

About two blocks north of the church, **Wat Lattanalangsi** is a large but modern temple whose claims to fame are its glazed windows and a large reclining Buddha image. Located on Sutthanu Road, about three blocks north of the Catholic Church, is a historically significant **statue of Than Kou Voravong** (1914–54), a hero in the resistance against the Japanese and minister of defence under the Royalist regime. The elegant statue, depicting him clad in the upper-class *sompot* (men's collarless shirt), was cast after Voravong's assassination, but changing political winds did not allow this allegory of the vicissitudes of Lao politics to be erected until 1995.

BELOW: St Teresa's Catholic Church.
RIGHT: riding to school.

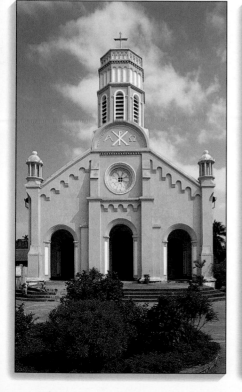

Markets and temples

To explore further in Savannakhet you need to hire a jumbo. Two kilometres (1 mile) east of the river, along Sisavangvong Road, is the **Talaat Singapore** (Singapore Market), so named because Singaporean aid paid for its construction. It offers an interesting mixture of upmarket goods and basic commodities; the vendors and their customers are even more interesting than the goods on sale. Further out of the town, along Route 13, a **dinosaur park** (open daily), complete with life-size replicas of the species which once inhabited Savannakhet, is scientifically dubious but, with tall trees, a large lake, a fish restaurant and quiet bungalows, makes an agreeable respite from urban Savannakhet.

Continuing a further 10 km (6 miles) east on Route 13 and then 3 km (2 miles) down a secondary road to the right, you come to **That Ing Hang ❹** (the Lao word *that* refers to any shrine said to contain a relic of the Lord Buddha). This is a site of great religious significance to the Lao. Both the site and the lower part of the structure itself date to later Khmer times (9th century AD), as indicated by the Hindu erotic art on the doorways. As with many Khmer religious sites in the region, That Ing Hang was restored and converted to a Buddhist place of worship during the time of the kingdom of Lan Xang – in the case of this *that*, during the 16th century. The French, during their rule in Laos, again restored the *that*. In spite of this mixture of cultural influences, the 25-metre (80-ft) -high *stupa*, which stands on top of a hollow chamber containing Buddha images (entry allowed only to men), retains an elegant and powerful presence.

For those with either a thirst for adventure or a profound interest in Khmer civilisation a trip to **Heuan Hin ❺** (literally, stone house) could be worthwhile. Located on the Mekong, 70 km (44 miles) south of Savannakhet, this Khmer

Map on page 150

A Hindu erotic door panel at That Ing Hang.

LEFT: That Ing Hang. **BELOW:** a market in Savannakhet.

temple, which dates from the 6th century, is set in a small grove of plumeria trees and is often the site of local fairs. The ruins themselves, which now contain a Buddha image, are unrestored, and most of the bas relief stone carvings which once decorated the site have been removed. Nonetheless, it's a pleasant three-hour cruise downriver from Savannakhet, and the village next to the ruins is prosperous and friendly.

Some 160 km (100 miles) east of Savannakhet lies the district of Xepon (also spelled Sepon), which can be used as a starting point for visits to what was once the Ho Chi Minh Trail (*see page 167*). But Xepon is reached via a very rough road, and the trail itself is 30 km (18 miles) further on. Most of the military detritus (tanks, trucks, artillery pieces) was destroyed during the war and is now half covered by the jungle, and the area is rife with unexploded ordnance (UXO). All things considered, Attapeu (*see page 167*) is a better venue for visiting the Trail.

Pakse and environs

The town of **Pakse** ❻, unlike Tha Kaek and Savannakhet, can lay no claim to having been home to ancient civilisations. The French founded it in 1905, possibly to offset the influence of nearby Champasak (Ban Wat Thong), which traces its lineage back to pre-Khmer inhabitants. Pakse (literally meaning "river mouth") is located at the confluence of the Don and Mekong rivers. It's about half the size of its northern neighbour Savannakhet, but Pakse's population of about 70,000 compensate for smaller numbers by the diversity and vivacious nature of the people. Pakse is home to many ethnic Chinese and Vietnamese, and one senses a less restrained, at times even cheeky, ambience here. Road travel

BELOW: Heuan Hin.

between Savannakhet and Pakse takes seven hours, with the condition of the road progressively deteriorating as you travel south. Again, extensive improvements are under way. Pakse is constructed on a grid of intersecting roads, so orientation is not difficult.

Map on page 150

The main sights of Pakse can be covered on foot within a day. A good walking tour would begin at the confluence of the two rivers; have coffee at one of the small **outdoor food stalls** just above the road leading down to the river ferry. Walking down the ferry road and bearing left, you will find small long-tail boats for hire. An interesting trip is to cross the Don River and visit **San Jao Suk Se**. Located on the northern bank of the Don where it meets the Mekong, this quiet and idyllic spirit temple, built in 1972, greets the devotees of the various deities of Mahayana Buddhism. Statues of a wide variety of wise men and minor gods line the walls of the incense-clouded temple.

Various other shrines dot the grounds, and the view of the Mekong and of Pakse is excellent. The best time to visit is morning, when the mainly elderly devotees come with offerings of food and drink for the gods and linger to chat among themselves. Be sure to negotiate a round trip with your boatman; the boat service to the temple is irregular.

The new bridge over the Mekong under construction at Pakse.

Returning to Pakse proper, walk along the bank of the Don and turn right at any of the main roads, all of which lead to the **central market**. A covered market building was completely destroyed by fire in 1997, so now the vendors operate around the periphery of the former site. Excellent fresh produce abounds, coming from the nearby temperate Bolaven Plateau. The far west end of the market (Road 10) specialises in local handwoven fabrics. A fine example of French colonial architecture, just north of the cloth shops, now houses the

BELOW: early morning in Pakse.

*Direct buses from
Vientiane to Pakse
take from around 16
to 18 hours.*

BELOW:
the Champasak
Palace Hotel.

Chinese Society. As you return towards the main road that parallels the Don River, the impressive compound of **Wat Luang** is hard to miss. Surrounded by large funerary urns, often shaped like *stupa*, this temple, which was built in 1935, contains the remains of many of the Champasak royal family, including Katay Don Sasorith, a staunch anti-Communist and prime minister during the Royalist period. The Communist regime removed his statue, that once stood in front of the temple, but wisely stopped short of disturbing his remains. The temple also houses a large school for monks, located in a beautiful wooden building behind the temple on the banks of the Don.

Champasak Palace Hotel

From Wat Luang, you could be forgiven for hailing a jumbo to the next point of interest, the **Champasak Palace Hotel**, about 400 metres (430 yards) east on busy Route 13. Construction of this edifice began in 1968; it was to serve as the residence of the last Prince of Champasak, Chao Boun Oum na Champasak. Boun Oum is remembered as a voluble and corpulent Oriental potentate, renowned more for his *joie de vivre* than his political prowess.

He served as prime minister of Laos from 1960 to 1962. As the tides of war turned against his faction he fled the country in 1974, dying in Paris a few years later and fated never to occupy his pleasure palace that commands lovely views of the Don River and the Bolaven Plateau. After the revolution the building was completed and served as a venue for Communist Party congresses and accommodation for visiting dignitaries. In 1995 a Thai company succeeded in its negotiations with the Lao government and, renovating the palace, converted it into a hotel. Although the hotel is highly recommended as

a place to stay in Pakse, it is worth a visit even if you are based elsewhere. The foyer uses gilt wood carvings to set an Oriental tone, but the meeting hall behind it, with its murals showing happily co-operating lowland Lao and hill tribes gathering the bountiful harvest, still recalls the building's days as a meeting place for the Party élite.

The atmosphere is relaxed, so it is not hard to wander to the upper floors where you can experience the effect that the building's intended inhabitant had planned. Huge pavilions (now hotel suites) are surrounded by private balconies, beneath which spread tiled terraces. The two top floors contain increasingly intimate reception rooms which command panoramic views of the entire region. Note the area just beneath the eaves on the upper floors of the building: as the Communists completed the building they added bas reliefs of the new national symbol of Laos, which included the obligatory hammer-and-sickle. Not content with merely painting over such images of the past, the new proprietors have placed bad luck-deflecting *feng shui* mirrors over the slogan that extols the virtues of socialism. Without ever intending to be so, the Champasak Palace Hotel is now a living historical museum.

Celebrating past and present

Directly east of the Champasak Palace Hotel lies **Wat Tham Fai** which, because of its sprawling grounds, is the site of many temple fairs. Should you be fortunate enough to be in Pakse when such an event is taking place (usually around the time of the major Buddhist holidays), be sure not to miss it; otherwise the temple has little to recommend it to the casual visitor. Another 200 metres (220 yards) east on Route 13 a small **Chinese temple** offers pleasant respite from the heat. Housed on two levels, it contains the garish images of the gods venerated by Mahayana Buddhism.

A further 400 metres (430 yards) east on Route 13 (it may be easier to hail another jumbo rather than walk) lies the **Champasak Heritage Historical Museum** (open daily 8am–4.30pm; entrance fee). Currently a bit rough and ready, the museum nevertheless has some beautiful pieces on the ground floor, including carved sandstone 7th-century Khmer lintels from Um Muang (*see page 164*) and some less interesting photographs of Communist Party officials greeting visiting dignitaries. (This emphasis is understandable since many of the party's leadership are from the south.) Many of the exhibits, however, are labelled in Lao or French (the Communist artefacts in Lao only, as a symbol of national pride), and the friendly guides speak only limited English. The first floor is more interesting, focusing on the various ethnic minorities who inhabit the region, including their jewellery and textiles.

After this admittedly lengthy day trip around Pakse (which, if you have the time, could be divided into two forays), a return to the starting point to watch the sunset at the confluence of the Don and Mekong rivers will provide an excellent perspective to reflect (over a chilled Lao beer) on this varied and vibrant southern terminus of the Mekong Valley. ❑

Map on page 150

BELOW: a small wall-mounted figure in a wat in Pakse.

SOUTHERN LAOS

Ancient temples, idyllic waterfalls, ethnic villages and captivating landscapes are just some of the attractions of the southern Lao regions, reached by scenic boat trips along the Mekong

Southern Laos offers a great diversity of attractions in close proximity. Travellers seeking insights into ancient history and culture will want to linger at the Khmer temple of **Wat Phu**, while the **Si Phan Don** (Four Thousand Islands) region will fascinate those with an interest in geology, colonial relics and current Lao rural lifestyle. The temperate **Bolaven Plateau** is home to a plethora of Mon-Khmer minorities; it offers superlative natural beauty, but still bears the scars of the Second Indochina War.

Travelling south from Pakse (*see page 156*) you leave a Laos bustling towards modernity and re-enter the past. Although land transport is feasible, via the same Route 13 that runs from the Cambodian border to Luang Prabang, the most atmospheric mode of travel is by boat. Depending upon your budget – and your pain threshold when seeking adventure – a variety of options is available for the 30-km (19-mile) cruise south to **Champasak** (Ban Wat Thong) on the western bank of the Mekong River. This is the starting-point for a visit to Wat Phu and nearby sights of historical interest. From what one might euphemistically call the Pakse ferry terminal, on the Se Don, about 200 metres (220 yards) upstream from its confluence with the Mekong, covered public boats leave throughout the morning. Each boat carries around 50 passengers, plus cargo.

LEFT: river boat to Champasak.
BELOW: the Katamtok Waterfall on the Bolaven Plateau.

Choice of seating is under or on the roof, although chivalry and Lao custom require that women do not ride on the roof. These vessels take two to three hours to reach Champasak, criss-crossing the river to deposit passengers at various riverside villages en route. The fare is minimal. A more comfortable alternative is to charter a smaller craft either from the same terminal or on the Mekong, just south of the two rivers' confluence. These vessels carry 10–20 passengers (avoid the smaller, uncovered long-tail boats) and take just over an hour to reach Champasak. Since the boat is chartered, smaller groups pay more per person.

A final alternative is to travel in style on the *Vat Phou*, a steel-hulled air-conditioned cruiser with private bathrooms and 12 state rooms. The company operating this vessel offers guided tours of the Wat Phu and Si Phan Don regions lasting four days, with French cuisine served on board. Bookings can be arranged through any of the travel agencies in Pakse. Prices vary according to season, but are never cheap.

Champasak

Prior to the establishment of Pakse by the French in 1905, the now sleepy **Champasak ❼** served as the administrative centre for the Champasak region, and the residence of Champasak's royal family when it was an independent kingdom. All that is left of this sumptuous past are two colonial era royal

residences, located just south of the now defunct fountain on the only paved street in the town.

While in Champasak, stroll along the tree-lined lanes and visit **Wat Thong**, located on the unpaved road directly west of the royal residences. Formerly the temple of the local royal family, it is now the final resting place of many of its members, and captures the essence of this city which time has eclipsed. Faded grandeur notwithstanding, Champasak has a very agreeable ambience. With comfortable accommodation available in the Sala Wat Phou, a restored colonial hotel, the town serves as an excellent base from which to explore Wat Phu.

Wat Phu and Um Muang

Wat Phu ❽ (literally "Mountain Temple") is located on a site which has been sacred to at least three cultures. The Chen La kingdom venerated the site from the 6th to the 8th centuries AD (reportedly placating the spirits with human sacrifices), and a pre-Angkor Khmer civilisation built most of the present edifices, beginning around the 9th century. Lastly, the Theravada Buddhist Kingdom of Lan Xang converted the Hindu temples into Buddhist ones.

What appears to have attracted the attention of all of these residents is an unusually shaped mountain behind the temple, Phu Pasak. The summit of this mountain juts skywards to a narrow precipice, which to the Hindu Khmers seemingly called to mind the holy Shiva *lingam*, or phallus. Locals still refer to the mountain, colloquially if somewhat irreverently, as Phu Kuai (Mount Penis). This geological formation also brings to mind a Buddhist *stupa*, which enhances its mystical significance. Adding to the symbolic power of the site, an underground spring flows from the mouth of a cave near the top of the temple complex. Although it lacks the grandeur of Angkor, Wat Phu nonetheless exudes a presence that even those not impressed by its architectural significance will find palpable.

BELOW: a fête at Champasak.

Located 9 km (5½ miles) south of Champasak, Wat Phu begins at river level and rises three levels to reach the foot of the mountain. Outside the complex is a large reservoir which in times past was the site of boat races and ritual bathing. The bathing (and fishing) continue, somewhat less ritualistically. As you go into the complex you see the remains of palaces built by Champasak royalty, towards the end of their dynasty, from which they viewed the annual festivities held on the full moon of the third lunar month, which continue to the present. An east-west axial promenade passes between two rectangular bathing ponds and leads to the base of the middle level. At the top of a flight of irregular stone stairs two large worship pavilions flank the central promenade. Scholars have deduced, from the deities carved into the stone, that the right-hand pavilion was used by male worshippers and the left by women. Currently only the former is open to visitors. As you climb through the small access door you can see Hindu bas reliefs on the lintels. Most of the free-standing statuary has been removed or damaged.

Returning to the central promenade you pass some pavilions whose function remains uncertain, owing to their state of disrepair. About 10 metres (30 ft) to the

the right of the central passageway is a stone *yoni*, a Hindu fertility and female well-being symbol. This artefact is constantly covered with offerings of flowers and incense, illustrating the continuing power of the ancient Hindu symbols among today's Buddhist Lao.

The third level of the temple, which contains the main sanctuary, is approached by a steep flight of stairs flanked by frangipani trees (*dok champa* in Lao, the national flower). Large trees and the remains of statuary surround the sanctuary, which is in a good state of preservation, as are the bas reliefs on the lintels. When this was a Hindu site of worship, a stone Shiva *lingam* occupied the central place of veneration bathed by spring water piped in from the cave; now large Buddha images take pride of place.

The mountain spring is still venerated by the Lao: bottles of the water are collected, and heads are held beneath the pipe emitting the spring water for both physical and spiritual refreshment. In the small cave behind the spring worshippers have collected a variety of Buddhist and Hindu religious statuary, including what appears to be a stone Shiva *lingam*. Behind and to the right of the sanctuary a stone carving depicts the Hindu trinity of Shiva, Vishnu and Brahma. Also to the right is a wooden Buddhist temple. A winding path leading from behind the temple (a small fee will secure the services of any of the young guides) leads to two interesting carvings of an elephant and a crocodile, probably by the first major group to venerate the site, the people of Chen La.

Wat Phu is famous for its *boon* (festival) which attracts visitors from throughout Laos and beyond. The precise dates vary, but usually the festival occurs in February. During the three-day event Wat Phu is filled with pilgrims who make offerings at various sites of the temple complex, particularly the sacred *yoni* and

Map on page 150

The ruins of the lower pavilion at Wat Phu, Champasak.

BELOW: the stairway and frangipani trees of Wat Phu.

Men and women of the southern minorities smoke long pipes filled with tobacco.

and the elephant and crocodile carvings. On the final day of the festival monks accept alms from the pilgrims, and in the evening a candlelight procession circles the worship pavilions at the lower level of the complex. Far from being a solemn event, the festival is characterised by a myriad of more worldly diversions such as boat races, cock fighting and kick-boxing competitions. In the evenings popular music and drinking add to the revelry.

Across the river from Wat Phu, located in a forest about 1 km (half a mile) north of the nearest village, Ban Nakham Noi, another Khmer ruin, **Um Muang** (also known as Um Tomo) is probably of interest only to serious aficionados of Khmer architecture, owing to its state of disrepair. A few carved lintels and Shiva *lingam* are all that remain of this 9th-century site.

Si Phan Don and Don Khong

After the historical and cultural focus of Wat Phu, the attractions of Si Phan Don and Don Khong are a pleasant change, offering scenic beauty and a glimpse into the life of Laos' rural population. The Mekong River is at its widest here: during the rainy season it is up to 12 km (7½ miles) across, and when the waters recede many small islands emerge. It is from this phenomenon that the Si Phan Don region takes its name, meaning "four thousand islands".

One of the larger and permanently inhabited islands – 6 km (4 miles) at it widest, 12 km (7½ miles) north to south – is **Don Khong ❾**, located about 120 km (75 miles) downstream from Wat Phu. Taking the public passenger ferry is for the hardy; depending on the passenger and cargo load, as well as the number of intermediate stops, the trip from Champasak can take from seven to nine hours. Charters can be arranged from either Pakse or Champasak. The journey can also be made by road, along Route 13 on the east bank of the Mekong; it takes about three hours in a public bus from Ban Muang across the river from Champasak. Direct buses from Pakse also reach Hat Xai Khun, a village east of Don Khong.

Don Khong offers no sites of historical significance, but compensates by giving the visitor a glimpse of southern Lao river life. Being the largest and most "developed" island it has decent accommodation in restored French villas from the colonial era, and even a Chinese restaurant in a breezy pavilion on the river. Don Khong is best explored by bicycle; a reasonable dirt road goes right round the island, and there are many interesting villages dotted along it. Since all overnight visitors will stay in Muang Khong, an exploration logically begins here. **Wat Phuang Kaew**, located directly behind the Sala Auberge Don Khong, greets visitors with a massive and gaudy stucco Buddha image.

Heading north you will find the oldest temple on the island, **Wat Jawm Thong**, which is in need of some restoration work. Interesting village temples can also be found at the southern tip of the island in Ban Huay and Ban Hang Khong, where the eponymous **Wat Hang Khong** temple is especially peaceful and attractive. Apart from the temples, Muang Khong is best enjoyed for its pleasant atmosphere and as a staging post en route to the islands further south.

Li Phi and Phapheng waterfalls

Located only 15 km (9 miles) by river south of Muang Khong, a one-hour trip which passes through a maze of small islands, **Don Khon** is the site of the **Li Phi Falls** (officially, though less commonly, known as Taat Somphamit). Also to be visited here are the remains of a 12-km (7½-mile) railway built by the French to allow cargo vessels to circumvent the rapids and waterfalls that abound on this section of the Mekong. During low water-level periods larger boats can reach only to **Don Det**, the island north of Don Khon, and a smaller long-tail boat navigates the channel between Don Det and Don Khon. Only basic accommodation is available in this area, so it is best explored on a day-trip from Don Khon. Any of the hotels in Don Khon can arrange such trips.

Disembarking on Don Khon you can pause for refreshment at a pleasant riverside café; across the road from it a French hospital from the colonial period is being converted into a small hotel. Turning right on the road in front of the hotel you pass through the village of **Ban Khon**, where a few colonial villas are shaded by trees. If you bear right where the road forks in the village you will reach the remains of a railway bridge built by the French. Passing beneath the bridge and turning left you come to the remains of an old steam locomotive which once plied the only railway ever constructed in Laos, in the early part of the 20th century. Two elderly Lao gentlemen who once served as railway engineers still live near the locomotive's final resting place and will proudly show visitors their certificates, in French, honouring their service. Although the locomotive itself is no more than a rusting hulk, the overall atmosphere is powerful. The hospital, villas and defunct railway all combine to epitomise the audacity and futility of the grand ambitions of *la mission civilasatrice*.

About 1 km (half a mile) further down what becomes more of a path than a road, the Li Phi falls rage over ragged boulders. Although the falls have a drop of only a few metres, their volume and power are impressive. A second set of falls is located about 500 metres (550 yards) further downstream. Fishermen use traps and nets in the pools at the base of the falls.

A unique attraction of Don Khon is a chance to view the endangered **Irrawaddy dolphin**. This mammal can survive in both fresh and salt water, but it is now mainly indigenous to the lower reaches of large Asian rivers, such as the Mekong and Irrawaddy. Held sacred by the Lao, they are not intentionally captured, but are nonetheless trapped in fishing nets and subsequently drown. Seemingly unafraid of humans, and thus a joy to observe, they travel in pods of fewer than 10. Every source queried has a different opinion on when and where to find them. Ask a local fisherman to guide you to the *plaa khaa*.

The **Khon Phapheng** (Phapheng Falls), are the largest set of waterfalls on the lower Mekong. What they lack in height they make up for in sheer volume. Several of the cascades are visible from the east bank of the Mekong, about 10 km (6 miles) south of the village of Ban Nakasong. From Don Khon or Don Det you must travel by boat to Ban Nakasong, and proceed south by land. The falls are an impressive sight, and are best viewed from a pavilion located

BELOW: Khon Phapheng.

above them – three separate cascades merge at this spot. Fishermen clamber precariously across the raging torrents on bamboo ladders to lay lines, while birds dive through the spray seeking smaller fry. Phapeng has its share of vendors of roasted chicken and other local delicacies, and plenty of cold beer: it's a lovely spot for a picnic and a great conclusion to this often arduous but certainly rewarding journey through a unique part of southern Laos.

The Bolaven Plateau

The Bolaven Plateau is known for its temperate climate and Mon-Khmer minority peoples; indeed, the name Bolaven means "place of the Laven", the predominant ethnic group in the region. Other attractions include waterfalls, boat cruises and, for those so inclined, visits to the Ho Chi Minh Trail (*see page 167*).

The plateau spreads over the Salavan, Sekong, Champasak and Attapeu provinces. The average altitude of 1,200 metres (4,000 ft) makes the area suitable for temperate crops. The French introduced the production of coffee, high-quality stock of both arabica and robusta strains; production declined during the Second Indochina War but is now experiencing a renaissance. In addition to the Laven minority, other groups include the Katu, Alak, Tahoy and Suay. All of these peoples have animist beliefs. The Laven in particular are famed for their handwoven cloth, with patterns of beads woven into the fabric. Foot looms are used to produce this cloth which, while not as fine as the work found in the north, certainly has a distinct style, more Khmer- than Thai-influenced.

Either Lan Xang Travel or SODETOUR in Pakse offers a variety of guided tours to the Bolaven Plateau, ranging from day trips to three- to four-day itineraries. Prices vary according to the size of the group and the itinerary. Since many of the attractions are located off the main road and are not signposted, some sort of guide is recommended; they are also available on a day basis in any of the major towns if you are not on a tour.

A good starting point for an exploration of the region is the **Taat Lo** (Lo Waterfall), 94 km (58 miles) northeast of Pakse. The road is paved throughout, and the journey time is no more than two hours; Laven villages can be visited en route. The falls drop only a few metres, but are wide and surrounded by lush vegetation. A restaurant at their base serves excellent French and Lao food. The Taat Lo Resort offers attractive chalets overlooking the falls. Alak, Katu and Suay villages can be found near the resort, which also arranges elephant day treks.

The town of **Salavan** is located 40 km (25 miles) northeast of Taat Lo Waterfall. Devastated during the Second Indochina War, the town has been rebuilt, and its only charm lies in its splendid isolation. Those interested in investigating the customs of the local Mon-Khmer ethic minorities might consider a visit.

A more interesting itinerary upon leaving the Taat Lo area would be to take the turn-off to **Sekong** ⑪ (Route 16), just east of the Taat Lo road. This two-hour journey passes through verdant coffee plantations with excellent views of the mountains above the plateau to the southwest. Sekong town, like Salavan, has been rebuilt since the war, and has a military

BELOW:
elephant trek at Taat Lo Resort.

presence. A decent hotel across from the market has an adjacent restaurant, and a good selection of minority handicrafts is available for sale. Otherwise the main reason to visit Sekong is to arrange a boat trip down the Kong River to Attapeu, which takes about seven hours. Although public transport exists, it's best to charter a long-tail boat, to allow stops at the many scenic spots along the way, including **Taat Hua Khon** (Human Head Waterfall) where, during a macabre World War II incident, the Japanese decapitated dozens of Lao partisans and threw the heads into the falls.

Attapeu and environs

Arriving in **Attapeu** ⑫ (officially Samakhi Xai, a piece of propaganda meaning "united people", which, deservedly, has failed to come into use), you see why the Lao call this their "garden city". All the houses seem to be surrounded by trees and shrubbery, both ornamental and agricultural. But, although strong on rural atmosphere, the town is without any specific attractions.

East of Attapeu, however, you can reach the **Ho Chi Minh Trail**. In the **Sansai** district you can see abandoned and damaged war equipment, and, near the village of **Paam**, an intact Russian Surface to Air missile and launcher, looking sad and incongruous in this rural setting. Although villages have rebuilt you can still see the crumbling foundations of temples destroyed by the bombing, and the defoliants used have left mainly scrub forests. Overall, the experience is unsettling but worthwhile. Those undertaking this trip should be particularly careful not to leave marked paths, since the concentration of unexploded ordnance (UXO) here is among the the highest in Laos.

Attapeu is literally the end of the line in terms of vehicle travel, so you must double back about 50 km (30 miles) towards Sekong in order to return to Pakse. Here a new road built to service a large hydroelectric project leads back to the Bolaven Plateau. About 30 km (19 miles) after starting this climb you reach **Nam Tok Katamtok** (Katamtok Waterfall). After you have become accustomed to the short but wide waterfalls of southern Laos, this cascade is spectacular in its 100-metre (300-ft) drop. A small pavilion provides a good viewing point, but no trails to the base are discernible, and the route would be precipitous, and also hazardous due to the possibility of UXO. About 2 km (1 mile) beyond the waterfall the road crosses a bridge, and to the right another small waterfall makes a pleasant picnic stop.

As you leave the more mountainous regions and re-emerge onto the plateau you come to prosperous-looking **Alak villages** which are accustomed to visitors and offer handicrafts for sale. **Paksong** ⑬ serves as a major market town where the region's farmers sell their crops, notably coffee, to middlemen from Pakse. The morning market is quite animated and filled with interesting minority groups who have descended from their home villages.

Beyond Paksong, on the way to Pakse, another spectacular waterfall, **Taat Fang** (also known as Dong Hua Sao), tumbles 120 metres (390 ft) – the tallest waterfall in Laos. Marked trails lead the physically fit 6 km (4 miles) to the base of the falls. ❑

Map on page 150

The six symbols of Laos' national seal: religion (the Pha Luang monument); industry (cogs); agriculture (rice fields); energy (a dam) transport (a road) and forestry (trees).

BELOW: war relic, east of Attapeu.

CAMBODIA

Cambodia's attractions include its historic sites, seaside resorts, cliff-top temples and the riverside city of Phnom Penh

A visit to Cambodia is truly a unique experience. Once the greatest city in the world, with over one million inhabitants, Angkor dominates the country's past and present, and will certainly make an invaluable commercial contribution to its future. Even after several visits one struggles to come to terms with the immensity of its scale; it is as though all the treasures of the Valley of the Nile were assembled in a single place. There is nowhere else like it on the face of the earth.

That Angkor is not listed as one of the Seven Wonders of classical antiquity is easy to explain – it hadn't yet been built, and the Greeks had no idea that Cambodia existed. But it surpasses them all, individually and even collectively. Truly, Angkor must be seen to be believed.

Yet Cambodia is more than just Angkor. There are wonderful temples, many hundreds of years old and still buried in the forests, waiting to be discovered. Some are not yet accessible, but each year clearance and restoration work is pressed forward, so that in time Cambodia is destined to become one of the world's major tourist destinations.

Then there is Phnom Penh, once an exquisite hybrid of Cambodian and French architecture and – despite the destruction of the war years and depopulation by the Khmer Rouge – destined to become so again. Like Laos, Cambodia has retained many of the beneficial aspects of French colonialism, and there can be few more romantic settings in which to sample French *haute cuisine* and sip a glass of wine than by the Chatomuk, or Quatre Bras, where the Mekong, Bassac and Sap Rivers come together. ❏

PRECEDING PAGES: helping out with the harvest; boat repairs in a fishing village on Tonlé Sap; preparing the land for the next crop; part of the Bayon, Angkor Thom. **LEFT:** Angkor Wat in silhouette.

Decisive Dates: Cambodia

EARLIEST TIMES

2000–1000 BC Early people, those on the flood-plains living in stilt houses while others inhabit caves, have a protein-rich diet of fish, rice and salt, and bake earthenware pots.

100 BC–AD 500 Establishment of a flourishing trading state called Funan in the Mekong Delta. Indian religious traditions – initially Shiva and Vishnu worship, but subsequently Buddhism – enter the region.

500–700 A proto-Khmer state is established inland from Funan near the confluence of the Mekong and Sap rivers, known to the Chinese as Chen La. The inhabitants speak a Mon-Khmer language, worship the goddess Shiva and begin to create a distinctive Khmer style of art at Vyadhapura (Angkor Borei). The first monumental Khmer architecture is produced during the reign of Insavarman I (616–65) at Sambor Prei Kuk.

THE GREATNESS OF ANGKOR

802–50 Reign of Jayavarman II, who proclaims himself a god-king and begins the great work of moving the capital to Roluos near Angkor.

877–89 Indravarman I creates a unified Khmer Empire and embarks on the construction of a massive irrigation system intended to underpin future expansion.

889–908 Yasovarman I moves the capital to Angkor.

1113–50 Surayavarman II begins the construction of Angkor Wat and conquers part of Champa.

1177 The Chams sack Angkor.

1181–1219 Jayavarman VII constructs the Bayon at Angkor Thom, establishing the rising influence of Buddhism, and defeats the Chams.

1296 The Siamese, a growing power to the north and the west, capture and pillage Angkor.

1297–8 Chou Ta-kuan, a Chinese visitor to Cambodia, writes an account of life and society in the Kingdom of Angkor.

1352–1430 The increasingly powerful Siamese Kingdom of Ayutthaya sacks and pillages Angkor four times, taking away the court regalia and many prisoners.

DIVISION AND DECLINE

1432 Under continuing pressure from the Siamese, the Khmer King Ponhea Yat abandons Angkor, moving the capital to the Phnom Penh region near the confluence of the Mekong, Sap and Bassac rivers. Subsequently Lovek, to the north of Phnom Penh, becomes the capital.

1593–4 Lovek is captured by King Naresuan of Siam.

1618–1866 The capital is moved to Udong, north of Phnom Penh, by Chey Chettha II.

1859 The French land at Saigon.

1862 French control three provinces of Cochin China.

THE FRENCH IN CAMBODIA

1863 The French force King Norodom to sign a treaty making Cambodia a French protectorate.

1866 A new capital is established at Phnom Penh.

1892 French troops seize the northwestern provinces of Cambodia from Siam and reincorporate them into the country.

1904 King Norodom dies and is succeeded by King Sisowath, who reigns until 1927.

1941 Thailand invades northwestern Cambodia.

1942 Norodom Sihanouk becomes king.

INDEPENDENCE AND THE INDOCHINA WARS

1945 King Sihanouk declares Cambodian independence with Japanese support.

1946 The Thais are expelled.

1953 Cambodia gains full independence from France under King Sihanouk.

1954 At the Geneva Conference, France formally confirms its withdrawal from Cambodia, Vietnam and Laos.

1955 Sihanouk abdicates, making his father, Suramarit, the king, while retaining real power for himself.

1959 Cambodia breaks off diplomatic relations with Thailand over ownership of Preah Vihear. The International Court at The Hague arbitrates and decides in favour of Cambodia.

1960 Sihanouk becomes increasingly autocratic. As the Second Indochina War develops Cambodia inclines towards North Vietnam and away from the United States.

1962 Disappearance of Cambodian Communist leader Tou Samouth. Pol Pot takes his place, and makes plans for a rebellion.

1965 Vietnam War escalates; Communist forces seek sanctuary in Cambodia. Sihanouk breaks off relations with USA but continues to repress domestic Communists and other dissenters.

1967 Pol Pot's group of Cambodian Communists – dubbed "Khmer Rouge" by Sihanouk – launches an insurgency in the northwest which the government brutally represses.

1969 US B-52 bombardment of Vietnamese sanctuaries in Cambodia begins.

1970 A coup is launched by right-wing General Lon Nol. Sihanouk takes refuge in Beijing.

1973 US troops begin to withdraw from Vietnam. In Cambodia B-52 carpet bombing peaks as 250,000 tonnes of bombs are dropped in seven months. The US Congress stops the bombing on 15 August.

THE ZERO YEARS

1975 Khmer Rouge forces led by Pol Pot defeat Lon Nol's army and take Phnom Penh on 17 April; cities are immediately evacuated, and the country is cut off from the outside world. Lon Nol officers, soldiers and officials killed; forced unpaid agricultural labour for all; brutal persecution of Buddhism and ethnic minorities.

1976 Massive starvation occurs in the northwest as hundreds of thousands of urban dwellers are deported there.

1977 Second wave of bloody purges centrally directed by Pol Pot group to try to eliminate all dissidents. Cambodia launches a series of military attacks across all three borders, massacring civilians in Thailand, Vietnam and Laos.

LEFT: stone image, the Bayon, Angkor Thom.
RIGHT: Cambodia-Vietnam monument, Phnom Penh.

1978 Refusal to negotiate with Vietnam over the border war. Massive purges spark an uprising in the east in opposition to Pol Pot regime. Rebels are defeated, regroup across the Vietnamese border and call for help from Hanoi.

1979 People's Republic of Kampuchea. Vietnamese troops invade and overthrow Pol Pot regime. Former eastern rebel Heng Samrin is president, Hun Sen foreign minister (who later becomes prime minister).

CAMBODIA REBORN

1979–88 Up to 100,000 Vietnamese forces are stationed in Cambodia to prevent a DK resurgence.

1989 Vietnamese forces start to withdraw.

1991 Prince Sihanouk returns to Phnom Penh.

1993 General elections are held, supervised by the United Nations. Coalition government of Prince Norodom Ranariddh's FUNCINPEC Party and Hun Sen's People's Party.

1996 Khmer Rouge forces split; Ieng Sary defects to the government in return for an amnesty.

1997 Turmoil increases within the Khmer Rouge. Pol Pot executes Son Sen and is placed under house arrest.

1998 Pol Pot dies in mysterious circumstances and the Khmer Rouge finally disintegrates. Hun Sen remains Cambodia's strongman.

1999 Cambodia joins ASEAN.   ❏

PRE-ANGKOREAN CIVILISATIONS

The early origins of the Cambodian people are not clear, but by the 8th century
"Land Chen La" was developing into a wealthy and centralised state

Experts tend to disagree as to the origins of the Cambodian people, some suggesting that they originated from the south, in present-day Malaysia and Indonesia, while others point to the southwards territorial imperative from what is now mainland China, which would indicate a Tai or Sinitic link. In fact, as is usual in these cases, the Cambodians as they exist at present are a racial and cultural mélange of many different peoples.

What is clear is that at least 4,000 years ago the fertile floodplains of the lower Mekong and Bassac rivers, as well as the Tonlé Sap (Great Lake of Cambodia), were inhabited by people of indeterminate origins, although logic dictates that they are at least partly ancestors of today's Cambodians.

Not a great deal is known about these people, but they certainly baked earthenware pots to hold water and fermented toddy palm, or to store the fish in which the region has always abounded. It was a forested area which flooded frequently, so it should be no surprise that they lived in stilt houses, just as most rural Cambodians do today.

Conditions for settled agriculture were unusually rich. The waters teemed with fish, rice could be grown with little effort, and primitive boats were built to travel from stilt house to stilt house and from village to village. The region, moreover, was close to the South China Sea, within easy access of the developing trade routes between China, South Asia and the Middle East. All the prerequisites existed for the development of a potentially rich and advanced civilisation, which began to happen around the 1st century AD.

The first kingdom

The first civilisation to appear was the Kingdom of Funan (1st–6th centuries AD), almost nothing of which survives today beyond the ruins of the supposed capital, Oc Eo, deep in

LEFT: ancient treasures buried in the jungle.
RIGHT: face of a Khmer statue.

the south Vietnamese delta province of An Giang. Oc Eo was a trading port which is thought to have flourished between about 100 and 400, after which it became submerged; it was discovered in the 1940s. Excavations reveal evidence of trade links, however tenuous, with Rome, the Middle East, India, South-

east Asia and China. In other words, Funan made up part of the flourishing coastal trade network which girdled Asia at that time, from the region of Canton to the Red Sea.

Rise of the Khmers

By 500 Funan appears to have been in decline, although the reason is unclear. It might have been the Arab discovery in the early centuries AD of the *mawsim*, monsoon winds, which allowed trans-oceanic rather than just coastal navigation, although this vital development could equally have led to Funan's commercial and economic growth. Meanwhile a new proto-Khmer state was developing further inland, the confluence of the Mekong and Sap rivers, in the region of present-day Phnom Penh. The inhabitants of this state, known to the Chinese annals (and therefore to subsequent history) as Chen La, spoke a Mon-Khmer language and were strongly influenced by Indian religious traditions. They may be regarded as the progenitors of the first authentically Cambodian state.

The first dated Khmer-language inscription known to history dates from 611, while the earliest known Sanskrit inscription from the region dates from just two years later. The historian David Chandler employs these and other, later, inscriptions to deduce that early Cambodian society was divided, in general terms, into two classes – those who understood both Sanskrit and Khmer, and those who only knew and spoke the latter.

The division between the the two classes was not just linguistic; it was also between those who grew rice and those who did not. "It was everyone's ambition to be 'rescued from the mud', but very few succeeded," Chandler explains. It was the destiny of almost all Khmers to work the land and to plant and harvest rice. All else rested on this fundamental, immutable fact. When sufficient surplus had

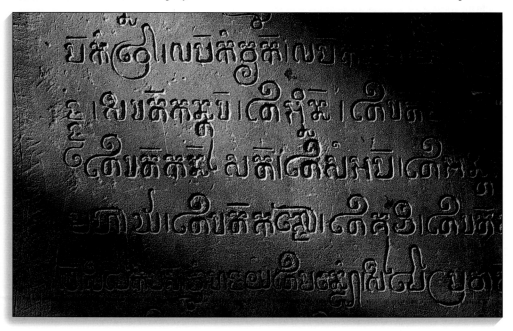

SANSKRIT AND KHMER

Sanskrit was the language of the gods and the priestly classes, and of matters of philosophic and esoteric concern. The records recount the genealogies of rulers, actions of the élite and meritorious deeds. They are all in highly polished verse. Khmer, by contrast, was the language of the *nak ta*, or "ancestor people", the indigenous, ordinary Cambodians. Inscriptions in Khmer are all in prose and record more mundane matters, such as temple administration, inventories of slaves, land-holdings, tax, and secular law. In this distinction between Sanskrit and Khmer lies much of the dichotomy which has distinguished Cambodian society to the present day.

been accumulated the "greater ones" – those "rescued from the mud" – could be maintained, and in turn they could devote their energies to maintaining the complex administration which would be required to build Angkor (*see pages 267–78*).

In early Cambodian society these privileged few, estimated by Chandler to make up around ten percent of the population, included clerks, artisans, concubines, artists, high officials and priests, as well as royal retainers and relatives, and finally soldiers. Khmer society, therefore, was divided into three separate and distinct groups: the summit symbolised by the king and his palace; the various groups, divided into *varna*, or castes, who did not have to grow rice; and the rice-growing peasantry on which the whole structure rested.

Life in Chen La

By around 800 the nascent Khmer state known to the Chinese as Chen La had developed into a fully fledged kingdom, with its capital at Isanapura (modern-day Sambor Prei Kuk, near Kompong Thom). At the time Isanapura was, according to one contemporary commentator, "the most extensive complex of stone buildings in all Southeast Asia, built a century ahead of similar constructions in Java."

Unfortunately, few records exist which can give an accurate picture of Cambodian society at this time. Historians are mostly limited to Sanskrit and Khmer inscriptions and the slightly more useful Chinese annals.

For several centuries, and certainly from the middle of the 3rd century AD, irregular tribute missions had been sent from the Lower Mekong Valley to China, and adventurous Chinese traders and other travellers had visited Funan and later Chen La. There is some confusion between descriptions of "Water Chen La", which may have been a Mekong Delta successor to Funan, with its capital at Vyadhapura (Angkor Borei, near Phnom Penh), and "Land Chen La", which lay further inland.

One Chinese description of Funan recounts: "The king's dwelling had a double terrace on it. Palisades take the place of walls in fortified places ... The king rides mounted on an elephant. His subjects are ugly and black; their hair is frizzy; they wear neither clothing nor shoes. For living, they cultivate the soil; they sow one year, and reap for three ... These barbarians are not without their own history books; they even have archives for their texts."

Yet such informative, albeit characteristically condescending, accounts are sadly few and far between, and we are therefore permitted little more than a momentary glimpse into the Khmer past. Around the middle of the 6th century, moreover, tribute missions seem to have stopped, perhaps at about the time that Funan was eclipsed by Chen La. Therefore very little is known of Chen La, or of why and how it developed. Current scholarship tends to take

the view that it was a loose confederation of small Khmer-speaking statelets (perhaps including "Water Chen La" and "Land Chen La") rather than, as was once thought, a powerful centralised state.

The move inland

By the 7th century "Land Chen La" seems to have eclipsed "Water Chen La" in importance as the centre of the polity moved northwestwards, beyond Isanapura and towards the region which would eventually become Angkor. At the same time the state seems to have acquired a new cohesiveness, though precisely why remains

uncertain. Chandler suggests that this may have resulted from increasing population density, improved wet-rice farming techniques and victories in local, unrecorded wars, the latter perhaps resulting in a protracted period of peace.

It is clear that by the 8th century "Land Chen La" was developing into an increasingly wealthy and centralised kingdom. Moreover, as the centre moved inland, away from the sea, it relied less on subsistence agriculture and trade, and more on manpower, irrigation technology and intensive rice production. In this way the foundations were gradually laid for the establishment of the Khmer Empire which would develop in the region of Angkor. ❑

LEFT: Khmer inscription at Lolei, Roluos.

RIGHT: Khmer sculpture of Durga Mahish.

THE ANGKOREAN ERA

The greatness of the Angkorean period was defined by its rulers who, apart from creating Angkor, unified the Khmer empire and introduced Buddhism

The Angkorean period of Cambodian history is generally considered to have extended from AD 802 to 1431, although these dates should not be interpreted too literally – there were Khmers in the Angkor region before it became the capital, and Angkor was not completely deserted when the capital was moved back towards Phnom Penh. Still, the six

centuries between these two dates mark the peak of Cambodia's power and influence in Southeast Asia, as well as the pinnacle of Khmer artistic and cultural achievement.

The god-king

The foundation of Angkor (meaning "city", from a Khmer variant of the Sanskrit *nagara*) is generally attributed to Jayavarman II. Little is known of him, but inscriptions dating from the 11th century – two centuries after the events in question – suggest that, as a young man, Jayavarman visited Java, returning in the late 8th century. He then travelled throughout the country from the Phnom Penh region, through the old capital at Sambor Prei Kuk, before settling in the region of Aninditapura, to the northeast of the Tonlé Sap.

Here he proclaimed himself a *devaraja*, or "god-king", creating a type of universal kingship clearly associating the ruler with the Hindu god Shiva. Although the records are few, it is clear that Jayavarman must have been a man of royal rank by birth and one who had already distinguished himself in various ways, not least in battle. Certainly his subsequent career involved numerous military campaigns, though the power he accrued also rested on a careful series of alliances, marriages and grants of land.

Jayavarman was undoubtedly successful: one inscription describes his realm as extending to "China, Champa, the ocean, and the land of cardamom and mangoes" (the latter is probably central Thailand). An exaggeration, certainly – even at its height the Khmer Empire never reached as far north as China. Nonetheless, it is probable that Jayavarman's influence extended over all of present-day Cambodia as well as to neighbouring territories which today constitute parts of eastern Thailand, southern Laos and the Mekong Delta region of Vietnam.

As a consequence of his successes, Jayavarman II is remembered as the founder of the first unified Cambodian state. He made his capital at Harlharalaya, an area today marked by the Roluos complex of monuments about 13 km (8 miles) southeast of Siem Reap, the oldest temples in the Angkor region.

Triad monarchs

Jayavarman was followed by a line of more than 30 monarchs who ruled from Angkor. Many of these incorporate the word *varman* (Sanskrit for "armour") in their titles. Not all are well known, nor did they all achieve greatness. Some, however, were clearly remarkable men, whose achievements, writ large in stone, retain the power to surprise and impress even today.

King Indravarman I (877–89) was one such, who during his rule established a "triadic" pattern that would be followed by many subsequent monarchs. Firstly, he busied himself with major irrigation works designed both to increase the agricultural production of the state and to indicate the extent of his power. Next, he commissioned statues of his parents and other relatives and ancestors shown as various gods. Statues of Jayavarman II and his queen, for example, depict them as Shiva and his consort, and were made for the temple complex of Preah Ko, near Roluos.

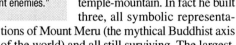

BRAVE WARRIOR

An inscription at Preah Ko tells of Indravarman as a monarch victorious at war: "In battle, which is like a difficult ocean to cross, he raised a pathway, made up of the heads of his arrogant enemies."

The third stage of Indravarman's rule was characterised by the construction of a temple-

Angkor, although the city that he founded was dignified by the Sanskrit name Yasodharapura in honour of its founder. The name Angkor does not come into general use until the 14th century.

Yasovarman's decision to move to Angkor was probably influenced by the presence in the region of a small hill on which he determined to build his own temple-mountain. In fact he built three, all symbolic representations of Mount Meru (the mythical Buddhist axis of the world) and all still surviving. The largest,

mountain, made in the form of a stepped pyramid and dedicated to him. It was designed to serve as both his tomb and a lasting monument to the glory of his rule. Known as the Bakong, the temple-mountain was the first great Khmer religious edifice to be made from stone rather than brick, and it still survives at Roluos.

Indravarman was succeeded in 899 by his son, Yasovarman, who ruled until about 908 and was the monarch who began the move to

LEFT: a 19th-century engraving by Delaporte of the upper courtyard of Angkor Wat.
ABOVE: Vishnu statue, Angkor Wat.
RIGHT: Khmer warriors, the Bayon, Angkor Thom.

Phnom Kandal or "Central Mountain", lies near the heart of the Angkor complex.

Building Angkor

To construct Angkor, Yasovarman needed to be both a ruler of vision and a great builder. He ordered the construction of a vast reservoir, the Yasodharatataka, along the southern shore of which he erected temples to honour Shiva, Vishnu and the Buddha, for by this time Buddhism had already started to make a serious impact on Khmer customs and religious beliefs. He also ordered the construction of numerous temples on hills throughout his domains. The most noteworthy of these is the great Preah

Vihear, set high on an all but inaccessible ridge of the Phnom Dangrek mountain range which separates Cambodia from northeast Thailand.

Over the next century Angkor continued to expand despite the construction of an elaborate rival city at Koh Ker, about 85 km (50 miles) to the north, by a usurper king. By the reign of Jayavarman V (968–1001) Angkor had grown considerably, and the ruler clearly commanded the loyalty of many thousands of field workers, stone masons and soldiers. Jayavarman V was a Shivaist but was very tolerant of Buddhism, which continued to exert an increasing influence at the royal court. One

of the most beautiful temples at Angkor, Banteay Srei or "Citadel of Women", dates from this time.

Inevitably a great city like Angkor attracted trade and foreign businessmen, but it seems that most international commerce was in the hands of the Chams, Chinese and Vietnamese rather than the Khmers. Goods traded included porcelain, cloth and textiles, forest produce, rice, buffalo and slaves. Unfortunately, little information regarding such matters survives, but some can be gleaned from the complex and detailed bas reliefs on the pediments of so many Angkorean monuments.

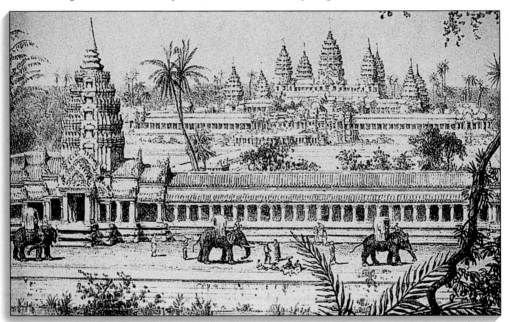

BUREAUCRATIC SYSTEM

Jayavarman V's successor, Surayavarman I (1002–50), emerged as a patron of Buddhism. He also expanded the Khmer territories, conquering the Theravada Buddhist kingdom of Louvo, which was centred on the town of Lopburi in present-day Thailand. Great hydraulic systems were built, and there is evidence of tight control over the people, who were obliged to live in close proximity in communities called *pura*. To meet the demands of his bureaucracy and the cost of running his kingdom, Surayavarman obliged the peasantry to work all year, utilising the reservoirs and irrigation canals to produce two harvests annually.

Jayavarman V's patronage of Buddhism was continued by his successor, Surayavarman I (1002–50). However, Utyadityavarman II, who ruled between 1050 and 1086, was a devotee of Shiva, and he built a great temple-mountain, the famed Baphuon, to house the Shiva *lingam* associated with his reign.

By the late 11th century the line of kings ruling at Angkor was in decline, with two or even three rivals competing for the position of "universal monarch". At the beginning of the 12th century, however, a new dynasty was founded by Jayavarman VI (1080–1107) which was to rule the Khmer Empire for more than 100 years.

Military power and diplomacy

Little is known about the first two kings in this dynastic line, but the third, Surayavarman II (1112–52), was a powerful ruler who presided over a unified kingdom in a manner reminiscent of Surayavarman I (no relation) and Yasovarman II.

As soon as Surayavarman II had ascended to the throne he began to act with vigour and speed to expand the territory and manpower under his control. His armies campaigned in the east, attacking both Vietnam and Champa. He employed mercenary troops drawn mainly from tributary regions in the west; it is likely dhism; rather, he was a devotee of the Hindu god Vishnu, and to the glory of this deity (and himself) he commissioned the largest and most magnificent of all the monuments at Angkor, the great temple complex of Angkor Wat (*see pages 269–73*). Construction of this monumental building was begun early in his reign, and was not completed until after his death in around 1150.

Kingship and religion

There is little information about the three decades between Surayavarman II's death and the coronation of Jayavarman VII in 1181 –

that these included Siamese, who appear in the bas reliefs at Angkor wearing grass skirts, carrying spears and marching out of step, in contrast to the serried ranks of Khmer soldiers.

Surayavarman II also established diplomatic relations with China – the first Angkorean monarch to do so, and possibly the first Khmer ruler since the days of "Water Chen La" to send missions to the Middle Kingdom. Unusually for a Khmer ruler, Surayavarman II was neither a partisan of Shiva nor a patron of Bud-

LEFT: a 19th-century engraving of Angkor Wat.
ABOVE: a stone carving in the South Gallery at Angkor Wat showing Surayavarman II surrounded by followers.

only one inscription survives from this period – but the latter's assumption of power represents a high point in Angkorean history.

As a young man Jayavarman VII (1181–1219) studied the doctrines of Mahayana Buddhism, the "Greater Vehicle" variant of the doctrine found in Vietnam, China and Northeast Asia rather than Theravada Buddhism, "The Way of the Elders", more generally associated with Southeast Asia. This devotion to Mahayana Buddhism was to become a major feature of Jayavarman VII's reign as he strove to associate traditional features of Khmer kingship – the *devaraja* concept of a universal god-king – with the teachings of Buddhism. This was at a variance with the concept of divine Khmer kingship, which generally associated the ruler with Shiva or, less often, Vishnu, or, on occasion, with Hari-Hara, a composite of the two. The Khmer kings employed this association to emphasise their grandeur, while in the minds of their subjects it had much to do with rice production, irrigation and adequate rainfall.

The new *bodhisattva*-kingship instituted and promoted by Jayavarman VII differed from the forms which had gone before in that the king no longer sought to be represented as the devotee of a divinity, or as a *devaraja* drawn up to divinity in death. Rather, through a combination of

Cham invasion

The French historians Paul Mus and Jean Boiselier identify the central event of Jayavarman VII's reign as the Cham invasion of 1177. The Chams had a powerful, marine-orientated kingdom in central and southern Indochina and controlled much of what is now central Vietnam between the 2nd and 12th centuries.

Jayavarman VII seems to have had some strong links with the Court of Champa and its capital at My Son, near present-day Da Nang. In the 1160s he seems to have spent some time there as either a guest or an exile, or perhaps leading a military campaign – as ever, the

meritorious acts, he sought to redeem both himself and his kingdom in the time-honoured Buddhist way. Apart from this, Jayavarman VII seems to have made little attempt to reform Khmer society or dismantle such Indian institutions as Brahmanism, slavery and universal kingship. Rather, he developed a synthesis of the two systems which effectively became one, and singularly Cambodian.

On a mundane level, Jayavarman VII was faced with a temporal threat which must have seriously shaken the Khmer regime and probably laid the initial foundations for the Cham-Cambodian mistrust that re-emerged in the brief but vicious holocaust of Democratic Kampuchea.

sources are sparse and imprecise. In 1177–8 the Chams invaded, first by water, and then by land. Their chief objectives seem to have been booty, prisoners-of-war and possibly revenge for earlier assaults against their own kingdom, especially by Surayavarman II. In 1178 they took the great city of Yasodharapura by surprise and pillaged it. According to a Cambodian stele the Cham King Jaya Indravarman IV "put the king to death, without listening to any proposal for peace".

Jayavarman, still three years away from his coronation, seems to have taken this invasion seriously. He defeated the Chams in a naval battle on the Tonlé Sap, while another Khmer prince killed the Cham king "with a hundred million arrows". On assuming his crown in 1181, Jayavarman VII found Angkor "plunged into a sea of misfortune and heavy with crimes".

As a Buddhist – as opposed to a Shivaist or Vishnuist – monarch, he believed he owed little to his predecessors, and so over the next three decades he sought to stamp his authority on his nation in a way which no other Cambodian attempted until such 20th-century figures as Norodom Sihanouk and Saloth Sar (Pol Pot) came to power.

CARING FOR THE SICK

Perhaps motivated by his Buddhist beliefs, Jayavarman VII departed from the Khmer norm in building numerous hospitals.

ents; this was followed by Preah Khan ("sacred sword") in 1191, and finally the famous Bayon, with its hundreds of enigmatic faces, each representing a Bodhisattva-like image of himself.

A new belief system

In many ways Jayavarman VII's reign can be seen as seminal for the development of Buddhism in Cambodia – not that he was anything but a syncretist: facilities and cells for Vishnuist and Shivaist devotees and for temple Brahmans

Once securely in power Jayavarman VII put in place a major series of road building and other public works programmes. He also built numerous public resthouses and reservoirs. He expanded the frontiers of his kingdom, bringing much of what is now central Thailand, southern Laos and southern Vietnam under his control. Jayavarman was also a temple builder *par excellence*. In 1186 he erected the Ta Prohm complex in honour of his parents.

LEFT: stone carving of Cham worshipping at the Bayon, Angkor Thom. **ABOVE:** portrait in stone of Jayavarman VII. **RIGHT:** Lochana, representing the ideal essence of Buddha.

were included in his major works. Nevertheless it was from this time that Buddhism began to supersede the Indic religions as the main belief system of the Cambodian people.

Still, the gradual conversion of the great majority of people to Theravada Buddhism during the 13th century is not solely attributable to Jayavarman's personal belief system – which was, in any case, Mahayanist. Equally important were his conquests to the west, where the south-moving Tai peoples and the long-established Mon population were already Theravada Buddhist. It also seems that wandering Sri Lankan monks may also have played a part in the conversion process. ❑

BACK TO WATER CHEN LA

The social and political upheaval which would leave the Khmer empire

at the mercy of its larger neighbours began early in the 15th century

Following the reign of Indravarman III, the Kingdom of Angkor entered a period of slow but terminal decline of which we know relatively little. Few inscribed stelae survive – if, indeed, they were ever created, as the old Hindu-orientated élite gradually embraced Theravada Buddhist values. Our knowledge of the period, such as it is, rests on Chinese records, one Cham inscription and a few Siamese ones, the evidence of archaeology and the uncertain process of logical deduction. As a result, historians tend to disagree about the progress of events in Cambodia in the two centuries between about 1350 and 1550.

Return to the coast

What is clear is that the country's political and economic centre of gravity began a long but inexorable shift back from "Land Chen La" – that is, the Roluos-Angkor region at the head of the Tonlé Sap – to "Water Chen La" – the region around Phnom Penh, Lovek and Udong – in the mid-14th century.

Some historians argue that this striking reversal of the Cambodian historical imperative was due to the rise of the Tai kingdoms (and especially that of the Kingdom of Ayutthaya) to the west and north of Angkor; others – notably Wolters and Vickery – contend that the shift back to the southeast was more probably linked to the rapid expansion of maritime trade between China and Southeast Asia which took place during the late Mongol and early Ming Dynasties in the 13th to 15th centuries. Proponents of the first school of thought tend to represent this as a period of Angkorean "decline", while those of the second, more recent school, see it as a period of Cambodian "change". As is usual in such dialogues, there is doubtless an element of truth in both hypotheses.

The most reliable references we have, as well as the most numerous, are Chinese. According to the historian David Chandler, more than a dozen tributary missions were sent from the Khmer Empire to China between 1371 and 1419 – more than were sent during the entire Angkorean period. The Chinese clearly valued these contacts which, as usual, were as much commercial as tributary missions, and afforded

the visiting Cambodian delegates appropriate dignity and respect.

But what actually happened "on the ground"? Viewed from an Angkorean perspective, the great temple complexes dedicated to Hindu deities such as Shiva and Vishnu may have declined in significance as Buddhism became the predominant religion of the state.

The Siamese threat

Then there was the unsettling question of the Siamese. Once tributary peoples who had served as mercenaries in the Angkorean armies, these relative newcomers to the region grew rapidly both in numbers and in strength, posing

LEFT: 16th-century mural on a *wat* wall depicting the Buddha taming the wild elephant, Nalagiri.
RIGHT: pagoda housing, Phnom Penh.

an increasing threat to the Kingdom of Angkor. This threat became palpable with the establishment, in 1350, of the Siamese Kingdom of Ayutthaya, centred on the Lower Chao Phraya River basin, within relatively easy striking distance of Angkor.

Wars soon broke out, with the Siamese generally, though not always, gaining the upper hand. Angkor was captured and sacked on several occasions, most notably in 1431. In sparsely populated Southeast Asia the "spoils of war" usually meant seizing people rather than land (*see page 28*), and these Siamese victories would have meant the large-scale transfer of

where in Southeast Asia must have appeared tremendously attractive. As the Angkor region came under repeated Siamese attack, this commercial alternative to an apparently endless cycle of war, temple-building and intensive rice cultivation must have become increasingly appealing. Accordingly, Chandler suggests that while one portion of Angkor's population departed westwards in a slow haemorrhage of power as prisoners of the Siamese, another portion – perhaps a trickle, not a stream – migrated southeast, to the vicinity of Phnom Penh, in search of a more prosperous and more secure existence.

captured Cambodian prisoners to the west, which deprived Angkor of much of the massed labour necessary for the maintenance of its great irrigation systems, not to mention skilled stonemasons and other temple builders.

On a more mundane level, the first- and second-quality sandstone used in temple construction had begun to run out, and the builders were increasingly obliged to use poorer-quality laterite. The time had come to move elsewhere.

Maritime trade

Viewed, on the other hand, from a Phnom Penh perspective, the rich and expanding possibilities of maritime trade with China and else-

VIETNAMESE RIDICULE

In the 19th century the Nguyen Lords of southern Vietnam began a sustained effort to "Vietnamise" Cambodian society, encouraging the wearing of Vietnamese clothes while also isolating Phnom Penh from direct contact with the outside world. Much of the hostility towards Vietnam which still represents an undercurrent in Cambodian society can be traced to this period. The Vietnamese tended to patronise the Cambodians, whom they saw as primitive children. According to the Emperor Minh Mang: "The people do not know the proper way to grow food... they do not know how to store rice for an emergency."

Significantly, this latter group of migrants would probably have included many of Angkor's richer and better educated classes – clerks, merchants, overseas businessmen such as the influential Chinese community, and perhaps even private slave-owners and landholders. To quote Chandler: "Once the choice had been made to become a trading kingdom – and it is impossible to say when, or how, this happened – locating the Cambodian capital at Angkor no longer made much sense."

Reasons for choosing the Phnom Penh region for a new capital were plentiful and logical. To begin with there seems to have been the well-therefore (for some time, at least) safe from Siamese attack, the Phnom Penh region was centred on the confluence of three rivers, the Mekong, Sap and Bassac, at a region known in Khmer as Chatomuk, or "four faces", subsequently known to the French as Quatre Bras, or "four arms" (*see page 209*).

A shrinking nation

The final move from Angkor seems to have taken place some time after 1432. Successive capitals were established, first at Lovek and then at Udong, both slightly to the north of Phnom Penh, and finally at Phnom Penh itself.

established tradition of royal rule from the Lower Mekong region dating back to "Water Chen La" and even Funan. In a way the Khmers were merely retracing their steps. It is also possible that the former royal region had resented the overlordship of Angkor, and that local chiefs, descendants or successors of an earlier élite, were anxious to reassert their independence from Angkor and to trade directly with China on their own behalf.

Beyond this there was the question of geographical location. Far from Ayutthaya and

During the subsequent two centuries the Khmer Empire frequently found itself at war with the Siamese court in Ayutthaya, sometimes emerging victorious, but more often on the losing side.

Meanwhile Vietnamese migrants began to move into the still predominantly Khmer region of the Mekong Delta until, by the 18th century, the new arrivals outnumbered the original Khmers by as many as ten times. The country was gradually being squeezed, but for the time being the commercial capital, Lovek, continued to prosper, with distinct trading communities of Chinese, Malays, Portuguese, Spanish, Japanese and Arabs established in the city.

LEFT: crude figures near a *stupa* in Udong.
ABOVE: Khmer statues, the Bayon, Angkor Thom.

A direct result of Cambodia's gradual shrinkage, caught between the Vietnamese hammer and the Siamese anvil, was a commensurate growth in both Siamese and Viet interference in Cambodian affairs. Relations with the Siamese court were better than those with the Vietnamese; a shared Indic perception of the world and many other similar values made the courts of Ayutthaya and Phnom Penh at least mutually comprehensible to each other. There was little understanding for or sympathy with the Vietnamese court at Hue, however, and anti-Vietnamese sentiment continued to grow apace.

bodia have become my children now, and you should help them and teach them our customs." He also advocated that Cambodians should be encouraged to speak Vietnamese, use Viet weights and measures, and even adopt Vietnamese table manners. Naturally enough, these policies sparked a long series of simmering rebellions. Meanwhile the Siamese court took advantage of the resulting instability to promote its own interests.

A number of the characteristics of anti-Vietnamese feeling, which would become so prevalent in the late 20th century among Cambodians of all walks of life, are apparent

Anti-Vietnam feelings

Had it not been for the arrival of French imperialism in the region during the 19th century, it is quite likely that the once-powerful Cambodian kingdom would have disintegrated completely. The western areas around Battambang and Angkor would probably have passed under Siamese control while Vietnam would have come to dominate Phnom Penh and the eastern regions of the country.

Certainly the paternalism of Vietnam's Minh Mang must have been humiliating for the Cambodians. In one lengthy memorial the Vietnamese leader addressed his administration in the following terms: "The barbarians in Cam-

from this time of petty risings. One rebel wrote: "We are happy killing Vietnamese. We no longer fear them. In all our battles we are mindful of the Three Jewels: the Buddha, the Law (*dhamma*) and the Monastic Community (*sangha*)." The Vietnamese responded by using Cham mercenaries – often Muslims – to put down the rebels, a development which would bode ill for Cambodia's Cham minority some hundred years later under the Khmer Rouge regime. ❑

LEFT: 18th-century map of Siam (Thailand), Laos and the Khmer Empire (Cambodia).
ABOVE: Cham fisherman, Tonlé Sap, *circa* 1890.

Pol Pot

The Khmer Rouge leader Pol Pot, known to his followers as "Brother No. 1", was born in 1928 in the village of Prek Sbauv, near the provincial capital of Kompong Thom, some 140 km (88 miles) north of Phnom Penh. He was the eighth of nine children of well-to-do farmers and was named Saloth Sar. In common with most revolutionary communist leaders, Saloth Sar was neither a peasant nor a proletarian; his family enjoyed close relations with the royal court in Phnom Penh. His cousin Meak had joined the Royal Ballet in the 1920s and was a consort of Prince (subsequently King) Monivong, to whom she bore a son. Saloth Sar's sister, Saroeun, also joined the Royal Ballet and became a royal consort; his elder brother, Loth Suong, worked at the palace as a clerk.

In 1934 Saloth Sar was sent to live with his relatives at court. During this time he spent several months as a novice monk at Vat Bottum Vaddei, a monastery near the palace which was favoured by the royal family, and studied the Buddhist scriptures and Khmer language. Later he learnt French and studied at Russei Keo Technical College in Phnom Penh. Although not an outstanding student he was chosen as one of a group sent for further education in Paris. Here he came into contact with Cambodian nationalists, including Ieng Sary, who would become one of his key associates.

In 1950 Saloth Sar visited Yugoslavia, and was apparently impressed by Tito's independent stand, rejecting both the West and the Soviet Union. In the same year he and Ieng Sary joined the French Communist Party. Two years later, having returned to Cambodia without any qualifications but with a newly acquired and keen sense of nationalism, he joined the Indo-Chinese Communist Party which was dominated by the Vietnamese. Although secretly nurturing an intense hatred for all things Vietnamese, Saloth Sar rose steadily through the ranks and became General Secretary of the (still clandestine) Cambodian Communist Party in 1962.

Soon after that Saloth Sar and his close colleagues disappeared into the jungled hills of Ratanakiri Province, where they began building the Communist guerrilla faction which King Sihanouk dubbed the "Khmer Rouge". During the subsequent years of civil war Saloth Sar used his increasingly powerful position to eliminate Hanoi-

ABOVE: Pol Pot, a lovely child who became a monster.

trained or pro-Vietnamese cadres – building, in essence, a movement which, though nominally internationalist, was deeply xenophobic, anti-urban and above all hostile to Vietnam.

In 1975 – Year Zero – the Khmer Rouge seized power and established the Democratic Kampuchea regime, but still Saloth Sar, now hiding behind the pseudonym "Pol Pot", remained out of the limelight. Between 1975 and his overthrow in 1979 he established what has been accurately characterised as "an indentured agrarian state". Brooking no rivals, he gradually eliminated all those whom he saw as a potential threat to his personal power – not to mention more than two million

ordinary Cambodians who were murdered, worked to death or died of starvation.

Overthrown by the Vietnamese in 1979, Pol Pot and his followers took to the jungles where, for almost 20 years, their numbers dwindled through desertion, disease and military attrition. Pol Pot was eventually arrested by his few remaining comrades, and either died or was killed near Anlong Veng in 1998. In retrospect it is difficult to see what inner demons drove Saloth Sar to develop into the paranoid political monster Pol Pot. Certainly his elder brother, Loth Suong, who survived the Zero Years, was unable to explain it, commenting with obvious bewilderment that Pol Pot was "a lovely child". ❑

THE KILLING FIELDS

The modern history of Cambodia is one of tragedy: it is estimated
that nearly a fifth of the population was killed in the late 20th century

Continuing Siamese-Vietnamese competition for domination over the rump of the Cambodian kingdom effectively came to an end in 1863, when King Norodom was persuaded to accept the establishment of a French protectorate over Cambodia. This had the somewhat contradictory effect of halting Viet-

namese political expansion into the country (as well as limiting Siamese influence) while at the same time encouraging Vietnamese immigration, for the French favoured the establishment of a predominantly Vietnamese civil service throughout Indochina.

French rule

Until 1941 all seemed to run smoothly in Cambodia. For example, in marked contrast to what happened in Vietnam, only one French official was assassinated during the entire pre-war colonial era, while the French helped transform Cambodia into a regional rice-bowl. Beyond this – starting with the traveller Henri Mouhot

(1826–61) – the French "rediscovered" the glories of Angkor, and contributed greatly to the establishment of two immensely significant and at least partially accurate truths, which form a central part of the Cambodian national psyche: firstly, that the Cambodians built Angkor; and, secondly, that French intervention saved most of Cambodia from division between Siam (later Thailand) and Vietnam. So maybe the French colonists were not too bad, in the short term. To quote the pleasure-loving and somewhat cynical King Sihanouk: "I am an anti-colonialist, but if one must be colonised, it is better to be colonised by gourmets."

Not everyone agreed, of course. And in the vanguard of the anti-colonialist forces, predictably, were the nationalists of the Indochinese Communist Party. Here, without descending too far into the racial maelstrom of Cambodian politics, a problem arises. Perhaps inevitably, the larger and more sophisticated Vietnamese element in the ICP dominated the lesser Lao and Cambodian contingents, leading to fears that "Big Brother" Vietnam might seek to replace the French as masters of a unified Indochina. Such, at least, were the fears of some revolutionaries: Lao and, especially, a group of ultra-nationalist Cambodians for whom hostility towards and fear of Vietnam was second nature.

The events which followed resulted in a bitter civil war and, after Democratic Kampuchea's seizure of power in 1975, the deaths of 2–3 million Cambodians – Khmers, Cham Muslims, ethnic Chinese, Thais, Vietnamese, Lao, Shan and various minority hill peoples.

How did this tragedy come about? As we have seen, Cambodian resistance to the French was of a very limited nature. A few teacher-intellectuals were active in producing nationalist literature – notably a Khmer language paper called *Nagara Vatta* (Angkor Wat) in the early 1940s. In 1940 France fell to the Germans; the colonial authorities in Indochina supported the Nazi-established Vichy regime, and in 1941, somewhat unexpectedly and with French backing, Norodom Sihanouk became king. On 9 March 1945 the Japanese armed forces moved to oust the Vichy administration, and on 13 March, in response to a direct request from Japan, King Sihanouk proclaimed Cambodia independent and changed the official name from Cambodge to Kampuchea. Within a few short weeks, however, the French were back in an ultimately doomed attempt to restore their colonial presence in Indochina.

LON NOL'S FANTASY

General Lon Nol believed that the Khmers were potential supermen, warriors who could defeat the Khmer Rouge and the NVA with charmed bullets and amulets.

The Indochina Wars

What followed, tragically, were three consecutive Indochina wars. The main protagonists were, of course, the Vietnamese, who took on and defeated first the French, then the United States, and finally an unlikely alliance of fellow "socialists" from China and Cambodia.

At first it appeared as though Cambodia might avoid serious involvement in Vietnam's long and vicious war with the French. Certainly most anti-colonialist fighting went on further to the north, culminating in the French debacle at Dien Bien Phu in 1954. Inevitably, however, as Ho Chi Minh's Hanoi-based government (The Democratic Republic of Vietnam) sought to take on and destabilise the Franco-American regime in Saigon (The Republic of Vietnam), Cambodia, together with neighbouring Laos, was drawn into the fray. Tentacles of the mighty "Ho Chi Minh Trail" crossed and recrossed each other throughout Laos and into the remote north-eastern Cambodian provinces of Ratanakiri and Mondulkiri – territories made familiar to Western filmgoers, albeit in a grossly exaggerated and stereotyped way, as the domain of the mad Colonel Kurtz in Francis Ford Coppola's *Apocalypse Now*.

In 1969, without Congressional approval, the USA began a series of massive air strikes against perceived Viet Cong and NVA (North Vietnamese Army) bases in Cambodia. Huge areas of the eastern part of Cambodia were carpet-bombed by B-52 bombers flying out of Thailand and Guam, devastating much of the country and driving the surviving Khmer peasantry to despair. They responded in one of three ways – massacring ethnic Vietnamese by way of "revenge"; flooding into an already bursting Phnom Penh; or joining the nascent Khmer Communist insurgency, dubbed by Sihanouk the "Khmer Rouge". Indeed, had not Kissinger's "sideshow" in Cambodia taken place it is doubtful whether the few hundred Khmer Communists hiding in remote Mondulkiri could have ever seized power.

As it was, the tragedy was played out. In March 1970, while on a visit to Beijing, Sihanouk was overthrown in a coup d'état by the Cambodian military headed by

General Lon Nol, who was bitterly anti-communist and hostile to the Vietnamese, and the coup was tacitly supported by the USA. Lon Nol then sent two major columns northwards into Communist territory. However, though grandiosely named Chen La 1 and Chen La 2, they were comprised mainly of ill-trained and poorly armed boys, who were cut to pieces by the insurgent forces.

Meanwhile, as territories under the control of the Lon Nol regime shrank, Sihanouk took up residence in Beijing and allied himself with his erstwhile Communist enemies, the Khmer Rouge. Embittered by its casualties and the failure of its strategy, the USA "Vietnamised" the war, withdrawing most or all of its combat

LEFT: a royal prince *circa* 1921.
RIGHT: Lon Nol leaves Phnom Penh.

troops from Vietnam by 1973 and leaving the troops of the Army of the Republic of Vietnam (ARVN) to fight the NVA with just US intelligence help and occasional air power.

The Khmer Rouge

Cambodia remained a sideshow – but word had spread amongst correspondents based in Phnom Penh that the Khmer Rouge were strangely different from the Viet Cong, the NVA and the Communist Pathet Lao. While they fought just as well, they were said to be quite merciless, and to be emptying small cities and towns of people as they fell under their control. More-

Almost the first order broadcast by the new regime, which called itself Democratic Kampuchea (DK), was the expulsion of the entire population of Phnom Penh on the pretext that a bombing raid was to be launched by the USAF. In fact, KR policy was the complete ruralisation of Cambodian society – all cities, towns and major villages were to be emptied, and the population sent to work in the fields. This policy was implemented with extraordinary ruthlessness – even patients in operating theatres were turned out onto the street to fend for themselves. Those who could not do so or who argued were shot or beaten to death. Meanwhile

over, they were increasingly hostile to their supposed Vietnamese "mentors" – by no means the puppet army of Hanoi that had been imagined.

The true nature of Cambodian Communism as interpreted by the Khmer Rouge leadership began to become clear on 17 April 1975, when Phnom Penh fell to the KR fully two weeks before the NVA rolled into Saigon. Most residents of the Cambodian capital were openly delighted the war was at last over, and were prepared to give the victorious Communist guerrillas a courteous if careful welcome. Instead they watched with mounting dismay as groups of sullen-faced, often openly hostile child-soldiers swarmed into the city.

ROYAL ALLIES CAST ASIDE

After the Khmer Rouge took power the former king, Sihanouk – the KR's their erstwhile ally – was flown back to Phnom Penh from Beijing, where he was held under de facto house arrest in the Royal Palace. He was then forcibly retired; a statue was to be built in his honour, and he was to receive a pension of US$8,000 a year, but neither of these ever materialised. During the Zero Years around 20 of Sihanouk's family were murdered by the Khmer Rouge, and it is more than likely that he too would have become a victim had it not been for direct appeals on his behalf from such Communist luminaries as Mao Tse-tung, Chou En-lai and Kim Il-sung.

a search was instituted for all members of the former Lon Nol army, who were marked for execution. A similar fate awaited all "intellectuals", from university professors and doctors to anybody who spoke a foreign language.

Meanwhile the shadowy élite of the Khmer Rouge, who would control the fate of Democratic Kampuchea, installed themselves in some considerable comfort in the administrative centre of Phnom Penh. The core group included, besides Pol Pot and Ieng Sary, the former schoolteacher Khieu Samphan, Thai-educated Nuon Chea – who would emerge as "Brother No 2", second only to Pol Pot, yet still more of an enigma – and Vorn Vet. Also of considerable importance were two sisters, Khieu Ponnary and Khieu Thirith, the former married to Pol Pot, the latter to Ieng Sary.

Once in power the DK élite began building a "new society" through what they called a "Super Great Leap" to socialism – clearly designed to surpass China's disastrous "Great Leap Forward". Society at all levels was divided and then subdivided into different groups. The "Old People" – those who had lived under KR rule before the fall of Phnom Penh – were most favoured, while the former city-dwellers, or "New People", were without any rights at all. In between were "Depositees": potential supporters of the revolution. A chilling but common threat made against New People in Democratic Kampuchea was "destroying you is no loss; keeping you is no gain". Tens of thousands were bludgeoned to death or forced to labour on massive construction sites, or sent to develop "new frontiers" in the malarial Elephant and Cardamom Mountains.

Frontiers were sealed. All religion was banned, the Buddhist supreme patriarch murdered, temples were turned into rice barns and mosques into pigsties. Pol Pot announced that feeding monks was a crime punishable by death, but his associate Nuon Chea kept one temple with four monks open for his pious old mother – DK rule was hypocrisy writ large. It was also paranoia. Pol Pot and his immediate henchmen saw traitors and Vietnamese agents everywhere they looked, and even as mad instructions were given for the country to be turned into a precise chequer-board of identi-

LEFT: Lon Nol's troops at the southern front.
RIGHT: King Sihanouk in Beijing.

cally-shaped rice fields, the dreaded *santebal* or secret police began a witch-hunt for opponents of the regime, real or imagined.

The Killing Fields

The interrogation and torture centre known as S21 or Tuol Sleng, a special prison under the direction of a high KR official known as Deuch, became the nerve centre of this operation. During 1975 and the first part of 1976 the majority of the victims of KR brutality were ordinary people, but as time passed so *angkar* – the organisation – began to consume more and more of its own. Pol Pot particularly dis-

trusted the khaki-clad troops of the Eastern Zone who had not been under his direct command during the civil war, denouncing them as "Khmer bodies with Vietnamese minds". In 1976–7 he unleashed his most loyal and most feared military commander, the one-legged General Ta Mok, against them.

Ta Mok and his dreaded *nirdei*, Southeast Zone soldiers, gradually extended their control – and thereby that of their master, Pol Pot – across the entire country. Communist cadres and party members arrested and taken to Tuol Sleng were forced, under the most barbarous tortures, to confess to ridiculous conspiracies. Old revolutionaries like Hu Nim and even Vorn

Vet were beaten and electrocuted until they signed statements that they worked for the CIA, Vietnam, the KGB or an unlikely combination of all three. Most were then taken to the nearby Killing Fields of Choeung Ek just south of Phnom Penh and executed with axe-handles or hoes "to avoid wasting bullets".

Attacks on Vietnam

It is now known that the DK regime systematically starved its population both as a method of political control and to raise rice exports to China and North Korea in exchange for armaments. But why did the KR need all this new

weaponry? The war with Lon Nol and the USA was over and won, the people were cowed and incapable of rebellion, but by 1977 relations with Hanoi had reached an all-time low. Vietnam was the new enemy.

Pol Pot openly announced his intention of retaking "Kampuchea Krom", or the Mekong Delta, from Vietnam (similar Khmer-speaking areas around Surin in Northeast Thailand would be recovered later). Vicious cross-border attacks resulting in vicious rapes and massacres were launched around the Parrot's Beak area of Vietnam. Vietnam responded by launching warning counter-attacks across the border,

HARD LABOUR AND ABSTINENCE

The barbarism of the Killing Fields apart, other KR policies made people miserable throughout the country, and the regime was increasingly despised. After the introduction of compulsory collectivised eating, in 1976, even the once-favoured Old People began to turn against the KR – though nobody questioned the regime directly and survived.

Orders were given to the effect that rice production should be increased threefold, and people laboured long into the night. They returned home to eat a thin gruel of rice chaff and morning glory vines, followed by long sessions of political propaganda, before being allowed a few hours' sleep. Marriage was permitted only with the per-

mission of *angkar* (the organisation) and extra-marital sex was punishable by death. Women were obliged to cut their hair short and wear identical black clothing.

Medical treatment was basic in the extreme because most doctors had been killed and those who had not were obliged to hide their identities to survive. KR "hospitals" were generally dirty shacks where illiterate teenagers administered injections of coconut juice. Schools were closed, money was banned and any form of trading was made illegal. Even "foraging" for food such as lizards and insects after work was made a capital offence, so people were in a state of perpetual hunger.

sometimes pushing 30 km (20 miles) into Cambodia before withdrawing. The once-formidable Khmer Rouge soldiers offered weak opposition to the Vietnamese. Many of them were purged and demoralised, sick of killing their own people and far from loyal to the regime in Phnom Penh.

As the Vietnamese withdrew, so thousands of Khmers fled with them, taking refuge across the frontier in Vietnam. Among those who deserted at this time was a young Khmer Rouge commander called Hun Sen. Subsequently, in collaboration with the Vietnamese, he began to build a Cambodian liberation army with the aim of overthrowing Pol Pot and establishing a regime friendly to Vietnam in Phnom Penh.

Vietnam intervenes

Khmer Rouge misrule came to a sudden end in December 1978 when Vietnam sent its forces rolling across the Cambodian frontier, seizing Phnom Penh and forcing the discredited DK leadership to take refuge in camps along the Thai border. The Viets were accompanied by around 20,000 members of the Vietnamese-backed Cambodian liberation army as well as Hun Sen himself and other Cambodian opponents of the Khmer Rouge regime.

There followed a cynical period of nine years when the regime established by the Vietnamese – which everyone, including most Cambodians, saw as a major improvement on DK – was made an international pariah, while the Khmer Rouge guerrillas received military and food aid from an unlikely collection of backers including China, the USA, Britain and Thailand.

In September 1989 Vietnam finally withdrew its forces from Cambodia, handing over control to the United Nations Transitional Authority in Cambodia (UNTAC). Elections were held in 1993 with an impressive 89 percent turnout The KR turned down the chance to stand as a legitimate political party and it has been in decline ever since. Ieng Sary, Nuon Chea and Khieu Samphan have all defected.

Pol Pot died at the remote jungle base of Anlong Veng in 1998, thereby avoiding impending arrest and trial. In March 1999, the one-legged general Ta Mok was arrested near

the Thai border, and later in the same year Deuch, the dreaded former commander of Tuol Sleng Prison, was discovered working anonymously with a Western NGO in Battambang Province. By then a born-again Christian, Deuch – uniquely among KR leaders – promptly admitted his guilt. Both men were sent for trial in Phnom Penh.

Cambodian politics today is dominated by a former middle-ranking KR general, Hun Sen, who has emerged as the *de facto* strongman of the Kingdom of Cambodia. In theory he shares power with Prince Ranarridh, King Sihanouk's son, while the king continues to spend most of

his time in either Beijing or Pyongyang. The situation is hardly perfect, and Hun Sen is much criticised for his occasional high-handedness and his firmness in dealing with the opposition.

Nevertheless, Cambodia is a country on the mend, and most professional or diplomatic observers acquainted with the scene feel that, for all his faults, Hun Sen is doing a reasonable job. Certainly personal freedoms are greater, the press is more independent and there is more evidence of increasing prosperity in Cambodia today than at any time in the past 50 years. After their experience of unparalleled suffering in the preceding quarter-century, most Cambodians are satisfied with the current order. ❏

LEFT: Cambodian "Map of Skulls" at the Tuol Sleng Museum of Genocidal Crime, Phnom Penh.
RIGHT: Hun Sen in Pochentoc.

AN ENVIRONMENT UNDER THREAT

*Cambodia, a land dominated by the Mekong River and the great lake of Tonlé Sap,
is finding it hard to reconcile ecological and economic priorities*

In contrast to its northeastern neighbour Laos, Cambodia is a relatively flat, low-lying land. Situated at the heart of Indochina, it has a total area of slightly over 180,000 sq. km (70,000 sq. miles), and shares land borders with Laos to the northeast, Vietnam to the east and southeast, and Thailand to the north and west. In addition, Cambodia has a 443-km (277-mile) coastline on the Gulf of Thailand in the southwest. The country is divided for administrative purposes into 20 provinces and three municipalities. The capital, Phnom Penh (population 1–1½ million), is in the southeast.

Two water features dominate the landscape: the Mekong River and the Tonlé Sap (Great Lake). The Mekong enters from Laos, close to Stung Treng in the north. It flows for around 500 km (300 miles) through Cambodia, up to 5 km (3 miles) wide in places, before passing into Vietnam bound for the South China Sea. The river splits in two at Phnom Penh, the first major division of its large delta, and the broader, eastern branch retains the name Mekong (strictly the Lower Mekong), while the western branch is known as the Bassac.

The Great Lake

The Tonlé Sap (*see page 209*) is a vast lake in Cambodia's central northwest, surrounded by a fertile lacustrine plain. The Sap River runs from the lake's southeastern end to join the Mekong in Phnom Penh, some 100 km (60 miles) distant. During the dry months, between November and May, the lake is at its smallest, though it still covers 2,500–3,000 sq. km (960–1,160 sq. miles), but when the rains fall, from mid-May to October, a rare hydrographic phenomenon occurs: the rising waters of the Mekong cause the flow of the Sap River to reverse. During this period the Tonlé Sap increases in surface area, sometimes to more

PRECEDING PAGES: Irrawaddy dolphins swimming in the Mekong River.
LEFT: typical countryside in central Cambodia.
RIGHT: wading through water in Lumphat.

than 8,000 sq. km (3,000 sq. miles). While the lake is at its lowest most of it is less than 2 metres (6½ ft) deep, and the whole area can resemble a marsh criss-crossed by navigable channels, but at its fullest its depth increases to as much as 14 metres (45 ft), and it gains up to 70 km (over 40 miles) in width.

Beyond the Mekong-Tonlé Sap Basin, Cambodia is fringed first by transitional plains, most of which are less than 100 metres (330 ft) high, and then by several mountain ranges on the peripheries of the country. The northern border with Thailand is marked by the Dangrek Mountains, a 350-km (220-mile) range of south-facing sheer sandstone cliffs rising 180–550 metres (585–1,800 ft) above the Cambodian plain. In the southwest, covering much of the region between the Tonlé Sap and the Gulf of Thailand, two separate ranges, the Kravanh (Cardamom Mountains) and the Damrei (Elephant Mountains), form a remote upland area. It is here that Cambodia's highest peak, Mount

Aoral (1,813 metres/5,892 ft), is found. Beyond these ranges, on the coast, is a narrow lowland strip, cut off from the central plains and sparsely populated. In the northeast of the country, occupying the remote provinces of Ratanakiri and Mondulkiri, the eastern highlands rise from the transitional plains. This region of thickly forested hills and isolated plateaus stretches east across the border into Vietnam, and north into Laos.

Most of Cambodia's approximately 11 million inhabitants live in small villages in the Mekong-Tonlé Sap Basin and practise subsistence wet-rice cultivation. The annual inunda-

tion of the Mekong and Tonlé Sap brings with it rich alluvial silt which makes for fertile soils throughout much of the central plains. The Tonlé Sap, due to the annual reversal of the Sap River, has a rich supply of freshwater fish. Many Cambodians rely on fishing the lake for income and as an important source of protein.

Ecology

Cambodia plays host to a diversity of natural environments. The central lowland plains are largely agricultural, but outside the cultivated fields of rice, maize and tobacco, and, in some places, the rubber plantations, they are thinly forested, with scrub-like areas of reeds and grasses covering large areas. Around the periphery, the transitional plains are covered with savanna grasses and small bushes.

The various mountain ranges in the country support several different forest types. Large areas of the Cardamom and Elephant mountains in the southwest are covered in virgin rainforest, where the upper canopy often reaches 50 metres (160 ft). Elsewhere in these mountains, at the highest elevations, are sub-tropical pine forests. The eastern mountain ranges bordering Vietnam and Laos are covered with deciduous forests and thick grasslands.

Over the past three decades large-scale logging has continued unabated throughout much of Cambodia; estimates put the reduction in forest cover at around one-third since 1970. While the Khmer Rouge started the exploitation of the forests, subsequent governments have helped to accelerate it. With international demand for timber high, and stricter controls on logging and the export of wood continually being

CAMBODIA'S CLIMATE

Cambodia's climate is governed by the annual monsoon cycle. From May to October the southwest monsoon carries heavy daily rainfall. The northwest monsoon, between November and March, brings slightly lower temperatures and less precipitation. In between are transitional periods, with changeable cloud cover, rainfall and high temperatures. The coolest months are between November and January, though even then temperatures rarely fall below 20°C (68°F): Cambodia is generally quite a few degrees hotter than Thailand and Laos. The driest months are January and February, when often there is no rainfall, and the wettest usually September and October. Rainfall actually varies

quite considerably from year to year and region to region. The southwestern highlands, with their seaward facing slopes, can exceed 5,000 mm (200 inches) a year, while the central plains generally average only 1,400 mm (55 inches). Greater problems arise when the southwest monsoon fails. This can cause severe food shortages for the many Cambodians dependent on the Tonlé Sap and its surrounding fertile soils for their sustenance. Droughts are not uncommon, and, despite the fact that historical evidence suggests they have always been a problem in the region, many blame irresponsible loggers in the more northerly countries on the Mekong for exacerbating the situation.

imposed in surrounding countries, Cambodia has not hesitated to cash in on its forests. Logging concessions have been sold to foreign nations, particularly Malaysia and Indonesia, bringing much needed cash to the ailing economy, but with little thought for the future. Several times the government in Phnom Penh has rescinded concessions, but greed always wins, and new concessions are sold.

Another habitat at risk is the salt marshes and mangroves which make up the narrow strip of land on the coast between the southwestern mountains and the Gulf of Thailand. The delicate ecology here is threatened by commercial

bear, deer and wild cattle. Many of these are threatened, along with a great many smaller mammals including monkeys, squirrels, voles and rats. The country is also rich in bird life: notable species include those found in wetland and grassland ecosystems such as cranes, herons, pelicans, cormorants, ducks and grouse.

Threats to the environment

As in neighbouring Laos, animal conservation still remains at best a minor issue. Many people still hunt – though, happily, the country is no longer a major game-hunting destination – and there is little education regarding the impor-

shrimp farming, largely the province of Thai entrepreneurs. To raise the profitable tiger-shrimps, mangroves must be cleared to make ponds. Fertilisers are added, and waste water is pumped out, an extremely destructive process which makes a farm useless within four years.

Loss of forest cover and encroachment on previously uninhabited forests, together with many years of war, also continue to pose a serious threat to the country's fauna. Among Cambodia's larger animals are tigers, leopards, rhinoceroses, elephants and various species of

LEFT: tending the crops.
ABOVE: slash-and-burn cultivation.

tance of maintaining a balanced ecosystem. Quite simply, most people are concerned only with finding their next meal. But large sections of the country are still virtually uninhabited, and little visited by locals or foreigners, so there remains a chance that some areas will be preserved untouched in their entirety.

Inevitably, the economic possibilities of the Mekong River have not gone unnoticed. As in other countries on the Mekong, various proposals have been made, mainly revolving around the establishment of hydro-electric facilities. So far nothing has come of these proposals, but they have brought to light the serious risks posed by similar projects upstream in Laos and

China. Because Cambodia is so dependent on the annual rise in the waters of the Mekong and the Tonlé Sap for the fertile deposits this brings, any change in the flow of the river could have disastrous effects on agriculture. The possibility of a decline in fish is a concern. Furthermore, future developments upriver could severely effect the performance of hydro-electric stations and dams within Cambodia.

Economy and industry

Twice in recent decades the Cambodian economy was virtually destroyed: first when the Khmer Rouge entered Phnom Penh in 1975,

and again with the 1989 withdrawal of the Vietnamese and the collapse of the Soviet Union, a major source of aid. Today, with Phnom Penh's move away from communist ideology to market economics, things are starting to improve.

By far the greatest sources of foreign revenue are wood exports and foreign aid, neither of which is sustainable. A third significant revenue, also with a dubious future, derives from the trans-shipment of gold and cigarettes from other Asian countries to Vietnam, where tariffs are significantly higher. Other than timber and gemstones, which are also a source of income, Cambodia has few natural resources. Rubber used to be a major export, with the Soviet Union purchasing almost the entire annual production, but it is now less important.

Cambodia is gradually starting to attract foreign investment – mainly Thai and Malaysian – in the services sector. With the nascent tourist industry growing stronger by the year, after being completely wiped out under the Khmer Rouge, there is potential for major expansion. Unfortunately, as a result of the lack of regulation in the country, much of this investment seems to be concentrated on casinos and the seedy entertainment scene.

As in neighbouring Laos, heavy investment is needed in education, basic infrastructure and telecommunications before Cambodia will start to look attractive to foreign investors. At the moment both the government and outsiders seem mainly interested in fast profits projects, and few are looking at longer-term positive development. This is perhaps not very surprising given the country's instability since 1975. It can only be hoped that a more responsible attitude will emerge before too much more damage is done.

For the foreseeable future, tourism may be Cambodia's greatest chance of securing sustainable foreign exchange. Tourist numbers are much lower than they were in the 1960s, but Angkor still stands, and remains one of the world's most marketable architectural and historical sites. As the clearing of land mines continues, and facilities for tourist accommodation and transport improve, there is no reason why this valuable resource should not be developed responsibly and successfully. ❏

PROTECTED ZONES

In the mid-1990s the first of 23 protected areas proposed by King Norodom Sihanouk was established in the southwestern province of Kompong Speu. Most of the areas have now been set up, and when completed will afford official protection to around 15 percent of Cambodia.

The various levels of protection include national parks, scenic zones, wild animal sanctuaries and, reminiscent of the Lao national parks, so-called multi-use zones in which some commercial activity will be permitted. The zoned areas are mainly located in the mountainous periphery of the country, but a few, including the Tonlé Sap area, are in the central plains.

LEFT: mine warning at Preah Vihear in northern Cambodia.

Tonlé Sap

The vast freshwater lake known as Tonlé Sap is truly a remarkable phenomenon. The very heart of Cambodia's rich agricultural and fishing economies, it is the riverine "lung" on which much of the country's prosperity depends. During the annual monsoon rains it swells greatly in size, becoming a natural reservoir which then gradually releases its accumulated waters during the long, hot months of the dry season. It also provides the surrounding plains with a never-ending supply of rich silt for farming, and is an equally reliable source of nutrition in the form of fish, snails, snakes, frogs and all manner of aquatic wildlife.

The Tonlé Sap, surrounded by a fertile rice-growing plain, dominates Cambodia's central northwest. During the dry season, approximately between November and May, the lake is at its smallest, though it still covers 2,500–3,000 sq. km (950–1,160 sq. miles). The Sap River runs from the lake's southeastern rim to join the Mekong and Bassac Rivers at Phnom Penh, some 100 km (60 miles) distant. The confluence of the rivers, known in Khmer as Chatomuk or "four faces", and in French as Quatres Bras or "four arms", is chiefly remarkable for a unique phenomenon, the reversal of the Sap River.

From May to October, during the annual southwest monsoon rains, the hugely increased volume of the Mekong forces the Sap River to back up, and finally reverse its course, flowing northwards to flood the Tonlé Sap with vast quantities of fresh water and rich sediment. During this period the Tonlé Sap almost trebles in size from 3,000 sq. km (1,160 sq. miles) to as much as 8,000 sq. km (3,100 sq. miles). At its lowest most of the lake is less than 2 metres (6½ ft) deep and is like a marsh with criss-crossing navigable channels; at its fullest the lake is as much as 14 metres (45 ft) deep, and it can gain 70 km (44 miles) in width.

Then, in mid-October, as the cool, dry winds begin to blow from the north and the level of the Mekong diminishes, the flow of the Sap is again reversed, carrying the surplus waters of the Tonlé Sap southwards to the Mekong and Bassac Deltas.

The annual flooding of the Tonlé Sap makes the lake an incredibly rich source of fish, while the farmland around it benefits from an annual deluge of rich sediment. It is impossible to make an absolute ethnographic distinction between lake-dwellers and nearby farmers, but on the whole the Tonlé Sap is fished by Muslim Chams and migrant communities of Vietnamese. These peoples are less concerned about taking life than the Theravada Buddhist Khmers who till the nearby fields – not that the latter show any concern at all about eating the fish once it has been caught and killed by someone else. There are few dinner tables anywhere in Cambodia that are without a supply of *prahok* – fermented fish paste from the great lake – and fish is a national staple.

The time of the October reversal of the waters is celebrated as Bon Om Tuk, one of Cambodia's most important festivals. For three days an estimated 250,000 revellers join in the festivities, which include long-boat races, music, dancing, fireworks and a great deal of eating and drinking. More than than 370 teams from Phnom Penh and the surrounding provinces compete in the traditional boat racing, which is said to celebrate an event in 1177. Angkor was invaded and sacked by a fleet of Cham warships which sailed up the Sap River and across the Tonlé Sap; the Chams were defeated by the country's most illustrious monarch, Jayavarman VII, and some bas reliefs in the Bayon at Angkor commemorate this. ❑

RIGHT: crossing the Tonlé Sap by boat.

AN ETHNIC LABYRINTH

*Ethnic Khmers dominate, but Cambodia has significant minority groups
and an old tradition of using female bodyguards to protect rulers*

Ethnic Khmers make up more than 90 percent of Cambodia's estimated 11 million people – although not the 96 percent often claimed by Cambodian government sources. The Khmers are a predominantly agricultural people, subsisting on a diet of rice and fish, and living in wooden stilted houses in villages of several hundred people. Farming has long been their main economic pursuit, but other traditional crafts include weaving, pottery making and metalworking.

In recent decades, as elsewhere in the developing world, there has been a marked degree of urbanisation as Khmers move to cities such as Phnom Penh, Battambang, Kompong Som (Sihanoukville) and Kompong Cham. The Khmers remain the dominant political and cultural section of the Cambodian population, although their economic influence is far less, on a per capita basis, than that of the ethnic Chinese and Vietnamese. Most Khmers are Theravada Buddhists, although Christianity made a small number of converts during the 20th century.

While most Khmers live within the frontiers of Cambodia, there are an estimated half a million Khmer-speaking people in southern Vietnam, especially in the Mekong Delta region, where they are known as Khmer Krom or "Lower Khmers". Similarly, as many as 200,000 live in the northeastern Thai provinces of Buriram, Surin and Si Saket. They are known to the Thais as Suay, and are famous for their skills as elephant handlers.

Beyond Southeast Asia a Khmer community has long been established in France, especially in and around Paris. More recently, as a result of the murder and mayhem that plagued their homeland for so many years, a substantial Khmer migrant community became established in Canada and the United States, especially in Toronto, California and Washington.

PRECEDING PAGES: harvesting rice.
LEFT: Cambodian man at the Bayon, Angkor Thom.
RIGHT: woman wearing a *krama*.

The Viet Kieu
The largest national minority in Cambodia is the Viet Kieu or migrant Vietnamese. Because traditionally little love has been lost between Khmer and Viet, there is a tendency on the part of the Cambodian authorities to underestimate the number of Vietnamese in the country.

According to figures published by the Cambodian government in 1995, there were just 100,000 Vietnamese residents, but independent estimates suggest there are between 500,000 and 1 million. They tend to live in the big cities, where they work as restaurateurs or in other small businesses, or make a living as fishermen along the Mekong and Sap rivers. Ethnic Vietnamese also make a disproportionately large contribution to Cambodia's sex industry.

Cambodia's Chams
A second distinctive minority in Cambodian society is the Cham Muslims, one of the oldest, but nowadays least considered, peoples of

Indochina. There are some 400,000–500,000 Chams in Cambodia, despite their having been particularly targeted for extermination by the Khmer Rouge in the 1970s. Gifted silversmiths, they also make a living by fishing and by butchering animals for their more fastidious Buddhist neighbours.

Chams are inheritors of a proud tradition that stretches back some 2,000 years: Champa was the first Indianised kingdom in Indochina, its founding predating both Chen La (6th century AD) and the first major expansion of the Vietnamese south from Tonkin (mid-10th century).

At the peak of their power, about 12 centuries ago, the Chams controlled rich and fertile lands stretching from north of Hue, in central Annam, to the Mekong Delta in Cochin China; yet today Vietnamese cities like Nha Trang and Da Nang dominate these regions. Only mysterious brick temples, known as "Cham towers", dot the skyline around Thap Cham and Po Nagar, while in Cambodia the name of an eastern province and its capital, Kompong Cham, remain as testimony to the lost kingdom.

The Chams are an Austronesian people, more closely linked with the islands of the Malay-Indonesian world and the Philippines than with the mainland. We can only surmise that at some

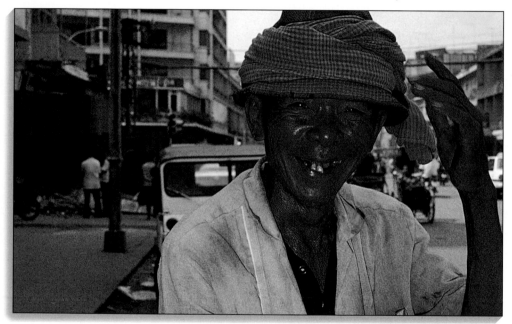

THE KINGDOM OF CHAMPA

The earliest records of the Kingdom of Champa are Chinese, dating from 192 AD. In these the Chams are described as having "dark skin, deep-set eyes, turned up noses and frizzy hair", characteristics which are often still recognisable in the modern descendants of the Chams. The annals record that the Chams dressed, like the Malays, "in a single piece of cotton or silk wrapped about the body. They wear their hair in a bun on the top of their head, and they pierce their ears in order to wear small metal rings. They are very clean. They wash themselves several times each day, wear perfume, and rub their bodies with a lotion made of camphor and musk."

distant time they migrated from the Indonesian archipelago and settled in what is now southern Vietnam, and what we know of early Cham society seems to bear this out. Unlike their Viet and Khmer neighbours, whose society is based on intensive rice cultivation, the Chams had little time for agriculture. Their prosperity was based on maritime trade – and probably on a certain amount of piracy.

Their principal exports were slaves (mainly prisoners of war) and sandalwood. This latter commodity, of great importance to the intensely religious societies of early Southeast Asia, brought considerable riches. It was also the Chams' proximity to the sea that first introduced them to Islam. Arab merchants reached southern China as early as the 7th century, and en route they stopped along the southern Vietnamese coast for provisions and trade. The first firm evidence of such visits is a 10th-century stone pillar inscribed in Arabic which was found near the coastal town of Phan Rang.

As happened elsewhere in Southeast Asia, from Aceh to Sulu, Islam seems to have spread its influence peacefully by means of commerce and intermarriage, but before the Cham people could

> ### A CALL TO PRAYER
> Unusually, the Cambodian Chams are called to prayer by drum-beats rather than by the *azaan* – the call of the *muezzin* to the faithful – which is so familiar in Muslim lands.

Cambodia, Thailand and Laos trace their common origin to this event.

Most Chams moved up the Mekong, into territories that now constitute the Cambodian heartland. They settled along the banks of the great river north and east of Phnom Penh, notably in the province and town of Kompong Cham, but also along the shores of the Tonlé Sap, Cambodia's great and fertile inland lake. Here they became well known and relatively prosperous through their skills as fishermen, settling into the ebb and

have been converted en masse their kingdom was swept away in a great disaster.

Disaster and diaspora

In 1471 the Chams suffered a terrible defeat at the hands of the Vietnamese. Champa was reduced to a sliver of territory in the region of Nha Trang, which survived until 1720 when the king and many subjects fled to Cambodia rather than submit to the Vietnamese. The Cham diaspora dates from this period, and the diverse Cham communities later established in

---

LEFT: posing for the camera in Phnom Penh.
ABOVE: New Year celebrations.

flow of Cambodian life, and acquiring a widespread reputation for their abilities as practitioners of traditional medicine.

During the 18th and 19th centuries Islam spread widely among the Cambodian Chams, who adopted Sunni Islam and maintained links with other Muslim communities in the region, whereas their fellows in Vietnam remained only partly Islamicised.

In 1975, when the Khmer Rouge seized power, nearly 400,000 Chams were living peacefully along the Mekong north and east of Phnom Penh. They followed the faith of their fathers in over a hundred mosques, caught fish, grew rice and tried to stay neutral in the war which was destroying Cambodia. Even before Pol Pot's seizure of power in 1975 the Khmer Rouge had begun implementing special policies towards Cambodia's various minority peoples. "Recent migrants" such as the ethnic Vietnamese, Chinese and Thai were marked for expulsion or death. By contrast, indigenous minorities, although mistreated by Cambodian rulers for centuries, were spared the worst of the Khmer Rouge excesses.

The one major exception to this policy was the Cham community, which was picked out for especially harsh treatment, probably because its members spoke a private commu-

much higher numbers, tens of thousands of Chams were murdered by the Khmer Rouge. By the time Vietnamese armed forces swept across the frontier in December 1978, between a half and two-thirds of the Cham community had been murdered, starved to death or driven out of the country.

Other minorities

Most of Cambodia's Hua Chiao, or Overseas Chinese, trace their origins to the southern coastal provinces of Hainan, Kwangtung and Fukien. Estimates of their numbers vary from 100,000 to 400,000. In recent years a new wave

nity language unintelligible to the Khmer Rouge, read Arabic, wore distinctive clothing and followed an "alien" religion – Islam. Whatever the logic behind the decision, after the Khmer Rouge seizure of power, in April 1975, anti-Cham policies were ruthlessly implemented.

During the three-and-a-half years of Khmer Rouge rule, Cambodia's Chams were systematically victimised. All mosques – traditionally the spiritual and social centres of Cham community life – were either demolished or turned over to secular purposes for use as ammunition stores and Khmer Rouge barracks. Like their Khmer compatriots, only proportionately in

of Chinese migration to Cambodia has started, and the presence of both Taiwanese and Malaysian Chinese in business circles is marked. The Chinese are almost exclusively urban, and, since they intermarry readily with urban Khmers, are not Muslim like the Chams, and are not disliked and feared like the Vietnamese, Chinese ethnicity is more readily subsumed within Khmer society.

Other minorities include the Khmer Loeu or Upland Khmer – hill tribes of Mondulkiri and Ratanakiri, such as the Kuy, Mnong, Brao, Tapuon and Jarai, as well as the Pear and Saoch of the southwest. Strangely, several of these groups fared comparatively well under the

Khmer Rouge – usually ruthless in their treatment of national minorities – because they were seen as "pure", unpolluted by capitalism and an urban environment, even models of primitive Communism. Collectively they probably number no more than 80,000.

Three groups who fared less well under the Khmer Rouge were the Thais, Lao and Shan. Faced with vicious discrimination in 1976–9, those Thais who were not killed fled to neighbouring Thailand. Surviving Lao also fled in droves. The Shan – a few thousand were long-term residents of Pailin, where they worked as gem miners – were even less fortunate, and seem to have been wiped out entirely.

Finally, mention should be made of the South Asians, a few hundred of whom live in the larger cities like Phnom Penh and Battambang, working chiefly as small businessmen and traders. In the late 1960s several thousand South Asians, mainly identified as "Pakistanis" because of their Sindhi or Pathan origins, lived in the countryside around Battambang, Poipet and Siem Reap where they specialised as cattle-breeders and milk producers. But they, too, fell foul of the Khmer Rouge – simply because of their ethnicity – and those not lucky enough to flee the country were killed en masse.

Khmer Loeu and Khmer Rouge

Before his capture and confinement in Phnom Penh, Ta Mok, the much-feared Khmer Rouge chief-of-staff, was reported to have surrounded himself with a special bodyguard of 30 hand-picked fighters. Strangely, all were from non-Khmer ethnic minorities, and all were female. Shades of Colonel Kurtz in Conrad's *Heart of Darkness* and Coppola's *Apocalypse Now*?

Although there never was a Kurtz – a crazed Caucasian renegade on the upper reaches of the Drang River – ironically, the territory he was supposed to occupy belonged, at the time in which the film was set, to the nascent Khmer Rouge. Here in the rainforests Pol Pot and his comrades had taken refuge from the Lon Nol regime, and were beginning their strange experiment in total collectivist agrarian revolution. Turning their backs on Phnom Penh – characterised as "the great whore on the Mekong" – they abandoned urban society

as hopelessly corrupt, and took refuge in the remotest parts of the country, as far from city life as possible.

In 1968, shortly after the KR (Communist Party of Kampuchea, or Khmer Rouge) took the decision to embark on an armed struggle, its leadership began operations in regions inhabited by non-Khmer upland minorities such as the Brao, the Tapuon and the Jarai. These people, traditionally looked down on by the Khmer and known by the derogatory term *phnong*, "savages", were of great interest to the KR's largely urban leadership for their knowledge of the jungle, survival skills and prowess as

LEFT: removing wheat husks.
RIGHT: selling fabric at the market.

hunters. They were also "poor and blank": in Maoist terms, ideal vessels for indoctrination. Finally, they are said to have shown great obedience to authority.

Because of this belief in "the noble savage", and in sharp contrast to the usual KR treatment of minorities, who were systematically persecuted and subjected to policies amounting to genocide, the Khmer Loeu were generally well treated and absorbed, wherever possible, into the ranks of the revolution.

Even before the KR seizure of power in 1975, many upland tribal people already served the KR leadership as special cadres,

messengers and bodyguards.

Some indication of the position of trust attained by these tribal minorities – and of the culture shock caused to ordinary Khmers on seeing people they traditionally perceived as "savages" bearing AK47s in the midst of the victorious Communist forces – can be gleaned from contemporary accounts of the KR seizure of power. Peang Sophi, a factory worker in Battambang, recalls that the peasant soldiers who occupied his city were "real country people, from very far away.

Many of them had never seen a city or printed words. They held Cambodian texts upside down, pretending to puzzle them out."

Still more telling is an account by Dith Pran (who became widely known in the West through the film *The Killing Fields*), who comments on KR troops entering his village in Siem Reap: "They didn't even look like Cambodians, they seemed to be from the jungle, or a different world."

It is not entirely clear whether the elusive, one-legged KR commander Chhit Chhoeun – better known as Ta Mok (Grandfather Mok) – employed specially trusted tribal cadres in his southwestern power base at this time; the area in question, around Takeo and Kampot, is far from the tribal uplands of Ratanakiri or the Cardamom Mountains. It is known, however, that as early as 1975 "Brother No. 1" – Pol Pot himself – was protected by two special bodyguards, both tribal people who could speak very little Khmer. Under these circumstances, Ta Mok's later choice of non-Khmer tribal minorities for his special bodyguard seems more predictable than extraordinary. The KR leadership, increasingly unable to retain or attract supporters, relied on such trustworthy followers for decades.

Women bodyguards

But what of the fact that Ta Mok's bodyguard were all women? In fact, this female entourage was rooted in long regional tradition. According to the Southeast Asia specialist Anthony Reid, the god-kings of Angkor surrounded themselves with 5,000 women, while Sultan Iskandar Muda maintained 3,000 in his palace at Aceh – a mere handful when compared with the 10,000 kept by Sultan Agung of Mataram. At both Aceh and Mataram, specially trained corps of female guards were maintained for the rulers' protection, while Sultan Al-Mukammil of the former state (1584–1604) employed a woman as the commander of his navy.

Ta Mok may have known nothing of these historical facts. What he clearly did know – perhaps intuitively – is that, in the words of the sagacious Professor Reid: "There appears to be no evidence that the confidence rulers placed in these women was ever betrayed by murder, as happened frequently at the hands of males." Like others before him, Ta Mok trusted his tribal women to protect him. ❏

LEFT: banana-leaf boats sail on the Mekong River during the New Year celebrations.

The Amazingly Versatile *Krama*

T he *krama*, more than any other item of clothing of everyday use, is quintessentially Khmer. No other country in Southeast Asia uses this scarf-like head-wrapping, and it is arguably a sign of Cambodia's ancient links with India, the land of turbans. *Krama*, which are made from cotton or silk, are most commonly found in red-and-white or blue-and-white check, and have a considerable variety of uses.

Just about every province of Cambodia produces *krama* in its own distinctive patterns. Kompong Cham produces large silk *krama* in shades of burgundy, maroon, crimson, indigo and emerald. Some *krama* are said to resemble Scottish tartans, others are more stripy. Quality varies from the simple, coarse cotton chequered scarf used by the poorest peasants to elegant, finely-woven silk *krama* with gold-fibre edgings. The colours of the cheaper cotton *krama* are usually duller, coming in shades of ochre, ginger and chocolate brown which are generally produced using natural dyes. The colours of the more expensive silk *krama* are often much brighter, today utilising chemical dyes which allow a wider range of hue. Such variations in colour took on a distinctly menacing tone under the Khmer Rouge, when special blue *krama* were issued to inhabitants of the Eastern Zone contiguous with Vietnam. These unfortunates were considered by the paranoid leadership to have "Khmer bodies with Vietnamese minds", and the wearing of one of the special blue *krama* marked the possessor for eventual execution.

Cambodians claim that there are more than 60 documented uses for *krama*. They are worn to provide protection from sun, dust, wind, cold and rain, and they may be wound around heads, necks, shoulders or hips. Wherever you go in Cambodia you will see them wrapped, knotted, slung casually over the shoulder, or worn as elaborate turbans – often in conjunction with hats. They are also regularly pressed into service as skirts, sarongs, aprons and even shorts.

Krama are also good for carrying things. Mothers use them to carry babies, children use them to heft kittens and puppies around, women going to market use them to carry bundles of chickens and other small livestock. They make excellent shopping bags; they are useful as covers for pillows, beds and chairs; they can be used as improvised fly-whisks and can be strung across the hood of a cyclo to rest the head of a weary driver. Folded, they form ideal cushions for the head on which large or heavy loads can be placed en route to market. In a sadder capacity, they can be used for leading blind people around as they seek charity. In short, there isn't much that the Cambodians don't use their ubiquitous *krama* for.

In some villages almost every family has a loom, often tucked beneath the stilts of the house to

take advantage of the shade, where fine cotton and silk *krama* can be produced. These *krama* are taken for sale in nearby markets where there are always ready buyers. Cambodians like to claim that the tradition of wearing *krama* dates back at least as far as the Angkor period. Certainly the Chinese Ambassador, Chou Ta-Kuan, who visited Angkor in the 13th century, commented that "every man or woman, from the sovereign down, knots the hair and leaves the shoulders bare. Round the waist they wear a strip of cloth, over which a larger piece is drawn when they leave their houses."

For many Cambodians – indeed, for the nation as a whole – wearing the *krama* is an affirmation of national and cultural identity. ❑

RIGHT: woman wearing a *krama* reproduced on an old 500 *riel* note.

THE CHAMS: SURVIVORS OF A LOST KINGDOM

When the Cham kingdom was conquered by the Vietnamese, many fled to Cambodia and lived in fishing villages along the Mekong and Sap rivers

▷ **CHAM FISHERMEN**
Cham fishermen's stilted village on the Sap River at Chruoy Changvar near Phnom Penh with traditional fishing boats.

In 1720 the last remnant of the ancient Kingdom of Champa was finally snuffed out by the Nguyen lords of southern Vietnam. In advance of this debacle the Cham king, together with many of his subjects, fled to Cambodia rather than submit to the Viets. They settled in the province and town that became Kompong Cham and also along the shores of the Tonlé Sap, Cambodia's large and fertile inland lake. Here they became prosperous fishermen, settled into the Cambodian way of life and acquired a reputation for their abilities as practitioners of magic and producers of love potions. During the 18th and 19th centuries Islam continued to spread among the Cambodian Chams, in marked contrast to its poor progress among those who remained in Vietnam. In part this may have been due to a Cham desire to maintain a separate ethnic and cultural identity among the Buddhist Khmers, in part also because their role as fishermen required the constant taking of life. Partly because of their Muslim religion, and also because they didn't speak Khmer, the Chams were treated very harshly by the Khmer Rouge. Many were killed, but one small group escaped along the Mekong River to Laos, and established a small community in Vientiane. Today other communities of Chams flourish in Thailand, Malaysia and their original homeland, the central-southern coastal provinces of Vietnam.

△ **CHAM TOWERS**
Brick towers, reminders of the Cham civilisation, can be seen in the central-southern coastal provinces of Vietnam.

△ **RELAXED ISLAM**
Chams practise a fairly relaxed form of Sunni Islam, fasting one day a week during Ramadan and not eating pork.

◁ **MASJID AL-AZHAR**
The spiritual and cultural centre of Laos' small Cham community, located in the Vientiane district of Chantabouli.

THE CHAM DRUMMERS

In Muslim communities all over the world the *azaan* (call to prayer) is heard five times a day. The *azaan,* always given in Arabic, dates back to the beginning of the Muslim era and later, as Islam spread, the familiar call to prayer travelled with it. Interestingly, some communities, while converting to Islam and adopting the familiar *azaan*, also preserved vestiges of earlier customs. Thus in the Maldives a conch shell was blown to announce the call to prayer, whilst in North Thailand a traditional temple gong may still be hung from the minaret and struck to call the faithful. Similarly, Cham Muslims of Indochina beat a drum to announce the time of prayer, a cultural reminder of the days, more than a thousand years ago, when Champa was a Hindu kingdom. Nowadays, Cham Muslim communities sound drumbeats rapidly and vigorously to signal the time to enter the mosque. In this way, the formal Arabic *azaan* is given at the start of communal prayers.

▽ **CHAM CLOTHING**
Cham men, especially of the older generation, still favour sarongs and prayer caps for everyday wear. Their batik sarongs resemble those worn in parts of Malaysia.

△ **SKILLED CRAFTSMEN**
Chams are famous for their weaving and dyeing abilities, with a deserved reputation for producing fine silk.

◁ **CALL TO PRAYER**
Free from persecution, Cham women, wearing veils for prayers, turn towards Mecca at a Cham mosque.

TALES AS OLD AS TIME

Despite attempts by the Khmer Rouge regime to destroy many of the traditional arts, Cambodian culture has managed to survive in all its forms

Defining the "cultural arts of Cambodia" is no simple matter. The main problem is deciding just where the "Cambodian" element starts and ends. To begin with, Khmer culture – together with that of the Mon and the Chams – is about the earliest known indigenous high culture in the region, yet even in the distant days of Chen La and early Angkor it drew heavily on Indian cultural, religious and artistic influences – so heavily, indeed, that Cambodian culture is generally defined as "Indic". The Khmers in turn went on to influence their neighbours, particularly the Lao and the Thais. Thai writing, for example, is derived from Khmer, as is much of Thai court language and culture.

But who gave what to whom? Indicisation may have started with the Khmer Empire, but at times of Cambodian weakness and Siamese strength the flow was often reversed. An interesting if little known example of this, through the unlikely medium of French colonialism, was the re-establishment of traditional court dance in the royal palace at Phnom Penh in the early 20th century. Standards had fallen so far in Phnom Penh that the French invited classical dance masters from the court of Bangkok to reinvigorate the tradition in Cambodia. Thus it is difficult to draw clear dividing lines between the Indic cultures of Southeast Asia. Much of what is Cambodian is also, with minor variations, Thai or Lao or, at one remove, Burmese or even Javanese.

The *Ramayana*

Perhaps the paramount example of this is the great Hindu epic, the *Ramayana*. In the context of this book the *Ramayana* influences both Cambodian and Lao culture (music, dance, literature, painting) to such an extent that it must be considered in depth. Because the great literary epic is essentially the same – *Reamker* in Khmer – it is dealt with in a single section, but

under Cambodian culture rather than Lao because of the great 19th-century murals of the *Ramayana* which exist at the Royal Palace in Phnom Penh; there is nothing so graphic in Laos. The tradition of the *Ramayana* as an all-pervading cultural influence is, however, as applicable to Laos as it is to Cambodia.

It is a story as old as time and – at least in the Indian subcontinent and across much of Southeast Asia – of unparalleled popularity. More than 2,300 years ago, at about the same time as Alexander the Great invaded northwest India, in another, less troubled part of that vast country the scholar-poet Valmiki sat down to write his definitive epic of love and war.

The poem Valmiki composed is in Sanskrit; its title means "Romance of Rama". The shorter of India's two great epic poems – the other being the *Mahabharata*, or "Great Epic of the Bharata Dynasty" – the *Ramayana* is, nevertheless, of considerable length. In its present form the Sanskrit version consists of some

---

LEFT: classical dancer, Phnom Penh.
RIGHT: stone carving at Preah Khan, Angkor.

24,000 couplets divided into seven books. It's astonishing, then, to think that people have memorised the entire work, and that since its initial composition it has enjoyed continual passionate recitation somewhere in Asia. Today it remains as vital as ever, though television, film and radio have brought it to a wider audience than Valmiki could ever have imagined – and its appeal continues to grow.

Prince Rama's story

The *Ramayana*, which scholars consider more of a romance than an epic, begins with the birth of Prince Rama in the Kingdom of Ayodhya

for 14 years. Sita accompanies Rama into exile, as does his half-brother, the loyal Lakshmana.

Word of Rama's exile then reaches Ravana, demon-king of the island of Lanka. Ravana lusts after Sita and, having sent a magical golden deer to lead Rama and Lakshmana off hunting, he seizes Sita and takes her to his palace in Lanka. Sita resists all his advances, whilst Rama and Lakshmana, realising they have been tricked, organise her rescue.

The defeat of Ravana and his devilish cohorts is no easy task, however, and the royal brothers need help in their endeavour. Fortunately, allies are found in Sugriva, King of the Monkeys,

(associated with the ancient city of Oudh) on the banks of the Sarayu River near Lucknow in northern India. Rama's youth is spent in the royal palace, under the tutelage of the sage Vishvamitra, from whom he learns patience, wisdom and insight, the qualities for a just and perfect king.

As a young man Rama enters a bridegroom contest for the hand of Sita, the beautiful daughter of King Janaka. Rama has the strength to bend the great bow of Shiva, and by this supernatural act he wins Sita. The couple marry, and for some time all is well – but then Rama falls victim to intrigue at the royal court, loses his position as heir, and withdraws to the forest

Ravana's own brother, Vibhishana, and above all the noble monkey-god Hanuman. Acting in unison and overcoming great difficulties, the forces of light invade Lanka, rescue Sita, and overthrow Ravana who is killed by Rama.

At this point in the story a darker side of Rama becomes apparent, as he accuses Sita of infidelity and requires her to undergo an ordeal by fire to prove her innocence. Rama seems satisfied, but on returning to Ayodhya he learns that the people still question Sita's virtue, and he banishes her to the forest. In exile, Sita meets the sage Valmiki and at his hermitage gives birth to Rama's two sons. The family is reunited when the sons become of age, but Sita, once again protesting her innocence, asks to be received by the earth, which swallows her up.

The impact of the *Ramayana* on Lao and Cambodian culture can scarcely be overstated. The love of Rama for Sita, the loyalty of Lakshmana and the heroism of Hanuman have left an indelible mark on many aspects of traditional drama, literature and dance.

The Phnom Penh murals

In 1831 King Rama III of Siam ordered master-painters to begin the great task of painting the *Ramayana* in murals at Wat Phra Kaew in Bangkok. Over several years the story of Rama,

Some 30 years later, following the completion of the Silver Pagoda at the Royal Palace in Phnom Penh, a decision was taken to tell the story of the *Ramayana* in murals along the inner face of the wall surrounding the complex. The resulting mural, which was not completed until the reign of King Sisowath, is protected by cloister-like arcades, and has been restored on a number of occasions, most recently in 1992.

King Norodom's decision to order the painting of the murals, together with the style and technique, was clearly influenced by the *Ramakien* murals at Bangkok, yet they have a

Sita, Ravana and Hanuman unfolded over hundreds of square metres of cloister wall, shaded from the sun by long roofs of orange tiles. At the time relations between the royal courts of Bangkok and Phnom Penh were close, and the *Ramayana* – in Thai, *Ramakien* – murals came to the notice of visiting Cambodian nobles. In 1866 Cambodia's King Norodom began building a new royal palace in Phnom Penh, using French and Cambodian architects but drawing much of his inspiration directly from the Chakri royal complex in Bangkok.

FAR LEFT, LEFT AND RIGHT: sections of a *Ramayana* mural in the Silver Pagoda, Phnom Penh.

WORLDWIDE INFLUENCE

The *Ramayana* quickly became popular in India, where its recitation is considered an act of great merit. It was translated from the original Sanskrit into numerous vernacular versions, often works of great literary merit themselves, including the Tamil version *Kampan*, the Bengali *Krttibas* and the popular Hindi version, the *Ramcaritmanas* of Tulsidas. Other celebrations of the poem which continue to flourish in India today include the annual Ram-Lila pageant of north India, and the Kathkali dance-drama of Kerala. So powerful was the *Ramayana* that it soon spread throughout the Hindu-Buddhist world, including Laos and Cambodia.

charm and distinction which are their own, and in some sections are better preserved than their Bangkok counterparts.

Dance

The beauty and elegance of the Cambodian Royal Ballet has to be seen to be believed. The writer Somerset Maugham was fortunate enough to witness a performance at Angkor in the 1920s, and enthused: "The beauty of these dances against the dark mystery of the temple made it the most beautiful and unearthly sight imaginable. It was certainly more than worthwhile to have travelled thousands of miles for

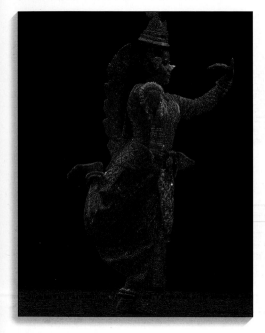

this." The dancers had an even greater impact on Auguste Rodin, who exclaimed on seeing a performance in Paris in 1906: "These Cambodian women have given us everything antiquity could hold. It's impossible to see human nature reaching such perfection. There is only this and the Greeks."

But this art form suffered under the Khmer Rouge regime. Under Pol Pot – who had relatives in the Royal Ballet and spent some time with them in his youth – an attempt was made to destroy the ballet. Instruments were smashed, costumes and books burnt, while musicians and dancers were brutally killed.

Fortunately one or two dancers survived, as did Princess Bupphadevi, a favourite daughter of King Sihanouk, who was in exile in France. In the two decades since the fall of the Khmer Rouge the Royal Ballet has been painstakingly rebuilt with her help, and today performances can be seen at the Hotel Cambodiana and elsewhere, as advertised in Phnom Penh (*see pages 230–1*).

Classical Khmer dance (*lamthon*) as performed by the Royal Ballet bears a striking resemblance to that of the Thai royal court, and indeed the two traditions influenced each other in turn until they have become practically a shared art form. Training takes many years, and elaborate costumes and headdresses are worn. It is a real spectacle that should not be missed. Cambodian masked theatre, known as *khaul*, is very similar to the Thai *khon*. Classical dances depicting incidents from the Buddha life-cycle stories, the *Jataka*, are often performed.

Music

Music has long flourished in both court and village settings, some kinds associated with specific functions, others with entertainment. In villages weddings are celebrated with *kar* music, communication with spirits is accompanied by *arakk* music, and entertainments include *ayai* repartee singing, *chrieng chapey* narrative, and *yike* and *basakk* theatres. At court, dance, masked and shadow plays and religious ceremonies are accompanied by *pinn peat* ensembles and entertainment by *mohori* ensembles. Temples often possess a *pinn peat* ensemble and a *korng skor* ensemble for funerals.

Traditional Cambodian music probably reached its zenith during the Angkor period. Carved on the walls of the great temples of

SHADOW PUPPETRY

Like the inhabitants of the Malay world and southern Thailand, the Cambodians have a strong tradition of shadow puppetry which they call *nang sbaek thom*, or "shadow plays". Generally performed during festivals, weddings and funerals, the plays are narrated by actors concealed beneath the puppet screen. A light behind the screen casts images of the puppets onto the screen for the audience to watch. The puppets are usually made of cow or buffalo hide, and can be very intricate in their design. Siem Reap in the northwest of the country (*see page 279*) is considered by many to be the original home of this art form.

Angkor and vicinity are the *apsara* (celestial dancer) figures along with musical instruments: the *pinn* (angular harp), *korng vung* (circular frame gongs), *skor yol* (suspended barrel drum), *chhing* (small cymbals) and *sralai* (quadruple-reed flute). These are believed to have developed into the *pinn peat* ensemble.

In about 1431 Angkor was looted by Siamese armies; the king and his musicians fled, and the city was abandoned and overrun by vegetation. Subsequently the capital was moved to Lovek, which itself was sacked by the Siamese in 1594. After this defeat, music and its functions were deeply affected, and a new style of melan-

flutes, gongs, xylophones and three-stringed guitars. Music is sometimes accompanied by song, either improvised ballads or court chants. At some festivals an orchestra known as *phleng pinpeat* will perform court music. Another type of orchestra is the *phleng khmer*, which performs at weddings. Popular music has been recently influenced by the Thai and Chinese.

Architecture

From an architectural perspective Cambodia is something of an enigma. Home to possibly the greatest and certainly the oldest high civilisation in mainland Southeast Asia, the country is

cholic and emotional music is said to have emerged. The period 1796–1859 was a renaissance for Cambodian music. King Ang Duong, the greatest of the monarchs of this period, ascended the throne in 1841 in the then capital, Udong, and under his rule Cambodian music and other art forms were revived and began to flourish again. There are two types of traditional orchestra in Cambodia, the all male *pip hat* and the all female *mohori*. Both comprise 11 traditional musical instruments, including

---

LEFT: dancer from the Cambodian Royal Ballet.
ABOVE: group of local musicians from Ta Prohm temple, Tonlé Bati.

studded with outstandingly beautiful temple complexes, both Hindu and Buddhist, dating from the 6th to the 15th centuries. Modern temple architecture, it must be said, is a disapointment by comparison, though due allowance must be made for the destruction and desecration wrought by the iconoclastic Khmer Rouge regime between 1975 and 1979.

Perhaps because Sihanouk was in residence under effective house arrest during much of this period, the Royal Palace and Silver Pagoda at Phnom Penh were spared. Elsewhere, however, Buddha images were decapitated, blown up or hurled into rivers, while temples and mosques were turned into storage barns or pigsties. Nor did Christian buildings fare any better: Phnom Penh Cathedral was levelled. Even the gods of Mammon were not spared as the National Bank was blown up. Fortunately there were limits to this iconoclasm – Angkor and other wonders of ancient Khmer civilisation were either protected or ignored and left to the encroaching jungle.

Temple styles

The temple architecture of ancient Khmer civilisation, both Hindu and Buddhist, is readily identifiable. Building mate-

rials include laterite (often as a plinth or base), surmounted by structures of sandstone and/or stucco-covered brick. Elaborately carved sandstone lintels feature scenes from the Hindu pantheon, commonly the churning of the primeval ocean of milk or Vishnu reclining on a lotus flower. Scenes from the *Ramayana* and, from around 1200 on, the Buddhist *Jataka*, illuminate bas reliefs of extraordinary quality. Everywhere, too, there are figures of *apsara* with jewellery and headdresses.

The central feature of the classical Khmer temple is often a stylised representation of Mount Meru of Hindu mythology. Main entranceways – with a few exceptions, notably at Angkor Wat

itself – are from the east, marked by decorated gateways or *gopura*. The central temple complex, generally set within several concentric enclosure walls, is usually characterised by the presence (in Hindu temples) of *lingam* (male phalli) and their counterpart, the female *yoni*. In times past lustral water was poured over *lingam* and *yoni*, often conjoined, before being used as a source of blessing and purification. Statues of the major Hindu deities Shiva, Vishnu and Brahma are often present.

Other commonly represented figures from Hinduism include Nandi, the bull mount of Shiva, and the *garuda*, the half-bird, half-human mount of Vishnu, also Parvati or Uma, the wife of Shiva, their sons Skanda, the God of War, and elephant-headed Ganesh, the God of Knowledge.

A particularly Khmer deity, Hari-Hara, represents a composite of Shiva and Vishnu. As Buddhism gradually replaced Hinduism from around the 11th century on, images of the Buddha and scenes from the *Ramayana* were used in temple consecration and decoration.

Buddhist temples built in and after the 19th century are less imposing, though artistic merit is not always lacking. The influence of Siam is dominant, though few contemporary Cambodian temples can match up to their Thai counterparts. The Royal Palace is based on the court in Bangkok, and was constructed under the supervision of French architects (*see page 225*). Other buildings of note in the capital include the National Museum and a plethora of early 20th-century French colonial architecture. Similar architecture can be found in Siem Reap, Kompong Cham, Battambang and Kampot.

The presence of Cham Muslims in many towns means that mosques and minarets also form part of the Cambodian skyline. They are mostly unremarkable imitations of Islamic architecture, but to the north of Phnom Penh some interesting mosques, painted in the Cham colour of pale blue in contrast to the traditional Islamic green, have been erected in the wake of Khmer Rouge persecution. ❏

LEFT: Ta Prohm temple, Angkor.
RIGHT: Banteay Kdei, Angkor.

THE ROYAL BALLET OF CAMBODIA

The elegant and sophisticated tradition of the Cambodian Royal Ballet is thought to date back to the times of the god-kings of Angkor

The tradition of royal dancing in Cambodia is at least 1,000 years old. Inscriptions indicate that the kings of Angkor maintained hundreds of dancers at their royal courts. The celebrated temple of Ta Prohm, endowed by Jayavarman VII in 1186, maintained no fewer than 615 dancers. The origins of Cambodian dance are not hard to discern – like so much in Khmer culture, they are rooted in Indic tradition, especially that of the *Ramayana*, though a great deal of cultural exchange has also taken place between the royal courts of Phnom Penh and Bangkok. The Royal Ballet suffered particularly badly during the vicious years of Khmer Rouge rule, when Pol Pot – who had relatives who danced with it – attempted to crush the tradition completely. Fortunately a handful of dancers survived, either in hiding in Cambodia or in exile in France, and today the ancient tradition is being carefully revived. There are currently around 50 teachers of classical dance and between 300 and 400 students at the School of Fine Arts in Phnom Penh, and there are plans to establish another school at Siem Reap near Angkor.

▷ THE APSARA
Ouk Phanith, a celebrated member of the Royal Ballet, performing the sacred dance of the *apsara* (celestial dancers – *see* the panel, *far right*).

△ STUDIED ELEGANCE
A troupe of dancers from the Royal Ballet performing at the Chatomuk Theatre in Phnom Penh.

▽ STORY TELLING
Hanuman, the heroic monkey-god, dances with Sita in a scene from the *Reamker* (derived from the Indian *Ramayana*).

CELESTIAL DANCERS

Cambodian mythology and, more particularly, Cambodian temples, are both richly endowed with bas reliefs and murals of *apsara* or celestial dancing girls. These nymphs are graceful, sensuous females who dance to please the gods and to keep the cosmos moving in an orderly fashion. In technical parlance, the term *apsara* refers to celestial females who dance or fly, while their sisters who merely stand, albeit with amazing grace, are called *devata* or "angels". Almost every temple has its quota of *apsara*, but it is generally agreed that the finest examples are to be found in the bas reliefs at Angkor, and that the best *apsara* are in the "Churning of the Ocean of Milk" in Angkor Wat's East Gallery. In this epic scene from the *Bhagavad Ghita* gods are encouraged in their creative endeavours by beautiful *apsara* flying above them.

△ **FEMALE DOMAIN**
Most dancers in the Royal Ballet are women and play male roles. Male and female roles are defined by elaborate costume.

◁ **SYMBOLIC GESTURES**
In classical Cambodian ballet great emphasis is placed on symbolic and graceful hand movements.

CAMBODIAN FOOD

Like many things in the country following the Khmer Rouge regime,
the national cuisine is experiencing a belated renaissance

Cambodia is a fertile land, rich in rice, vegetables, fruit and all manner of fish. Nobody in Cambodia should go hungry, and until the late 20th century almost nobody did. It is impossible to keep the Khmer Rouge out of contemporary Cambodian matters, even if the subject is cuisine – during the "Zero Years" of Democratic Kampuchea, between 1975 and 1978, more than a million people starved to death as a direct result of government policy and an indirect result of administrative incompetence.

Almost nobody in Cambodia (except, of course, the Khmer Rouge leadership) had enough to eat; nearly everyone was malnourished to the point of starvation. Rice was a rarity because the KR government was exporting it en masse to buy Chinese and North Korean arms. People were reduced to eating rice-gruel and nutritious but tasteless morning glory vine. Independent "foraging" for food was a crime punishable by death, and communal eating was enforced – when anything was available to eat, that is.

Although this period was over by 1979 the Cambodian people have not forgotten the years of starvation and are still obsessed with food. Fortunately there is plenty of it to go round now, and moreover the quality of the ingredients available and the standards of the restaurants and street stalls are improving rapidly. The quality of Cambodian cuisine may not match that of Thailand, but it is inherently more sophisticated than that of Laos, and is fast catching up in terms of variety and quality with that of Vietnam.

The national diet

Cambodian cuisine, though uniquely Khmer, draws heavily on the traditions of both its Thai neighbours and its Chinese residents. It is often said, and with some accuracy, that Cambodian

LEFT: street vendor preparing food in Phnom Penh.
RIGHT: baguette seller at Kompong Cham by the bank of the Mekong River.

food is similar to Thai food but without the spiciness. The main national staple is of course rice, but French colonial influence has dictated that the Cambodians eat more bread – generally French-style *baguettes* – than any other Southeast Asian country. The country's incredible richness in waterways, including the Mekong,

Sap and Bassac rivers, not to mention the Tonlé Sap, means that freshwater fish and prawns are especially popular – and plenty of fresh seafood is available from the Gulf of Thailand.

Beef, pork, chicken, duck and other poultry are widely available but more expensive than fish dishes, while other less well known Cambodian delicacies include locusts, field rats, snakes and land crabs.

The small town of Skon, for example, on the main route between Phnom Penh and Kompong Cham, specialises in deep-fried spiders – but the visitor need not despair. With major hotel chains like Raffles investing heavily in the tourist infrastructure, sophisticated

Cambodian cuisine (as well as Vietnamese, Chinese, French and Italian) is well on the road to recovery.

Popular dishes

In Cambodia soup is served as an accompaniment to almost all main courses, not before them as in the West. Some of the better-known soups include *somla machou banle* (sour fish soup), *somla machou bangkang* (sour and spicy prawn soup, akin to Thai *tom yam gung*), *somla chapek* (pork soup with ginger) and *moan sngor* (chicken and coriander soup). *Num banh choc* (rice-noodle and fish soup) is a common Cam-

chicken, *trey saich koh* is grilled beef, and so on. Fish and meat dishes not served with noodles are generally accompanied by rice. Indispensable condiments are *prahok* (fish paste) and *tuk trey*, a fish sauce like Thai *nam pla* and Vietnamese *nuoc mam* but with ground roasted peanuts added.

Ethnic influences

Travellers upcountry will generally find themselves limited to Cambodian cuisine or to the fairly ubiquitous *baguette* and pâté. In towns of any size Chinese food is widely available, and generally reflects the southern coastal ori-

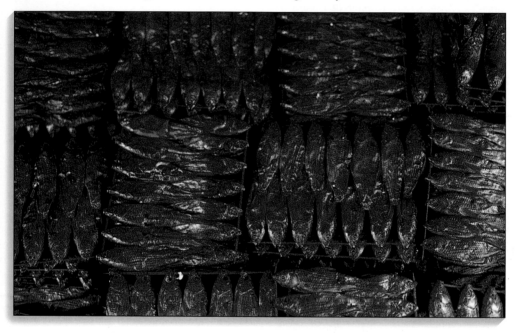

bodian breakfast. Other well-known dishes include *khao poun* (rice noodles in a coconut-based sauce), *hamok* (fish with coconut milk steamed in a banana leaf), *saich moan chha khnhei* (stir-fried chicken with ginger) and *somla machou saich koh* (sour beef stew). *An sam jruk* (pork and soybeans marinated in ginger and chilli) can be delicious, but is very rich. Watch out for *pong tea kon* (fertilised duck egg containing an embryo, like the Filipino *balut*) which is not to everybody's taste. Many dishes are served *trey*, or grilled, so *trey aing* (grilled fish) is available just about everywhere, as is *trey chean neung spey* (fried fish with vegetables). By extension, *trey moan* is grilled

gin of most of Cambodia's Overseas Chinese migrants. Expect, therefore, Cantonese, Hokkien, Teochou and Hailam fare. In the west of the country, notably at Poipet, Sisophon, Battambang and Siem Reap, Thai cuisine is widespread, while in the east, at Kampot, Takeo, Kompong Cham and Svay Rieng, Vietnamese culinary influence is common. Kompong Som excels at seafood and also has a small number of Western food outlets – French, Italian, British, German and Australian.

Phnom Penh has, naturally enough, the widest range of restaurants in the country. Here the visitor can find everything listed above as well as Greek, Turkish, North Indian, South

Indian, Sri Lankan, Malay and – increasingly – fast food restaurants. Pizza is now popular, but the "Pizza Hut" restaurant near the Cambodia-Vietnam Friendship Monument is a copycat operation.

Traditional cuisine

Just as neighbouring Laos has at least one good cookbook (*see page 81*), Cambodia now has a distinctly upmarket offering, prepared and published in the USA, which bodes extremely well for the future of the restaurant business in contemporary Cambodia. *The Elephant Walk Cookbook*, the first volume of traditional Cambodian cookery published in English, is promoted as a cultural as well as a culinary adventure.

It is also the story of its author Longteine De Monteiro, and the way in which she and her husband were forced into exile in 1975 by the Khmer Rouge takeover of Cambodia, eventually coming to own three restaurants and a market in and around Boston. An important objective of this work is to preserve traditional dishes that may now no longer be served in Cambodia because everyone who knew how to make them was either exterminated by the Khmer Rouge or fled.

The recipes in *The Elephant Walk* blend influences from Asia and the West, including China, Vietnam, Thailand, India, Spain and France. It is a balancing act of colours, textures and, most of all, salty, sour, sweet, hot and bitter flavours. Rice and fish are important, particularly freshwater-lake fish and a fermented fish paste, *prahok*, and so are coconut milk, lemongrass, and a list of other ingredients that are increasingly available outside Southeast Asia.

Dishes described include salads, pickles and the ever-popular *loc lac* – beef marinated in mushroom soy sauce, sautéed, and served on crisp lettuce with lime juice. Cambodian dishes are presented as being less salty than Vietnamese, less sweet than Thai and subtler than both. The author states: "Cambodian dishes feature a rich interweaving of cultural influences... Some of the recipes in the book, like catfish with coconut milk and red chillies, were

COLONIAL INFLUENCE

The capital serves some of the best French food in Indochina, as well as colonial bequests from the Middle East and North Africa, notably *cous-cous* and *merguez* (spicy Moroccan sausage).

created in the kitchens of Cambodian aristocrats... others, like stuffed cabbage with lemongrass, have simpler origins."

It will take a little time before the sophisticated dishes presented in *The Elephant Walk Cookbook* are widely available in Phnom Penh, but there is currently an explosion of Cambodian restaurants amongst overseas Khmers in France and the USA, and under this influence the restaurateurs of Phnom Penh are gradually rediscovering their culinary heritage.

Traditional dishes making a comeback and recommended by *The Elephant Walk Cookbook* include:

Soups: *somla machou*, a tangy soup combining shrimp, tomatoes and fried garlic garnished with fresh mint; *s'ngao moan*, shredded chicken breast simmered with lemongrass, holy basil, scallions and fresh lime; *b'baw moan*, a "hearty rice soup" with chicken, cilantro, bean sprouts and fried garlic; and *kuy tieu*, or rice-noodles cooked with sliced pork, beansprouts, red onions and fish sauce.

Other dishes eaten with rice: *nataing*, ground pork simmered in coconut milk, sliced garlic, peanuts and chilli peppers, served as a

LEFT: dried fish.
RIGHT: limes and chillies.

dip with rice; *leah chah*, green mussels cooked with garlic, holy basil, red onions, chilli peppers and lime; *mee siem*, rice-noodles sautéed with shredded chicken, soya beans, chives, red peppers, beansprouts and fried egg; *cha'ung cha'ni jruk ang*, spareribs marinated with mushrooms, soy sauce, garlic and black pepper, served with pickled cabbage; *trey ang k'nyei*, grilled catfish served with a sauce of ginger, salted soy beans and coconut milk; *moan dhomrei*, sliced chicken sautéed

> ## FRUIT
>
> There is an abundance of fruit in Cambodia all year round, including mango, coconut, rambutan, durian, mangosteen, star fruit, pineapple, watermelon and a wide variety of bananas.

Indochina, Vietnamese cuisine reflects long years of cultural exchange with China, the host country and, more recently, France. As in Cambodian restaurants, dishes are served at the same time rather than by course, and eaten with long-grain rice, *nuoc mam* (fish sauce) and a range of herbs and vegetables, generally with chopsticks.

Some of the more popular Vietnamese dishes include *cha gio*, small spring rolls of minced pork, prawn, crabmeat, mushrooms and vegetables wrapped in rice paper and then deep fried. The *cha gio* are rolled in a lettuce leaf with fresh mint and other herbs, then dipped in a sweet sauce. Another dish eaten in a similar fashion is *cuon diep*: shrimp, noodles, mint, coriander and pork wrapped in lettuce leaves.

Soups are popular. *Mien ga* is a noodle soup blending chicken, coriander, fish sauce and scallions; *canh chua*, a sour soup served with shrimp or fishhead, is a blend of tomato, pineapple, star fruit, beansprouts, fried onion, bamboo shoots, coriander and cinnamon, and *pho*, often eaten for breakfast or as a late-night snack, is a broth of rice noodles topped with beef or chicken, fresh herbs and onion. Egg yolk is often added, as may be lime juice, chilli peppers or vinegar. *Pho* is generally served with *quay* – fried flour dough.

with holy basil, bamboo shoots, pineapple and kaffir lime leaves; and finally *chau haun*, mixed chicken, beef and shrimp cooked in a sauce of garlic, shallots, ginger, lemongrass and peanuts. Some of these dishes are already available at upmarket restaurants in Phnom Penh and Siem Reap, but if you fancy trying one and it is not on the menu, just ask.

Vietnamese dishes

As well as "Khmer" food, Vietnamese cuisine is widely available throughout the country. Indeed, despite the ethnic rivalry, there are probably more Vietnamese restaurants than there are Khmer. As it does elsewhere in

Drinks

Branded soft drinks are available everywhere, as is canned and bottled beer. Local beers include Angkor, Angkor Stout and Bayon, but beer in Cambodia is inferior to that of Vietnam, Laos or Thailand. By contrast, imported and domestic wine is available. Avoid fresh fruit juices and sugar-cane juice. Cartons and cans of fruit juice, milk and drinking yoghurt are available in supermarkets. Coffee and tea are available throughout the country and are of good quality.

Tap water should not be consumed: buy bottled water, and avoid ice from street stalls – the source of the water is uncertain and it is common for blocks of ice to be dragged unprotected along dirty streets. ❑

LEFT: collecting fruit from the top of the tree.
RIGHT: freshly fried snacks for sale.

CAMBODIA: PLACES

*A detailed guide to the entire country, with principal sites
clearly cross-referenced by number to the maps*

L ike Laos, Cambodia is often described as a small place. True, at 181,036 sq. km (69,898 sq. miles) it's not large – about the same size as Missouri, but still nearly twice as big as Portugal. However, it has more historic sites per square kilometre than almost anywhere else on earth. The Khmers were master builders, and the product of more than a millennium of magnificent temple construction awaits the visitor.

Of course, the most important site in the country, if not in all of Southeast Asia, is the great temple-city of Angkor, which must not be missed. Other great temples, too, are now open to visitors – Ta Prohm and Phnom Chisor near Phnom Penh, as well as the mountain-top sanctuary of Preah Vihear (the latter currently only accessible from Thailand).

Cambodia is also geographically unique. Tonlé Sap, the great lake which dominates the northwest of the country, expands and shrinks with the rainy and dry seasons, providing a vast natural reservoir for the waters of the Mekong River. One way to visit Angkor is to take the boat from Phnom Penh, the country's shabbily elegant capital, across the Tonlé Sap to Siem Reap. En route it is possible to see something of the lifestyle of Cham and Vietnamese fisherfolk, many of whom spend all their lives on the water.

Finally, Cambodia has at least one thing that neighbouring Laos lacks – a coastline. Although seriously dilapidated by years of neglect and deliberate destruction by the Khmer Rouge, Cambodia's "Riviera" is fast coming back into fashion. The port city of Kompong Som, once known as Sihanoukville, offers a choice of four beaches and some fine seafood, while the old resort town of Kep, once known to the French as Kep-sur-Mer, is gradually being rebuilt and refurbished. ❏

PRECEDING PAGES: boats passing in a waterway; fishing on a lake.
LEFT: palm trees and canal near Angkor Wat.

Cambodia

0   50 km
0   50 miles

Buntherik
Sukhuma
Pakse
Sanamxai Ban Uk
Da Nang
Tan Canh
Cong Co Do
Chuong Nghia
L A O S
Ban Phonsaat
Ban Sompoy
Tri Dao
Koh Brahi
Ban Huayxai
Tam Nyik
Sankeo
Kon Tum
Munlapamok
Ban Phonsaat
Plei Morr
Ban Vip Tai
Ban Taseun
Ban Kanluang
Muang Khong
Siëmpang
Phievleu
Plei Ken Ngo
Dinh Dien
Dak Quon
Chu Pnan
1571
Kompong Srâlau
Ban Xot
Virachai
Pakâp
Plei Doch
Play Cu
Plei Rongol
Dogrong
Plei Klane Kla
Mu Prey
Srâlau
**Stoëng Trêng
(Stung Treng)**
San
Khsach Thmei
Chhêp Kândal
Bùng Lũng
(Ban Lung)
Bô Kheo
**Rotanokiri
(Ratanakiri)**
Thang Duc
Phu Nhon
Thalabârivath
23
Kamäng Chông
Stoëng Trêng
(Stung Treng)
Sângkùm Ân Dêt
Srêpôk
Lumphät
13
Siëmbok
Srê Pông
Kaöh Nhek
Méreuch
Ban Ay Rieng
Kompong Tabên
Srê Sbov
Mondolkiri
Kaöh Mayeul
Krong Buk
Sâmbor
Chbar
Ban Don
Quang Nhieu
22
Sândan
Khlêk Khlâk
Prek Te
Buon Ma Thout
Nong Trai
**Krâcheh
(Kratie)**
Préap
Xenmonorom
Xa Tho Thanh
Spoê Tbong
21
Krâcheh
(Kratie)
O Rang
Dak Dam
Duc Lap
Buon Phoke
Lac Thien
Prêk Kak
Krach Chhma
Srê Rônéan
Tuy Duc
1578
Bôs Khanaôr
Chhlong
Snuol
Lou
Dong Krola
Kompong Cham
20
Kompong Cham
Dang Boa
Kien Duc
Dak Nong
Duc Trong
Wat kor yon
Tonle Bêt
Suông
Loc Ninh
Ba Ra
Duc Phong
Da Dung
Phum Krêk
Mémút
Dia Diem Bunard
Bao Loc
Di Linh
Binh Long
V I E T N A M
Kâmchay Méa
Tan Bien
Dong Xoai
Da Hoa
Gia Bac
Prey Vêng
Kompong Trach
Chon Thanh
Xa Phuong Lam
Dinh Dien
Dak Menou
Prey Vêng
Tay Ninh
Phu Giao
Dinh Quan
Xa Hieu Tin
Ham Thuan Nam
Ap Long Hoa
Khsach Sa
Hoa Thanh
Ho Tri An
Duc Linh
1302
Mui Ne
Banam
Svay Riêng
Svay Riêng
Go Dau
Ben Cat
Tan Uyen
Xa Gia Kiem
Dau Giay
Song Dinh
Xa Phu Sung
Phan Thiet
Kompong Trâbêk
Chiphu
Kompong Rou
Cu Chi
Thu Dau Mot
Bien Hoa
Ap Binh Chau
Moc Hoa
Hoc Mon
Thu Duc
Xuan Loc
Cam My
Ap Rung La
Song Phan
Hong Ngu
Tien Giang (Mekong)
Ben Luc
Binh Chanh
Nha Be
Long Thanh
Ho Chi Minh
Long Le
Ham Tan
Pho Tri
Ap Bac
Can Duoc
Long Dat
Cho Moi
Tan An
Xom Vam Lang
Ba Ria
Phuoc Tuy
Cho Phuoc
Cao Lanh
Cai Lay
Go Cong
Vung Tau
**SOUTH CHINA
SEA**
Chau Thanh
Cai Be
My Tho
Xom Cua Tieu
Long Xuyen
Thanh Hung
Sa Dec
Can Tho
Thot Not
Nha Trang

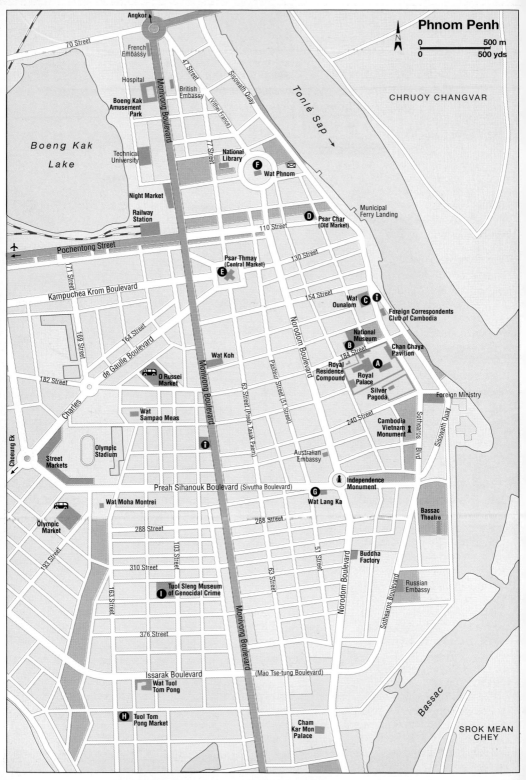

Phnom Penh

N

| 0 | 500 m |
| 0 | 500 yds |

Angkor ↑

French Embassy

70 Street

Hospital

British Embassy

(Vithei France)

47 Street

Ssowath Quay

Tonlé Sap →

CHRUOY CHANGVAR

Boeng Kak Amusement Park

Technical University

Monivong Boulevard

77 Street

National Library

Boeng Kak Lake

F Wat Phnom

Night Market

Railway Station

110 Street

D Psar Char (Old Market)

Municipal Ferry Landing

Pochentong Street

171 Street

130 Street

Kampuchea Krom Boulevard

Psar Thmay (Central Market) E

154 Street

Wat Ounalom C f

Foreign Correspondents Club of Cambodia

169 Street

164 Street

de Gaulle Boulevard

182 Street

Charles

O Russei Market

Wat Koh

Norodom Boulevard

Pasteur Street (51 Street)

B National Museum

184 Street

A Royal Palace

Chan Chaya Pavilion

Royal Residence Compound

Silver Pagoda

Foreign Ministry

63 Street (Preah Tasak Paem)

Wat Sampao Meas

Olympic Stadium

f

240 Street

Cambodia Vietnam Monument

Sothearos Blvd

Ssowath Quay

Choeung Ek

Street Markets

Australian Embassy

Preah Sihanouk Boulevard (Sivutha Boulevard)

Independence Monument

G Wat Lang Ka

Bassac Theatre

Wat Moha Montrei

Olympic Market

193 Street

288 Street

288 Street

103 Street

310 Street

163 Street

I Tuol Sleng Museum of Genocidal Crime

51 Street

63 Street

Norodom Boulevard

Buddha Factory

Sothearos Boulevard

Russian Embassy

376 Street

Issarak Boulevard

(Mao Tse-tung Boulevard)

Wat Tuol Tom Pong

H Tuol Tom Pong Market

Cham Kar Mon Palace

Bassac

SROK MEAN CHEY

PHNOM PENH

Phnom Penh's fortunes have risen and fallen with Cambodia's turbulent history and its streets and buildings echo past glories and defeats

Maps:
Area 244
City 248

Phnom Penh ❶, the Cambodian capital, is an attractive riverside city of broad boulevards and there are numerous sights to please the visitor. Not withstanding this, it is still a rather shabby and run-down place owing to the long years of war, and four years of Khmer Rouge abandonment, although improvements are now well under way. All of the more important attractions for the tourist are located beside, or within walking distance of, the Phnom Penh riverside, and this area also contains many of the best restaurants and cafés in the city.

The Royal Palace

Immediately to the south of the National Museum, on Sothearos Boulevard, lie the extensive grounds of the **Royal Palace** Ⓐ (open daily 7.30–11.30am, 2.30–5pm; entrance fee). The palace was built in Khmer style with French assistance in 1866, and it has functioned as the official residence of King Norodom Sihanouk since his return to the capital in 1992.

The public entrance to the palace is opposite the attractive, colonial-style Renakse Hotel, to the east of the palace grounds. Certain areas within the complex, including the king's residential quarters, are not open to the general public, but much of the rest of it is accessible. Just beyond the entrance gate stands the **Chan Chaya Pavilion**, formerly used by Cambodian monarchs to review parades, and for performances of classical Khmer dancing. Nowadays dance performances are regularly presented at the nearby Cambodiana Hotel.

Dominating the centre of the larger, northern section of the royal compound is the **Royal Throne Hall**. This was built as recently as 1917 in the Khmer style, the architect self-consciously borrowing extensively from the Bayon at Angkor. Inside the Throne Hall, the walls are painted with murals from the *Reamker*, the Khmer version of the *Ramayana*. As well as coronations, the Throne Hall is used for important constitutional events and, on occasion, for the acceptance of ambassadorial credentials.

To the right (north-west) of the Throne Hall stands the restricted **Royal Residence Compound** of King Sihanouk, while to the left (south) are several structures of interest. These include the **Royal Treasury**, the **Royal Banqueting Hall** and the **Napoleon III Pavilion**.

The pavilion, which has recently been renovated by French volunteers using French money, was originally given by Emperor Napoleon III to his wife, Empress Eugénie. She had it dismantled and sent the prefabricated folly across the seas to Phnom Penh as a gift for King Norodom in the 1870s.

PRECEDING PAGES: UNESCO building, Phnom Penh. **BELOW:** street corner in Phnom Penh.

Stained glass window in the Napoleon III Pavilion of the Royal Palace, Phnom Penh.

The Silver Pagoda

Leaving the main northern compound of the palace by a clearly marked gateway in the southeastern corner, you should then proceed along a narrow southwesterly route that leads to the North Gate of the celebrated **Silver Pagoda** compound. This structure has been dubbed "Silver Pagoda" because its floor is lined with more than 5,000 silver tiles weighing more than 1 kg each, or 5 tonnes in total; it is also known as **Wat Preah Keo**, or "Temple of the Emerald Buddha". It houses the sacred symbol of the nation, and photography within the building is therefore forbidden. The Silver Pagoda was built by King Norodom in 1892, and then extensively rebuilt half a century later by Sihanouk (in 1962). The temple houses two priceless Buddha figures, one of which – the Emerald Buddha, from which the temple gets its name – dates from the 17th century and is made of crystal. The other Buddha is a much larger affair, being made of 90 kg of pure gold, encrusted with 9,584 diamonds, the largest of which is 25 carats.

Continuing northwards from the Royal Palace on Sothearos Boulevard you will soon come to a small public garden, and behind the garden is the **National Museum** Ⓑ (open Tues–Sun 8am–noon, 2–5pm; entrance fee). The museum, housed in a red pavilion built in 1918, holds a wonderful collection of Khmer art, including some of the finest pieces in existence. Unofficially, it also "houses" an estimated 2 million bats, which explains the sharp, acrid smell and the constant squeaking and twittering from above the specially strengthened ceiling. As you enter, buy a copy of the museum guidebook, *Khmer Art in Stone*, which identifies and discusses the most important exhibits, including a 6th-century statue of Vishnu, a 9th-century statue of Shiva and the famous sculpted

BELOW: the National Museum.

head of Jayavarman VII in meditative pose. Particularly impressive is a damaged bust of a reclining Vishnu which was once part of a massive bronze statue found at the Occidental Mebon Temple in Angkor.

Map on page 248

Wat Ounalom

The headquarters of the Cambodian Buddhist *sangha* and Phnom Penh's most important wat, **Wat Ounalom** ❻ stands just behind the **Foreign Correspondents Club of Cambodia** (FCCC; 363 Sisowath Quay; tel: 427757) and slightly north of the Royal Palace. Founded in 1443, this extensive temple suffered badly at the hands of the iconoclastic Khmer Rouge but is fast recovering. Unfortunately the once extensive library, of the Buddhist Institute, which is also housed here, will take many years to replace.

To the west of the main temple stands a *stupa* said to contain an eyebrow hair of the Buddha. Within the temple are several archaic Buddha figures, smashed to pieces by the Khmer Rouge but since reassembled. Also on display is a statue of Samdech Huot Tat, head of the *sangha* when Pol Pot came to power and subsequently killed by the Khmer Rouge, which was recovered from the nearby Mekong and reinstalled after the collapse of Democratic Kampuchea. On leaving the temple turn right (south) along Sisowath Quay, the road that runs along the Sap River. This is a delightful area of small riverside cafés and restaurants where it is possible to savour the French influence in Cambodia's past – a good place to stop for coffee and croissants, or a *baguette* with *pâté*. Alternatively, the FCCC is open to all comers, has a well-stocked bookshop on the first floor, and offers unsurpassed views across the Sap and Mekong rivers from its well-appointed second-floor restaurant.

BELOW:
the interior of the FCCC restaurant.

A selection of blue and white china in contemporary and traditional designs at the Central Market.

BELOW: Wat Phnom.

North of Wat Ounalom

The market with the longest history in Phnom Penh is the *psar char*, or **Old Market D**, located near the riverfront at the junction of 108th and 13th Streets: a densely packed locale offering a wide selection of tapes, books, clothing, jewellery, dry goods and fresh vegetables. Unlike some of the markets it stays open late into the evening. A short distance to the southwest, at the commercial heart of Phnom Penh, is the extraordinary *psar thmay*, literally "new market", but generally known in English as **Central Market E**. Built in 1937 during the French colonial period, it is Art Deco style and is painted bright ochre. The design is cruciform, with four wings dominated by a central dome, and the overall effect has been likened to a Babylonian ziggurat. In and around the four wings almost anything you can think of is for sale, including electronic equipment, tapes, videos, clothing, watches, bags and suitcases, and a wide variety of dried and fresh foodstuffs. There are many gold and silver shops beneath the central dome which sell skilfully crafted jewellery as well as Khmer *krama* (scarves), antiques, pseudo-antiques and other souvenirs.

Built on a small mound in the north of the city not far from the banks of the Sap River, **Wat Phnom F** is perhaps the most important temple in Phnom Penh, and from it the capital takes its name. According to legend, around six centuries ago a Cambodian woman called Penh found some Buddha figures washed up on the bank of the Sap. Being both rich and pious, she had a temple constructed to house them on top of a nearby hill – in fact a mound just 27 metres (88 ft) high, but for all that the highest natural point in the vicinity – hence "Phnom Penh" ("the hill of Penh").

Wat Phnom, the temple built to house the figures, is entered from the east via

a short stairway with *naga* balustrades. The main *vihara*, or temple sanctuary, has been rebuilt several times, most recently in 1926. There are some interesting murals from the *Reamker* – the Khmer version of the Indian *Ramayana* – and in a small pavilion to the south is a statue of Penh, the temple's founder.

Wat Phnom is eclectic, to say the least. Although dedicated to Theravada Buddhism, it also houses (to the north of the *vihara*) a shrine to Preah Chau, who is especially revered by the Vietnamese community, while on the table in front are representations of Confucius and two Chinese sages. Finally, to the left of the central altar is an eight-armed statue of the Hindu deity Vishnu. The large *stupa* to the west of the *vihara* contains the ashes of King Ponhea Yat (1405–67).

To the north and east of Wat Phnom, along 94th Street and 47th Street (also known as Vithei France), lie many dilapidated old colonial buildings, increasing numbers of which are being renovated. This is the old **French Quarter**. Should you wish to explore it, leave Wat Phnom by the main eastern stairway and walk due east to the Sap River, noting en route the colonial-style Post Office building, usually resplendent with large portraits of King Sihanouk and Queen Monique. At the river turn left onto Sisowath Quay and then take the next left turn down onto 47th Street. Walk north along 47th Street to the roundabout, turn south down Monivong Boulevard, past the French Embassy (on the right) and the British Embassy (on the left), and then turn east by the Railway Station along 106th Street. This route takes you past many examples of French colonial-style architecture.

Map on page 248

South of the Royal Palace

As you walk south along Sothearos Boulevard from the palace you will pass an extensive park, in the centre of which stands a statue in heroic Social-Realist style depicting two soldiers – one Vietnamese, the other Cambodian – protecting a Cambodian woman and child. This is the **Cambodia-Vietnam Monument**, dedicated to the supposedly unbreakable friendship that links the two peoples.

At the southern end of the park, turning west along Sihanouk Boulevard, you will reach the pineapple-shaped **Independence Monument** – in fact, it represents a lotus – built to celebrate Cambodia's independence from France in 1953. Immediately to the south of this monolith is **Wat Lang Ka G**, the second Phnom Penh temple (after Wat Ounalom) to have been restored after the overthrow of the Khmer Rouge regime. Today it is a flourishing example of the revival of Buddhism in Cambodia. Saffron-robed monks abound, while newly painted murals from the *jataka* (Buddha life-cycles) fairly gleam from the restored *vihara* walls.

While the Sisowath Quay offers wonderful views over the junction of the Sap and Mekong rivers, to understand the unique confluence of waters at Phnom Penh properly you should also see the Bassac River. This is best viewed from the Monivong Bridge, south of the city centre, which marks the start of Route 1

BELOW: the Central Post Office.

to Ho Chi Minh City. The confluence of the rivers, known in Khmer as **Chatomuk** or "four faces", is remarkable for a unique phenomenon: the reversal, from May to October, of the Sap River, which more than doubles the size of the Tonlé Sap. Then, in mid-October, as the level of the Mekong diminishes, the flow of the Sap is again reversed, carrying the surplus waters of the Tonlé Sap southwards to the Mekong and Bassac deltas. The time in October when the waters return to their normal course is celebrated as *Bon Om Tuk*, one of Cambodia's most important festivals.

The Independence Monument lit up against the night sky.

Antiquities and a museum of torture

Perhaps the most interesting market for the visitor, after the Art Deco Central Market, is **Tuol Tom Pong ⊕** in the southern part of the town, beyond Issarak Boulevard (also known as Mao Tse-tung Boulevard) at the junction of 163rd and 432nd Streets. This is probably the best place to shop for genuine and imitation antiquities, Buddha figures, silk clothing, silver jewellery and ornaments, gems and old bank notes from previous regimes.

Interestingly, the notes for sale include those of the Khmer Rouge, which had currency printed in China but then had a change of mind, outlawed money and markets, blew up the central bank and ultimately never issued any notes to the public. The Khmer Rouge money is readily recognised by both its pristine condition – it was never circulated – and the war-like themes on the notes: look for rocket-toting guerrillas, howitzers, machine guns and fierce-faced Khmer Rouge girl soldiers.

Not for the weak-hearted, just over 1 km (half a mile) from Tuol Tom Pong market, to the north of Mao Tse-tung Boulevard, stands the former Tuol Sleng

BELOW: the river community along the Bassac River.

Prison, now **Tuol Sleng Museum of Genocidal Crime ❶** (open daily 7–11.30am; 2–5.30pm; entrance fee). Here, during Pol Pot's years in power, around 20,000 people were interrogated under torture and subsequently murdered, generally together with their families.

The former prison – once a school – is a chilling sight; the pictures of many of those killed stare out at the visitor in black and white from the museum walls, and primitive instruments of torture and execution are on display, as is a bust of Pol Pot. Many of the former classrooms were divided up in an incredibly primitive fashion into tiny cells. Everywhere there are crude shackles and cuffs. Initially those executed here were people the Khmer Rouge perceived as "class enemies" and supporters of the former regime, but soon the Communist regime began to consume itself in a frenzy of paranoia. By the time Tuol Sleng was liberated, in 1979, nearly all those suffering torture and execution were Khmer Rouge officials who had fallen from grace.

The Killing Fields

Finally, for those with the stomach for the experience after visiting Tuol Sleng, about 12 km (7 miles) south of the town lie the infamous **Killing Fields of Choeung Ek**. Here victims of the Khmer Rouge, including many from Tuol Sleng, were executed and buried in mass graves. Many of these graves have now been exhumed, and a *stupa*-shaped mausoleum has been erected to the victims' memory. It's a disturbing experience to view row upon row of skulls arranged in tiers in a tall plexi-glass case in the middle of the mausoleum. The easiest way to get there is by taxi from the vicinity of the Central Market, though motos waiting outside Tuol Sleng will also make the journey. ❑

Map on page 248

BELOW: a reminder of the Khmer Rouge regime's brutality.

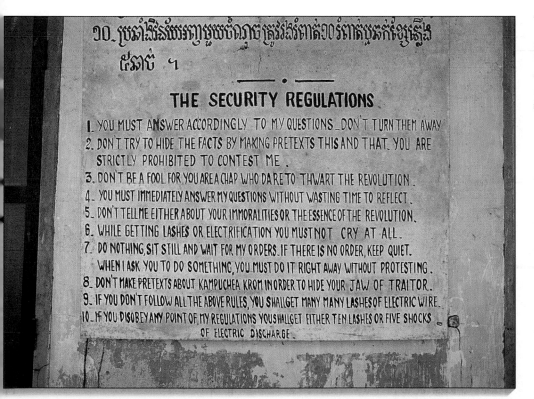

PHNOM PENH ENVIRONS

Map on page 244–5

There are many places to visit from Phnom Penh which take in fine examples of classical Khmer temple architecture and are a good introduction to the Cambodian countryside

Phnom Penh

Although the most important classical Khmer antiquities are either clustered at Angkor or scattered around the still relatively inaccessible fringes of the country, worthwhile historical sites within a short driving distance of Phnom Penh exist at Tonlé Bati and Angkor Borei to the south of the city, and at Udong, a former capital, to the north. Phnom Penh is also well placed for visiting Kompong Cham, the country's third city, which is the site of an important new road bridge across the Mekong, scheduled to open in 2002.

South to Tonlé Bati

Takeo Province, due south of Phnom Penh and bordering Vietnam, is a very worthwhile destination where you can see some fine examples of classical Khmer temple architecture. Because the province is so close to Phnom Penh it is relatively simple to visit some of these temples on a day trip from the capital. Air-conditioned taxis are available in the vicinity of the Diamond Hotel on Monivong Boulevard and should cost between US$30 and US$50 per day, depending on the distance to be travelled and your bargaining skills.

Route 2 from Phnom Penh to **Takeo** is a good road, and the journey should only take 1–1½ hours. This is a quiet, sleepy country town that makes a pleasant enough place to stop for a meal or – at a pinch – the night. Hotels are adequate, and Khmer, Vietnamese and Chinese food available. Looking around, you would scarcely guess that, during the Khmer Rouge period, Takeo was the headquarters of Ta Mok, the much-feared one-legged general who was arrested in 1999 and imprisoned in Phnom Penh. "Grandfather Mok" and his fanatical southwestern cadre made Takeo just about the most feared zone in the whole country, though happily there is no sign of such repression now.

You can take two days over this southward route, setting out from Phnom Penh early in the morning and heading directly to **Tonlé Bati ②** which is about 32 km (20 miles) distant. The chief attraction here is the laterite temple of **Ta Prohm** built by King Jayavarman VII on top of an earlier 6th-century Khmer shrine. The result is a well-preserved gem of a temple, not unduly large, but with some splendid decorative features. The main sanctuary has five chambers, in each of which is a statue or a Shiva *lingam*. Generally the shrine is favoured by fortune-tellers who will predict your future and read your palm for a few *riel*. At almost any time a traditional orchestra will be playing outside the inner sanctum of the shrine, attracting offerings from pious visitors from Phnom Penh. Clouds of incense waft through the air, and the atmosphere is very much that of a living shrine.

LEFT: houses and fishing nets at Kompong Cham.
BELOW: Apsura, Ta Prohm temple, Tonlé Bati.

An unusual feature of the temple may be found on the inner east wall of the sanctuary, about 3 metres (10 ft) above the ground. This is a bas relief which shows a woman carrying a box on her head while a man bows in supplication to another, larger woman. The scene purportedly represents a pregnant woman who gave birth to a child with the assistance of a midwife, but then failed to show the latter appropriate gratitude and respect. As a punishment, the midwife has condemned the woman to carry the afterbirth in a box on her head for the rest of her life. The crouching man is begging the midwife to forgive his wife. Another small but unusual bas relief on the inner north wall of the central sanctuary shows, in the upper part, a king sitting with his wife; in the lower part, because the wife was unfaithful, there is a representation of a servant putting her to death by trampling her under his horse's hooves.

A short distance from Ta Prohm – about five minutes' walk, on the north side of the approach road in the grounds of a modern temple – is the second of Tonlé Bati's attractions, the small temple of **Yeay Peau**. According to legend, during the early 12th century King Preah Ket Mealea was travelling in the Tonlé Bati area when he met and fell in love with a young girl called Peau. Soon Peau became pregnant, and after a while gave birth to a boy whom she named Prohm. The king, meanwhile, had returned to Angkor, leaving a ring and a sacred dagger so that the boy could travel to Angkor and identify himself to his father when he had come of age. In time this came to pass, and Prohm visited Angkor where he lived with his father for several years. On his return to Tonlé Bati Prohm failed to recognise his mother, seeing instead a woman so beautiful that he asked her to become his wife. Peau objected that she was his mother, but the young man refused to believe this. Accordingly, it was decided that a contest

BELOW: picking lotuses at Ta Prohm Temple, Tonlé Bati.

should be held to see what should happen. If Prohm, assisted by the local men, could build a temple before Peau, assisted by the local women, could do so, then she would marry him. In the event the wily Peau released an artificial morning star using candles. The men, thinking that it was dawn and the women could not possibly beat them, went to sleep. The women went on to win the contest, and Prohm was obliged to acknowledge Peau as his mother.

That, at least, is the legend. Whatever the real facts behind the building of the temples at Tonlé Bati, two classical Khmer temples exist, one named for Prohm and the other for his mother Peau. The latter is much smaller in size and less impressive than Ta Prohm; inside there is a headless statue of Peau standing beside a seated Buddha.

*Window with
elaborate shutters
at Phnom Chisor.*

Chisor Mountain

After visiting Tonlé Bati you should continue south on Route 2 for around 23 km (14 miles). The intersection for **Phnom Chisor ❸** (Chisor Mountain) is located close by the two brick towers of **Prasat Neang Khmau** – the "Temple of the Black Virgin", once probably dedicated to the Hindu goddess Kali. A side road heads eastwards at this point, leading to the foot of Phnom Chisor which is about 4 km (2½ miles) distant. The climb to the top of the hill is 100-metre (325-ft) up and involves tackling as many as 750 unevenly-spaced concrete steps, but the effort is worth it because of the spectacular views from the top over the surrounding countryside. Snacks and cold drinks are available on the way up and at the top, but it is still a hot and exhausting climb in the heat of the day. Anyone less than superlatively fit should make at least two rest stops on the way up, as there is plenty of time to take in the sights.

BELOW:
small stone figure,
Phnom Chisor.

The main temple at Phnom Chisor stands on the eastern side of the hill. Constructed of brick and laterite, with lintels and doorways of sandstone, the complex dates from the 11th century, when it was known as Suryagiri. The isolation of the site, and the way the temple suddenly appears as you struggle over the crest of the hill, have led some writers to liken the temple's atmosphere to that of a Southeast Asian Stonehenge or Macchu Pichu. Views from the far side of the temple, looking east, are spectacular. The long, straight old road built by the original temple architects is clearly visible, and would make a far more appropriate access point if reclaimed from encroaching nature. Two lesser temples punctuate the progress of this road, and a large natural lake glistens in the distance.

When you have visited Phnom Chisor it is probably best to press on to Takeo for lunch, bypassing nearby Angkor Borei and Phnom Da, which can be visited during the afternoon. There won't be much happening in Takeo – you should eat, have a few quiet drinks, and then make arrangements to visit Angkor Borei in the mid afternoon to view the temples by the warm light of the descending sun.

Angkor Borei

To reach **Angkor Borei** from Takeo, head back northwards along Route 2 until you reach the turn east to Phnom Chisor. Follow this road beyond the hilltop temple, through the town of Sai Waa, until you reach the town of Prey Kabas. Just before you enter this settlement a side road leads away to the south-west and, about 5 km (3 miles) along this road, the busy little market town that is your destination. It is believed that, almost 1,500 years ago, **Angkor Borei** was the site of Vyadhapura, the capital of "Water Chen La" before the centre of Khmer civilisation moved north-westwards to Angkor, but unfortunately there is little evidence of this to be seen at present. The area has yet to be thoroughly excavated, though American archaeologists from the University of Hawaii have recently been collaborating with their local counterparts in a preliminary survey. You should visit Angkor Borei District Office, a pleasant old colonial-style building, where some Chen La artefacts are displayed; they include temple carvings, early inscriptions and a Shiva *lingam*.

The temple of **Phnom Da ❹** can be reached by crossing the bridge to the south of Angkor Borei and driving – in the dry season – for around 5 km (3 miles). The hilltop temple, which may date from as far back as the 7th or 8th centuries, is of brick and sandstone. Although one of the oldest stone structures in Cambodia, it is in a surprisingly good state of preservation. Nearby on another hilly outcrop is a smaller sandstone temple, thought to have been built about a century after Phnom Da, called **Asram Taa Asey**. This structure was probably dedicated to Hari-Hara, a distinctively Khmer god combining manifestations of Vishnu and Shiva in the same deity.

A word of caution about the whole Phnom Da region: during the hot and dry season it's easy to drive or be driven around, but during the rains the whole area from around Takeo to the Vietnam frontier is flooded and it is necessary to hire a small boat in Angkor Borei and be taken to the temple sites by water.

BELOW: buffalo grazing near Phnom Penh.

North to Udong

Udong, a former capital of Cambodia, can be visited with ease from Phnom Penh on a day trip. Should you have the time and the inclination, however, a more rewarding and informative trip can be made by continuing by road to stay overnight in the large Mekong River city-port of Kompong Cham, returning by boat to Phnom Penh the next day. In this way a small circular tour can be completed, encompassing royal tombs, rubber plantations, an archaic Hindu temple and a fast and comfortable voyage down the Mekong.

The city of Udong is located on low hills about 35 km (22 miles) north of Phnom Penh. The road to follow is Route 5, which continues to Kompong Cham, an important port on the Sap River 60 km (38 miles) north of Udong. Route 5 winds north out of Phnom Penh on the west bank of the Sap River.

As you drive north, you will notice the **Chruoy Changvar** Peninsula between the Sap and Mekong rivers to the east. If you look closely, small minarets indicate the presence of two or three mosques in the rural villages of the peninsula, so near to and yet so far from Phnom Penh. In fact, the name "Changvar" is said to be derived from the island of Java in Indonesia, and the peninsula is home to one of Cambodia's fascinating but sadly decimated Cham Muslim communities – the Cham people suffered particularly badly under the Khmer Rouge regime.

Chruoy Changvar is reached by the Japanese Bridge (so named because in 1993 it was rebuilt with Japanese aid) and makes an interesting two-hour side trip from Phnom Penh, being particularly popular with city residents for its dozens of fine riverside restaurants. For Udong, however, ignore the bridge and continue north; you will pass through several prosperous Cham villages with

Map on page 244–5

Cattle are still widely used to till the fields in Cambodia.

BELOW: an aerial view of the central Cambodian countryside.

Map on page 244–5

newly restored mosques and silversmiths' workshops. The local Muslims are friendly, and it is quite all right to visit the mosques and photograph the turbaned Cham men, though – as with Buddhist temples throughout the country and mosques everywhere – shoes should be removed before entering a place of worship, and women should cover their heads.

A ruined capital

Udong ❺ – the name means "victorious" – was the capital of Cambodia on several occasions between 1618 and 1866. Today little remains of the former capital's days of glory, but the site is still certainly worth a visit. Two low ridges rise from the surrounding plains; unfortunately both bear the marks of extensive bombing during the years of the Second and Third Indochina Wars, and several of the *stupas* have been destroyed or are in ruins. The larger of the two hills is called Phnom Reach Throap, or "hill of the royal treasury". Here one can see the remains of an enormous Buddha figure – blown up by the Khmer Rouge – as well as *stupas* containing the ashes of King Monivong (who ruled 1927–41), King Norodom (who ruled 1845–59) and the 17th-century ruler King Soriyopor.

A naga balustrade: the hand represents Muchalinda, who sheltered the Buddha from a rainstorm.

BELOW:
a Buddha in Udong.
RIGHT:
temple at Udong.

A short distance north-east of Udong, but only accessible by boat from Prek Kdam, is the former royal city of **Lovek**. Situated on the west bank of the Sap River, Lovek was an interim Cambodian capital, between the times of Angkor and Udong, which flourished in the 16th century, but in 1594 it was captured and looted by the burgeoning Kingdom of Ayutthaya, or Siam.

According to legend, the Siamese beseiged the city in 1593 but were beaten back. Before leaving, however, they used cannon to fire silver shot into the bamboo fortifications surrounding the city. After the Siamese withdrawal the Cambodians tore down these barricades to get at the silver and, as a consequence, when the Siamese returned a year later, they took the city with ease. This legend may not be true, but it is closely associated with the years of Cambodian decay which followed the abandonment of Angkor, and when you look at Lovek today – or what can be seen from the banks of the Sap River – the former city seems symbolic of that period of decay.

After visiting Udong retrace your drive down Route 5 for 4 km (2½ miles) to the small town of **Prek Kdam** on the banks of the Sap River. From here it's a short ferry ride – via a ferry donated and maintained by Denmark – to the east bank of the river, then a 42-km (26-mile) drive along Route 6 to the junction town of Skon (pronounced Skoon). The countryside is fertile and verdant (especially during the rainy season), with rice paddies and thousands of sugar palms stretching in every direction.

From Skon follow Route 7 for 47 km (30 miles) to Cambodia's third-largest city **Kompong Cham** *(see page 286)*. The journey along an excellent road, takes you through countryside rich in rubber plantations. Just outside the town – about 2 km (1 mile) to the north-west – is the **Wat Nokor Bayon** temple complex, a modern temple set amid ancient ruins, which is best visited at sunset. ❑

ANGKOR

This ancient capital of the Khmer kingdom is the cultural and spiritual heart of Cambodia. Although monumental in scale, it offers intimate glimpses into lives lived in a distant past

Map on page 268

Angkor

Phnom Penh

Angkor is one of the wonders of the world. Perhaps nowhere else on earth, unless in the Valley of the Nile in Egypt, are the relics of antiquity found on so monumental a scale. When the French first opened Angkor to tourism it was usual to distinguish between the "Small Circuit" comprising the central temples of the complex, and the "Great Circuit", taking in the outer temples. Today, when air-conditioned taxis have replaced elephants and horses as the most popular means of transportation here, it still makes a great deal of sense to follow – at least approximately – these designated routes. Therefore in this chapter the two circuits are described in turn; the Great Circuit starts on *page 273* and descriptions of sites beyond the circuits start on *page 277*.

The Small Circuit: Angkor Thom

The road to Angkor leads north from Siem Reap, past the Angkor Conservatory, to a tollbooth. Here you must pay a fairly hefty charge – for a day, three days or up to a week – before proceeding to view the monuments. About 1 km (half a mile) beyond the tollbooth the road reaches the south side of Angkor Wat, and you will catch your first sight of the justly famed monument. For the moment, however, it is probably better to drive past Angkor Wat by the west road and visit the city of Angkor Thom, as the former should be visited in the afternoon when the complex is best illuminated by the sun.

Angkor Thom ❻ or "Great City" encompasses a huge, square area of land enclosed within an 8-metre (26-ft) -high defensive wall and outer moats approximately 100 metres (325 ft) wide. Each side of the wall is about 3 km (2 miles) long, and it has been speculated that, at the height of its wealth and power, the city may have supported as many as 1 million people. The founder and architect was the Buddhist King Jayavarman VII (1181–1220), probably the most prolific builder the Khmer Empire ever produced.

There are five gateways into the city, each approached by a causeway built across the moat. As you approach from the south the view of the fortifications is impressive. The causeway is flanked by 108 large stone figures, 54 gods on the left and an equivalent number of demons on the right. In the distance, at the far end of the causeway, the southern gateway bears four huge enigmatic faces facing in the cardinal directions.

The Bayon

Passing through this prodigious gateway, the road continues northwards for around 1.5 km (1 mile) to reach the **Bayon**. This temple, which should be entered from the east, was built in the late 12th century by Jayavarman VII. Always a favourite with visitors,

PRECEDING PAGES: North gate, Angkor Thom. **LEFT:** Ta Prohm covered with the roots of a banyan tree. **BELOW:** gate at Angkor Wat.

Stone carving depicting daily life at Angkor Thom.

is possibly the most celebrated structure at Angkor after Angkor Wat itself, and justly so. It is thought to represent a symbolic temple mountain and rises on three levels, the first of which bears eight cruciform gateways. These are linked by galleries that contain some of the most remarkable bas reliefs at Angkor; they combine numerous domestic and everyday scenes with historical details of battles won and lost by the Khmers. The domestic scenes, many of which are in smaller bas reliefs below the main war scenes, show details of fishermen, market scenes, festivals, cockfights, removing lice, hunting, women giving birth, and so on. There are also everyday scenes from the royal palace – princes and princesses, wrestlers and sword fighters.

To view the bas reliefs, which are well worth an hour or two of your time, it is best to start near the east entrance to the Bayon and proceed clockwise, via the south wall, keeping the carvings to your right. The **East Gallery**, which is in an excellent state of preservation, features a military procession of Khmer troops, elephants, ox carts, horsemen and musicians. Parasols shield the commanders of the troops, who include Jayavarman VII. The **South Gallery** is spectacular and contains some of the finest bas reliefs at Angkor. The early panels depict the great naval battle that took place on the Tonlé Sap in 1177. The Khmers have no head coverings and short hair, while the Cham invaders wear strange hats which resemble long hair. The fighting is intense, with bodies falling from the boats and sometimes being taken by crocodiles.

Having viewed the galleries, you should climb to the third level and spend some time examining the vast, mysterious faces with their sublime smiles. The central shrine, which is circular, is also at the third level, and features the faces of the *bodhisattva* Avalokitesvara.

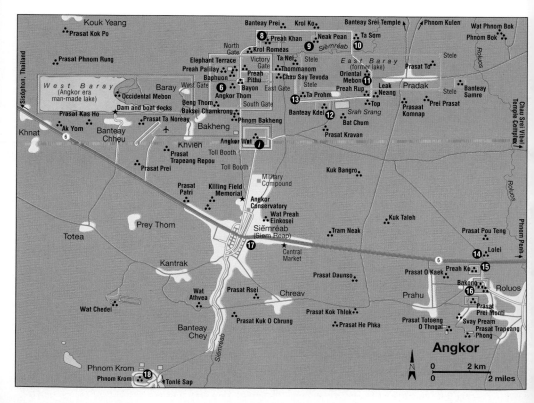

Angkor

Kings' terraces

Passing the once mighty Baphuon – now undergoing extensive restoration – and the former royal palace of Phimeanakas, you reach the celebrated **Elephant Terrace**. Also built by the Jayavarman VII, this structure is over 300 metres (970 ft) long, and has three main platforms and two lesser ones. The terrace was probably used by the king, the royal family, ministers and generals to review their forces, and perhaps to watch other entertainments. The whole terrace is elaborately decorated not only with the sandstone elephants which give the terrace its name, but also with detailed tigers, lions, geese and lotus flowers.

Immediately to the north of the Elephant Terrace and in a direct line with it stands the **Terrace of the Leper King**. Like the Elephant Terrace, this much smaller structure dates from the late 12th century and is chiefly remarkable for its many bas reliefs. After seeing this, you should head southwards back to the Bayon and leave Angkor Thom by the South Gate. A few hundred metres beyond the South Gate, to the west side of the road, the hill of **Phnom Bakheng** rises 67 metres (218 ft) above the surrounding plains. This is an ideal spot from which to view the distant spires of Angkor Wat at sunset, but it is worth climbing at any time of the day. On the east side a steep and treacherous stairway provides a swift but difficult means of ascent. Alternatively, and much more easily, a winding elephant path leads to the summit via the south side of the hill.

Angkor Wat

After Phnom Bakheng, you should continue south to **Angkor Wat ❼**. By any standards this must be the highlight of any visit to the Angkor region – the great temple is simply unsurpassed by any other monument. Construction of this

Map on page 268

BELOW: the Elephant Terrace at Angkor Thom.

A security guard at Angkor Wat with pet lizard for company. Visitors should stay on the well used paths as there are mines on some outlying paths.

BELOW: Angkor Wat.

masterpiece is thought to have begun during the reign of Surayavarman II (1112–52), and to have been completed some time after his death. Authorities claim that the amount of stone used in creating this massive edifice is about the same as that used in building the Great Pyramid of Cheops in Egypt, though Angkor Wat has many more exposed surfaces, nearly all of which are elaborately carved to a remarkable standard.

Angkor Wat was established as a Hindu temple dedicated to the god Shiva, but it is also thought to have been envisaged as a mausoleum for Surayavarman II. Its orientation is different from that of most temples at Angkor, as the main entrance is from the west rather than the east. The bas reliefs – one of the most important elements of the temple – are intended to be viewed from left to right, conforming to Hindu practice.

The westward orientation of the temple is supposed to be related to the association between the setting sun and death. The sheer scale of Angkor Wat is difficult to grasp in a single visit. Just walking to the central shrine across the moat and along the main causeway is a humbling experience. At the end, the main towers of the temple rise to an astonishing 65 metres (210 ft) through three separate levels.

At the third level there are five great towers – one at each corner – and the great central spire. These towers are conical, tapering to a lotus-shaped point. Angkor Wat is built on a massive scale: the area of land covered by the complex is around 210 hectares (500 acres) and it is surrounded by a moat which is 200 metres (650 ft) wide. Yet, despite these overwhelming statistics, it is generally very much alive, a very human place indeed. Vendors of all kinds of goods, from cold drinks and snacks to the ubiquitous sarongs, *krama* (Khmer scarves)

and cast heads of Jayavarman VII and other kings, are everywhere. Cattle wander across the main temple enclosure and drink at the tanks there, while buffalo laze and flick their tails in the broad moats surrounding the complex.

Map
on page
271

Angkor Wat: first level

Proceeding along the central causeway you should enter the central sanctuary at the first level and turn right to walk round the entire gallery of bas reliefs – no small feat, as there is much to see. Near the entrance to the first gallery there is a huge stone standing figure with eight arms bearing symbols which indicate that the statue was of Vishnu. In recent times, however, a Buddha head has replaced that of Vishnu, and the statue is now much venerated by local Buddhists.

The bas reliefs of Angkor's first-level galleries are all truly remarkable, but even so some stand out. Thus the visitor should look for:

In the West Gallery Ⓐ
- The Battle of Kurukshetra: The southern part of the west gallery depicts a scene from the great Hindu epic, the *Mahabharata*, in which the opposing Kauravas and Pandavas clash with each other.
- The Battle of Lanka: This panel depicts a well-known scene from the *Ramayana* and must be considered one of the finest bas reliefs at Angkor Wat. It depicts a long struggle between Rama and the demon-king of the island of Lanka, Ravana.

In the South Gallery Ⓑ
- The Army of King Surayavarman II: This splendid panel shows the victorious army of Surayavarman II in triumphal march. Surayavarman rides a great war elephant and carries a battle axe. He is shaded by 15 umbrellas and fanned by

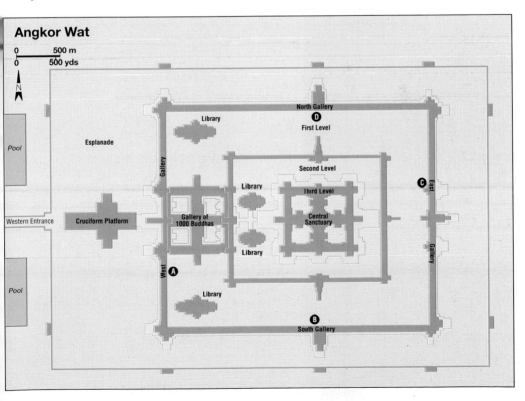

Angkor Wat

0 — 500 m
0 — 500 yds

N

Pool

Esplanade

Library

North Gallery Ⓓ
First Level

Second Level

Gallery

Library

Third Level

East Gallery

Ⓒ East

Western Entrance

Cruciform Platform

Gallery of 1000 Buddhas

Central Sanctuary

Library

West Gallery Ⓐ

Pool

Library

South Gallery Ⓑ

Exploring Angkor Wat can be thirsty work, but there are plenty of vendors around with a supply of cool drinks.

BELOW: stone carving showing sinners being taken to hell, Angkor Wat.

numerous servants. The main ranks of Khmer soldiery march in close order and look like serious warriors. To the west is one of the earliest representations of Thais, at this time fighting as mercenary troops for the Khmer Empire. Contrasting with the serried ranks of the Khmers, the Thais march out of step and wear long, dress-like sarongs.

● The Scenes of Heaven and Hell: The scenes on this panel, depicting the various rewards and punishments of heaven and hell, are truly terrifying. Those who have done well and accumulated merit in this life seem to be fine – they approach Yama, the judge of the dead, apparently confident of passage to heaven – but, beneath them, sinners are being dragged to hell by hideous devils wielding heavy clubs.

In the East Gallery ☉

● The Churning of the Ocean of Milk: This is probably the best executed and most spectacular of all the bas reliefs at Angkor. In one huge, brilliantly carved panel, 88 *asura* (devils) on the left (south side) and 92 *deva* (gods) on the right (north side) churn the ocean of milk with a giant serpent for a thousand years. Their purpose is to extract the elixir of immortality, which both covet. Overhead finely carved *apsara* sing and dance to encourage the gods and devils in their endeavour.

● The Victory of Vishnu over the Demons: Vishnu, riding on a *garuda*, is engaged in mortal combat with legions of devils. Perhaps predictably, the powerful god takes on all comers and, despite the odds, emerges victorious.

In the North Gallery ☉

● The Victory of Krishna over Bana: In this panel Vishnu, as Krishna, rides a *garuda*. A burning walled city is the residence of Bana, the demon king. The

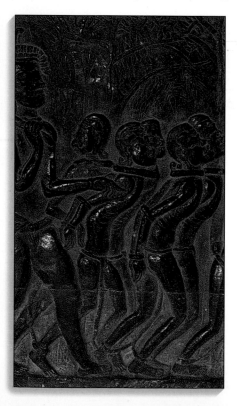

garuda puts out the fire and captures Bana; then, in a spirit of mercy, Krishna kneels before Shiva and asks that the life of the demon king be spared.

● The Battle between the Gods and the Demons: This finely carved panel features yet another battle scene. Here gods of the Brahmanic pantheon struggle with various devils. The gods are distinguishable by their traditional mounts and aspects: Shiva, for example, rides a sacred goose, while Vishnu has four arms and is seated on a *garuda*.

Angkor Wat: upper levels

After examining the galleries of bas reliefs, you should enter the central complex and climb up to the second level by the usual steep flights of steps. The exterior of this level is rather plain, but within more than 1,500 *apsara* – celestial dancers – grace the walls.

In times past, only the king and the high priest were allowed on the top (third) gallery of Angkor Wat. The central sanctuary rises 42 metres (137 ft) above the top level, bringing the overall height of the central tower to the same height as that of the cathedral of Notre Dame in Paris.

The central sanctuary and the third level of Angkor Wat are ideal places to visit at sunset. Clear, stunning views are available across the entire temple, and – perhaps for the first time – it is possible to grasp clearly the stupendous size of the entire complex. As the sun sinks, warm, golden or red rays of sunshine pierce the elaborately carved sandstone window buttresses, illuminating the very finest and best preserved *apsara* to be found anywhere at Angkor. It is truly an unforgettable experience.

The Great Circuit: Preah Khan

From Siem Reap head north past Angkor Wat, through Angkor Thom, to the North Gate. Next, turning due east, stop opposite the row of cold-drink stalls directly in front of the west entrance to **Preah Khan ❽**, the temple of the "sacred sword", also founded by the Buddhist King Jayavarman VII. Built in the style of the Bayon and dedicated to Buddhism, the temple served as both a monastery and the centre of the former royal city. There is a magical quality about Preah Khan which comes from the feeling of proximity to nature; this is because the temple still awaits full restoration, and great trees with smothering roots still cling to the sandstone and laterite walls.

An inscribed stone stele, found at Preah Khan in 1939 and removed for safe keeping to the Angkor Conservatory, indicates that the temple was once the heart of the ancient city of Nagarajayacri. The central sanctuary was dedicated in 1191, during Jayavarman VII's reign. However, Jayavarman was followed by a series of Hindu-oriented kings who did their best to Hinduise the great Buddhist sanctuary. Accordingly, images of the Buddha were chipped out of their niches, and elsewhere in the interior of the shrines Buddha images were transformed into *rishi*, or ascetics, by the simple addition of beards.

The central sanctuary of Preah Khan is cruciform, with four entrances. Look for the "Hall of Dancers", named for the finely carved rows of *apsara* which decorate the walls. If you are feeling fit and agile enough to clamber over (and

Maps on pages 268/271

LEFT: Preah Khan.
BELOW: sunlight catching pillars at Angkor Wat.

sometimes under) the great piles of fallen stone in the northeastern section of the main sanctuary you may visit "the Shrine of the White Lady": an elegant figure, supposedly not an *apsara* but the wife of Jayavarman VII, tucked away in a hidden room. The shrine is still venerated, and supplicants light incense and leave offerings of money. You will need a guide to find this out-of-the-way spot, but the effort is worth it.

Neak Pean

After leaving Preah Khan you should head eastwards along the road leading to the East Baray. About 2.5 km (1½ miles) from Preah Khan a track leads south-wards for around 300 metres (975 ft) to the unusual temple of **Neak Pean ❾**, or "the coiled serpents". This structure, which dates from the second half of the 12th century, was built by Jayavarman VII and dedicated to Buddhism. Located in the midst of the Jayatataka on the North Baray, Neak Pean now remains dry for most of the year, but it was once an island, and its whole pur-pose is closely connected with water.

The temple, which is quite small by Angkorean standards, is set in an artifi-cial pond 70 metres (230 ft) square. This central pool is surrounded at the car-dinal points by four smaller square pools which are set somewhat more deeply into the earth. In the centre of the main pool is a circular island bearing a stepped laterite shrine dedicated to the *bodhisattva* Avalokitesvara. Two intertwined ser-pents circle the base of the island and give the complex its name. The central pool is said to represent the Himalayan Lake Anavatapta, located at the summit of the universe, which was believed to give birth to the four great rivers of the world. These four rivers are represented at Neak Pean by four gargoyle-like

BELOW:
shrine at the Bayon, Angkor Thom.

heads which, when opened, would permit water to flow from the main pool to the four smaller pools. The heads are located in small stone-roofed buildings between the main pool and the lesser square ponds. The east head represents a human being, the south a lion, the west a horse and the north an elephant. In times past, pilgrims to Neak Pean would consult with resident priests and then repair to the appropriate pool, where servants of the shrine would release a plug and allow the magical waters of the central pool to pour out over the supplicant.

About 2 km (just over a mile) from Neak Pean stands the tranquil and charming temple of **Ta Som** . Built in the late 12th century by the indefatigable Jayavarman VII, and inevitably dedicated by him to Buddhism, the Bayon-style temple was also built to honour Jayavarman's father. Ta Som is not one of the "great" temples of Angkor in that it is not monumental in size. What makes it special, however, is its setting on the northeastern limits of the great Angkorean complex. It is off the beaten track, sees relatively few visitors, and as a consequence is filled with birdsong and the sound of cicadas.

In the East Baray

Located in the midst of the East Baray, the 10th-century **Oriental Mebon** is another example of an artificial temple mountain representing Mount Meru – one of the enduring themes of classical Khmer architecture. Surrounded by three laterite enclosure walls, the "mountain" rises through three levels before culminating in a central platform bearing four smaller outer towers and one larger central tower. The stairways at the foot of the artificial mound are flanked by carved sandstone lions, while elephants stand astride the corners of the second and third levels. Quite close by is **Preah Rup** , a Hindu temple dedicated

One of the four stone gargoyles at Neak Pean, used to divert water from the main pool into smaller pools below.

BELOW:
the ruins of the temple of Ta Som.

Looking out from the landing stage over Srah Srang (Royal Bath).

BELOW:
Ta Prohm temple.

to the god Shiva, which also dates from the 10th century. Visitors to Preah Rup should climb to the top of the monument for excellent views north across the East Baray, as well as southwest, where the distant spires of Angkor Wat can be distinguished in clear weather.

As you leave Preah Rup the road passes the great reservoir of **Srah Srang**, or "royal bath". This large body of water, 300 metres (970 ft) by 700 metres (2,270 ft), was built on the orders of Jayavarman VII and, especially in the late afternoon and evening, makes a delightful sight as buffaloes bath in its tranquil waters. At the western side of the lake is a sandstone landing stage flanked by lions and bearing a large *garuda* on the back of a three-headed serpent. Immediately west of the landing stage a gateway in a high laterite wall gives access to **Banteay Kdei** ⑫, the "citadel of the cells". Also commissioned by Jayavarman VII, the temple was used as a Buddhist monastic complex until the mid-20th century. As a consequence it is less overgrown than some of the other outer temples, and very pleasant to stroll through. Visitors are advised to follow the central corridor through the "hall of the dancing girls" – so called from a bas relief of dancers cut into the wall – and on to the central sanctuary which contains a recent Buddha image, still much venerated by the local people.

Finally, and ideally towards the end of the day, the route leads past Banteay Kdei for a distance of about 1 km to reach the spectacular temple of **Ta Prohm** ⑬ or "ancestor of Brahma". This very large complex was, yet again, the work of Jayavarman VII and dedicated to Buddhism. A stone stele, now removed to the Angkor Conservatory, tells us quite a lot about it: for example, in its prime the temple owned 3,140 villages and was maintained by 79,365 people including 18 high priests, 2,740 officials, 2,202 assistants and 615 dancers.

Ta Prohm is a long, low complex of buildings all on the same level, with a series of concentric galleries connected by passages that provide shade in the heat of the day. The entire complex is surrounded by a rectangular laterite wall of around 700 metres (2,270 ft) in width by 1,000 metres (3,300 ft) in length. What makes Ta Prohm so special is that, following an unusual archaeological decision, the jungle has been only partly cut back, so that the buildings are covered with the roots of huge banyan and kapok trees which rise high above the temple. Spectacular roots bind lintels and crack vaulted passageways, while parrots fly in the upper canopy and break the stillness with their sharp cries.

Map on page 268

Beyond the circuits: the Roluos complex

Some 11 centuries ago King Jayavarman II (802–50), remembered as the founder of the first unified Khmer state, made his capital at Hariharalaya ("the dwelling place of Hari-Hara", a deity combining the attributes of both Vishnu and Shiva). Today the Roluos complex of temples, which are the oldest in Angkor, marks the site of this first Angkorean capital.

Founded by King Yasovarman I (889–908), **Lolei ⓮** was dedicated to the Hindu deity Shiva. Most people come here to see the magnificent carvings and well-preserved stone inscriptions, though the four central brick towers are somewhat tumbledown and covered with shrubbery. Just to the south stands **Preah Ko ⓯**, the "sacred bull". Built by King Indravarman I (877–89), it is set amidst attractive rural scenery and, being somewhat off the beaten track, is usually tranquil and rarely visited. The main sanctuary consists of six brick towers set on a low laterite platform. A short distance beyond Preah Ko rises the solid mass of **Bakong ⓰**, a late 9th-century Hindu temple dedicated to Shiva. A

BELOW:
the roots of banyan and kapok trees, Ta Prohm temple.

thousand years ago Bakong was the central feature of Hariharalaya. It is built as a temple mountain on an artificial mound surrounded by a moat and outer enclosure walls. Bakong, which is easily the largest monument of the Roluos Group, is best entered from the east by a processional way decorated with seven-headed *naga* serpents.

The justly famed temple of **Banteay Srei** lies about 30 km (18 miles) northeast of Siem Reap, and is generally reached by taxi. While Angkor Wat, Angkor Thom and the Bayon impress by their sheer size, Banteay Srei inspires through meticulous detail. It is, indeed, a scrupulously executed miniature temple complex carved in fine pink sandstone – and in the quality of the stone and the soft, almost mellifluous charm of the colour lies much of the temple's appeal.

Founded in the second half of the 10th century by two Shivaist priests, Banteay Srei is of rectangular design, enclosed by three walls and the remains of a moat. The central complex consists of a number of structures including, most importantly, shrines dedicated to Shiva (the central and southern buildings) and to Vishnu (the northern building). The main themes represented in the many elaborately carved lintels and frontons are derived from the Hindu epic, the *Ramayana*. Also worthy of note are the finely carved figures of male and female divinities set in recessed niches of the central towers.

Base town attractions

Siem Reap ⓱, the base town for people visiting the nearby temples of Angkor, is a relaxing and pleasant place located by the shady banks of the Siem Reap River. Near the centre stands the celebrated **Grand Hotel d'Angkor**, recently completely renovated by the Singapore Raffles Group. Over the years many

BELOW: library buildings at Banteay Srei.
RIGHT: elaborate door lintel, Banteay Srei.

Map on page 268

well-known visitors to Angkor have stayed here, including such luminaries as W. Somerset Maugham, Noël Coward, Charlie Chaplin and Jacqueline Kennedy Onassis. After watching traditional Cambodian dancers performing at Angkor during the 1920s, Maugham was moved to write: "The beauty of these dances against the mystery of the temple made it the most unearthly and strangely beautiful sight imaginable. It was certainly more than worthwhile to have travelled thousands of miles for this, and I returned to the hotel with the exciting prospect of seeing the city and its monuments by daylight".

Truth to tell, Siem Reap itself has few monuments, though with Angkor so close at hand this is perhaps a good thing – the visitor will certainly feel the need to relax after a long day's sight-seeing. Directly opposite and south of the Grand Hotel stands **King Sihanouk's Villa**, a small palace rarely visited by the reigning monarch, who spends much of his time in Beijing. Foreign visitors to Siem Reap are usually permitted to walk in front of the attractive colonial-style building, though locals without appropriate business are generally shooed away.

Southwards, along the bank of the river, lies the delightful old **French Quarter**, which could as well be in Djibouti or Algiers were it not for the Khmer sights and sounds which pervade the area. There are numerous pleasant guesthouses and restaurants here, and this is certainly the best place to relax during the quiet Siem Reap evenings. Just south of the French Quarter is the recently built **New Market** (in Khmer, Psar Thca), one of the best places in the town to buy souvenirs of Angkor. Some of these are cheap and unattractive, but look for the wonderful temple-rubbings on rice paper which are most reasonably priced and look very attractive when framed. The vendors will roll them up and insert them into decorated round rattan carrying-cases for the

Locally brewed Angkor Beer is widely available in bottles, cans and on tap.

BELOW: street in the French Quarter, Siem Reap.

Map
on page
268

journey home. Other good places to look for superior quality souvenirs such as carved sandstone replicas of Angkor pieces, leather puppets and woodcarvings may be found near the Angkor Conservatory, about 1.5 km (1 mile) out of town on the right side of the road to Angkor.

A good Siem Reap option, particularly during the early evening, is to stroll southwards along the riverbank into the southern suburbs of the town. Under the shady trees there are many attractive, blue-painted and decorated Cambodian stilt houses as well as rustic bamboo **water-wheels**, some as much as 3 metres (10 ft) high, which creak as they raise the waters of the Siem Reap River to irrigate nearby rice paddies and fruit orchards.

Tonlé Sap excursion

A particularly worthwhile excursion from Siem Reap lies south on the nearby **Tonlé Sap**, Cambodia's Great Lake. The road from the town leads towards **Phnom Krom** ⓲, the only hill in an otherwise completely flat landscape. Phnom Krom – which is gradually being quarried away – is surmounted by a 10th-century sandstone temple of the same name which may be reached by a long flight of steps. The climb, while tiring, is well worth it for the view over the nearby lake and north towards Angkor. The scenery varies greatly from season to season, as during the rains the Tonlé Sap expands considerably. In consequence the last section of road run along a narrow causeway leading to the "port" for Battambang and Phnom Penh. At the end of the causeway is a small and rather malodorous fishing village. Here, a very reasonable charge, one can hire a boat to explore the nearby **Floating Village**. Be sure to choose a boat with a good roof as a sun-shield, especially during the hot season. The sun, already fierce, is reflected back by the still waters of the Tonlé Sap and can prove very trying; a sunscreen and hat are recommended, especially for the fair skinned.

BELOW: fish and winkles caught at Siem Reap.

The "village" consists of a fairly wide main thoroughfare, with many turnings off leading to narrow passages between houseboats, stilt houses and extensive fish traps. The water isn't deep – in the dry season it would be possible to stand in some places – but it is immensely rich in silt and sediment, so the propellers of the boats look almost as though they are churning warm chocolate. The people clearly aren't rich, but their unusual community boasts all kinds of unexpected amenities. There's a police station, a couple of floating petrol stations, fish farms, floating restaurants and – amazingly – pig sties. Men fish and repair vessels or extend their houses, women cook and wash up in kitchens invariably at the sterns of the boats, and children play on the wooden decks and landings, or swim in the muddy waters of the lake.

Inshore most villagers seem to be Khmer, but further out in an extended area of houseboats most of the people are Vietnamese. One sure way of distinguishing is to look for the Chinese characters and small red altars characteristic of Vietnamese homes ashore or afloat. Another is to watch for the *non la*, or conical hats, worn by Vietnamese women everywhere to protect their complexions, generally fairer than those of their Khmer neighbours. ❑

Indic Traditions

A Chinese envoy, Chou Ta-kuan, visited the Khmer capital, Angkor, during the reign of Indravarman III (1296–1308) and left a detailed manuscript describing his experiences which now acts like a window on all aspects of 13th-century Angkorean life as it is unconstrained by the Indic tradition of excluding ordinary people from literature. Chou Ta-kuan tells us that the Khmer Empire, known to its inhabitants as Kan-po-chih (Cambodia), began at present-day Vung Tau; all the southern Mekong region belonged to it.

Chou recognised three religious traditions established at Angkor: Brahmanism, Buddhism and Shivaism. Most familiar, both to him and to the present-day visitor, were the Theravadan Buddhists, known by a Tai term, Chao Ku. The Shivaists were already a declining influence at this time; Chou found their temples poorer than those of the Buddhists, housing a shiva *lingam*.

Chou records: "The walled city of Angkor was some five miles in circumference. It had five gates, with five portals. Outside the wall stretched a great moat across which massive causeways gave access to the city. The Palace stands to the north of the Golden Tower and the Bridge of Gold; starting from the gate its circumference is nearly one-and-a-half miles. The tiles of the central dwelling are of lead; other parts of the palace are covered with pottery tiles, yellow in colour... Out of the Palace rises a golden tower, to the top of which the ruler ascends nightly to sleep. By contrast, the houses of the ordinary folk were thatched with straw, for 'no one would venture to vie with the nobility'."

In fact, as Chou makes clear, late-13th century Khmer society was rigidly stratified by class. At the base of the pyramid were slaves, many of whom were reportedly captured "mountain tribes". They were set apart from free people by various prohibitions: they could not sleep in houses, though they could lie beneath them; on entering a house they had to prostrate themselves before beginning work; they had no civil rights; their marriages were not recognised by the state; and they were obliged to call their owners "father" and "mother". Slaves often tried to run away, and when caught would be tattooed, mutilated and shackled.

Above the slaves were a number of classes who were free but not part of the nobility. These included slave-owners, landholders, resident and visiting traders and, most probably, market traders, who according to Chou were mainly women. The position of other "free" people outside the élite is a matter for speculation.

The king and his immediate entourage, the high élite, topped the pyramid. Chou was perplexed by the king's relative accessibility, which was so unlike the Emperor of China's court. In fact, his approach to royal audiences seems closer to the Sukhothai system than to the Chinese (or Viet).

Chou may not have known it but, by the end of the 13th century, the Khmers, influenced by both the rising power of their Tai neighbours and the growing strength of Theravada Buddhism, were reaffirming their Indic identity even as they paid tribute to China. ❑

RIGHT: the Leper King terrace, Angkor Thom.

CENTRAL CAMBODIA

The Mekong River is essential to life in Cambodia. This chapter follows a route south and then north along its banks, stopping off at interesting places along the way

Map on page 244–5

Phnom Penh

Around 1,500 years ago, when an independent kingdom centred on the Phnom Penh region first emerged, it was dubbed "Water Chen La" by the Chinese annalists because of its proximity to, and dependence on, the Mekong River (*see page 44*). Over the intervening centuries little has occurred to change the Cambodian people's reliance on the Mekong for their fundamental existence. If it has aptly been said that "Egypt is the gift of the Nile", then the Mekong – together with its related rivers the Sap and the Bassac – remains Cambodia's lifeline.

In the 18th century the Khmers lost control of Prey Nokor – subsequently renamed Saigon – and the Mekong Delta to Vietnam, but continued to rely on the Mekong and Bassac rivers for access to the sea. The French colonial interlude saw the construction of a basic road network, and a narrow-gauge railway was built linking Phnom Penh with Bangkok, but still the Mekong River remained Cambodia's major link with the outside world. In 1955, in an attempt to change this and loosen the country's reliance upon Vietnam, construction of a new deepwater seaport at Kompong Som – briefly known as Sihanoukville – was begun, but by 1967, when a rail link was finally completed to Phnom Penh, Cambodia was already engulfed in war.

The great river played a central role in the turbulent events that followed. By 1973 Phnom Penh, swollen with refugees from Vietnam and surrounded by Communist forces, was completely dependent on the Mekong supply route for its survival. When, in early 1975, the insurgents blocked the river with floating mines and halted the convoys, the Communist seizure of power was assured. Khmer Rouge radio subsequently declared in triumphalist tones: "The Mekong was the key to our great victory. It was also the enemy's weakest point. Blocking the Mekong meant completely defeating the enemy and and winning total victory." Subsequently, economic mismanagement, technical incompetence and, above all, continuing warfare would combine to reduce Cambodia's nascent transport infrastructure to a complete shambles – but through it all the waters of the Mekong continued to pour into the South China Sea.

LEFT: girl at Wat Nokor Bayon.
BELOW: Mekong River traffic.

The flow of the Mekong River

It is difficult to overstate the importance of the Mekong to Cambodia. Rising in a remote region of China's Qinghai Province, it flows for more than 4,000 km (2,500 miles) through six different countries before reaching the sea – but it is in Cambodia that the river is at its most complex. After passing through the Si Phan Don or "four thousand islands" region of southernmost Laos and roaring over the

Chinese sailors coming to the country note with pleasure that it is not necessary to wear clothes and, since rice is easily available, women easily married, houses easily run and trade easily carried on, a great many sailors desert to take up permanent residence.

— CHUA TA-KUAN

BELOW:
lush paddy fields.

mighty Khone Falls, the Mekong enters Cambodia and flows south through Stung Treng, Kratie and Kompong Cham provinces. Up to this point it is still just a large river. When the waters reach Phnom Penh, however, they are joined by the Sap River from the northwest, while the Bassac River breaks away towards the southeast.

This confluence of the rivers, known in Khmer as Chatomuk or "four faces", and in French as Quatre Bras or "four arms", is remarkable for a unique phenomenon, the reversal of the Sap River. From May to October, during the annual rainy season, the hugely increased volume of the Mekong forces the Sap River to back up, and finally reverse its course, flowing northwards to flood the Tonlé Sap with vast quantities of fresh water and rich sediment. During this period the Tonlé Sap more than doubles in size, from 3,000 sq. km (1,160 sq. miles) to as much as 8,000 sq. km (3,100 sq. miles). Then, in mid-October, as the level of the Mekong diminishes, the flow of the Sap is again reversed, carrying the surplus waters of the Tonlé Sap southwards to the Mekong and Bassac deltas. The time of the October reversal of the waters is celebrated as *Bon Om Tuk*, one of Cambodia's most important festivals. The annual flooding of the Tonlé Sap makes the lake a rich source of fish, while the farmland around the lakes benefits from an annual deluge of rich sediment. There's even a special variety of rice which has adapted itself to these unusual conditions: rising and falling with the waters, it uses its long root system to float at times of flood.

Visitors to Cambodia have long remarked on the spectacular fertility brought about by this unique relationship between the Mekong and its tributary, the Sap; Chou Ta-kuan, a Chinese ambassador who visited Angkor in 1296–7, recorded: "Generally speaking, three or four crops a year can be counted on, for

the entire Cambodian year resembles the Chinese summer, and frost and snows are unknown." Elsewhere he notes that the Tonlé Sap is so rich in fish that it is possible to catch them by hand, while the soil is so naturally rich that there is no need to use fertiliser. Chou also wrote admiringly of the scenery along the great river: "The heavy shade of old trees and trailing rattan-vines form a luxuriant cover. Cries of birds and animals weave a tissue of sound." For broad reaches of the Mekong, comparatively little has changed.

Map on page 244–5

South down the Mekong

The easiest and most convenient way to explore the Cambodian Mekong, at least for the present, is to set out by riverboat from Phnom Penh. In years to come it will be possible to enter Cambodia from Laos by way of the river – plans are already afoot, but for the present remain in their infancy. Similarly, while many locals use the Upper Mekong or Tien Giang, and more particularly the Bassac (Lower Mekong or Hau Giang) as a means of voyaging between Cambodia and Vietnam, this option is not at present open to foreigners. Given this fact, there isn't much point in travelling south along the Mekong or the Bassac from Phnom Penh, since the only destinations of any consequence are over the border in Vietnam.

If you do decide to go south – there are boats departing from the Phnom Penh riverside on a regular if unscheduled basis – you will come to the rather inappropriately named **Koki Beach** ⑲, a popular picnicking spot for people from Phnom Penh at weekends and holidays. A low area of mudflats by the west bank of the Mekong, Koki is covered with restaurants on stilts specialising in freshwater and seafood delicacies. Although more generally reached by way

Avoid touching people on the head. Cambodians believe that's where one's vital essence resides. Even a hairdresser will ask permission before touching.

BELOW: local children.

of Route 1 from the Monivong Bridge, Koki can also be reached by boat, which allows a brief (1-hour) trip on the Mekong. Further downstream, and also more generally reached by Route 1, is the ferry town of **Neak Luong**. It was here that, in August 1973, a USAF B-52 accidentally dropped its entire load of bombs, levelling much of the town and killing or wounding more than 400 civilians – an incident which features prominently at the start of the movie *The Killing Fields*, and which was instrumental in bringing about a halt to the US bombing of Cambodia. Today there are no visible reminders of the tragedy, and it's possible to take a boat to this busy little town on the east bank of the Mekong and catch a bus or local taxi back to Phnom Penh. After Neak Luong the next stop is Vietnam, so for now this is as far as river travel goes south of Phnom Penh.

North up the Mekong

If you want to experience the Mekong and visit the friendly if isolated towns along its banks, you will do far better to head north from Phnom Penh on one of the numerous express river boats. Schedules vary and are apt to change suddenly, but services are regular, seemingly safe and fairly comfortable – if somewhat noisy, as the air-conditioned vessels nearly all show non-stop videos, generally of the kung fu variety. The first important stop north of the capital is **Kompong Cham ⓴**, Cambodia's third largest city and a notable rubber port. The journey should take between two and three hours, with brief stops at Prek Tamerk and Turi, small fishing settlements on the east bank of the great river. The approach to Kompong Cham (*see page 262*) is signalled by the unexpected appearance of an impressive new bridge across the Mekong. Although still under construction at time of writing, this bridge will soon provide direct road

BELOW: police building at Kompong Cham.

access between Phnom Penh and Ho Chi Minh City for the first time. Kompong Cham is a good place to spend the night as there are adequate hotels and restaurants, as well as the entrancing ruins of **Wat Nokor Bayon**, an 11th-century sandstone and laterite temple, originally dedicated to Mahayana Buddhism. At some time, probably during the 15th century, it was re-dedicated to Theravada Buddhism, and a modern temple set amid the ancient ruins still functions as a Buddhist centre. The complex, which is located about 2 km (1 mile) to the northwest of the town, is a fascinating blend of the contemporary and the archaic.

Beyond Kompong Cham the journey back up the Mekong winds north and then sharply east for around 100 km (60 miles), or about three hours' journey by express boat, to **Kratie ㉑**. There is an unexpected charm to this isolated riverside port which still retains some fine, if decaying, examples of French colonial architecture. One reason for Kratie's relatively good state of preservation is that it fell under Khmer Rouge control at an early stage in the civil war, and was not subjected to either fierce fighting or subsequent bombing. There are three or four hotels along the waterfront by the boat dock, and several passable restaurants serving variations on Cambodian, Chinese and Vietnamese cookery. The waterfront also has several small establishments selling beer and soft drinks which make an excellent place to sit and watch the sunset over the Mekong. The administrative section of the town lies to the south of the dock beyond the hotels, while a large market beside the dilapidated road leading east to Phumi Samraong and Snuol, towards the Vietnamese frontier, serves most of Kratie Province. Except in the immediate vicinity of Kratie it's best to stay away from the various roads leading north, east and south from the town. Not only are

Map on page 244–5

Guardian at the entrance of Wat Nokor Bayon.

BELOW: the ruins of Wat Nokor Bayon.

The Mekong River is essential to life throughout Cambodia – it's also good fun to splash around in and cool off on a hot day.

they in an execrable state of repair, but also the very real risks of banditry and unexploded ordnance do still exist, and are likely to do so for some years to come. Instead it is safer, easier and more pleasant to stick to the river when exploring, and there are indeed things worth seeing.

The Mekong dolphin

It's possible to charter a boat or take a taxi – the latter without risk, as the distance is not great – the 30 km (20 miles) north of the town to the peaceful riverside village of **Sambor ㉒**. In the vicinity are pre-Angkorean ruins dating from the 8th century, but pending excavation and restoration there is little to see. More rewarding is the trip along the river and the probability of seeing the rare **Mekong dolphin**, an endangered species which is making something of a come-back in the waters near Kratie, and which may soon become a major attraction in the area. More correctly known as the Irrawaddy Dolphin, this is a delight-ful and sociable mammal which has been driven to the verge of extinction by fishermen using explosives and nets, collisions with rafts of teak logs, and fatal encounters with the sharp propellers of speeding "long-tail" boats.

In Cambodia nowadays it is common to blame the Khmer Rouge for all man-ner of ills, from the looting of ancient temples to the destruction of the country's natural habitat. In line with this, Cambodian fisheries experts assert that Mekong dolphins were slaughtered wholesale by the Khmer Rouge for their meat and oil, claiming that "five dolphins a day were killed in the Tonlé Sap alone". Be this as it may, there were recently thought to be no more than 150 of these rare creatures surviving in the waters of the Middle Mekong, about half in Laos and the remainder in the Cambodian provinces of Kratie and Stung Treng.

BELOW: the Mekong (Irrawaddy) dolphin.

Fortunately tourism may provide an economic stim-ulus for the protection and preservation of this unique species; certainly the Cambodian Ministry of Tourism is conscious of the potential attraction of dolphin watching, and has recently announced its intention of promoting the natural environment of the Middle Mekong as "an alternative destination to Angkor". The boatmen of Kratie claim never to kill dolphins intentionally, but they certainly know where they are to be found and will take visitors to see them for a small hourly charge.

One such destination is the village of **Prek Kampi**, about 17 km (11 miles) south of Kratie, where a group of around 20 dolphins can be found. Visitors report that here it is generally possible to see several of these large mammals, which grow to 2–3 metres (6–10 ft) in length, hunting and playing offshore. They appear reg-ularly each morning and evening, but the locals claim that the best time to see them is around 3pm.

Beyond Kratie, the Mekong continues due north for 140 km (88 miles) to the even more isolated riverside town of Stung Treng. The appallingly bad road from Kratie to Stung Treng runs inland, well away from the river, whilst the latter attains widths of several kilometres in these remote reaches. It takes between three and four hours to reach Stung Treng by express boat from Kratie, and services are far from regular. Until mid-1997 the river journey was considered unsafe, as attacks by marauding Khmer Rouge guerrillas were not uncommon. Nowadays the journey is considered quite safe, however, as all Khmer Rouge in the area have surrendered to the Royal Cambodian Government and, more often than not, joined the government forces.

Map on page 244–5

Stung Treng

The town of **Stung Treng** ㉓ nestles on the banks of the Tonlé Sekong a short distance from the east bank of the Mekong. It is a small place, surprisingly clean, with a well-maintained park beside the waterfront. Passable accommodation is available, and the usual selection of Khmer and Chinese dishes is served in a couple of small restaurants located to the west of the covered market – the latter has a dubious reputation as an important centre for trading in endangered species including tiger and bear parts. There's nothing much to do or see in this sleepy backwater, but Stung Treng does make a suitable base for trips upriver. At time of writing it cost very little to charter a boat for a day trip to the Lao frontier about 50 km (30 miles) north of the town. The journey is very quiet, for there is little in the way of riverine trade between Cambodia and Laos at present.

It is possible to visit some of the former Khmer Rouge guerrillas in Thala Barivat and Samaki districts, both within a short jeep drive of Stung Treng. Despite their fearsome reputation they seem friendly enough.

Still, this is a major improvement on the situation in the 1970s when the Khmer Rouge were in power. Suspicious of all foreigners – even fellow Communists – and hostile to the Lao as allies of their perceived arch enemies, the Viets, the Khmer Rouge barred all travel on the Mekong near the Lao frontier, tore up the few primitive road links between the two countries, and fired at anything moving on the Lao side of the frontier, including innocent Lao fishermen.

Today the Cambodian border post at the hamlet of Phumi Kompong Sralau is marked by a small thatched hut flying the Cambodian flag, while a little upstream at the Lao settlement of Thai Boei a slightly more salubrious building flying the Lao flag marks the frontier of the Lao province of Champasak (*see page 161*). It is not yet possible for foreigners to cross into Laos at this point, though locals are free to do so. Plans are well advanced to make this an international border crossing, however, and when this comes to fruition it will be possible to proceed up river to the Lao town of Hat Xai Khun and thence to Pakse and Champasak.

BELOW:
Kreung girl from Ratanakiri province.

It is also possible to cross the Mekong by boat from Stung Treng to the small settlement of Phumi Thalabarivat where the ruins of a pre-Angkorean temple may be seen. Similarly, a weekly boat runs from Stung Treng up the Tonlé Sekong to Siempang.

To the east of Stung Treng and away from the river lies the beautiful and undeveloped upland province of **Ratanakiri**, home to some of Cambodia's least known tribal peoples. It is possible to reach Ban Lung, the provincial capital, by road from Stung Treng, but the journey is arduous and takes at least 10 hours – far longer in the rainy season when the road becomes impassable. There are five flights a week between Phnom Penh and Ban Lung, most of which stop over at Stung Treng. The Ministry of Tourism is keen to promote both Ratanakiri and the adjoining province of **Mondolkiri** as destinations for eco-tourism and trekking, but this project remains in its infancy. ❑

THE CAMBODIAN COAST

Having spent many years out of bounds during the Khmer Rouge regime, the region is reviving its French colonial and Thai border atmosphere and is welcoming back foreign tourists

Map on page 244–5

I n times past, before the years of the Indochina Wars, the Cambodian coast enjoyed an idyllic reputation among middle-class Cambodians, French colonialists and wealthy foreign visitors alike. Perhaps because of this historical association with domestic and foreign élites, the palm-fringed southern coast – a region studded with the elaborate villas of the wealthy, including that of King Sihanouk at Kep – fared particularly badly under the harsh rule of the obsessively anti-urban Khmer Rouge. Kep, in particular, was systematically razed to the ground, while ordinary people (except fishermen) were moved away from the coast to prevent the possibility of flight from the DK "people's paradise" by way of the sea. Even the movements of those permitted to fish were tightly monitored by Khmer Rouge cadres, while traffic through the port of Kompong Som was limited to the occasional exchange of Cambodian raw materials for Chinese and North Korean armaments and other aid.

Today all this is changing, and relatively fast. The coast is once again being developed as a tourist destination, and foreign investors are joining local businessmen in developing hotels, resorts and better quality restaurants. To be sure, there is still a long way to go – but for the people of Phnom Penh and for foreign travellers, trips to the coast and long hours of swimming and sunbathing by the Gulf of Thailand are coming back into vogue.

There are basically two roads south from Phnom Penh to the coast: the dilapidated Route 3 via Angk Tasaom to Kampot, or the much better US-financed Route 4 via Kompong Speu to Kompong Som, the latter considered by many to be the best road in the country. The 150-km (95-mile) drive from Phnom Penh to Kampot takes about two and a half hours by taxi or three hours by bus. The train, though functioning, cannot yet be recommended; in addition to the rundown state of both railway lines and rolling stock, it was near Kampot in 1994 that three young Western backpackers were abducted from the train and subsequently murdered by the then-still-active Khmer Rouge guerrillas.

PRECEDING PAGES: hotel pool. **LEFT:** sunset on the River Mekong. **BELOW:** girl in a yellow dress.

Kampot

Kampot ㉔, the capital of the province of the same name, is a small, relaxed town of around 15,000 people. Just 5 km (3 miles) inland, by the banks of the Sanke River, there is a coastal feel to the place which adds to its rather languid attraction. "Downtown" Kampot – if such a phrase can aptly be applied to this laid-back provincial town which still feels very much on the road to nowhere – centres on a large roundabout space about 400 metres (1,300 ft) east of the river. This area is the main commercial hub and also the location of Kampot's two best hotels, each of which offers adequate if basic facilities. The road north from the roundabout leads out past a large covered market – a favourite with visitors from Phnom Penh, who stop off here to buy the fresh seafood for which Kampot is renowned. Of more interest to the foreign visitor, however, is the series of narrow, colonnaded streets leading west from the roundabout to the riverfront. Although badly in need of restoration, there are some fine examples of French and Chinese colonial architecture to be seen in this warren, as well as the best of Kampot's handful of restaurants.

Travellers staying overnight in Kampot should check into one of the hotels at the roundabout, head east towards the river for a bite to eat, then walk the length of the delightful riverfront which, shaded by casuarina trees, offers fine views of the nearby Chuor Phnom Damrei (Elephant Mountains). There are some particularly fine colonial buildings in this area, notably the **Governor's Residence** and the main post office at the southern end of the riverfront.

Fishing boats cluster on the far side of the Sanke River, which is reached by a delightful but rather unsafe bridge comprised of a patchwork of wooden planks and twisted iron girders. Not far to the north, an equally decrepit bridge carries the single-track railway connecting Phnom Penh to Kompong Som; a span of this clanking antique collapsed in 1998, disrupting train services between Phnom Penh and Kompong Som, and has yet to be repaired.

Around Kampot

Kampot shelters in the lee of the Chuor Phnom Damrei, a wild region of trackless forests and sheer, unclimbed rock outcrops. Just two hours northwest of Kampot, along a very dubious road, is the former hill station of **Bokor** ㉕.

Bamboo pipes are used for carrying palm toddy (made from the juice of the coconut palms). Toddy is widely collected in Cambodia and used for making sugar or alcoholic drinks.

BELOW:
street scene in Kampot.

Map
on page
244–5

Renowned in pre-war days for its pleasant climate, cool mountain streams, forested walks and distant panoramic view of the Gulf of Thailand, Bokor fell on hard times under the Khmer Rouge and has not yet really recovered. Still, it is worth a trip if you are in the vicinity. The 1,079-metre (3,506-ft) -high resort is often shrouded in mist which drifts through the ruined casino and abandoned church. Soon, no doubt, it will be rehabilitated as Kampot has been and once again echo to the sound of day-trippers from nearby Kompong Som and Phnom Penh.

Another formerly celebrated resort is **Kep** ㉖, known to the French as Kep-sur-Mer. In pre-war times the 7-km (4-mile) stretch of palm-fringed beach was lined with the villas of rich Cambodians and French settlers. Then the Khmer Rouge arrived and took a special vengeance on the place, destroying virtually every building in town and turning the Shell petrol station into the site of a mass grave. Today Kep is back on the tourist circuit, though much rebuilding remains to be done. It's a 30-km (20-mile) drive from Kampot and can be reached by *moto*. Although there are hotels and restaurants – indeed these are multiplying at quite a rate – most visitors will prefer to stay in Kampot, driving out to Kep for a day of sunbathing, fishing, swimming and indulging in the excellent local seafood. It will not be long before Kep, like Bokor, is once again firmly back on the tourist map.

A short distance off the Kep shore lies **Koh Tunsay**, also known as "Rabbit Island", which can easily be reached by boat and makes a popular excursion. The island has four small but beautiful beaches with good swimming and snorkelling. The large island clearly visible to the south is Phu Quoc and belongs to Vietnam, as does the smaller Hai Tac archipelago scattered to the south-east.

BELOW: the beachfront at Kep.

The sea frontier in this region is still in dispute between Cambodia and Vietnam, and ownership of Phu Quoc in particular remains a serious bone of contention between the two countries. As a consequence, visitors sailing in the vicinity of Kep should remember to keep well inshore and to the west to avoid possible confrontations with Vietnamese patrol boats. The land frontier with Vietnam is only about 50 km (30 miles) east of Kep, and the border crossing to the Mekong Delta town of Ha Tien may one day be opened to international travellers; for the present, however, its use is strictly limited to locals.

Kompong Som

It is possible to travel directly from Kampot to Kompong Som using the extremely poor road paralleling the rundown railway line, but most people will prefer to use Route 4 from Phnom Penh. This is 230 km (144 miles) long and takes between two and three hours by bus or taxi. It is also possible to fly to Kompong Som from Phnom Penh's Pochentong International Airport, and there is talk of plans to open an international airport in Kompong Som itself. The road passes through the small provincial capital of Kompong Speu before rising over a forested spur of the Chuor Phnom Damrei.

Just before the small settlement of Sre Khlong a dusty road rising into the mountains leads to the former hill station of **Kirirom** – a sign to the right of the road announces Preah Sumarit Kossomak National Park in Roman script. Once the hot season retreat of wealthy Phnom Penh residents, Kirirom was – like Kep – deliberately blown up by the vengeful Khmer Rouge. At present it remains largely unvisited, but as the site of Cambodia's first officially designated national park it should come to flourish again, given time. After crossing the Chuor Phnom

BELOW: street in Kompong Som.

Map
on page
244–5

Damrei, Route 4 forks as it drops down to the coast; the eastern fork leads to the fishing village of Phesar Ream while the western one continues to **Kompong Som** ㉗, commonly known as Sihanoukville. For the forseeable future, Kompong Som will remain the heart of Cambodia's "Riviera". Like Kep, this town was once a holiday haven for the rich, and fortunately the Khmer Rouge wrought less thorough destruction here, probably because the deep-water port and railway terminus provided a key communications link with Phnom Penh.

Nowadays the resort is well into the process of reconstruction. There are numerous hotels and guesthouses of all classes, quite a few run by expatriate Australian, French and British entrepreneurs. Kompong Som's restaurants offer a wide choice of cuisine, the seafood is fresh and plentiful, and the traffic relatively light. The main activities are, as one might suspect, sunbathing and swimming. There's also good snorkelling and fishing, while diving trips are available with experienced dive instructors. Kompong Som also has a (limited) nightlife, with several discos and nightclubs as well as numerous examples of the increasingly ubiquitous karaoke bar.

The Golden Lions monument at Kompong Som.

In all, Kompong Som has about 10 km (6 miles) of beachfront, divided into four main beaches. Starting in the north, the first is **Victory Beach** between the harbour and Koh Pos Island – really two beaches divided by a rocky point and a small hillock – about 2 km (1 mile) long; the north end is more developed, with several restaurants and budget-priced bungalows. **Independence Beach**, between the old Independence Hotel and the southwestern peninsula, is popular with weekenders from the capital but is often deserted mid-week. It has few facilities. **Sokha Beach**, between the peninsula and a Cambodian army base, is perhaps the most popular of Kompong Som's seaside attractions, offering a wide strip of sand, shady palm trees and adequate facilities including a good seafood restaurant.

BELOW: sunset on the beach.

Finally, **Ochheuteal Beach**, stretching away to the south of the town, is around 3 km (2 miles) long, relatively undeveloped and very tranquil. Of the beaches, this is probably the most attractive, though all offer the casuarinas, palm trees and clear blue waters one would expect from the Gulf of Thailand.

Visitors should note that Kompong Som is a surprisingly spread-out place. The rundown town centre, with its busy markets, torn-up asphalt-and-rubble streets, rooting pigs and somnolent dogs, is about 2 km (1 mile) away from the port and railway station. Although not particularly attractive and utterly devoid of any historical or cultural buildings, this is probably the best place to look for accommodation, restaurants and transport to the various beaches – all of which are some distance away. A less central but more attractive alternative is to stay out at one of the beaches; Ochheuteal offers the best standards of food and accommodation, while Victory is popular with backpackers and budget travellers.

The Gulf islands

There are a number of offshore islands which can be visited by arrangement with one of several companies offering reasonably priced boat charters. Locals divide these islands into three groups: the **Kompong Som**

Portable street vendor's wagon selling baguettes and snacks.

Islands, which lie close to the west of the port within an easy half-day's trip; the **Ream Islands**, which are scattered to the east towards the fishing village of Phsar Ream; and, finally and more distantly, the **Koh Tang Islands**, which lie further out to sea, between four and eight hours' journey from Kompong Som.

Local diving companies recommend the Kompong Som group, and more especially Koh Koang Kang together with Koh Rong Samloem, for swimming and snorkelling when the prevailing winds are from the southwest (March to October). The Ream Group, more protected by the bulk of the mainland, is reportedly a better bet during the cool season (November to February) when the winds blow from the north. For snorkelling, the waters around Koh Chraloh, Koh Ta Kiev and Koh Khteah are highly recommended, though the proximity of the mainland and related higher levels of silt can reduce visibility, especially in choppy weather. Finally, Koh Tang and the nearby islands are recommended for more serious divers who may wish to spend a night or two away from Kompong Som, either moored in the lee of one of the islands or camping on shore. This whole area is rich in a diverse marine life, with large fish, excellent visibility and sunken wrecks that can be explored with appropriate supervision.

The coastal "Wild West"

The coast to the west of Kompong Som is almost completely undeveloped. There are no roads hugging the coastline around Kompong Som Bay, and a journey overland to the isolated but beautiful province of Koh Kong requires a long detour inland by roads which can only be described as execrable. Happily there is an alternative. **Tunlop Rolork**, a small fishing port about 2 km (1 mile) north of Kompong Som's main harbour, maintains a small fleet of fast boats

BELOW: a bay on the south coast.

which provide a passenger service to Koh Kong, where Cambodia's coast meets the southeasternmost part of Thailand. These Malay-built vessels are really intended to serve as river ferries and are ill-suited for rough weather in open seas, so are certainly best avoided during the southwest monsoons which blow between June and October. During the cool season, however, they provide a fast and convenient way of travelling along the coast to Thailand. The journey from Kompong Som to Koh Kong takes between three and four hours, with boats leaving daily at noon (times are variable and it is better to check).

An alternative is to travel back up Route 4 to Phnom Penh as far as the small junction village of Kaong – a distance of about 60 km (40 miles) – and then turn left for 15 km (9 miles) to reach the small port of **Sre Amben**. This is really the start of the Cambodian coast's "Wild West". It soon becomes apparent from the wide range of Thai goods available in town that Sre Ambel, although notionally a fishing port, is a smugglers' haven which flourishes on illicit trade with nearby Trat and Koh Kong. Goods are brought in by sea from Thailand and discreetly despatched to Phnom Penh and all points north via Route 4, thereby avoiding the docks and customs officials of Kompong Som.

There are a couple of dubious guesthouses, but Sre Amben really is not a place to stay overnight. It does, however, have an attractive Buddhist temple, located on the hill behind the main market. Shared taxis from Kompong Som take about one-and-a-half hours to Sre Amben. Fast boats for Koh Kong depart every day between about 10.30 and 11.30 am; the harbour is near the taxi stand. Whichever port you choose, if the seas look a little rough and you are not a good sailor, remember that discretion is the better part of valour – seasickness pills are available at pharmacies in Kompong Som though not in tiny Sre Amben.

Map on page 244–5

BELOW: river-dwelling family.

Map on page 244–5

A taste of Thailand

The route that the fast boats take to Koh Kong cuts west across Kompong Som Bay before turning into the open waters of the Gulf of Thailand and heading north along the coast. Most boats take the opportunity to stop briefly at Koh Sdech, the most important of the tiny and remote **Samit Islands**, where the really adventurous traveller may choose to stop overnight and take another boat in the morning. At the time of writing there was one small guesthouse plus a number of fishermen's restaurants – though, as with Sre Ambel, smuggling is clearly a lucrative pastime in these waters and Koh Sdech is, by any standards, a smugglers' den. There is not a great deal to do or to see there, but there is a wide range of beers available, including Singha Beer from nearby Thailand and, more surprisingly, Surya Beer from distant Indonesia. Most travellers, however, will prefer to head straight on towards Koh Kong.

About two hours distant from Koh Sdech, **Koh Kong** ❷ – confusingly the name of the province, the provincial capital *and* an offshore island – is a fast-developing coastal resort designed especially to appeal to visitors from neighbouring Thailand. It is also a convenient point for entering or leaving Cambodia by land. Hardly surprisingly, the place has something of a Thai feel to it, being a clearing point for imported Thai goods, both legal and illegal, where the Thai *baht* is as welcome – probably more welcome – than the Cambodian *riel*. Before the "Zero Years" of the Khmer Rouge, Koh Kong was largely settled by ethnic Thais who had lived there for generations. After the Khmer Rouge victory most of them fled across the nearby border to Thailand, though some remained to carry on a surprisingly successful resistance from the jungles of the interior. Those who fell into KR hands, like most minorities elsewhere in Cambodia, were simply killed. In the years since the Khmer Rouge were toppled from power, local Thais have moved back to Koh Kong in serious numbers, and Thai is widely spoken and understood.

At present Koh Kong has something of a frontier atmosphere. It's just 10 km (6 miles) by taxi from the border post of Ban Hat Lek, and the presence of Cambodia's larger neighbour is everywhere to be felt. Nearly all the consumer goods on sale in town are brought in by road or ferried in from Thailand. A new casino has been built on Cambodian territory just opposite Ban Hat Lek, which attracts many Thais keen to enjoy the gambling denied them by law at home. Perhaps inevitably, numerous bars and brothels have also sprung up to cater to this rapidly expanding trade. Should you decide to leave Cambodia at Koh Kong, fast air-conditioned buses leave the city of Trat on the Thai side of the border on a regular basis. Depending on the traffic and the time of day, it takes around five hours to reach Bangkok's eastern bus terminal at Ekkamai.

It is not possible to return to Phnom Penh by road – a single unpaved track, which is both dangerous and all but impassable, winds across the Chuor Phnom Kravanh or "Cardamom Mountains" which isolate Koh Kong from the rest of Cambodia. Koh Kong does have an airport, however, with direct flights to and from Phnom Penh on Tuesdays, Fridays and Sundays. ❑

BELOW:
Koh Kong village.
RIGHT: barbecue lunch on the beach at Koh Kong.

Maps
on pages
244/303

PREAH VIHEAR

*The temple of Preah Vihear, closed by war for more than 20 years
and now accessible through Thailand, is one of the most
impressive Khmer historical sites in the region*

Set high on a cliff on the edge of the Dongrak Mountains overlooking Cambodia, **Preah Vihear** ㉙ (known to the Thais as Khao Phra Viharn) is remarkable both for its outstanding Khmer architecture and for its stunning location. Long claimed by both Thailand and Cambodia, the temple complex was finally awarded to the latter by the World Court in 1963, though the question of ownership still rankles with many Thais. Whatever the rights and wrongs, for the foreseeable future the only practical way of access – short of climbing hundreds of feet up a sheer and treacherous rock face – will remain via the province of Si Saket, in Thailand's remote northeast.

Possible bases for the exploration of Preah Vihear are the northeastern Thai cities of Surin, Si Saket and Ubon Ratchathani. All three towns have adequate accommodation, though only Surin and Ubon Ratchathani have first-class hotels. An alternative is to stay in the small Thai town of Kantharalak, which is just 30 km (20 miles) from Preah Vihear. The temple is best visited as a day trip. Be sure to leave early in the morning to allow enough time to explore it properly, for the site is large and it closes early.

Closed for decades because of civil war and general brigandage, Preah Vihear opened briefly between 1991 and 1993, only to become off-limits again as a result of the presence of Khmer Rouge forces in the region. Then in August 1998, following the death of Pol Pot and the expulsion of the Khmer Rouge from its nearby base at Anlong Veng, the temple opened once more – this time, it is hoped, for good.

BELOW:
overlooking a cliff
face, Preah Vihear.

Temple on a peak

Preah Vihear is an extraordinary place, possibly the most impressive Khmer historical site after Angkor. Although in need of restoration the temple is quite magnificent, and one is left wondering how the original builders transported such massive block of stone to the peak of the Dongrak escarpment – a height of 600 metres (1,950 ft). In fact, Preah Vihear took around 200 years to build, starting during the reign of Rajendravarman II in the mid-10th century and reaching completion in the early 12th century during the reign of Surayavarman II. It was the latter monarch, beyond doubt a visionary builder, who also began the construction of Angkor Wat. It is thought that the site of Preah Vihear had long been holy to the Khmers, who are believed to have held the locality in reverence for at least 500 years before the building of the temple.

Constructed in the Baphuon and early Angkor styles, Preah Vihear was built originally as a Hindu temple dedicated to the god Shiva. Of the four main *gopura*, or elaborately decorated gateways, the first two are in serious disrepair, though fine examples of carving – *apsaras* and divinities – are still visible. The third *gopura* is comparatively well preserved, with a finely carved lintel depicting Shiva and his consort Uma sitting on Nandi, the bull, Shiva's traditional mount.

The tricky ascent

Foreign (non-Thai) visitors to Preah Vihear must pay a 100 *baht* entry fee per head and deposit their passports with the Thai border police. The new black-top road to the temple stops abruptly at the Thai frontier, and visitors must proceed on foot across a rocky plateau, down a steep embankment, and then up a long slope to the initial – steep and tricky – temple steps. It is not a climb for the old or unfit, though elderly Thai pilgrims, tiny old ladies prominent among them, pull themselves to the top of the hill. Such Thai visitors often complain bitterly about the damage to the site, insisting that things would be very different if the temple was still in Thai hands.

The temple extends for around 900 metres (3,000 ft), through five separate stages, before culminating in the massive bulk of the main sanctuary perched high on the cliff top. Here the great *prasat* or central spire has been thrown to the ground, and mighty blocks of carved stone lie in a tumbled heap, awaiting eventual restoration. Everywhere there are signs warning visitors not to stray off the sanctioned paths, for the danger of mines remains very real.

The temple is now firmly under the control of the Cambodian army, and young soldiers – some little more than children – watch silently as a regular stream of Thai and other visitors picks its way over the stones. Once through the main temple complex, head for the nearby cliff top and gaze across the Cambodian plains below, so near but so inaccessible. It would be easy to fall, but any other sort of descent is all but impossible. ❑

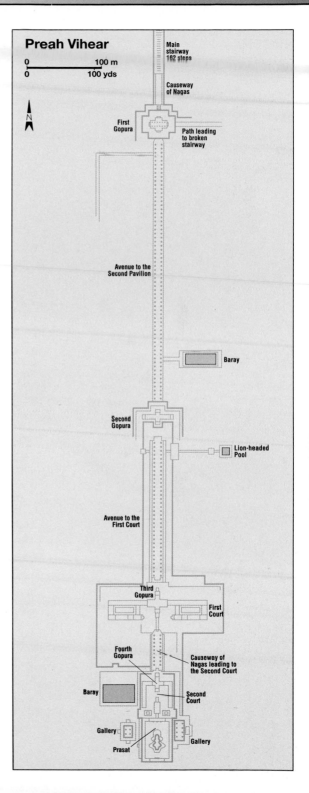

INSIGHT GUIDES
TRAVEL TIPS

New Insight Maps

Maps in Insight Guides are tailored to complement the text. But when you're on the road you sometimes need the big picture that only a large-scale map can provide. This new range of durable Insight Fleximaps has been designed to meet just that need.

Detailed, clear cartography
makes the comprehensive route and city maps easy to follow, highlights all the major tourist sites and provides valuable motoring information plus a full index.

Informative and easy to use
with additional text and photographs covering a destination's top 10 essential sites, plus useful addresses, facts about the destination and handy tips on getting around.

Laminated finish
allows you to mark your route on the map using a non-permanent marker pen, and wipe it off. It makes the maps more durable and easier to fold than traditional maps.

The first titles
cover many popular destinations. They include Algarve, Amsterdam, Bangkok, California, Cyprus, Dominican Republic, Florence, Hong Kong, Ireland, London, Mallorca, Paris, Prague, Rome, San Francisco, Sydney, Thailand, Tuscany, USA Southwest, Venice, and Vienna.

𒀸 INSIGHT GUIDES

The world's largest collection of visual travel guides

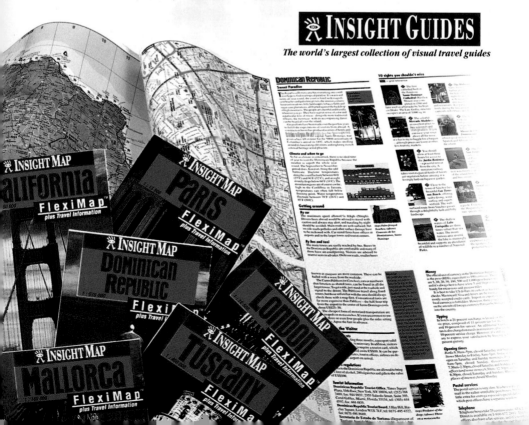

CONTENTS

Getting Acquainted

Area Laos covers an area of about 235,000 sq. km (90,730 sq. miles), dominated by the Mekong River, the twelfth longest river in the world.
Capital Vientiane
Population just under 5 million
Language Lao
Religion Theravada Buddhism
Currency Kip
Weights and Measures Metric
Time Zone Laos is 7 hours ahead of Greenwich Mean Time (GMT).
Electricity The electric system in Laos runs on a 220v AC circuit, and most outlets use two-prong flat or round sockets. Bring any adaptors you think you might need. Even in Vientiane, blackouts do happen, most often when the rains are heaviest in July and August. Some rural areas receive electricity only at certain times, while many villages manage to survive without any power at all.
International dialling code 856

Geography

What you first notice about a map of Laos is the country's most mixed of blessings: it is entirely land-locked, sharing borders with China, Burma (Myanmar), Thailand, Cambodia and Vietnam. It has had little easy access to international trade over the centuries, but at the same time has suffered from heavy-handed meddling by its neighbours and other outside powers as a result of its location at the heart of Southeast Asia. The perception in the USA that Laos was central to the Cold War "domino" theory, and thus could not be "lost" to the

Communists, led to the Americans' intense (but secret) involvement in the course of Lao history. On the other hand, Laos today has the opportunity to capitalise on its strategic location at the intersection of major trading routes in the region.

There is more of the great Mekong River (Mae Nam Khong means "Mother of Waters") in Laos than any other country in Southeast Asia, and most of it flows freely. This promises to soon change, as at least 20 damming schemes are now in the planning stages in Laos; every week in Vientiane, it seems, one hears of another hydroelectric project "in the works". The Mekong River Valley provides Laos with its best agricultural zones, and with the fish that – along with rice – is a staple of the Lao diet. The Anna-mite mountain chain runs parallel to the Mekong through almost half the length of Laos. The terrain in the north is marked by steep, jagged mountain slopes, while the south benefits from fertile plains such as the Bolaven Plateau, where most of Laos' coffee is grown. The highest peak is Phu Bia, which lies just south of the Plain of Jars, one of Laos' major tourist attractions.

People

The population of Laos now stands at a density of only 20 people per square kilometre, one of the lowest in Asia (in neighbouring Vietnam it is 230 people per square kilo-metre). The Lao government likes to divide the population into three main ethnic categories, ostensibly according to the height at which they live: Lao Soung (higher mountain), Lao Theung (lower mountain) and Lao Loum (lowland). Some 50–60 percent of the population are Lao Loum, 20–30 percent are Lao Theung and 10–20 percent are Lao Soung. Female representatives of each group can often be seen on printed currency and government billboards, and in official festivals and parades.

This is, however, a somewhat arbitrary categorisation, as there

Climate

Laos, like most of mainland Southeast Asia, has three main seasons. The rainy season, marked by the arrival of the monsoon between May and July, can last until as late at November. During this season, the weather is hot, sticky and, as one would expect, wet; temperatures during the day average around 30° C (86° F) in the lowlands and 25° C (77° F) in the mountain valleys.

The monsoon is followed by a dry, cool season, from November until mid-February, during which the temperature in the Mekong River Valley can drop to as low as 15° C (59° F). During this season – the best time to visit Laos – cool breezes make life more pleasant, and it can be downright cold after the sun goes down. The third season, dry and hot, begins in late February and lasts until May; temperatures in the Mekong River Valley reach 38° C (100° F) in March and April.

are at least 68 different ethnic groups in Laos, each with its own linguistic, religious and culinary traditions. In general, however, the Lao Loum live in the Mekong River Valley, subsist on wet-rice culti-vation, and practise Theravada Buddhism. The Lao Theung live on mid-altitude mountain slopes, are largely animist, and suffer from the lowest standard of living of the three groups. The Lao Soung live at altitudes of 1,000 metres (3,280 ft) above sea level and higher, and have traditionally relied on the cultivation of dry rice and opium. Ethnic Chinese in Laos, as indeed throughout the region, tend to dominate the business commu-nities urban centres. Viets also make up a large portion of the traders and small business owners in Laos – not to mention the continuing Vietnamese military presence in some provinces.

The European expatriate community in Laos is relatively

small (less than 1,000), and is made up mostly of temporary residents working in Vientiane for international aid organisations like the UNDP or smaller NGOs.

Government

The Lao People's Democratic Republic (Lao PDR) was formed on 2 December 1975, when the Communist Lao People's Revolutionary Party took over from the Royal Lao Government in the wake of the Second Indochina War. To this day the PDR remains the primary ruling institution in the country, exerting considerable influence on people's everyday lives. Power within the PDR lies in the nine-member Politburo, the 49-member Central Committee and the Permanent Secretariat. Currently, the Secretary General of all three bodies is the same man, President Khamtay Siphandone. State administration is made up of the Council of Government, which includes the 12 ministries, the Office of the Prime Minister and the National Planning Committee. The National Assembly is the nation's sole legislative body.

Representatives, almost all of whom are party members, are elected by the public and meet once a year to rubber-stamp Central Committee decisions and prime ministerial declarations. The state is divided into 16 different provinces (kweng), one municipality, Vientiane, and one "Special Zone", Saisomboun, which continues to be administered by the Lao military, owing to recurring armed bandit attacks in the region. Each province is further divided into district, subdistrict and village levels.

Education

Public education in Laos involves five years of primary school, three of middle school and three of high school. The National University in Vientiane provides what is really the only opportunity for higher education inside the country. Most Lao complete less than three years of formal education. Public-school

teachers are notoriously under-educated, and educational facilities throughout the country, from the capital city of Vientiane to the most remote of rural villages, are abysmal. While the government claims a national literacy rate of 84 percent, this figure falls by nearly half when urban areas are excluded. Almost all Lao men spend at least a part of their youth studying at the local wat, or Buddhist temple; for Lao boys in rural areas, the wat might offer the only chance to obtain an education and to work their way up in society.

Public education was introduced into Laos under the French in 1902, when the first public elementary schools were opened in Vientiane and Luang Prabang. Children of the Lao upper classes would study at French lycées in the country's urban centres, while royalty were sent off to study in France. There is a good chance that any Lao older than 40 whom you encounter during your visit will have a solid knowledge of French. After the revolution in 1975 there was a marked decline in the quality of public education. While the number of schools expanded rapidly, the limited facilities served as little more than centres for political indoctrination. Lack of funding for buildings and books, and a serious lack of qualified teachers (most of the educated population fled after 1975), plague the system to this day. During the Cold War, Laos' best students completed their education abroad, usually in Eastern Bloc countries like Hungary, East Germany and Bulgaria. Most of these Lao, now in their early thirties, are struggling to replace whatever mildly useful language they learnt overseas with English, but scholarships to study abroad are in far shorter supply than in the past.

Religion

Buddhism is the dominant religion in Laos; nearly two-thirds of the population are Theravada Buddhists. Introduced to Laos in the

late 13th and early 14th centuries, Buddhism was heavily promoted by King Fa Ngum, the first monarch of the unified Lan Xang kingdom. Fa Ngum declared Buddhism the official state religion, and carried the important Prabang Buddha image from Cambodia to Luang Prabang in the mid-14th century. Theravada, or Hinayana (Lesser Vehicle), Buddhism, which originated in India and reached Laos via Southeast Asia, is the earlier and more "pure" of the two major schools. The other school, Mahayana (Greater Vehicle), is a more expansive Buddhism practised in North and East Asia. The objective of Theravada Buddhism is to attain nirvana, the ultimate end of physical existence – and thus of all suffering – on this earth. Most Lao Buddhists are of the Lao Loum ethnic majority, and regularly donate money and food to the monks at their village wats in order to acquire merit and bring them closer to this end, or at least to a better life. A Lao will visit the local temple whenever he or she feels moved to do so, but most often on days favoured by the lunar calendar and during Buddhist festivals.

Buddhism has been intimately tied to Lao politics since the days of King Fa Ngum. Buddhist monks supported the Pathet Lao in the 1960s and 1970s, impressed by their simple lifestyles and the hardships they willingly endured – in stark contrast to the corrupt Royal Lao Government. After 1975, however, the Communists initiated a brief period of strict religious sanctions, forbidding citizens to donate food and money to temples and forcing monks to work the land and raise animals. By the end of 1976 the government had responded to popular dissatisfaction with this policy and reversed the ban. While the Buddhist leadership is still controlled by the party, and monks must go through a Marxist political education, the government has become increasingly supportive of Buddhist ritual in recent decades. Deceased party members are now accorded traditional Buddhist funeral rites, statues of Communist leaders openly incorporate Buddhist imagery, and the That Luang *stupa* is once again the national symbol, replacing the hammer-and-sickle. The state seems to have realised that, as a leading Lao Buddhist claimed in 1995, "Buddhism is inseparable from the Lao nation."

Most Lao Loum practise Buddhism alongside traditional Lao spirit (*phii*) worship. The most common method of such worship is the *basi* ceremony given in honour of the guardian spirits, usually performed on the occasion of an important journey, the development of a new project or a wedding. The *basi* is conducted by a village elder, seated on the floor along with the guest of honour and all other participants around a tiered centrepiece that is decorated with flowers and banana leaves, draped with white cotton strings, and surrounded by offerings of food and drink to the spirits. After the village elder offers his blessings to the guest of honour and communicates with the guardian spirits, attendants tie white strings around each of the guest's wrists while offering their best wishes. The strings must be worn for at least three full days following the ceremony in order to ensure good luck.

Economy

When the current government took control in 1975 it implemented a brief, disastrous programme of nationalisation and collectivisation of agriculture. In 1979 it abruptly reversed course, and embarked on a process of reform in agriculture, monetary policy and commodity pricing that still continues. The economies of urban centres like Vientiane have been transformed since the mid-1980s, when restrictions on private enterprise and ownership of private property began to be lifted, and the economy is now "socialist" in name only (and rarely even that). Laos now has a liberal foreign investment code – at least on paper – which allows 100

percent foreign ownership for government-approved projects. Thailand, the USA and Australia now top the list of foreign investors.

However, Laos remains one of the ten poorest nations in the world. Eighty percent of the population work in agriculture, fishing and forestry, and 10 percent in the armed forces or the civil service. Industry is almost non-existent, and the economy is over-whelmingly dependent on foreign aid, pumped into the country by bodies like the UN, the ADB and the World Bank. Annual per capita income hovers just below US$400. The Asian economic crisis of the mid-1990s, particularly the currency woes in Thailand, also had a devastating effect on the Lao economy, sending the *kip* on a deflationary free-fall. Civil servant salaries have not kept pace with the resulting inflation, and have been rendered almost worthless. Despite government attempts to keep it under control, Laos has a thriving black market for currency exchange and the trade of untaxed imports from Thailand and Vietnam.

Planning the Trip

Getting There

There are two international airports in Laos, Wattay Airport in Vientiane and Luang Prabang Airport. Regular flights from Vientiane to Bangkok, Chiang Mai, Phnom Penh, Hanoi, Ho Chi Minh City and Kunming, China, are available. Only one international flight is available from Luang Prabang to Chiang Mai.

Lao Aviation has been a troubled airline for years – it was still mostly off limits to UNDP employees and foreign diplomats in Vientiane at the time of publication owing to safety concerns – and relies on foreign airlines to provide much of the service. Lao Aviation alternates with Thai Airways to service flights to Bangkok, with Vietnam Airlines for flights to Hanoi and Ho Chi Minh City, with China Yunnan Airlines for Kunming, and with Royal Air Cam-bodge for Phnom Penh. Remember that an airport tax must be paid by all passengers departing on interna-tional and domestic flights in Laos.

There are now eight border checkpoints through which travel-lers can (relatively) freely enter Laos on the ground. From China, tourists enter by road through the Mengla/Boten (China/Laos) check-point. From Thailand you can enter Laos by crossing the Mekong River at four points – Cheng Kong/Houey Say (Thailand/Laos), Nakon Panoum/Tha Kaek and Mukdahan/Savannakhet via a short river ferry trip, or Nong Kai/ Vientiane by crossing the Friendship (Mittaphap) Bridge – or by road at Chong Mek/Champasak. From Vietnam you can cross by road at Vinh/Kaew Neua (Vietnam/Laos) or Dansavanh/Lao Bao.

Entry Regulations

Visas and Passports

To enter Laos you must have a valid passport and proper visa. Your best bet is to obtain a 15 or 30-day tourist visa in advance of your trip at the Lao consulate or embassy nearest you. This is a relatively trouble-free process, though costs vary depending on which consulate or embassy you visit. The 15-day tourist visas are now available on arrival at major checkpoints, but nothing but US dollars cash (US$30 at time of publication) is accepted. The 10-day transit visas for tourists travelling through Laos from one country to another (from, say, Vietnam to Thailand) are also available. Be sure to double-check this information, as it is highly subject to change as Laos struggles to develop a coherent approach to tourism.

Extension of Stay

Tourist visas to Laos can be extended (currently for US$1 per day) at the Immigration Office in Vientiane only. There is no limit to the number of extensions, as long as you are willing to pay. Transit visas cannot be extended. Upon departure from Laos, travellers who have overstayed their visas will be expected to pay a fine (currently US$5) for every day beyond the expiration date marked on the visa.

Customs

There is little security at Laos' border checkpoints (though be sure to hang on to your baggage claim tickets when flying – employees tend to be strict about collecting them after arrival). Travellers are rarely issued customs declaration forms, and even completed forms go unchecked. Restrictions on drugs, weapons and pornography apply, but there is no limit on the amount of Lao and foreign currency you can bring into the country.

The duty-free allowance for each visitor is 1 litre of spirits and 500 cigarettes and a reasonable amount of perfume. One regulation worth keeping in mind is the restriction on sacred Buddha images; travellers have been known to be stopped on exit and detained while authorities examine a purchase to ensure that it is not a national treasure.

Health

Laos is still a developing country, and it is a good idea to take the necessary health precautions before arriving. The following immunisations, some of which require multiple injections, are recommended: Hepatitis A, Typhoid, Diptheria, Tetanus, Hepatitis B, Polio and Tuberculosis. Optional vaccinations include Rabies and Japanese B Encephalitis, a mosquito-borne disease that is very rare. Medicine to combat malaria – common in Laos outside Vientiane – is available, but consult a doctor before beginning any medication.

While in the country, be particularly careful of water and ice; only consume water that comes from carefully sealed containers or has been boiled thoroughly. Heat exhaustion and prickly heat can result from dehydration and salt

Lao Embassies

Australia
1 Dalman Crescent, O'Malley
Canberra, ACT 2606.
Tel: (61 26) 286 4595, 286 6933,
Fax: (61 26) 290 1910.
Burma (Myanmar)
NA1 Diplomatic Headquarters
Tawwin Road, Yangon.
Tel: (95 1) 22482
Fax: (95 1) 227466.
Cambodia
15–17 Thanon Keomani
Phnom Penh.
Tel: (855 23) 26441
Fax: (855 23) 27454.
China
11 East Fourth Street
Santilun, Chao Yang
Beijing.
Tel: (86 1) 532 1224
Fax: (86 1) 532 6748.
France
74 Avenue Raymond Poincaré
75116 Paris.
Tel: (33 1) 45 53 02 98

Fax: (33 1) 47 27 57 89.
Germany
Amlessing 6
D-53639 Königswinter 1, Bonn.
Tel: (49 2223) 21501.
India
E53 Panchsheet Park
New Delhi 17.
Tel: (91 11) 642 7447
Fax: (91 11) 642 8588.
Indonesia
Jalan Kintamani Raya C15 No 33
Kuningan Timur, Jakarta 12950.
Tel: (62 21) 520 9602
Fax: (62 21) 522 9601.
Japan
3-21, 3-Chome, Nishi Azabu
Minato-ku, Tokyo.
Tel: (81 3) 54112291
Fax: (81 3) 54112293.
Malaysia
2 Loront Damai
55000 Kuala Lumpur.
Tel: (60 3) 248 3895
Fax: (60 3) 2420344.

Philippines
34 Lao-Lappu Street
Magallaness Village
Makati City, Manila.
Tel: 833 5759.
Singapore
179-B Gold Hill Centre
Thomson Road.
Tel: (65) 250 6044, 250 6741.
Thailand
520, 502/13 Soi Ramkhamhaeng
39, Bang Kapi, Bangkok.
Tel: (66 2) 538 3696, 539 6667
Fax: (66 2) 539 6678.
United States
2222 S Street NW
Washington
D.C.20008.
Tel: (1 202) 332 6416
Fax: (1 202) 332 4923.
Vietnam
22 Tran Bing Trong
Hanoi.
Tel: (84 4) 254 576
Fax: (84 4) 228 414.

deficiency, so drink lots of fluids, avoid intense activity when the sun is strongest, and rest frequently during the day. Travellers' diarrhoea is quite common, though usually not serious; be sure to avoid dehydration problems by replacing the fluids your body will lose.

Currency and Exchange

The unit of currency is the *kip*, and bills are now issued in the following denominations: 100, 500, 1000, 2000 and 5000. There are no coins, and notes smaller than 100 have been rendered obsolete. While stores and services in Laos are officially forbidden to use any other currency, virtually any merchant will (gladly) accept US dollars or Thai *baht* in lieu of the shaky *kip*. You can buy *kip* at foreign exchange banks and other exchange offices with a valid passport, or a photo-copy of the photo and visa pages.

Travellers' cheques can be exchanged at major hotels and banks only. The Lao almost always use cash, and, as a result of the recent downward slide of the *kip*, lots of it. However, credit cards are accepted at a few upmarket hotels, restaurants and shops in Vientiane, where a five percent service charge is usually added to the bill. You can get a cash advance on a VISA card at some banks in Vientiane for a 3.5 percent (for dollars) or 2.5 percent (for *kip*) transaction fee. At the time of publication there are no ATM machines in the country. Banks are open 8.30am–4pm, Monday to Friday.

What to Wear

In general, the Lao seem quite happy with the recent influx of tourists to their country. One aspect of this trend they tend to despise, however, is the way many travellers dress while in Laos. The Lao are very conservative when it comes to dress, and expect foreign visitors to respect this custom.

Women should avoid clothing that bares the thighs, shoulders or breasts; long trousers, walking shorts and skirts are acceptable, while tank tops, short skirts and running shorts are not. Both men and women should dress conservatively, especially when making a visit to a temple or government office.

Sandals or shoes that can be taken off and on easily are a sensible idea, as shoes must always be removed before entering a Lao house or temple.

Whatever the season, bring lightweight cotton clothing and a light jacket or pullover for those rare, welcome, cool nights during December and January.

Photography

Film is available in Laos, and at very reasonable prices, but in limited quantities. Print film can be bought almost everywhere, but slide film is really only obtainable in the larger towns. Avoid buying film from non-air-conditioned shops. There are places to get print films processed, although quality varies, and on the whole it would be safer to have slide film developed back in your own country.

On the whole Lao people do not mind having their pictures taken, but it is still advisable to ask permission before photographing anyone. The hill tribes are a little different, and some of them actively dislike having their pictures taken. Never force anyone, and always ask permission. Show restraint when photographing people at prayer, and monks. Avoid photographing anything that may have connections with the military.

Practical Tips

Media

Newspapers & magazines

The national Lao-language news-paper is *Pasason* (*The People*), which is very popular, although dubious as a source of accurate information about the country. In Vientiane you will also find people reading the *Viang Chan Mai* (*New Vientiane*) city newspaper. The Lao government now produces two newspapers for the expatriate community in Vientiane: the English-language *Vientiane Times* and the French-language *Le Renovateur*. Both concentrate on news in the world of development, and are full of details of the latest agreements between the Lao government and its foreign donors. *Le Renovateur* has a far snappier design, and also tends to be more up-to-date on current events in town, so go for that one if you can read French. The state-run KPL News Service puts out an uninformative daily news bulletin in English and French. *The Bangkok Post* and *The Nation*, the two main English-language dailies from Bangkok, are available in hotels, shops and restaurants in Vientiane.

Raintrees bookshop sells current issues of *Time* and *Newsweek*, and cafés and restaurants carry back issues of Western magazines. The government-run **State Bookshop** sells Lao and Thai textbooks and western magazines, in addition to stamps, postcards and posters of Marx and Lenin.

Raintrees Books
52 Nokeo Khumman Road, Vientiane
Tel: (21) 213060,
Fax: (21) 215208.
State Bookshop
Setthathirat Road, Vientiane
Tel: (21) 212475.

Le Renovateur
Pangkham Street, Vientiane.
Tel: (21) 217872,
Fax: (21) 216365,
e-mail: lerenovateur@laonet.net

Vientiane Times
Pangkham Street, Vientiane.
Tel: (21) 216364,
Fax: (21) 216365,
website: www.vlentianetimes.com

Television & radio

The Lao government broadcasts on one radio station throughout the country, but most Lao rely on Thai radio for entertainment. Expats often use short-wave to pick up programmes from the BBC, VOA, Radio Australia and Radio Free Asia.

Lao National Television now has two channels but, again, almost all Lao prefer Thai television; as you make your way around the country, you will probably find most televisions tuned to one of the popular Thai soap operas. Satellite TV is now widely available in Vientiane, offering channels like CNN, MTV and BBC World Service.

Postal Services

The Lao postal service offers reliable service at reasonable prices. There are post offices in every provincial capital, painted with the same colour scheme of mustard yellow. For sending packages abroad, most expats use the **Express Mail Service (EMS)**.

Receiving incoming mail at the main post office in Vientiane is possible, although remember that all packages must be opened and their contents displayed for inspection. Residents check their boxes at the post office daily, as there is no home delivery service.

A number of international courier agencies offer their services in the capital city of Vientiane:

DHL Worldwide Express
52 Nokeo Khumman Road.
Tel: (21) 214868,
Fax: (21) 216830.

Express Mail Service (EMS)
Vientiane Post Office.
Tel: (21) 217245, 215767,
Fax: (21) 212779.

Federal Express
Vientiane Post Office.
Tel: (21) 223278, 223279,
Fax: (21) 223280.

Lao Freight Forwarder
Km 3, Thadeua Road.
Tel: (21) 313321,
Fax: (21) 314831.

Overseas Courier Service
First Floor, Lao Plaza Hotel,
63 Samsenthai Road.
Tel: (21) 218839,
Fax: (21) 218840.

TNT Express Worldwide
8/3 Lan Xang Avenue.
Tel: (21) 214361.

United Parcel Service
12/26 Nong Bone Street.
Tel: (21) 414392

Telecommunications

Until 1990, Laos was connected with the world, except Thailand and the USSR, by only one phone line – only one incoming or outgoing international call could be placed at a time. Things have changed a lot since then, and International Direct Dialling (IDD) is now available in Laos. While expensive, it provides a reliable service to more than 150 international destinations.

In Vientiane the Public Call Office on Setthathirat Road, near the Presidential Palace, is where most travellers make international phone calls. In the provinces international calls can be made from the local post or telephone office, or from one of the phone booths which have reached some towns. To use these booths for both international and domestic calls you need a phonecard, which can be purchased at post offices, telephone offices, or some shops.

To call long distance within the country, dial 0 first, then the provincial area code and number. For international calls, dial 00, the country code, then the area code and number.

Internet

Until very recently there was no e-mail service in Laos. The government seems to have resigned itself to the inevitability of Internet access, however, and it is now easily available to foreigners in Vientiane and Luang Prabang (and before long in smaller cities as well). While some residents still prefer to dial long-distance to an Internet provider in Bangkok, there is a local server in Vientiane run by the American **Globenet** company. While its lines are notoriously busy, Globenet does offer reliable Internet service, which is accessible from its office on the second floor of the Lao Hotel Plaza and in computer shops and cafés in the town.

Vientiane
Globenet
Second Floor, Lao Plaza Hotel,
63 Samsenthai Road.
Tel: (21) 218841, 218842,
Fax: (21) 222740,
web: www.laonet.net

Malic Cybercafé
1 Luang Prabang Road.
Tel: (21) 222646,
e-mail: malic@laonet.net

Microtec Computers
168-69 Luang Prabang Road.
Tel: (21) 213836,
Fax: (21) 212933.

Planet Computers
205 Setthathirat Road.
Tel: (21) 218972,
Fax: (21) 216387,
e-mail: planet@laonet.net

Telephone Area Codes

Attapeu	31	Sam Neua	64
Huay Xai	84	Savannakhet	41
Luang Nam Tha	86	Sekong	31
Luang Prabang	71	Tha Kaek	52
Pakse	31	Udomxai	81
Pakxan	54	Vang Vieng	21
Phongsali	88	Vientiane	21
Sainyabuli	74	Xieng Khuang	61

Emergency Numbers

Police Tel: 91
Fire Tel: 190
Ambulance Tel: 195

Luang Prabang
Planet Computers
Phothisarat Road.
Tel: (71) 252291,
e-mail: planet@laonet.net

Tipping

Tipping is not expected in Laos,
except at a few upmarket
restaurants in Vientiane and Luang
Prabang, where you might leave
10–15 percent if a service charge
has not already been added to your
bill. Taxi and *tuk-tuk* drivers
certainly do not expect to be tipped,
unless the trip was unusually
difficult or much longer than
originally expected.

Business Hours

Government offices are officially
open 8am–noon and 1–4pm,
Monday to Friday. But don't expect
to get anything done after 11.30am
or before 2pm, during which time
most employees are enjoying lunch
and a midday rest at home.
    Most shops close for an hour
during lunch, and are open for a
half-day on Saturday. Almost all
businesses are closed on Sunday.

Medical Services

Medical services in Laos are
limited; the most extensive are in
Vientiane, where even the two state
hospitals, **Mahosot** and **Setthathirat**, are not up to international
standards. Even the **International
Clinic** at Mahosot is best reserved
for only minor injuries. The **Friendship
Hospital** is a specialised medical
centre for trauma and orthopedics.
Most foreign residents requiring
medical attention choose to visit
the **Australian Embassy's Clinic**. All
numbers are for Vientiane.
Friendship Hospital
Phontong Road,

Ban Phonsavang.
Tel: (21) 413306.
International Clinic
Fa Ngum Road, Ban Kaonyot.
Tel: (21) 214022.
Mahosot Hospital
Fa Ngum Road, Ban Kaonyot.
Tel: (21) 214018.
Setthathirat Hospital
Nong Bone Road, Ban That Luang.
Tel: (21) 413720.
Australian Clinic
Australian Embassy, Phonxay Road.
Tel: (21) 413603, (020) 511462.
Many Vientiane residents opt for
facilities just across the river in
Thailand:

Wattana Private Hospital
Nong Khai, Thailand.
Tel: (66-42) 465201.
AEK Udon International Hospital
Udon Thani, Thailand.
Tel: (66-42) 342555,
Fax: (66-42) 341033.

Travel Agencies

Vientiane
DAI Travel
093/4 Samsenthai Road.
Tel: (21) 214667,
Fax: (21) 213558.
Diethelm Travel Laos, Ltd.
Namphu Circle.

Foreign Embassies in Vientiane

Australia
Phonxay Road.
Tel: (21) 413600.
Burma (Myanmar)
Sokpaluang Road.
Tel: (21) 314910,
Fax: (21) 312439.
Cambodia
Tha Deua Road.
Tel: (21) 314952,
Fax: (21) 312584.
China
Wat Nak Nyai Road.
Tel: (21) 315100, 315103.
France
Setthathirat Road.
Tel: (21) 215253, 215258/9,
Fax: (21) 215255.
Germany
Sokpaluang Road.
Tel: (21) 312110, 312111,
Fax: (21) 314322.
India
That Luang Road.
Tel: (21) 413801, 413802.
Indonesia
Phon Kheng Road.
Tel: (21) 413907, 413909.
Japan
Sisangvone Road.
Tel: (21) 414400, 414402,
Fax: (21) 414403.
North Korea
Wat Nak Road.
Tel: (21) 315260, 315261.
South Korea
13 Phon Kheng Road
Tel: (21) 415833,

Fax: (21) 415831.
Malaysia
That Luang Road.
Tel: (21) 414205.
Mongolia
Thadeua Road.
Tel: (21) 315220.
Philippines
Salakokthan Road.
Tel: (21) 315179,
Fax: (21) 314732.
Poland
Thadeua Road.
Tel: (21) 312940,
Fax: (21) 312085.
Russia
Thaphalanxay.
Tel: (21) 312218.
Singapore
Nong Bone Road.
Tel: (21) 416860,
Fax: (21) 416855.
Sweden
Sokpaluang Road.
Tel: (21) 315018,
Fax: (21) 315001.
Thailand
Phon Kheng Road.
Tel: (21) 214582, 214585,
Fax: (21) 214584.
United States
That Dam Road.
Tel: (21) 212581, 212582,
Fax: (21) 212548.
Vietnam
That Luang Road.
Tel: (21) 413400, 413403.

Tel: (21) 213833,
Fax: (21) 216294,
e-mail: dtllvte@pan-laos. net.la
Inter-Lao Tourisme
7/73 Setthathirat Road.
Tel: (21) 214832,
Fax: (21) 216306.
Lane Xang Travel
Pangkham Street.
Tel: (21) 214509,
Fax: (21) 215804.
Lao Travel Service
08/3 Lane Xang Avenue.
Tel: (21) 216603, 216604,
Fax: (21) 216150,
e-mail: lts@pan-laos.net.la
SODETOUR
114 Fa Ngum Road.
Tel: (21) 216313, 216314.

Luang Prabang
Diethelm Travel Laos, Ltd.
Phothisarat Road.
Tel: (71) 212277.
Lan Xang Travel
Wisunalat Road.
Tel: (71) 212753.
Lao Travel Service
Navang Road.
Tel: (71) 212317.
SODETOUR
Navang Road.
Tel: (71) 212199.

Banks

Vientiane
**Banque pour le Commerce
Exterieur Lao**
1 Pangkham Street.
Tel: (21) 213200,
Fax: (21) 213202.
Joint Development Bank
75/1-5 Lane Xang Avenue.
Tel: (21) 213535,
Fax: (21) 213530.
Setthathirat Bank
6-10 Setthathirat Road.
Tel: (21) 213400.
Siam Commercial Bank
117 Lan Xang Avenue.
Tel: (21) 213500, 213501.
Thai Farmers' Bank
08/4 Lan Xang Avenue.
Tel: (21) 213550.
Vientiane Commercial Bank
33 Lan Xang Avenue.
Tel: (21) 222700,
Fax: (21) 213513.

Luang Prabang
Lan Xang Bank
65 Sisavangvong Road.
Tel: (71) 212186.

Savannakhet
Lao May Bank
Khanthabouli Road.
Tel: (41) 212703.

Pakse
Phak Tai Bank
Road No. 13.
Tel: (31) 212168,
Fax: (31) 212173.

Religious Services

A number of religious communities
in Vientiane offer services to the
public:

Christian
Catholic Centre
193 Samsenthai Road.
Tel: (21) 216219.
Church of the Holy Spirit
ARDA Center,
93 Luang Prabang Road.
Tel: (21) 217162.
Church of the Sacred Heart
193 Samsenthai Road.
Tel: (21) 216219.
Lao Evangelical Church
Luang Prabang Road.
Tel: (21) 216052, 216222.
Seventh Day Adventist
Nong Bone Road.
Tel: (21) 412270, 412701.

Baha'i
Baha'i Faith Centre
Luang Prabang Road.
Tel: (21) 216996.

Muslim
Jama' Masjid Mosque
Namphu Circle.

Getting Around

On Arrival

From Vientiane's Wattay
International Airport the journey into
the centre of the city is a painless
15-minute taxi drive. Large hotels
often provide limousine service
from the airport if arranged prior to
check-in. There is no airport bus
service or public transport.

From the Luang Prabang Airport
the journey into the centre of the
city takes about 15 -minutes by
taxi, *tuk-tuk* or minitruck. Again,
large hotels often provide limousine
service from the airport if arranged
prior to check-in. No public
transport is available.

From the Friendship Bridge into
the centre of Vientiane takes about
30 minutes by *tuk-tuk*, fewer by taxi
or private car. Larger hotels often
provide limousine service from the
bridge if arranged prior to check-in.
A rather unreliable public bus service is available for a minimal fee.

By Air

All flights in Laos are handled by
the state-run **Lao Aviation**. The
main aircraft used for Lao Aviation's
domestic flights are the Chinese
Y-12 and Y-7 planes. One ATR-72 is
available for international flights
and the popular Vientiane-Luang
Prabang route. There is also a daily
flight from Vientiane to Pakse in the
south. Flights to Savannakhet leave
every day except Friday. These
three destinations, Luang Prabang,
Pakse and Savannakhet, have the
only scheduled flights you can really
rely on. There are flights to and
from other places such as Luang
Nam Tha, Muang Sing, Phonsavan,
Sam Neua and Muang Xai.

It is hard to know just how safe air travel is in Laos, as official safety records are not made public. The Chinese planes must rely on visual flying techniques, while the ATR does have radar capability. But the main problem with the Y-7 and the Y-12 seems to be one of maintenance, as neither the technical ability nor the funds are available to keep the planes in top condition. The scheduling system at Lao Aviation is laughable, and it is often impossible to know precisely when your flight is departing until the day before it leaves, even if you have booked a seat far in advance. Tickets for foreigners are more than twice the price of those for Lao citizens, and, unless handled by a travel agent, all domestic ticket purchases must be made in US dollars cash.

If you have the budget, it is possible to charter a helicopter with a foreign pilot through **Westcoast Helicopter** in Vientiane for about US$1,000 per hour. A number of regional airlines also have offices in Vientiane.

Lao Aviation
2 Pangkham Street.
Tel: (21) 212051,
Fax: (21) 212056.
Lao Westcoast Helicopter
Wattay Airport,
Vientiane.
Tel: (21) 512023,
Fax: (21) 512055.
Malaysia Airlines
Plaza Hotel,
63 Samsenthai Road.
Tel: (21) 218800.
Royal Air Cambodge
First Floor,
Lao Plaza Hotel,
63 Samsenthai Road.
Tel: (21) 218816,
Fax: (21) 218815.
Silk Air
Royal Dokmaideng Hotel
Lan Xang Avenue.
Tel: (21) 217492
Thai Airways
119 Pangkham Street.
Tel: (21) 222527, 222528.
Vietnam Airlines
First Floor, Lao Plaza Hotel,
63 Samsenthai Road.

Tel: (21) 217562,
Fax: (21) 222379.

By Road

The road system in Laos is improving with every passing year. An array of foreign governments and international aid organisations is currently funding road improvement projects, and the nation's main highway, Route 13, originally built by the French during the colonial period, is now fully paved from Luang Prabang in the north to Savannakhet in the south. However, most roads remain in poor condition – less than a quarter are tarred. Interprovincial transport by bus and truck is widely available, which makes it possible to visit at least part of every province in Laos.

Regular buses, a few air conditioned, supply Route 13 between Luang Prabang and Savannakhet. For more remote routes, large flat-bed trucks fitted with wooden seats, pick-ups, or trucks converted into passenger vehicles by the addition of two long wooden benches in the back are the most common forms of road transport.

By Boat

Not so long ago the 7,400 km (4,600 miles) of navigable waterways in Laos constituted the country's only transport network. Today, they remain a great way to get around the country. The main long-distance river trip for tourists in Laos runs from Huay Xai in the north down to Luang Prabang. These days, the route from Vientiane to Pakse in the south is mainly used for cargo traffic, but smaller passenger ferries from Pakse to Champasak and Don Khong still run. Throughout the country, river taxis are available for short trips to sites such as temples and caves that are inaccessible by road. Luxury river cruises are now available in the north and the south through a French-owned cruise company, **Indocruise**.
Indocruise
Francois Nginn Road, Vientiane.

Tel: (21) 216886,
Fax: (21) 216886,
e-mail: gbcruise@loxinfo.co.th

Public Transport

For short trips in the centres of town, stick to *tuk-tuks* and jumbos; the pedicab (*samlo*) has virtually disappeared with the increase in motorcycle and car traffic. In Vientiane the city bus system is of little use to tourists, as it only runs between the centre of the city and outlying villages. Car taxis in Vientiane can be found in front of major hotels, the morning market and the airport – always negotiate the price before you set out.

Private Transport

Perhaps the best way to get around any town in Laos is to hire a bicycle, or, for more ambitious day trips, a motorcycle. Bicycles can be hired for the day from restaurants and guesthouses in towns throughout Laos, and small motorcycles can be hired from dealers in Vientiane, Luang Prabang and Savannakhet. Cars, pick-ups and 4WD vehicles are available for hire from private operators in Vientiane.
Asia Vehicle Rental
08/3 Lan Xang Avenue,
Vientiane.
Tel: (21) 217493,
Fax: (21) 217493,
e-mail: avr@loxinfo.co.th
Khounta Rental
Luang Prabang Road,
Vientiane.
Tel: (21) 513127.

Where to Stay

Choosing Accommodation

Laos is working to upgrade the availability and quality of its tourist accommodation. Currently there are very few luxury hotels, and all are located in the larger cities. Elsewhere what you will most often find is simple guesthouses, very cheap by western standards (though backpackers often complain that the prices are expensive compared to Laos' neighbours). As there are no tourism industry associations it is hard to apply common standards of quality and service to facilities in Laos hotels.

Hotel Listings

VIENTIANE

Expensive

Lao Plaza Hotel
63 Samsenthai Road.
Tel: (21) 222741,
Fax: (21) 222740.
Built by the Thai-owned Felix chain, this is Vientiane's newest luxury hotel, located right in the centre of the city. It comes complete with all the services you would expect from an international standard luxury hotel, including a pool, a fitness centre and a nightclub, e-mail access and a piano bar where you can enjoy free drinks and listen to a lounge singer. Credit cards accepted.

Novotel
Samsenthai Road.
Tel: (21) 213570,
Fax: (21) 213572,
e-mail: novotlao@loxinfo.co.th
Located just out of town near the airport, the Novotel has recently been refurbished in elegant European style, and is known for its excellent bakery, beautiful swimming pool and popular nightclub. Credit cards accepted.

Royal Dokmaideng Hotel
Lan Xang Avenue.
Tel: (21) 214455,
Fax: (21) 214454.
A drab structure near the morning market on Vientiane's main avenue, the Royal offers a Chinese restaurant and nightclub (with occasional traditional Lao music and dance performances), and a swimming pool and fitness centre.

Settha Palace Hotel
6 Pangkham Street.
Tel: (21) 217581,
Fax: (21) 217583,
e-mail: settha@laonet.net
Once known as one of the grandest hotels in Indochina, the Settha Palace was originally built by the French in the early part of the last century and has just undergone a magnificent renovation. This is certainly the most elegant place to stay in town, the Settha Palace is a welcome addition to Vientiane's hotel scene, offering spacious guest rooms and suites with private terraces in a graceful colonial-era building. This historical landmark features period furniture, a first-class restaurant, a beautiful swimming pool and a sidewalk café.

Moderate

Asian Pavilion Hotel
379 Samsenthai Road.
Tel: (21) 213430,
Fax: (21) 213432,
e-mail: asianlao@loxinfo.co.th
Nothing to get excited about, this hotel offers clean rooms and an efficient staff at reasonable prices.

Day Inn Hotel
59/3 Pangkham Street.
Tel: (21) 223847, 223848,
Fax: (21) 222984.
Popular with UNDP staff on temporary stints in Vientiane, this recently refurbished colonial structure downtown has a refreshingly light and airy interior, large rooms and an excellent location.

Lan Xang Hotel
Fa Ngum Road.
Tel: (21) 214102,
Fax: (21) 214108.
This four-storey concrete behemoth on the banks of the Mekong River was once Vientiane's premier hotel. It no longer holds any claim to that title, but as it has pool tables, a tennis court, badminton courts and its own temple, a stay here can be good fun. While the shabby interior reminds one only of glory days gone by, the hotel remains popular among the Vientiane élite for wedding parties.

Price Guide

The following price categories indicate the cost of a double room in high season:
Expensive: $80 and above.
Moderate: $20–60.
Budget: under $20.

Lani Guest House
281 Setthathirat Road.
Tel: (21) 214919,
Fax: (21) 215639.
A charming converted residence set back from a main road in the heart of Vientiane's central district, the Lani offers 12 spacious rooms, each with phone and hot shower, and a nice outdoor terrace.

Lani Two Guest House
268 Saylom Road.
Tel: (21) 213022,
Fax: (21) 215639.
So successful with his first guesthouse, Mr Lani opened a second one that is smaller, slightly cheaper and less centrally located. Some rooms have direct access a pleasant balcony overlooking the large garden. Chinese food is served on the outdoor terrace – the menu is that of the Ban Haysok restaurant, also owned by Mr Lani.

Le Parasol Blanc Hotel
263 Sibounheuang Road.
Tel: (21) 215090, 216091,
Fax: (21) 222290, 215444.
Among the best in this category, the hotel has bungalow-style rooms with beautiful hardwood floors, satellite TV, swimming pool and a shaded garden. A bar and a restaurant (with occasional live piano music) serve

good French, Lao and Thai food in one of the more charming surroundings in town.

Tai Pan Hotel
2-12 François Nginn Road.
Tel: (21) 216907,
Fax: (21) 216 223.
A pleasant, sparsely decorated hotel just around the corner from the Mekong. The rooms come with beautiful wooden floors, individual balconies overlooking the street below, breakfast and airport pick-up. Credit cards accepted.

Vansana Hotel
Phon Than Road.
Tel: (21) 414189,
Fax: (21) 413171.
Quite a way out of town, but quiet as a result, the Vansana offers a swimming pool and sauna, massage service, restaurant and a nightclub famous for traditional ballroom dancing. Credit cards accepted.

Price Guide

The following price categories indicate the cost of a double room in high season:
$$$: Expensive: $80 and above.
$$: Moderate: $20–60.
$: Budget: under $20.

Budget

L'Auberge du Temple
184/1 Sikhotabang Road.
Tel: (21) 214844,
Fax: (21) 214844.
A small, recently renovated villa just out of town, the French-owned auberge offers large rooms, verandahs with a nice view of Wat Khunta just across the street and free breakfast.

Heuane Lao Guest House
055 Ban Simuang.
Tel: (21) 216258,
Fax: (21) 215628.
A traditional Lao structure near Wat Simuang with 12 rooms and two large suites, each with bathroom.

Lao Paris Hotel
100 Samsenthai Road.
Tel: (21) 215639.
Good location, in the heart of downtown Vientiane, if the hotel itself is nothing special; restaurant with Lao, Thai, Vietnamese and western food.

Pangkham Guest House
72/6 Pangkham Street.
Tel: (21) 217053,
Fax: (21) 217053.
This Chinese-owned guesthouse located on Vientiane's Tailor Street offers adequate, unremarkable rooms; bicycle and motorcycle hire is available.

Saylomyen Guest House
Saylom Road.
Tel: (21) 214246.
This two-storey structure offers eight simple rooms of varying degrees of comfort; the rather odd garden behind adds some colour.

Sisangvone Guesthouse
Sisangvone Road.
Tel: (21) 414753,
Fax: (21) 414753.
A villa-style guesthouse with 15 very basic rooms; the large house faces the active Wat Sisanvone in a quiet and pleasant neighbourhood just a short walk from That Luang.

Vannasinh Guest House
051 Phnom Penh Street.
Tel: (21) 222020.
Clean, quiet and well-run, the Vannasinh is located on the outskirts of Chinatown and serves pretty good breakfasts.

Villa Manoly
Ban Simuang.
Tel: (21) 212282,
Fax: (21) 218907.
A large villa in a peaceful neighbourhood around the corner from Wat Simuang, the Manoly has a quiet sitting terrace, beautifully landscaped grounds and spacious rooms.

CHAMPASAK

Moderate

Sala Wat Phu
Main Street.
Tel: (31) 212175.
Pleasant rooms and a good attached restaurant in a French-era building which has been well-restored; bookings are made through its agent in Pakse.

LAO PAKO

Moderate

Lao Pako Resort
Tel: (21) 222925,
Fax: (21) 212981.
The best way to reach Lao Pako is to drive or take the public bus as far as Som Sa Mai village, then a short local boat-trip downstream.

LUANG PRABANG

Moderate

Auberge Le Calao
Rim Khong Road.
Tel: (71) 212100.
Beautifully restored colonial mansion near Vat Xieng Thong, with great views of the Mekong from each room's private balcony.

Mouang Luang Hotel
Bunkhong Road.
Tel: (71) 212790.
One of the largest hotels in Luang Prabang, built in a mixture of traditional and modern styles.

Phousi Hotel
Kitsalat Road.
Tel: (71) 212292,
Fax: (71) 212719.
Well located for trips up Phousi Hill, this hotel also has a very pleasant garden.

Phu Vao Hotel
Phu Vao Street.
Tel: (71) 212194,
Fax: (71) 212534.
The only place in the town with a swimming pool, this hotel has great views of Luang Prabang.

Saynamkhan Guesthouse
Kingkitsalat Road.
Tel: (71) 212976,
Fax: (71) 212719.
Situated at the foot of Phousi Hill, the Saynamkhan offers great value in a renovated colonial villa.

Souvannaphoum Hotel
Phothisarat Road.
Tel: (71) 212200,
Fax: (71) 212577.
Originally Prince Souvanna Phouma's official residence, this place has 25 rooms, all with terraces, and a garden. You might even be able to sleep in the

prince's old room but you need to book in advance.

Villa Santi
Sakkarin Road.
Tel: (71) 212267,
Fax: (71) 212267.
A colonial villa that is owned by a princess – what could be more exotic? There is also a very comfortable guesthouse attached.

PAKSE

Moderate

Champasak Palace Hotel
718 Ban Pra Bath Road.
Tel: (31) 212263,
Fax: (31) 212781.
This huge hotel, overlooking the town of Pakse and the Sekong River, is the former residence of the last Prince of Champasak, Boun Oum. Facilities include a fitness club, a bar and a somewhat tacky garden overlooking the river. The only place in the town that accepts credit cards.

Hotel Residence du Champa
Champasak Road.
Tel: (31) 212120,
Fax: (31) 212765.
Slightly out of town, this hotel offers rooms with air-conditioning and satellite television.

SAVANNAKHET

Moderate

Hoongtip Hotel
Phetsarath Road.
Tel: (41) 212262,
Fax: (41) 213230.
One of the better hotels in the town, but still nothing special.

Nanhai Hotel
Latsavongseuk Road.
Tel: (41) 212371,
Fax: (41) 212381.
The largest and possibly the most luxurious place in Savannakhet, this is a Chinese-style hotel with a good restaurant attached.

Phonepaseut Hotel
Santisouk Road.
Tel: (41) 212158.
A little way away from the river, but nevertheless a very comfortable,

clean hotel. Across the road there is an excellent swimming pool with free access for guests.

Sala Savanh Guesthouse
Kuvoravong Road.
Tel: (41) 212445.
Offers large air-conditioned rooms in an old colonial mansion near the centre of the town.

Budget

Mekong Hotel
Tha He Road.
Tel: (41) 212249.
Old colonial building on the river-front with an attached nightclub.

Riverside Resort
Tel: (41) 212775.
Located 1 km (half a mile) south of the town on the Mekong, offering idyllic bungalows in a quiet compound with lovely gardens.

TAAT LO WATERFALL

Moderate

Taat Lo Resort
Taat Lo Waterfall.
This offers attractive chalets over-looking the falls; bookings can be made through Pakse travel agents.

THA KHAEK

Budget

Khammouane Hotel
Setthathirat Road.
Tel: (52) 212216,
Fax: (52) 212370.
Large hotel with air-conditioned rooms and a restaurant.

Phoudoi Hotel
Kuvoravong Road.
Tel: (52) 212048.
Located quite some distance from the river and the main part of the town, near the airfield, this place has comfortable, cosy rooms.

Souksomboon Hotel
Setthathirat Road.
Tel: (52) 212254.
Built in the 1930s; the style seems to reach for Art Deco, but stumbles into neo-Rococo. The hotel has an attached disco.

Where to Eat

What to Eat

Lao food is quite simple, making use of the country's abundant fresh vegetables, freshwater fish, chicken, duck, pork and beef (see page 79). The staple of the Lao diet is sticky rice, which is used as a tool to eat most food by hand. Chopsticks are used only for Chinese and Vietnamese dishes. Spices used in Lao cuisine include lemongrass, hot chillies, peanuts, coconut milk, ginger and the unique *paa daek*, or fermented fish paste. One of the most common Lao dishes is *laap*, a "salad" made from minced meat, chicken or fish, mixed with lime juice, mint leaves and other spices. *Laap* is served with a pile of fresh leaves and eaten with sticky rice. Papaya salad (*tam mak hong*), another favourite, is a mix of green (unripe) papaya, lime, hot chillies and fish paste, to which can be added ingredients like peanuts and tomatoes.

Thai, Chinese and Vietnamese food are common in Laos, a testa-mony to the political and cultural influences of the three surrounding powers. Chinese rice-noodle soup (*foe*) is often eaten for breakfast, lunch or a snack, and is served with a variety of fresh vegetables and condiments. Vietnamese spring rolls (*yaw*) are very popular, and are usually served with fresh leaves, cold rice-noodles and assorted dipping sauces. The French left their mark with *baguettes* (*khao jii*), which are widely available and usually served as sandwiches with paté, sliced meats and vegetables.

Lao sweets often involve sticky rice and coconut, and are sold at markets in little packages made from banana leaves.

Drinking Notes

Certainly the most popular beverage in Laos is the domestically produced Beer Lao, a mild and refreshing beer served in glass bottles and cans. Draught or "fresh" beer (*bia sot*) is also served in pitchers at simple bars and beer gardens in Vientiane. Lao men certainly like to drink, and you can find them at these establishments every night of the week, and even during the day at weekends. *Lau-lao* is an incredibly strong rice whisky served at parties and important occasions such as weddings. At a private function the host will always empty the first glass of *lau-lao* on the floor in deference to the house spirits, and then drink a glass himself. He will then offer a glass to each guest in turn – drinking at least one glass is imperative, and always in one quick gulp. *Khao kham* is a deliciously sweet wine, red in colour and made from sticky rice; it makes a nice after-dinner liqueur.

Lao coffee, grown in the fertile Bolaven Plateau in the south of the country, is some of the best in the world. It is usually served in a glass, not a cup or mug, mixed with both sugar and sweetened condensed milk. As this mixture results in a very strong, very sweet taste, Lao coffee is often served with a glass of weak tea or hot water as a chaser. Iced milk coffee (*café nom yen*) is popular as well, served with sweetened condensed milk over ice. Fresh fruit juice – lemon, orange, coconut and sugar cane, among others – is served in outdoor stalls throughout Vientiane and other cities, and fruit shakes are widely available.

Restaurant Listings

VIENTIANE

In addition to being the political and economic centre of Laos, Vientiane is a culinary capital as well, where an enormous variety of excellent food can be found at reasonable prices. Thanks to both its wide choice and its great value, Vientiane is arguably the best place to dine in Southeast Asia.

Lao

Banmala
Khu Vieng Road.
Tel: (21) 313249.
Famous among Lao and expats alike for its excellent grilled chicken, duck and fish, papaya salad, sticky rice and fresh beer. Always crowded with Lao men passing the time for hours on end on weekend afternoons or weekday evenings. **$**

Kua Lao
111 Samsenthai Road.
Tel: (21) 215777.
An upmarket Lao restaurant which offers good quality Lao and Thai food in a beautiful French colonial mansion. Nightly traditional Lao music and dance performances. **$$**

Nang Kham Bang
97/2 Khun Bulom Road.
Tel: (21) 217198.
This place offers some of the best Lao food in the town, including specialities such as stuffed frogs, roasted quail, grilled chicken and fish. Always crowded with a mix of expats, government officials and Thai businessmen. **$**

Salongxay Restaurant
Fa Ngum Road.
Tel: (21) 214112.
Located just opposite the Lan Xang Hotel, the Salongxay offers a Lao set menu accompanied by classical music and dancing. **$$**

Soukvimane Lao Food
That Dam.
Tel: (21) 214441.
A small but highly regarded Lao restaurant just around the corner from the That Dam stupa, Soukmivane serves excellent Lao meat, fish and soup dishes. **$$**

Tamnak Lao (Lao Residence)
That Luang Road.
Tel: (21) 413562.
Near the Patuxai, victory monument, this place is generally frequented by package tourists and offers expensive Lao food in a formal environment. **$$**

Italian

L'Opera
Namphu Circle.
Tel: (21) 215099.
One of the most upmarket restaurants in the town, L'Opera offers excellent Italian food in a romantic setting. The charismatic Italian owner ensures that the service is impeccable and that opera music is always playing. Frequented by the diplomatic and business communities the restaurant's takeaway *gelati* bar is a highlight. **$$$**

Lo Stivale
44/2 Setthathirat Road.
Tel: (21) 215651.
The less formal of the two Italian choices, with an extensive menu featuring pasta dishes, soups, salads and good desserts. **$$**

Chinese

Ban Haysok
34 Heng Boun Street.
Tel: (21) 215417.
Solid Southern Chinese cuisine in a clean and upmarket environment. The absurdly extensive menu also includes Lao and Thai food. **$$**

Beijing Restaurant
Mekong Hotel,
Luang Prabang Road.
Tel: (21) 212938,
Fax: (21) 212822.
Known for its crispy duck, this clean, basic restaurant offers a variety of Chinese dishes. **$$$**

Guang Dong
91-93 Chao Anou Street.
Tel: (21) 217364.
Located in the heart of Chinatown, this place offers *dim sum* and other Chinese specialities with an emphasis on Cantonese dishes. **$$**

Mai Yuan
Second Floor, Lao Hotel Plaza,

63 Samsenthai Road.
Tel: (21) 218800.
Elegant dining room specialises in *dim sum* and offers lunch specials in addition to the à la carte menu. **$$$**

Vietnamese

PVO
344 Samsenthai Road.
Tel: (21) 214444.
This simple shop only has about six items on the menu, but they are among the best in the town. Spring roll sets served with fresh vegetable leaves, cold rice-noodles and peanut dipping sauce are the speciality of the house, as is the ballroom-dance music that the proprietor, Mr Chantha, a connoisseur of the best places to tango, likes to play on his stereo. **$**

Viengsavanh
Heng Boun Street.
Tel: (21) 213990.
A small, clean, very popular restaurant in Chinatown known for two dishes: barbecued pork meatball sets served with a peanut sauce and fresh greens like mint, basil and mango, and raw beef strips that diners boil themselves in pots of coconut water on the tables and eat with various sauces. **$**

Thai

Just for Fun
Pangkham Street.
Tel: (21) 213642.
This funky little shop serves a remarkable variety of Thai and Lao dishes (all available in vegetarian varieties), every imaginable herbal tea, great coffee and the best chocolate cake in the town. You can also buy traditional Lao handicrafts in the low-key atmosphere. **$**

Sathapone Restaurant
Dongpalan Road.
Tel: (21) 416214.
A bit far out of town, the Sathapone serves all sorts of Thai curry and noodle dishes in its spacious dining room, or for takeaway. **$**

French

La Belle Epoque
Settha Palace Hotel,
6 Pangkham Street.
Tel: (21) 217581,
Fax: (21) 217583.
The newest and priciest French restaurant in the town offers a nostalgic and elegant dining experience inside the recently renovated Settha Palace Hotel. The Swiss chef serves the best desserts in Laos. **$$$**

Le Côte d'Azur
Fa Ngum Road.
Tel: (21) 217252.
One of the newest and hottest spots in the town, this French restaurant offers a bright, spacious and comfortable dining room and an extensive menu featuring excellent Provençal fare – fresh seafood, creative salads and the best pizza around. **$$$**

Le Provençal
Namphu Circle.
Tel: (21) 217251.
Located on Vientiane's central circle, this place offers French and Mediterranean cuisine, including pizzas, pastas, seafood, grilled steaks, salad Niçoise and a good wine selection. **$$$**

Le Souriya
15 Pangkham Street.
Tel: (21) 215887.
An elegant and intimate eatery just off Vientiane's central circle. The menu is small, but filled with rich sauces and fine wines; the peppersteak and chocolate soufflé are a highlight. **$$$**

La Terrasse
Nokeo Khumman Road.
Tel: (21) 218550.
Busy almost every night of the week, La Terrasse is one of the best deals in the town, serving hamburgers, pizzas, large salads, grilled brochettes, Tex-Mex fare like burritos, and an array of mixed drinks (including Margaritas) at remarkably low prices. **$$**

Le Vendome
Wat Inpeng Road.
Tel: (21) 216402.
A less expensive French option, this

Vientiane Bars

Anousone Bar and Brasserie
Fa Ngum Road,
Tel: (21) 222347.
Housed in a simple but somehow elegant wooden structure near the Mekong River, the Anousone serves good mixed drinks and basic Lao and western food at reasonable prices.

La Cave des Châteaux
Namphu Circle.
Tel: (21) 212192.
A French-style wine merchant offering imported French wines, cheeses and meats for tasting and takeaway.

Kop Chai Deu
Samsenthai Road.
Tel: (21) 223022.
A lovely outdoor food garden in the grounds of an illuminated (and nicely dilapidated) French mansion, this place serves simple snack foods, Korean barbecue and beer.

Malic Cybercafé
1 Luang Prabang Road.
Tel: (21) 222646.
Just like an English pub, only with better food and e-mail access (free drink included); can be very crowded, particularly when there is a football match on the satellite television.

Namphu Fountain Bar
Namphu Circle.
Tel: (21) 216775.
While offering one of the best locations among the city's drinking establishments, the Namphu serves truly mediocre food in a seedy environment.

Samlo Pub
Setthathirat Road.
Tel: (21) 222308.
An old-fashioned pub catering shamelessly to older male expats, complete with darts, snack food, and other entertainment.

Sala Khounta (Sunset Bar)
Fa Ngum Road.
A simple wooden structure in a row of similar establishments overlooking the Mekong, this bar is a popular place for Vientiane residents to meet after work, drink beer and watch the sun hit the horizon.

cosy little restaurant is hidden on a back road just opposite Wat Inpeng and offers traditional French dishes; the candlelit outdoor terrace is a nice touch. **$$**

Namphu
Namphu Circle.
Tel: (21) 216248.
One of the oldest upmarket establishments in the town, the Namphu has a good bar and serves excellent French and German food, including patés and some impressive desserts. Expats rave about the blue-cheese hamburgers. **$$$**

Santisouk Restaurant
Nokeo Khumman Road.
Tel: (21) 215303.
This place has been around since before the revolution, and was once known as Café La Pagode. It is known for its sizzling steak and *filet mignon* platters, good breakfasts and retro atmosphere. Also serves Lao food. **$**

German/Swiss

Europe Restaurant
Dong Palan Road.
Tel: (21) 413651.
Offers a full range of continental cuisine, including Swiss, German,

and Italian, and good wine in an elegant setting. The restaurant features solid service, complimentary appetisers, and a nice garden at the back. Order ahead for specialities like fondue and roast lamb. **$$$**

German Sausage Grill
Setthathirat Road.
An odd addition to the Vientiane culinary world, this German-owned outdoor stall serves fried *bratwurst*, frankfurters and meatloaf. **$$**

Weinstub (La Taverne Alsacienne)
Nokeo Khumman Road.
Tel: (21) 222997.
If you feel the need to pretend that you are not in the tropics, escape into this dark wood-and-stucco interior, which serves Alsatian cuisine, including smoked meats, potato salad and stews. The special platter of meats, paté and cured vegetables is great value. **$$**

Indian

Khyber Pass
071 Samsenthai Road.
Tel: (020) 511112.
Despite the fact that "Southeast Asian cuisine" is written on the sign

outside, this is an Indian/Pakistani restaurant which often feels like a family affair, as the owner's relatives always seem to be hanging around. **$$**

Nazim Restaurant
Fa Ngum Road.
Tel: (21) 223480.
Extremely popular with tourists and expats alike, the menu has a southern feel. Though the service can be slow and sloppy, and the interior is plain, the food is cheap and tasty, especially the vegetarian dishes. **$$**

The Taj
75/4 Pangkham Street.
Tel: (21) 212890.
The high end of Indian cuisine in Vientiane, the Taj offers North Indian curries, vegetarian dishes and tandoor specialities in a quiet, well-designed dining room. Try the daily lunch buffet. **$$$**

Japanese/Korean

Korean Restaurant
Nong Bone Road.
Tel: (21) 412662.
A simple affair with very reasonable prices and great service, this place serves Korean barbecue, authentic *kimchi* dishes and tasty meat stews. **$$**

Koto Japanese Restaurant
229 Nong Bone Road.
Tel: (21) 412849.
A small, *ryoka*-style restaurant and guesthouse serving all the usual Japanese favourites, including excellent *sushi*, *katsu* and *teriyaki* dishes. **$$**

Sakura Japanese Restaurant
Km 2, Luang Prabang Road.
Tel: (21) 212274.
By far the better of the two Japanese options, Sakura is perennially popular among Japanese expats for its high quality (and highly priced) *sushi* sets and *teishokus* and traditional Japanese ambience. **$$$**

Bakeries/Sweets

Le Croissant D'Or
Nokeo Khumman Road.
Tel: (21) 223740.
The best croissants and French pastries in Vientiane, and a nice

Vientiane Nightclubs

Broadway Nightclub
Lao Hotel Plaza,
63 Samsenthai Road.
Tel: (21) 218800.
In the basement of the Lao Hotel Plaza, the Broadway has good dance music, live and recorded.

Chess Café
Sakkarin Road.
Tel: (21) 217798.
One of the most popular spots for young singles, Lao and expat alike, this disco offers a mixture of live songs (including the obligatory *Hotel California*) and contemporary DJ mixes.

D'Tech Disco
Novotel, Samsenthai Road,
Tel: (21) 213570.
Standard nightclub and disco serving up expensive drinks and high-energy dance music.

Image Pub
Heng Boun Street.
A small nightclub with an innovative interior, a good bar and small dance floor on which you can boogie to contemporary Thai hits.

Marina Nightclub
Km 3, Luang Prabang Road.
Tel: (21) 216978.
Popular with the Vientiane high-school and college set; the DJ at Marina plays Thai and western pop hits accompanied by bright flashing lights and TV screens in a classy interior.

Viengratry May
Lan Xang Avenue.
Tel: (21) 215326.
A traditional Lao nightclub (a dance floor surrounded by sofas and tables) featuring live music; it is packed full almost every night of the week.

outdoor seating area just across from Wat Mixay. **$$**

Healthy and Fresh Bakery
14/4 Setthathirat Road.
Tel: (21) 215265.
The Canadian-owned Healthy and Fresh serves fruit, yogurt, granola, salads, quiches, soups and sandwiches; in addition there are wonderful (certainly fresh, but not so healthy) baked goods. **$$**

Liang Xiang Bakery
111 Chao Anou Road.
Tel: (21) 212284.
On the main street in Chinatown, this small shop sells pastries of an entirely different quality, but the prices are cheaper and the ice cream sundaes excellent. **$**

Nai Xiang Chai Yene
Chao Anou Road.
Just down the street from the Liang Xiang are the best fruit juices and shakes in town, complete with outdoor seating in this bustling neighbourhood. **$**

Paradice Ice Cream
Luang Prabang Road.
Tel: (21) 218599.
A French-owned ice cream parlour serving delicious fresh-fruit sorbets in homemade cones. **$$**

Scandinavian Bakery
74/1 Nam Phu Circle.
Tel: (21) 215199,
Fax: (21) 215231.
Run by a Swede, the bakery serves fresh bread, pastries, sandwiches, cakes and good European-style coffee (with free refills). Outdoor seating on the fountain circle is available, CNN is always on the satellite TV, and the message board will give you a taste of expat life in Vientiane. **$$**

Sweet Home
118/1-3 Thadeua Road.
Tel: (21) 314046.
A Chinese owned bakery, restaurant and guesthouse, Sweet Home serves cakes, pies, pastries, and ice cream. **$**

Xang Coffee House
0/32 Khun Bulom Road.
Tel: (21) 223173.
A mildly successful attempt at a funky urban coffee house, serving expensive coffee drinks, smoothies and desserts in addition to a full selection of sandwiches, snacks and salads. **$$**

LUANG PRABANG

Ban Lao
Ban Mano.
Tel: (71) 212438.
A solid restaurant serving mostly Lao and Chinese food. **$$**

Le Calao
Rim Khong Road.
Tel: (71) 212100.
An extensive western menu with Lao specialities. **$$**

Le Saladier
Sisavang Vong Road.
A French restaurant with good steaks and salads. **$$**

Luang Prabang Bakery
Sisavang Vong Road.
Tel: (71) 212617.
Café-style establishment serving excellent salads, quiches, sandwiches and tasty pastries. **$**

Price Guide

The following price categories indicate the cost of a meal for one without drinks:

$$$: Expensive: above $15
$$: Moderate: $2–15
$: Budget: under $2

Pak Huoy Mixay
47/5 Ban Vatnong, Savang Vatthana Road.
Tel: (71) 212260.
Probably the best place in town for Lao specialities, this place serves excellent fresh fish from the Mekong; they also have a barbecue out on the terrace. **$$**

Villa Santi
Sakkarine Road.
Tel: (71) 212 267, Fax: (71) 212267.
This place has connections with the last king's personal chef, so the food ought to be good; it serves both traditional Lao and French cuisine. **$$**

Visoun Restaurant
Wisunalat Road.
Tel: (71) 212268.

Some Lao favourites, but mostly Chinese food. Open from early morning to late at night. **$**

PAKSE

Champasak Palace Hotel
718 Ban Pra Bath Road.
Tel: (31) 212263.
A variety of Lao, Chinese and Thai dishes at reasonable prices, considering that it was a palace. **$$**

SAVANNAKHET

Haan Ahaan Lao-Paris
Tha He Road.
Tel: (41) 212792.
Offering a wide variety of Lao, Vietnamese and French food, this place even serves French wine. **$$**

Savanhlaty Food Garden
Si Muang Road, near the Sala Savanh Guesthouse.
Only open in the evening, this small night market serves a variety of Lao, Thai and Chinese dishes as well as the ubiquitous Beer Lao. **$**

TAAT LO WATERFALL

Heaun Mittaphap Lao-Thai
Tat Lo Resort.
A restaurant at the base of the falls serving excellent French and Lao food in a lovely atmosphere. **$$**

THA KHAEK

Floating Restaurant
Setthathirat Road.
Serves fresh fish dishes; shoes are removed people sit cross-legged at low tables in dining enclosures. **$**

Noodle Shops
Riverside, Setthathirat Road.
Large shade trees cover a few tables; a good place to sit and have a cold drink or order noodles from the across the road. **$**

Phavilai Restaurant
Kuvoravong Road, near the ferry landing point.
A good place for basic Lao cuisine and Chinese noodle dishes. **$**

Festivals

International New Year's Day
A public holiday celebrated with private *basi* ceremonies (*see page 316*) and, now, large parties.

Boun Pha Vet
During this festival, the birth story, or *Jataka*, of Prince Vessantara, the Buddha's penultimate existence, is told. It is regarded as an auspicious time for Lao males to be ordained into the monkhood. Temples in villages throughout Laos celebrate the three-day festival with sermons, fortune-telling, processions, and dance and drama performances.

Boun Makkha Busaa
This festival commemorates a central speech given by the Buddha to a group of enlightened monks in which he is said to have set out the first series of monastic regulations and predicted his own death. It is celebrated with chanting, offerings and candlelit processions at temples throughout the country.

Boun Makkha Busaa is celebrated with particular aplomb at the ruins of Wat Phu outside Champasak, where it includes elephant races, water buffalo and cock fighting, and traditional music and dance performances.

Vietnamese Tet/Chinese New Year
The Chinese and Vietnamese communities in Vientiane, Pakse and Savannakhet celebrate the lunar new year with private parties, firecrackers, parades and visits to Vietnamese and Chinese temples. In Vientiane, Chinese opera is often performed near the waterfront.

Lao Women's Day
Lao Women's Day is an official public holiday for women only, but as the absence from the office of nearly half the workforce makes getting anything done even harder than it already is, it has become a popular day for men to take off too.

Lao New Year
In Laos, *pi mai*, or new year, is the most fervently celebrated event of the year. It is a time when the entire country stops working and begins to party – only three days are official public holidays, but most Lao take the whole week off. Citizens remove Buddha images from the temples in order to clean them with scented water, and then take to the streets to dowse one another – an act of cleansing and purification in anticipation of the end of the dry season. Foreigners are a particular target. Offerings are made at temples, and small mounds of sand or stone are built in temple courtyards and (in Luang Prabang) on the banks of the Mekong River to request health and happiness in the new year.

In Luang Prabang the celebration is especially beautiful, and includes a large, colourful parade filled with traditional Lao costumes, music and dance, the procession of the sacred Prabang Buddha image, a Miss New Year beauty contest, and a handicraft fair.

International Labour Day
A public holiday occasionally marked by trade fairs and parades in the capital.

Boun Visakha Busaa
Starting on the 15th day of the sixth lunar month, this festival celebrates the Buddha's birth, enlightenment and passing away, and is marked at temples by ancestor worship, chanting and preaching, and candlelit processions in the evening.

Boun Bang Fai
The *bang fai*, or rocket, festival is a pre-Buddhist ceremony in which villages compete to produce the highest-flying homemade bamboo rockets, fired into the sky in order to celebrate fertility and call for the rains. The festival is filled with traditional music, dance, folk-theatre performances, processions, and lots of sexual imagery. Men and women alike will cross-dress and display oversized wooden phalli and small statues depicting sexual acts. Participants perform crude acts, it is said, in order to anger the gods, who retaliate by sending thunderstorms down on the fields.

The Lao take this ceremony very seriously: when it was banned by the Communists in 1976 the Party was blamed for that year's poor harvest – and the festival was reinstated the next year.

Boun Khao Phansa/Khao Watsa
This festival marks the beginning of the three-month Buddhist "rains retreat", during which time monks are forbidden to wander outside their temples and must spend their time in prayer and meditation. It is the traditional time of year for Lao men to enter monkhood temporarily. The *tak baat*, or alms-giving ritual, can be seen at temples around the oountry.

Boun Haw Khao Padap Dinh
During this festival the living pay respect to the dead, usually by making an offering at the local temple so that the monks will chant on behalf of the deceased.

Boun Ok Phansa/Ok Watsa
Ok Phansa marks the end of the monks' three-month fast and retreat during the rainy season. In Vientiane the water festival is quite spectacular; on the first day at dawn, donations and offerings are made at temples around the city; in

the evening, candlelit processions are held around the temples, and hundreds of colourful floats decorated with flowers, incense and candles are set adrift down the Mekong River in thanksgiving to the river spirits; the next day an exciting longboat racing competition is held on the Mekong.

November

Boun That Luang

This three-day religious festival is held in and around That Luang *stupa*, the national symbol of Laos, where hundreds of monks gather to accept alms and floral offerings from Lao and Thai worshippers alike. The festival includes a candlelit procession circling That Luang, a grand fireworks display, and an international trade fair near the temple that lasts for one week.

December

Lao National Day

This public holiday commemorating the 1975 Communist victory in Laos is marked by military parades and official speeches, and is probably the only time in Laos that you will ever see the hammer and sickle displayed in public.

Hmong New Year

Hmong New Year celebrations occur throughout the month on different dates in different villages, and include colourful displays of traditional costumes made from silk and silver jewellery. Performances of musical instruments like the *teun* flute and Hmong-style *khene* pipe are common. The Hmong also enjoy activities such as the *mak khon* cotton-ball throwing ceremony, ox fighting, spinning-top races and cross-bow demonstrations.

Shopping

Vientiane

A number of shops featuring Lao textiles, wood carvings, jewellery and traditional handicrafts have sprung up on the streets of downtown Vientiane. Upmarket boutiques selling home furnishings and interior designs cater to tourists and expats alike. The Morning Market on Lan Xang Avenue is certainly the best place to check for any of these items; it is open all day, and sells almost anything you could possibly want.

Textiles

Laos has a rich and now thriving textile tradition. Textile production has traditionally been performed exclusively by women, and the art is now being encouraged by the UN and other development agencies as a means of income for Lao women. Lao textile weavers use silk and cotton fabrics, and natural dyes of five main colours: black, orange, red, yellow and blue. Central motifs include animals such as the river serpent, dragon, deer and lion, and geometric symbols like triangles and spirals.

Main products include women's wraparound skirts, shoulder bags, shawls, shoulder sashes for men and women, and blankets. At specialised shops you can also find antique textiles, wall hangings and furniture coverings. Weaving styles and techniques, including even loom design, vary widely by region and ethnic group. In general Southern Laos is known for its *ikat*, or tie-dye, designs and foot-loom weaving technique, while in the north weavers use frame looms and the weft brocade style.

Art of Silk

Manthatoulath Road, Vientiane.
Tel: (21) 216167.
This shop is supported by the Lao Women's Union, UNICEF and SIDA as part of a project to provide jobs for Lao women. It offers silk and cotton weaving for sale, and the building houses a small textile museum.

Lao Antique Textiles

Stall A-24, Morning Market, Vientiane.
Tel: (21) 212381.
This small shop offers one of the best selections of antique textiles in Vientiane, as the owner draws upon her connections with dealers throughout the country. The authenticity seems reliable, and the owner is willing to bargain.

Lao Textiles

82/5 Nokeo Khumman Road, Vientiane.
Tel: (21) 212123,
Fax: (21) 216205.
The most famous textile shop in the country, Lao Textiles sells beautiful silk fabrics using a mixture of tapestry, brocade and *ikat* techniques, all hand-dyed with natural dyes. Housed in a French colonial mansion, it is run by an American woman, Carol Cassidy, who uses Lao textile patterns combined with her own contemporary designs. The pieces, including scarves, home accessories and wall hangings, are very expensive, as many end up in museums and private galleries overseas. The dyeing, spinning and weaving process can be seen at the workshop behind the shop.

Nikone Handicraft Centre

Dong Mieng Road, Vientiane.
Tel: (21) 212191,
Fax: (21) 215628,
e-mail: nikone@pan-laos.net.la
Popular among the Vientiane expat community, this large shop near the Russian Circus sells textiles and other Lao handicrafts.

Jewellery

Bari Jewellers

366-8 Samsenthai Road, Vientiane.
Tel: (21) 212680,
Fax: (21) 222974.
This Indian-owned shop sells

traditional Lao jewellery in addition to gold and silver pieces and precious stones.

Saigon Bijoux
367-369 Samsenthai Road, Vientiane.
Tel: (21) 214783.
A well-established boutique with an extensive selection of gold and silver; the jeweller can make new pieces as well.

Furnishings & Gifts

Couleur d'Asie
Khun Bulom Road, Vientiane.
Tel: (21) 223008.
This chic boutique sells beautiful home furnishings and interior design accessories with a Lao accent. Coffee, tea and snacks are served in the tea corner.

Ikho Boutique
Nam Phu Circle, Vientiane.
Tel: (21) 517 247.
One of the newest shops in the town, Ikho sells coffee-table books, picture frames and other trinkets in addition to original silk fashions.

Mandalay
François Nginn Street, Vientiane.
Tel: (21) 216886.
A French-owned boutique featuring Southeast Asian styles of rosewood, teak and ebony furniture.

Phai Exclusive Trading Co. Ltd.
Ground Floor, Lao Plaza Hotel, 63 Samsenthai Road, Vientiane.
Tel: (21) 218800.
An upmarket shop featuring expensive furniture, home accessories, jewellery and bamboo crafts.

Satri Soie Lao
79/4 Setthathirat Road, Vientiane.
Tel: (21) 219295,
Fax: (21) 219295.
A four-storey wonder of a shop offering antique textiles, traditional Lao jewellery, antique coins and silverware, contemporary furniture and reams of beautiful silk.

Yani
82/6 Setthathirat Road, Vientiane.
Tel: (21) 212918,
Fax: (21) 215802.
Small French–Vietnamese boutique selling Lao fabrics, contemporary jewellery and women's fashions.

Clothing

Kinnaly Fashion
397/6 Samsenthai Road, Vientiane.
Tel: (21) 223457.
Selling silk and cotton clothing for men and women, and cushions and curtains made to order.

Lao Cotton Co.
Luang Prabang Road, Vientiane.
Tel: (21) 215840,
Fax: (21) 222443.
A state enterprise formed in 1996, Lao Cotton offers lightweight good quality shirts and other casual wear, linens and decorative fabrics, and cotton-leather products like purses and handbags.

Galleries

Lao Gallery
092/2 Nokeo Khumman Road, Vientiane.
Tel: (21) 212943,
Fax: (21) 215628.
This small gallery showcases oils, acrylics, pastels and watercolours by Lao and Vietnamese artists.

T'Shop Lai Gallery
Wat Inpeng Street, Vientiane.
Tel: (21) 223178,
Fax: (21) 223178.
A French-owned gallery showing traditional and contemporary prints and paintings, stylish Lao-accented furniture and a few interesting antique maps of the region.

Sport

Badminton

This is one of the most popular recreational activities in Lao, badminton is played on courts throughout the country's larger towns – there are courts in people's backyards, hotel and guesthouse grounds, or just in the street.

Fitness Centres & Swimming

A number of hotels in Vientiane operate swimming pools and fitness centres that are open for public use for a small fee, usually between US$5 and $10 per day.

The Australian Embassy Recreation Club is private, and you need to be a guest of a member in order to use the pool.

Australian Embassy Recreation Club
Km 3, Thadeua Road, Vientiane.
Tel: (21) 314921

Lan Xang Hotel
Fa Ngum Road, Vientiane.
Tel: (21) 214102,
Fax: (21) 214108.

Lao Plaza Hotel
63 Samsenthai Road, Vientiane.
Tel: (21) 222741,
Fax: (21) 222740.

Novotel
Samsenthai Road, Vientiane.
Tel: (21) 213570,
Fax: (21) 213572.

Royal Dokmaideng Hotel
Lan Xang Avenue, Vientiane.
Tel: (21) 214455,
Fax: (21) 214454.

Taipan Hotel
2-12 François Nginn Street, Vientiane.
Tel: (21) 216907,
Fax: (21) 216 223.

Football

Increasingly popular as a national sport, football (soccer) matches can be seen every weekend at the National Stadium in Vientiane. Government offices, high schools, local companies, villages and even expat groups organise teams to compete. Interprovince matches are played on fields and stadiums in the provincial capitals.

Golf

Vientiane has two golf courses catering to the local business community, but owing to the limited facilities many expats head for a newer resort complex over the border in Nong Khai at weekends.

Santisuk Lan Xang Golf Course & Resort
Km 14, 555 Thadeua Road, Vientiane.
Tel: (21) 812022.
A nine-hole course with a club house that serves European food.

Vientiane Golf Club
Km 6, Route 13 South, Vientiane.
Tel: (020) 511314.
A nine-hole course with a small pro shop that sells and hires supplies, and a club house offering refreshments and a social atmosphere.

Victory Park Golf & Country Club
Nong Khai, Thailand.
Tel: (66-42) 407296, 407297,
Fax: (66-42) 407299.
A new complex featuring an 18-hole course, an extensive club house and a swimming pool.

Kattor

Kattor is a traditional Lao sport in which a woven rattan (or, increasingly these days, plastic) ball is kicked around a circle. The objective is to keep the ball in play, and players earn points for the style and level of difficulty of their kicks. These days, *kattor* is often played with a volleyball net, using the same rules as volleyball, except that only the foot and head can be used to direct the ball.

The skills of some incredibly agile players can be witnessed in public places in the late weekday afternoons in cities and towns throughout Laos.

Lao Massage

In addition to the services of major hotels, excellent massage parlours can be found in major cities around the country. Traditional Lao massage can be quite rigorous, so be prepared to have every part of the body worked.

Vientiane
Mixay Massage
73/3 Nokeo Khumman Road.
Tel: (21) 312628.
Traditional massage parlour.

Running

The Hash House Harriers is an international expat organisation founded by British civil service officers in Kuala Lumpur just after World War II, named after the restaurant where they would meet after work to drink and organise a run. The chapter in Vientiane holds a run each Monday at 5pm. The course, different every week, may take you through forests and rice fields in addition to dusty roads. Check the notice boards at the Scandinavian Bakery (*see page 329*) and Phimphone Market for the week's location. The run is followed by dinner and drinking.

By contrast, the Vientiane Bush Hash is a more intense affair (and not just the running) which meets every Saturday at Nam Phu Circle before heading off to a challenging running course outside the city.

Softball

Every Saturday at 3.30pm a group of Lao locals and expats (these days, predominantly Japanese) get together at the sports field near the US Ambassador's Residence in Vientiane to play a very informal game of softball. If you would like to be a spectator, telephone (21) 413273 or (21) 313848 for up-to-date details.

Sokpaluang Temple
Sokpaluang Road.
Traditional massage, herbal saunas, herbal tea.

Luang Prabang
Lao Red Cross
Wisunalat Road.
Housed in a beautifully restored Lao-French building, the Red Cross offers traditional herbal saunas and a combination Swedish-Lao massage.

Squash & Tennis

The Australian Embassy Recreation Club operates a squash court available to members and their guests. A number of hotels in Vientiane have tennis courts that are open to the public for a fee (*see Fitness Centres & Swimming*, page 324). A cheaper option would be one of the city's private tennis clubs, though they have none of the amenities of a hotel facility.

Sokpaluang Tennis Club
Sokpaluang Road.
Tel: (21) 312383.
Vientiane Tennis Club
National Stadium.

Thai Kickboxing

Thai kickboxing, or *muay thai*, has become quite popular among Lao, where it has risen above the rank of an amateur activity with the recent success of Lao boxers in international competitions. In the game any part of the body except the head can be struck or used to strike the opponent. Spectators often wonder at the remarkably high kicks to the neck, but the emphasis in *muay thai* boxing is on neither kicking nor punching – blows by the elbow and knee are the most effective way to win.

Language

What?	*nyang?*
Who?	*pai?*
When?	*vila?*
Where?	*sai?*
Why?	*ben nyang?*
How?	*nyow dai?*
What is this?	*an nee men nyang?*
Do you speak English/French/ Lao?	*wow dai baw passa ungkit/ falang/lao?*

Greetings

Thank you	*kop chai*
You're welcome	*baw pen nyang*
Hello	*sabai dee*
Goodbye (person leaving)	*la gon*
Goodbye (person staying)	*sok dee*
Nice to meet you	*nyin dee tee hu chak*
What is your name?	*chao seu nyang?*
My name is ...	*koy seu ...*
Where are you from?	*chao ma tae sai?*
I come from the USA/England/ Canada/France	*koy ma tae amelikaa/ungkit/ kanada/falang*
How are you?	*sabai dee baw?*
I'm fine	*sabai dee*
Excuse me	*kho thoht*

Directions/Transport

Where is ...?	*you sai ...?*
Toilet	*hong nam*
Restaurant	*han ahan*
Hotel	*hong haem*
Bank	*tanakan*
Hospital	*hong maw*
Police station	*satanee tamluat*
Left	*sai*

Right	*kua*
Car	*lot nyai*
Bus	*lot meh*
Bus Station	*satanee lotmeh*
Bicycle	*lot teep*
Aeroplane	*nyon*
Motorcycle	*lot chak*
Pedicab	*sam law*
Post office	*bai sanee*
Tourist office	*hong kan tong teeow*
Embassy	*satantut*

Shopping

How much is ...?	*tow dai ...?*
This one	*toh nee*
That one	*toh nan*
Money	*ngeun*
Change	*ngeun noi*
Price	*lakaa*
Cheap	*teuk*
Expensive	*peng*

Restaurants

Eat	*gin khao*
Drink	*deum*
Drinking water	*nam deum*
Cold water	*nam yen*
Ice	*nam kon*
Tea	*nam saa*
Coffee	*ka fei*
Milk	*nom*
Sugar	*nam tan*
Rice	*khao*
Fish	*bpa*
Beef	*sin ngua*
Pork	*moo*
Chicken	*gai*
Plate	*chan*
Glass	*jok*

Days & Time

Sunday	*wan ateet*
Monday	*wan chan*
Tuesday	*wan angkan*
Wednesday	*wan put*
Thursday	*wan pahad*
Friday	*wan souk*
Saturday	*wan sao*
Today	*meu nee*
This morning	*sao nee*
This evening	*meu leng*
Tomorrow	*meu eun*
Yesterday	*meu wan nee*
What time is it?	*chak mong laeoh?*

Numbers

Zero	*soun*
One	*neung*
Two	*song*
Three	*sam*
Four	*see*
Five	*ha*
Six	*hok*
Seven	*jet*
Eight	*baet*
Nine	*gao*
Ten	*sip*
Eleven	*sip-et*
Twenty	*sao*
Twenty-one	*sao-et*
Twenty-two	*sao-song*
Thirty	*sam-sip*
Thirty-two	*sam-sip-song*
Hundred	*loi*
Two hundred	*song loi*
Thousand	*pan*
Million	*lan*

Language Schools

A number of language schools in Vientiane offer short-term Lao language classes.

Centre du Langue Français
Lan Xang Avenue.
Tel: (21) 215764.

Lao-American Language Center
232 Phon Kheng Road.
Tel: (21) 414321,
Fax: (21) 413760.

Saysettha Language Centre
374 Nong Bone Road.
Tel: (21) 414480,
Fax: (21) 413382.

SDM Services
Sisangvone Road.
Tel: (21) 414383.

Vientiane University College
That Luang Road.
Tel: (21) 414873,
Fax: (21) 414346.

Further Reading

Where to Buy Books

Good reading material about Laos is hard to find, and Laos itself is often the last place to come across anything worthwhile written about the country. There are, however, some excellent volumes available on Lao history, politics, culture and religion.

Culture & Religion

Aspect du Pays Laos by Thao Nhouy Abhay (Vientiane: Editions Comité Littéraire Lao, 1956). An excellent overview of Lao culture and religion, written in French by a high-ranking official in the Royal Lao Government and member of the former royal family of Champasak.
Lao Textiles and Traditions by Mary Connors (Oxford University Press, 1998). The authoritative text on Lao textiles, this widely-quoted volume offers a clear introduction to history, style and technique.
Traditional Recipes of Laos by Phia Sing (Devon: Prospect Books, 1995). This book, written by the former chef and social director at the royal palace in Luang Prabang, contains recipes for traditional Lao dishes and Luang Prabang specialities.

History & Politics

Laos: Keystone of Indochina by Arthur J. Dommen (Boulder: Westview Press, 1985). An informative, if slightly out of date, look at the political history of the Lao People's Democratic Republic.
Lao Peasants Under Socialism by Grant Evans (Yale University Press, 1990). A harsh analysis of the Communist programme in Laos and the failure of socialism to better the lives of rural Lao citizens.
Politics of Ritual and Remembrance: Laos since 1975 by Grant Evans (Chiang Mai: Silkworm Books, 1998). An engaging work on contemporary Lao politics and society, full of provocative observations about the period between the pre- and postwar regimes, the exploitation by the party of religious symbols and traditions, and the challenges facing the current Communist regime.
Tragic Mountains: The Hmong, the Americans and the Secret Wars for Laos, 1942–1992 by Jane Hamilton-Merritt (University of Indiana Press, 1992). A former foreign correspondent in Laos, Hamilton-Merritt documents the Hmong struggle for freedom from the end of World War II through the Indochina Wars to the Communist takeover.
Stalking the Elephant Kings: In Search of Laos by Christopher Kremmer (Chiang Mai: Silkworm Books, 1997). An Australian journalist attempts, unsuccessfully, to uncover the mystery surrounding the disappearance of the royal family after the 1975 Communist takeover in Laos.
The Politics of Heroin in Southeast Asia by Alfred W. McCoy (Harper and Row, 1972). The classic work on the politics and economics of opium production in the region.
The Ravens: Pilots of the Secret War of Laos by Christopher Robbins (New York: Bantam Press, 1989). Great for military buffs, this entertaining and informative book relates the story of the American air war in Laos with an emphasis on tactical details.
In Search of Southeast Asia: A Modern History edited by David J. Steinberg (University of Hawaii Press, 1987). One of the most highly regarded introductions to the history of the region, this text includes limited material on Laos, but offers a discussion of the larger historical context from which the country has never been separate.
Buddhist Kingdom, Marxist State: The Making of Modern Laos by Martin Stuart-Fox (Bangkok: White Lotus, 1996). In this work on post-1975 Lao politics and history, the Eest's pre-eminent modern Laos scholar provides one of the clearest discussions of the emergence, victory and rule of the Pathet Lao.
A History of Laos by Martin Stuart-Fox (Cambridge University Press, 1997). The best English-language general history of Laos in print, this Stuart-Fox volume offers a clear and comprehensive – if a bit dry – narrative that focuses on the development of Lao nationalism in the years since World War II.
Shooting at the Moon: The Story of America's Clandestine War in Laos by Roger Warner (South Royalton: Steerforth Press, 1996). An enjoyable, though profoundly disturbing, history of the secret American war in Laos, using material gleaned from declassified US government material and extensive interviews with relevant actors.

Travel

A Dragon Apparent: Travels in Cambodia, Laos and Vietnam by Norman Lewis (London: Eland, 1982). A first-class travel narrative of the 1950s that gives you a sense of just how much – and how little – has changed in Indochina since the early postwar days.
Travels in Indochina by Henri Mouhot (Bangkok: White Lotus, 1986). Travel narrative documenting Mouhot's 1858–60 trip to Southeast Asia, which ended in the explorer's death in Luang Prabang.
The Lands of Charm and Cruelty: Travels in Southeast Asia by Stan Stesser (New York: Vintage Books, 1994). Originally published in The New Yorker, Stesser's section on Laos is now slightly dated, but it provides an entertaining and insightful look at Lao politics and society in the early 1990s.

Internet Sites

Visit Laos: The official website of the National Tourism Authority of Lao PDR, this well-designed site offers general information on Lao language, history and culture in addition to specific destination sections on each province. www.visit-laos.com

Laos – A Country Study: A US Library of Congress Federal Research Division site with comprehensive sections on the geography, history, politics and economics of Laos. lcweb2.loc.gov.frd/cs/latoc.html

Lao Embassy in the US: A good place to check for current information on visa regulations, this site includes helpful links to government departments and affiliated organisations. www.laoembassy.com

Vientiane Times: The website of the Ministry of Information and Culture's English-language newspaper, offering archived articles and good links to other news sources about Laos. www.vientianetimes.com

Mekong Express: A business-orientated site, edited by a Vientiane-based American publisher, which offers helpful information about Laos and the other states of the Greater Mekong Subregion: China, Burma (Myanmar), Thailand, Vietnam and Cambodia. www.mekongexpress.com

Lao Human Rights Council: To get a sense of the concerns of overseas Hmong and Lao about human rights violations in Laos and the country's current relations with Thailand and Vietnam, visit this unashamedly biased site. http://home.earthlink.net/~laohumrights/

LaoNet: One of the more interesting and well-designed among the deluge of Lao immigrant community web pages that have hit the web, this site caters for young Lao–Americans struggling with questions of identity, culture and heritage. http://www.global.lao.net/

Getting Acquainted

The Place

Area Cambodia covers an area of 181,035 sq. km (69,900 sq. miles) and is bordered by Thailand, Vietnam and Laos.

Capital Phnom Penh

Population 11 million

Language Khmer

Religion Theravada Buddhism (90 per cent); Cham Muslim; Christian

Currency riel (CR)

Weights and Measures Metric

Time Zone Cambodia is 7 hours ahead of Greenwich Mean Time (GMT).

Electricity The electric system runs on a 220V AC circuit, and most outlets use two-prong flat or round sockets. Bring any adaptors you think you might need.

International dialling code 855

Geography

Cambodia should be – indeed, by many accounts used to be, and may with luck become again – a tropical paradise. To borrow from a 12th-century inscription attributed to King Ramkhamhaeng of Sukhothai: "In the waters there are fish, in the fields there is rice." Cambodia is immensely fertile, capable of supporting with ease a population several times its current level. There is fruit aplenty, vegetables grow, quite literally, at the drop of a seed, and it is warm the year round, so heating and warm clothing are never a problem. And yet the very name "Cambodia" has become synonymous with hatred and murder. During the mid- and late 20th century the lush green rice paddies of this gentle land were first raped by B-52 bomber strikes

and then converted into the Killing Fields of the genocidal Khmer Rouge regime.

It will take a long time to overcome the results, but the process is now well under way. Cambodia is, for the first time for decades, at peace. The former leaders of the Khmer Rouge are either dead in prison, or have surrendered to the government. Major problems still exist – land mines, poverty, a devastated infrastructure, banditry and the scourge of AIDS – but Phnom Penh and the other major cities are slowly being rebuilt. Meanwhile the ancient monuments of Angkor have been declared safe and opened to international tourism, as have the hilltop sanctuary of Preah Vihear and many other historical sites throughout the country. Roads are being resurfaced railways upgraded, and international airports are functioning at Phnom Penh and Siem Reap. Hunger is a thing of the past, and everywhere Cambodians are eager to rebuild their ancient land as a prosperous new country.

Climate

Cambodia's climate is based on the annual monsoon cycle. Between May and October the southwest monsoon carries heavy daily rainfall, usually for a few hours in the late afternoon. The northwest monsoon, between November and March, brings somewhat cooler temperatures and lower rainfall. The coolest months are between November and January, though even then temperatures rarely fall below 20° C (68° F). The driest months are January and February, when there is little or no rainfall, and the wettest months are usually September and October. The best time to visit is certainly during the cool season; April, which can be furnace-like, is best avoided.

Government

The Kingdom of Cambodia is, as the name indicates, a monarchy. Samdech Preah Norodom Sihanouk,

King of Cambodia, was born in Phnom Penh in 1922, the most recent in a long line of Cambodian monarchs stretching back to the *devaraja* "god-kings" of Angkor. He succeeded to the throne in 1941 and ruled as king until 1955, when he abdicated but retained power as variously, prime minister, head of state and president. Ousted by the military coup of General Lon Nol in 1970, Sihanouk moved to Beijing and allied himself with the Communist Khmer Rouge. After the Khmer Rouge seizure of power in 1975, he returned to Phnom Penh, only to be put under house arrest by his erstwhile "allies". Following the Vietnamese expulsion of the KR in 1979, Sihanouk became president-in-exile of the anti-Vietnamese coalition forces, spending most of his time in China or North Korea.

In May 1993, following the elections organised by the United Nations', Cambodia officially became a constitutional monarchy with King Norodom Sihanouk as head of state. His son Norodom Ranariddh became "First Prime Minister", while the head of the former Vietnamese-backed regime, Hun Sen, became "Second Prime Minister". In July 1997 Hun Sen moved against Ranariddh through a coup d'état, forcing the First Prime Minister to take refuge in France. At the time of publication the situation remains unchanged, with Hun Sen in power and the nation effectively at peace. In recognition of this new stability, Cambodia was admitted to ASEAN in April 1999.

Religion

About 90 percent of Cambodians are Buddhists, followers of the dominant Southeast Asian school known as Theravada or "Way of the Elders". At the central core of Buddhist belief are the Four Noble Truths – that there can be no existence without suffering, that the cause of suffering is desire, that the elimination of desire extinguishes suffering, and that the way to extinguish suffering is the Noble Eightfold Path. For most ordinary

The People

Around 90 percent of Cambodian people are Khmer. Farming has long been their main economic pursuit, but in recent decades many have moved to cities such as Phnom Penh, Battambang, Kompong Som and Kompong Cham. The Khmers remain the dominant political and cultural section of the Cambodian population, though their economic influence is far less on a per capita basis than that of the ethnic Chinese and Vietnamese.

The second largest ethnic group in the country is the Vietnamese, of whom there may be as many as one million living mainly in the large cities and around the Tonlé Sap. A second distinctive national minority is the Cham Muslims, of whom there are around half a million. Originally migrants from Vietnam, the Chams live in scattered rural communities along the banks of the Sap and Mekong rivers, especially to the north of Phnom Penh. There are probably 400,000 ethnic Chinese in Cambodia, involved in business and living in cities and towns.

Other minorities include the Khmer Loeu or "Upland Khmer" – hill tribes of Mondulkiri and Ratanakiri, such as the Kuy, Mnong, Brao, Tapuon and Jarai, as well as the Pear and Saoch of the southwest. Collectively they probably number no more than 80,000 persons. Other smaller groups deserving of mention include small numbers of Thai and Lao living mainly along the frontiers with those countries, and a handful of economically significant South Asian Muslims, often from the former French enclaves of Pondicherry and Mahe in India.

Cambodians, however, Buddhist practice centres around gaining merit and acting in a correct and proper way. Simple and effective ways of achieving this are abstaining from taking life; refraining from drunkenness, gambling and sexual promiscuity; keeping calm; and honouring the elderly. A popular way of achieving merit is to give donations to temples and monks. Above all, honour and respect should be paid to the Buddha, the *sangha* (order of monks) and the *dhamma* (sacred teachings). Nearly all Cambodian Buddhist men become monks at least once in their lives. Women, too, may become nuns, though the percentage is lower and the decision is often delayed until middle or old age when the task of raising children has been achieved. Buddhism, like other religions, suffered badly under the atheistic Democratic Kampuchean regime, but today it is making a comeback.

Other religions include Islam, with around half a million Cham adherents and a handful of urban-based South Asians; Christianity, both Catholic and Protestant, chiefly practised by ethnic Vietnamese and Chinese; and Vietnamese religions such as Mahayana Buddhism and Cao Daism. Although most Cambodian Buddhists believe in locality spirits and other manifestations of animism, pure animism is by and large limited to upland minority peoples – Khmer Loeu – such as the Kuy, Mnong, Brao and Jarai of north-eastern Mondulkiri and Ratanakiri, and the Pear and Saoch of the southwestern Cardamom and Elephant mountain ranges.

Economy

Currently the greatest sources of Cambodian government revenue are logging exports and foreign aid, neither of which is sustainable in the long term. Rubber was once an important export, and may become so again. Fortunately Cambodia has major reserves of fishing waters and farmland, and in years to come the country is likely to become a major rice exporter like nearby Thailand and Vietnam.

As in Laos, heavy investment is needed in education, basic infrastructure and telecommunications before Cambodia will start to look attractive to foreign investors. The railway line between Bangkok and Phnom Penh is in urgent need of upgrading, as is the rail link between Phnom Penh and Kompong Som. In time, and given satisfactory investment, the latter should make Cambodian imports and exports less dependent on the Mekong River route through Vietnam.

Inevitably, the economic possibilities of the Mekong River have not gone unnoticed in Cambodia. As in other countries on the Mekong, various proposals have been made, mainly revolving around the establishment of hydroelectric facilities.

In the near future, tourism is likely to become a major source of foreign exchange. Current annual tourist arrivals are still lower than they were in the 1960s. But Angkor is one of the world's most remarkable destinations. As the opening of other historical sites continues, and as facilities for accommodation and transport improve, tourism is bound to become of central importance to the Cambodian economy.

Planning the Trip

Getting There

By Plane
Cambodia is served by nine regional airlines including its own national carrier, Royal Air Cambodge. These international flights land at Phnom Penh's Pochentong Airport and Siem Reap Airport. At the moment Pochentong is unable to accept long-haul flights, though there are plans to upgrade the airport. Regional airports serving international flights from Europe and the United States include Bangkok, Ho Chi Minh City, Kuala Lumpur, Hong Kong and Singapore. There are daily flights between Bangkok and Phnom Penh with Thai International Airways, Royal Air Cambodge and Bangkok Airways, and also daily flights from Ho Chi Minh City with Vietnam Airlines and Royal Air Cambodge. Singapore provides daily connections through Silk Air and Royal Air Cambodge. Less frequently there are flights from Vientiane (Lao Aviation), Hong Kong (Dragonair) and Kuala Lumpur (Malaysia Airlines). Bangkok Airways have daily flights to Siem Reap, although recently the government has shown its disapproval of this particular route, preferring foreign visitors to enter through Phnom Penh.

It is advisable to reconfirm all your flights 72 hours before take-off. A departure tax of US$20 is levied for all international flights.

By Road
There are two points of entry by road: Moc Bai on the Vietnamese border and Poipet on the Thai border. Usually the trip between Ho Chi Minh City and Phnom Penh takes five or six hours by taxi. If you are entering by this route make sure that you already have a Cambodian visa, and that your Vietnamese visa states clearly that Moc Bai is your exit point. You will be turned back if this is not the case. Similarly, if you are entering from Thailand you will need to get your visa in Bangkok. At the moment this is not a good way to enter as the roads leading to both Siem Reap and Battambang are in dreadful condition.

By Sea
It is now possible to enter Cambodia by boat. Speedboats travel between Ban Hat Lek in Trat Province, Thailand, and Koh Kong Town. You will need to have collected your Cambodian visa in Bangkok before embarking on this option. From Koh Kong there are boats twice daily to Kompong Som (Sihanoukville).

Entry Regulations

Visas and Passports
You must have a valid passport to enter Cambodia. Transit visas are available for most nationalities at Pochentong and Siem Reap airports; you need one passport photo and US$20. These are valid for 30 days and can also be obtained through the Cambodian Embassy or Consulate in your own country. If you are entering the country overland then a visa must be obtained in either Ho Chi Minh City or Bangkok.

Extension of Stay
If you are planning to stay longer than 30 days extensions are granted at the immigration office situated at 5, Street 200, Phnom Penh, Tel: (23) 424 794. A 30-day extension costs US$30. Some travel agencies in Phnom Penh will handle extensions for a small fee.

Customs
Travelling to and from the country is reasonably trouble-free (Cambodia wants to attract tourists and knows that fewer formalities will encourage

Cambodian Embassies Overseas

Australia
5 Canterbury Court, Deakin,
ACT 2600, Canberra.
Tel: (616) 273 1259,
Fax: (616) 272 1053.

Bulgaria
Mladost 1, Block Salvador Allende,
Residenz 2, Sofia.
Tel: (3529) 757 135,
Fax: (3529) 754 009.

China
9 Dong Zhi Men Wai Dajie,
100600 Beijing.
Tel: (861) 06532 2101,
Fax: (861) 06532 3507.

Cuba
No. 7001, 6ta AV. ESQ.
70 Miramar, Havana.
Tel: (537) 336 151,
Fax: (537) 336 400.

Czech Republic
Na. Hubalc1,
6900 Prague 6.
Tel: (422) 352 603,
Fax: (422) 351 078.

France
4 Rue Adolphe Yvon,
75016 Paris.
Tel: (331) 4503 4720,
Fax: (331) 4503 4740.

Germany
Groner Weg 8,
D53343 Wachtberg Pech, Bonn.
Tel/Fax: (492) 2832 8572.

Hungary
Rath Gyorgy 48, 1122 XII,
Budapest.
Tel: (361) 155 5165,
Fax: (361) 155 2376.

India
B47 Soami Nagar,
110017 New Delhi.
Tel: (9111) 642 3782,
Fax: (9111) 642 5363.

Indonesia
4th Floor, Panin Bank Plaza,
Jalan 52 Palmerah Utara,
11480 Jakarta.
Tel: (6221) 548 3716,
Fax: (6221) 548 3684.

Japan, 8-6-9 Akasaka, Minato-ku,
107 Tokyo.
Tel: (813) 3478 0861,
Fax: (813) 3478 0865.

Laos
Ban Saphanthong Nou,
ABP/34, Vientiane.
Tel/Fax: (85621) 314 951.

Russia
Strakopuchemy Per. 16, Moscow.
Tel/Fax: (7095) 956 6573.

Thailand
185 Rajadamri Road,
10330 Bangkok.
Tel: (662) 254 6630,
Fax: (662) 253 9859.

United States
4500-16th Street, N.W.,
20011 Washington D.C.
Tel: (1 202) 726 7742,
Fax: (1 202) 726 8381.

Vietnam
71 Tran Hung Dao Street, Hanoi.
Tel: (844) 825 3788,
Fax: (844) 826 5225.

more visitors). However, if you are bringing a video or photographic equipment make a list of it before you arrive at the customs declaration counter and be ready to show it to the customs officials. Hold on to this list for your departure. The duty-free allowance for each visitor is 1 bottle of spirits, 200 cigarettes and a reasonable amount of perfume.

Health

Unfortunately Cambodia's health infrastructure is still rather rudimentary, so it is advisable to take all the necessary precautions for a safe trip before you arrive. Immunisation is recommended for cholera, typhoid, tetanus, hepatitis A and B, polio and tuberculosis.

Malarial mosquitoes are widespread in the countryside, but as long as you are staying close to the tourist areas there should be no real problems. Nevertheless it is advisable to bring along some good mosquito repellent for use on exposed skin at night. After dark it

is advisable to wear long-sleeved shirts and long trousers.

Always try to avoid drinking water offered to you that has not come directly from a bottle. Bottled water is widely available. Ice should also be avoided. When travelling around the country, and especially walking, carry your own water bottle. Apart from being guaranteed clean, it will also help prevent dehydration. Heat exhaustion, salt deficiency and dehydration cause more problems than anything else, so don't forget sun block and keep drinking liquids.

It is recommended that visitors arrange a comprehensive overseas travel sickness insurance before leaving, including transport home if necessary. If you were to have a major health problem or an accident, it would be wise to consider evacuation to Bangkok where emergency health facilities are better.

Currency & Exchange

The Cambodian currency is called the riel, although you will have precious little use for it. Almost all

transactions in Phnom Penh, Kompong Som and Siem Reap are made in US dollars. With the recent Southeast Asian economic crisis the value of the riel has dropped, although at the time of writing it had remained stable for more than a year, with around 3750 riel to US$1. Notes come in denominations of 100,000, 50,000, 20,000, 10,000, 5,000, 2,000, 1,000, 500, 200 and 100. The import and export of riel is prohibited.

It is a good idea to have plenty of small denomination US dollars, as they are far easier to change than the larger notes. Thai baht is also widely accepted.

Travellers' Cheques & Credit Cards

Travellers' cheques are on the whole difficult to change upcountry. Most banks in Phnom Penh will deal with them, also a few in Siem Reap, but surcharges are very high. It is best to have US dollar cheques.

Credit cards are still a fairly new phenomenon in Cambodia. Most decent hotels will accept VISA and

MasterCard for hotel or restaurant bills. Cash advances on cards are possible in certain banks in Phnom Penh, Siem Reap, Battambang and Kompong Som. Most banks charge a minimum US$10 for transactions.

Photography

Film is readily available in Phnom Penh. Agfa and Kodak print films and Fuji slide films are all on sale, and there are plenty of places to get these films processed, although quality varies. Video film is also available at very reasonable prices.

Cambodians are usually quiet, polite people and on the whole do not mind being photographed, although it is always advisable to ask first. Show restraint when photographing people at prayer, and monks. Also, be careful when photographing soldiers or anything military. Children are a great subject for photography, and at Angkor there is no shortage of willing subjects.

What to Wear

Cambodia is hot all year round, so it is unnecessary to bring a lot of heavy clothes. During the monsoon season things get pretty wet, so do remember to bring along some lightweight protection against the rain. A strong pair of shoes is essential if you are visiting the temples at Angkor. You will find yourself doing a lot of clambering about. A hat is also recommended when visiting Angkor: much of the site is exposed, and it is amazing how quickly you can feel debilitated without something covering your head. When visiting temples and mosques men and women should dress appropriately: no skimpy clothing. Knee-length shorts are acceptable, but running shorts are not. To visit one of Phnom Penh or Siem Reap's more exclusive restaurants you will require reasonably smart clothes. If you do forget anything you believe is essential you will almost certainly be able to pick it up in Phnom Penh at one of the many very good markets.

Practical Tips

Media

Newpapers & Magazines

There is a variety of English- and French-language publications available in Cambodia. The *Phnom Penh Post* is a tabloid newspaper printed once a fortnight and sticks fairly solidly with events within the country. The *Cambodia Daily* is available every day except Sunday and will keep you up-to-date with world events, but in a rather limited format. The *Bangkok Post* and the *International Herald Tribune* are flown in daily from Thailand, and provide a far more comprehensive view of regional and world events. The French language *Cambodge Soir* is a twice-weekly tabloid. Young newspaper boys hawk all these publications around Phnom Penh.

There is a free monthly English-language magazine called *Bayon Pearnik* that contains listings of the latest restaurants and all the local events that might interest a visitor.

The following shops sell English-language publications:

London Book Centre
65, Street 240, Phnom Penh.
Tel/Fax: (23) 214 258
E-mail:
jwalterphysics@camnet.com.kh
Monument Books
228 Monivong Blvd, Phnom Penh.
Tel/Fax: (23) 426 586.

Postal Services

The postal service, like many other services, has improved over the last few years. Mail is forwarded via Bangkok and therefore arrives much more quickly than ever before. Costs are very reasonable: a 10-gram airmail letter costs between 1,800 and 2,400 riel. Postcards

are anything from 1,500 to 2,000 riel to anywhere in the world.
Ministry Of Posts and Telecommunication
East of Wat Phnom on Street 13, Phnom Penh.
Tel: (23) 426832,
Fax: (23) 426001.

Courier Services

A number of international courier agencies offer their services in Phnom Penh:
DHL Worldwide Express
28 Monivong Boulevard, Sangkat Sras Chark.
Tel: (23) 427 726.
Open Mon–Fri 8am–6pm, Sat 8am–5pm.
Federal Express (FedEx)
Transport Cargo (Cambodia) Co., Ltd., 19 106th Road, Sangkat Wat Phnom.
Tel: (23) 426 931,
Fax: (23) 427 633.
Open Mon–Sat 7.30am–5.30pm.
TNT Express Worldwide
139 Monireth Boulevard.
Tel: (23) 424 022,
Fax: (23) 880 661,
E-mail:
TNT-Logistics@bigpond.com.kh

Telecommunications

Telephone costs in Cambodia are high – international calls vary between US$5 and $7 per minute, domestic calls between US$1 and $2 per minute. The Ministry of Posts and Telecommunications has recently installed new phone boxes around Phnom Penh and other major tourist destinations. Many of these boxes take phonecards, and it is possible to telephone most countries directly. Cards for US$2, $5, $20, $50 and $100 can be purchased at the central Post Office in Phnom Penh and at various good hotels. Cards are available in Kompong Som (Sihanoukville) at the Camintel office on Ekareach Street.

Internet

There are two Internet providers in Cambodia at present, Camnet and

BigPond. They both offer full access, but can be quite expensive.

BigPond
56 Norodom Boulevard,
Phnom Penh.
Tel: (23) 430 000,
Fax: (23) 430 001,
E-mail: support@bigpond. com.kh
Full Internet access for US$60 per month, US$6 per hour.

Camnet
Full Internet access for US$25 per month, US$6 per hour.

Phnom Penh
LIDEE Khmer's Internet Café
Street 53 (just north of the Central Market).
Tel (23) 725 245
E-mail: postmaster@pic.forum.org.kh

FCCC Internet Café
363 Sisowath Quay.
Tel: (23) 210 142,
Fax: (23) 427 758,
E-mail: postmaster@fcc.forum.org.kh

KIDS (Khmer Internet Development Service)
47, Street 178 (across from the National Museum).
E-mail: kids@forum.org.kh

Siem Reap
Lotus Temple
In front of the Psar Tcha (New Market).
Tel: (63) 964 032,
Fax: (63) 380 065,
E-mail: lotus@worldmail.com.kh

Medical Services

Good hospitals in Cambodia are few and far between, and only a limited range of medicines is available. Minor ailments can be treated, but for anything major it would be best to go to Bangkok.

Calmette Hospital
Monivong Boulevard, Phnom Penh.
Tel: (23) 723 173.
The Calmette is the largest hospital in Phnom Penh and has some French staff.

Community and Family Medical Clinic
262, B Street 63, P.O. Box 2548,
Phnom Penh.
Tel: (012) 803 610.
Clinic run by Dr. Marissa Regino.

European Medical Clinic
Hong Kong Centre,
Sisowath Boulevard, Phnom Penh.
Tel: (015) 916 413,
Fax: (23) 364 656.

International Medical Institute, Dental Department
193, Street 63, Phnom Penh.
Tel: (015) 836 609.

Phnom Penh Medical Services
181 Norodom Boulevard,
Phnom Penh.
Tel.: (23) 300 311, 212 670,
Fax: (23) 212 842.

Raffles Medical Centre
Sofitel Cambodiana,
313 Sisowath Quay, Office No. 3,
Ground Floor, Phnom Penh.
Tel: (23) 426 288.

Ta Cheng Hospital
160 Mao Tse Tung Boulevard
(Issarak Street), Phnom Penh.
Tel: (23) 219 247.

Tropical and Travellers Medical Clinic
88, Street 108, Wat Phnom Quarter,
Phnom Penh.
Tel/Fax: (23) 366 302.
The best pharmacy in Phnom Penh is the **Pharmacie de la Gare**, near the railway station, recommended for all medicines.

Telephone Area Codes

Phnom Penh	23
Kandal	24
Kompong Speu	25
Kompong Chhnang	26
Takeo	32
Kampot	33
Kompong Som (Sihanoukville)	34
Koh Kong	35
Kep	36
Kompong Cham	42
Prey Veng	43
Svay Rieng	44
Pursat	52
Battambang	53
Banteay Meanchey	54
Kompong Thom	62
Siem Reap	63
Preah Vihear	64
Udor Meanchey	65
Mondulkiri	73
Stung Treng	74
Ratanakiri	75

Tipping

Tipping is not a traditional part of Khmer culture, but with wages being so low it is appreciated. If you feel you have been well treated a small token of your gratitude would not be out of place. Hotels and top restaurants will have already added a service charge to your bill.

Business Hours

Banks are normally open Monday to Friday, 8.30am–3.30pm. Government offices and official bodies open Monday to Saturday, 7.30am–11.30am and 2pm– 5.30pm. Post offices open Monday to Saturday, 7am–7pm. Banks, administrative offices and museums are closed on all public holidays and occasionally on religious festivals. Shops and supermarkets are usually open for longer hours.

Travel Agencies

Phnom Penh
Angkor Tourism
178C, Street 63,
Boeung Keng Kong 1.
Tel/Fax: (23) 362 169, 427 676
E-mail: AKTPNH@bigpond.com.kh

Apex
53, Street 63.
Tel: (23) 217 787, 216 595,
Fax: (23) 210 200,
E-mail: apexcam@camnet.com.kh
Will arrange tour packages to Angkor Wat, Battambang, Angkor Borei and other destinations.

Apsara Tours
8 Street 254, R. V. Vinnavaut Oum.
Tel: (23) 216 562, 212 019,
Fax: (23) 426 705, 217 334,
E-mail:
apsaratours@camnet.com.kh

Diethelm Travel
65, Street 240.
Tel: (23) 219 151,
Fax: (23) 219 150,
E-mail: dtc@bigpond.com.kh
Years of experience with travel to Southeast Asia.

Discover Cambodia Ltd
366 Monivong Boulevard.
Tel/Fax: (23) 212 280,
E-mail: discover@bigpond.com.kh

East-West Travel (Cambodia) Ltd
182A, Street 208.
Tel: (23) 427 118, 426 189,
Fax: (23) 426 189,
E-mail: eastwest@bigpond.com.kh
Another experienced company.
Eurasie Phnom Penh Travel
86 Pasteur Road.
Tel: (23) 427 114, 426 456,
Fax: (23) 725 008,
E-mail: et.tvl@bigpond.com.kh
Can arrange car hire, international
and domestic tickets and cruises.
Eureka Travel
158 Sihanouk Boulevard,
Lucky Complex.
Tel: (23) 218 9386,
Fax: (23) 218 939,
E-mail:
eureka.travel@bigpond.com.kh
Hanuman Tours
233, Street 13.
Tel: (23) 724 022, 428 883,
Fax: (23) 426 194, 427 865
E-mail: hanuman@bigpond.com.kh
KU Travel & Tours
200 Norodom Boulevard.
Tel: (23) 723 456,
Fax: (23) 427 425,
E-mail: ku@camnet.com.kh

Sampan Tour
43, Street 240.
Tel/Fax: (23) 211 906,
E-mail:
sampan.tour@worldmail.com.kh
Transpeed Travel
19, Street 106.
Tel: (23) 723 999,
Fax: (23) 722 533,
E-mail: transpeed@bigpond.com.kh

Siem Reap
Eurasie Phnom Penh Travel
Sivutha Road.
Tel.: (015) 634 014,
Fax: (63) 963 449,
E-mail: et.tvl@bigpond.com.kh
Lotus Temple
In front of Psar Thas Market.
Tel: (63) 964 930,
Fax: (63) 380 065,
E-mail: lotus@worldmail.com.kh

Banking and Finance

Phnom Penh
Angkor Bank
PO Box 1063, 116 Sihanouk Blvd.
Tel: (23) 721 527,
Fax: (23) 721 520.

Bangkok Bank
26 Norodom Boulevard.
Tel: (23) 725 398,
Fax: (23) 426 593.
Banque Indosuez
70 Norodom Boulevard.
Tel: (23) 428 112,
Fax: (23) 427 235.
Cambodian Commercial Bank
26 Monivong Boulevard.
Tel: (23) 261 208,
Fax: (23) 426 116.
Emperor International Bank Ltd.
230 Monivong Boulevard.
Tel: (23) 426 254,
Fax: (23) 426 417.
Ernst & Young
124 Norodom Boulevard.
Tel: (23) 211 431,
Fax: (23) 360 437.
Global Commercial Bank
337 Monivong Boulevard.
Tel: (23) 721 567,
Fax: (23) 426 612.
PricewaterhouseCoopers
41 Norodom Boulevard.
Tel: (23) 218 086,
Fax: (23) 428 076.
Singapore Banking Corporation Ltd.
68, Street 214, PO Box 688.

Foreign Embassies in Phnom Penh

Australia: 11, 254 Street
Tel: (23) 426 000/1,
Fax: (23) 426 003.
Bulgaria: 227 Norodom Boulevard
Tel: (23) 723 181/2,
Fax: (23) 426 491.
Burma (Myanmar):
181 Norodom Boulevard
Tel: (23) 213 664,
Fax: (23) 213 665.
Brunei Darussalam: 237 Street 51
Tel: (23) 211 457/8,
Fax: (23) 211 456.
Canada: 11, 254 Street
Tel: (23) 426 000/1,
Fax: (23) 426 003.
China: 256 Mao Tse Tung
Boulevard (Issarak Street)
Tel: (23) 427 428,
Fax: (23) 426 271.
Cuba: 98 Street 214
Tel: (23) 368 610,
Fax: (23) 217 428.
France: 1 Monivong Boulevard
Tel: (23) 430 020,

Fax: (23) 430 038.
Germany: 76–78, Street 214
Tel: (23) 426 381,
Fax: (23) 427 746.
India: 777 Monivong Boulevard
Tel: (23) 210 912/4,
Fax: (23) 634 480.
Indonesia: 90 Norodom Boulevard
Tel: (23) 217 934,
Fax: (23) 217 566.
Japan: 75 Norodom Boulevard
Tel: (23) 217 161,
Fax: (23) 216 162.
Korea (South): 64 Street 214
Tel/Fax: (23) 211 902,
Fax: (23) 211 903.
Laos: 15–17 Mao Tse Tung
Boulevard (Issarak Street)
Tel: (23) 982 632,
Fax: (23) 720 407.
Malaysia: 161, Street 51
Tel: (23) 216 176,
Fax: (23) 216 004.
Malta: 10 Street 370.
Tel/Fax: (23) 368 184.

Philippines: 33 Street 294
Tel: (23) 428 592,
Fax: (23) 428 048.
Poland: 767 Monivong Blvd
Tel: (23) 426 250,
Fax: (23) 426 516.
Russia: 213 Sothearos Boulevard
Tel: (23) 722 081,
Fax: (23) 426 776.
Singapore: 92 Street & Norodom
Boulevard
Tel: (23) 360 855/6,
Fax: (23) 360 850.
Thailand: 4 Monivong Boulvard
Tel: (23) 363 870,
Fax: (23) 810 860.
United Kingdom: 27-29, Street 75
Tel: (23) 428 295,
Fax: (23) 427 125.
United States: 27, Street 240
Tel: (23) 216 436,
Fax: (23) 216 437.
Vietnam: 436 Monivong Blvd
Tel: (23) 362 531,
Fax: (23) 362 610.

Tel: (23) 427 555,
Fax: (23) 427 277.
Standard Chartered Bank
89 Norodom Boulevard.
Tel: (23) 216 685,
Fax: (23) 216 687.
Union Commercial Bank Ltd.
UCB Building,
61, Street 130.
Tel: (23) 427 995,
Fax: (23) 427 997.

Kompong Som (Sihanoukville)
Canadia Bank
Ekareach Street.
Tel: (34) 933 490.
Cambodia Commercial Bank
Ekareach Street.
Tel: (015) 345 295.
First Overseas Bank
Ekareach Street.
Tel: (34) 933 694.
Pacific Commercial Bank Ltd.
Omui Street.
Tel: (34) 933 508.

Airline Offices

Aeroflot Airways
101, Street 128,
Phnom Penh.
Tel: (23) 362 008,
Fax: (23) 362 018.
Air France
Hotel Sofitel Cambodiana Business
Centre, Office 11,
313 Sisowath Quay,
Phnom Penh.
Tel: (23) 219 220, 426 426,
Fax: (23) 426 426.
Bangkok Airways
61A, Street 214,
Phnom Penh.
Tel: (23) 426 624, 426 707,
Fax: (23) 310 409.
China Southern Airlines Co., Ltd.
Suite A3, Regency Square,
168 Monireth Road,
Phnom Penh.
Tel: (23) 424 588, 424 577,
Fax: (23) 424 082.
Dragonair
19, Street 106,
Phnom Penh.
Tel: (23) 427 665,
Fax: (23) 427 652.
Kampuchea Airlines
19, Kossamak Street,
Phnom Penh.

Tel: (23) 427 868,
Fax: (23) 427 869.
Lao Aviation
58, Sihanouk Boulevard,
Phnom Penh.
Tel: (23) 216 563.
Malaysia Airlines
172–184, Monivong Boulevard,
Phnom Penh.
Tel: (23) 426 688,
Fax: (23) 426 665.
Royal Air Cambodge
24 Kramoun Sar Avenue and
Monivong Bridge,
Phnom Penh.
Tel: (23) 428 830, 428 831,
Fax: (23) 428 803,
e-mail:
Royal-Air-Cambodge@camnet.com.kh
206 Norodom Boulevard,
Phnom Penh.
Tel: (23) 428 891, 428 055,
Fax: (23) 427 910.
Thai Airways
19, Street 106,
Sangkat Wat Phnom,
Phnom Penh.
Tel: (23) 72 335, 722 470,
Fax: (23) 427 211.
Vietnam Airlines
35 Sihanouk Boulevard,
Phnom Penh,
Tel: (23) 363 396,
Fax: (23) 364 460.

Religious Services

Christian
**Cambodia District Church of the
Nazarene**
3A Monireth Road.
Tel: (23) 366 109.
**International Christian Assembly of
Phnom Penh**
20, Street 71.
Tel: (23) 426 057,
Fax: (23) 720 597.
Phnom Penh Presbyterian Church
131, Street 192.

Muslim
The International Mosque
Beside Boeng Kak Lake.
Nur ul-ihsan Mosque
Khet Chreng Chamres,
National Route 5, Km7.
An-Nur an-Na'im Mosque
Khet Chreng Chamres,
Route 5, Km8.

Getting Around

On Arrival

Pochentong Airport
Pochentong Airport is 10 km
(6 miles) from the centre of Phnom
Penh, and the journey into the town
takes around 20 minutes. Taxis can
be hired in front of the main
terminal building. Be prepared for a
lot of jostling from the ever-eager
taxi drivers. The average fare for
downtown Phnom Penh at the time
of publication is US$5. Motorcycle
taxis are also available for around
US$2. Some of the better hotels
offer a free limousine service to
and from the airport.

Siem Reap Airport
The airport for the Angkor temple
complex is 7 km (4.5 miles) from
the centre of Siem Reap, the
nearest town. Taxis can be hired in
front of the main terminal building.
There are plenty to choose from,
and most of the drivers will speak
some English. Some will offer trips
to the hotel of your choice for as
little as US$1 in the hope that they
can secure your custom over the
few days you are touring the
temples. Certain larger hotels have
their own courtesy buses for
collecting guests.

By Air

Royal Air Cambodge runs a limited
domestic operation. New ATR-72
turboprop aircraft are used for
flights between Phnom Penh and
Siem Reap, Battambang, Koh Kong,
Stung Treng and Ratanakiri. There
are at least four flights per day to
Siem Reap. Domestic airport tax at
Phnom Penh is US$10, and to other
airports US$4 at publication.

By Bus

There are three air-conditioned bus services now offering comfortable trips between Phnom Penh and the seaside resort of Kompong Som (Sihanoukville). The road to Kompong Som (Sihanoukville) is by far the best in the country. There are buses to Siem Reap, but as the road is still in poor condition it is a long and tedious journey. For shorter trips to, say, Oudong or Kompong Chhnang there are air-conditioned buses, and these roads are in better condition than those further upcountry.

By Train

Train travel in Cambodia is to be avoided. The rolling stock is old, slow and uncomfortable. Trains to Kompong Som and Kampot run every other day, and the journey takes approximately six hours. The other route runs to Battambang and also leaves Phnom Penh every other day. It takes 10 hours to get to Battambang. An interesting aside on the Battambang train is that the first two carriages are used as mine sweepers – travel on these is free, so they are always crowded.

By Boat

Comfortable modern boats now ply the routes between Phnom Penh and Siem Reap/Stung Treng. Boats for Siem Reap depart just beyond the Japanese Bridge at the northern end of Phnom Penh. Travelling up the Sap River you will pass Cham fishing communities, and as the boat enters the Tonlé Sap large Vietnamese and Khmer boat communities can be seen. The journey takes six hours and costs approximately US$20. There is a daily boat to Kompong Cham with a journey time of two hours. The fare is payable in riel (10,000) or US dollars ($3).

Public Transport

In Phnom Penh the "cyclo" or pedicab can be seen on every street corner. It costs a little less than a moto, but is not as quick. The cyclo has three wheels, and the driver sits behind you. Cyclos can be hired by the hour or by the day and are a great way to see the sights (not applicable to Angkor). Agree a price in advance.

Motorcycle taxis, or "motos", as they are known, can be found all over the country. The drivers are usually recognisable by the fact that they wear hats of some sort (crash helmets are not compulsory in Cambodia), and the motorcycles have larger seats than usual. Because taxis are sometimes hard to find in Phnom Penh the moto is the best way to get somewhere quickly. Many moto drivers speak some English. Expect to pay 1,000–1,500 riel for a short journey, and 2,000 riel for longer ones. Always agree the fare beforehand, and remember: hold on tight; there are lots of potholes in the roads. Motos wait at the airport, and this can be a viable way into town if you arrive alone. The fare is usually US$1–$2.

Taxis are available at Pochentong airport, but they can be difficult to locate quickly in Phnom Penh. For trips in Phnom Penh expect to pay US$5 an hour; outside the price is negotiable. There are plenty of taxis ready and willing to take you around the temples at Angkor. It costs about US$20 a day in and around Angkor and Siem Reap; you will have to pay double that to visit the temples further afield such as Banteay Srei. Another option for long-distance travel is a shared taxi. These vehicles ply the routes between Phnom Penh and all the major towns. The drivers will usually wait until they have filled the vehicle to overflowing, so this is not always a good way to travel, although it is a cheap way to get around.

Private Transport

Hotels and travel agents can arrange cars with drivers. It is still not possible to hire your own vehicle, which is probably a good thing as Cambodia's roads are dangerous. Motorcycle hire is now becoming possible outside Phnom Penh. In Siem Reap certain cafés hire them for around US$8 a day. In Phnom Penh the charge per day is slightly less.

It is possible to hire a car and driver in Phnom Penh from the following addresses:

Koum Sokly
79, Street 130.
Tel: (23) 720 147.
Las Sokha
26, Street 288.
Tel: (015) 910 685.
Nop Sovan
164, Street 369.
Tel: (015) 883 296.
Saren
19, Sothearos Boulevard.
Tel: (015) 915 428.
Sokha Car Rental
26, Street 288.
Tel: (015) 910 685.
Som Sokha
34, Street 93.
Tel: (017) 817 355.

Where to Stay

Good accommodation in Cambodia is limited to a few major centres: Phnom Penh, Siem Reap, Kompong Som (Sihanoukville) and Battambang. These days Phnom Penh offers a fine choice of luxury accommodation at very reasonable, prices considering their amenities. Mid-level accommodation can be found in abundance and is usually quite comfortable. At the lower end, guesthouses are now becoming more and more common, and some of them are really quite excellent. Compared with what was available a few years ago, the general situation in Cambodia has improved tremendously. Above the US$20 point all rooms will be air-conditioned and normally have satellite television and a refrigerator. Hot water is usually available, even in the cheaper guesthouses.

Hotel Listings

PHNOM PENH

Expensive

Diamond Hotel
172–184 Monivong Boulevard.
Tel: (23) 426 636,
Fax: (23) 426 635.
Centrally located in Phnom Penh's commercial district.

Hotel Le Royal
92 Rukhak Vithei Daun Penh (off Monivong Boulevard).
Tel: (23) 981 888,
Fax: (23) 981 168.
A luxury hotel with a history, it has seen a succession of foreign guests including journalists of the Vietnam War and UN aid workers after the defeat of the Khmer Rouge.

Hotel Sofitel Cambodiana
313 Sisowath Quay.
Tel: (23) 426 288,
Fax: (23) 426 290,
E-mail: sofitel.cambodiana@worldmall.com.kh
A splendid hotel overlooking the confluence of the Sap, Bassac and Mekong rivers. Contains all the amenities of a top modern hotel.

Inter-Continental
Regency Square,
296 Mao Tse Tung Boulevard (Issarak Street).
Tel: (23) 720 888,
Fax: (23) 720 885,
E-mail: phnompenh@intercontl.com
A five-star hotel with all the facilities of this worldwide chain.

Royal Phnom Penh
Samdech Sothearos Street.
Tel: (23) 360 026,
Fax: (23) 360 036.
South of the centre, with restaurants, pool and fitness centre.

Sunway
No. 1, Street 92,
Sangkat Wat Phnom.
Tel: (23) 430 333,
Fax: (23) 430 339.
A new hotel with a weekly *apsara* dance performance between November and March.

The Juliana Hotel
16 Juliana, 152 Street,
Sangkat Veal Vong.
Tel/Fax: (23) 366 070–72.
Away from the city centre, with health club, sauna and a good pool. Regards itself as Phnom Penh's premier business hotel.

Moderate

Beauty Inn Hotel
100 Sihanouk Boulevard.
Tel: (23) 721 616,
Fax: (23) 722 677.
Situated in the heart of Phnom Penh's business district.

Goldiana Hotel
10–12, 280 Street.
Tel: (23) 727 085.
An excellent mid-range hotel. Very popular with NGOs and consultants.

Holiday International
84 Monivong Boulevard.
Tel: (23) 427 402,
Fax: (23) 427 401.

A 24-hour coffee shop, casino and the Manhattan disco.

Renakse Hotel
40 Sothearos Boulevard.
Tel: (23) 722 457,
Fax: (23) 428 785.
Beautiful French colonial-style hotel superbly located opposite the Royal Palace and close to the riverfront.

Sheraton Cambodia Hotel
Street 47,
near Wat Phnom Penh.
Tel: (23) 360 395,
Fax: (23) 426 858.
Well located for Wat Phnom and the Sap Riverfront.

Tai Ming Plaza Hotel
281 Norodom Boulevard.
Tel: (23) 363 168,
Fax: (23) 363 010.

The following price categories are based on a double room in high season:

$$$ Expensive: $60 and above.
$$ Moderate: $20–$60.
$ Budget: $20 and under.

Budget

Mittapheap Hotel
262 Monivong Boulevard.
Tel: (23) 213 331,
Fax: (23) 426 492.
If you enjoy a game of snooker this is the place to come.

One Way Guesthouse
136 Norodom Boulevard.
Tel: (23) 12 849 871
E-mail: oneway@cambodia-web.net

SIEM REAP

Expensive

Grand Hotel D'Angkor
1 Vithei Charles de Gaulle.
Tel: (63) 963 888,
Fax: (63) 963 168,
E-mail: ghda@worldmail. com.kh
This fabulous hotel sits in the centre of Siem Reap opposite King Sihanouk's villa. It was recently refurbished by the Raffles Group and can rightly claim to be one of Southeast Asia's grandest hotels.

Moderate
Angkor Hotel
Street 6, Phum Sala Kanseng.
Tel: (63) 964 301,
Fax: (63) 963 302.
One of the newest hotels in Siem
Reap with an excellent restaurant
and a large swimming pool.
Angkor Village
Wat Bo Road.
Tel: (63) 963 561-3,
Fax: (63) 380 104.
Has its own elephants available for
rides.
Banteay Srei Hotel
St. No. 6, Airport Road.
Tel/Fax: (63) 913 839.
Good value considering all its
facilities.
Bayon Hotel
Phoum Wat Bo, Sangkat 4.
Tel: (63) 631 769,
Fax: (63) 963 993.
Great location in the heart of Siem
Reap old town, next to the small
winding river.
Nokor Kok Thlok Hotel
Airport Road.
Tel: (63) 380 200,
Fax: (63) 380 022.
Well located for the airport.
Ta Prohm Hotel
Near Old Market.
Tel: (63) 380 117,
Fax: (63) 380 116.
Very well situated next to the river,
in the old French quarter.

Price Guide

The following price categories are
based on a double room in high
season:

$$$ Expensive: $60 and above.
$$ Moderate: $20–$60.
$ Budget: $20 and under.

Budget
Freedom Hotel
Route 6, near Central Market.
Tel: (63) 963 473,
Fax: (63) 964 274,
E-mail:
freedom_hotel.boc@worldmail.com.kh
A very reasonable restaurant
attached to the hotel, and a free
pick-up service from the airport.

Garden Guest House
99 Wat Bo Road.
Tel: (63) 914494
This clean, friendly place is run by
the local doctor's wife.
Ivy Guesthouse
Between Ta Prohm and Psar Tcha
markets.
Tel: (63) 800 860,
Fax: (63) 380 065.
A good place to get local information.
Popular Guest House
33 Boboos Street,
Vihear Chin Village.
Tel: (015) 917 377.
A new guesthouse where all your
sightseeing trips can be organsied.

BATTAMBANG

Budget
Angkor Hotel
Street No. 1.
Overlooks the Sangker River.
Khemara Hotel.
Near the railway station.
All rooms have air-conditioning and
satellite television.
ODA Hotel
Route 5.
The largest hotel in Battambang.

KOMPONG SOM (SIHANOUKVILLE)

Moderate
Chhne Chulasa Hotel
Ekareach Street.
Tel: (34) 320 071,
Fax: (34) 347 501.
Located near the centre, not far
from Ochatial Beach. Apart from the
hotel it has very good bungalows on
offer.
Seaside Hotel
4th Quarter, Mittapheap Section,
Ochatial.
Tel: (34) 933 662,
Fax: (34) 933 640.
The largest and probably the best
hotel on Ochatial Beach.

Budget
Chez Mari-Yan Bungalows
Sangkat 3, Khan Mittapheap.
Tel: (34) 933 709.
Close to Independence Square,

near Victory Beach. Has a good
open air restaurant and the
bungalows provide a great
view of the ocean.
Marlin Semsak Hotel
Ekareach Street.
Tel: (34) 320 169,
Fax: (34) 933 480.
Located in downtown Kompong Som
with a good bar and restuarant. The
Australian owner offers excellent
deep sea diving trips.
Mealy Chenda Guesthouse
Mondul 3, Sangkat 3,
Khan Mittapheap.
Tel: (34) 933 472.
Overlooking Victory Beach.
Victory Hotel
Sangkat 2, Khan Mittapheap.
Tel: (34) 933 468.
Close to the main market.
Yang Chou
Street 19, Sangkat 2,
Khan Mittapheap.
Tel: (34) 933 522.
Centrally located with satellite TV;
pretty good value for what you get.

KAMPOT

Budget
Phnom Kamchay Hotel
Central roundabout.
Virtually the same as the Phnom
Khieu Hotel, but does have a rather
rundown bar attached.
Phnom Khieu Hotel
Central roundabout.
Well located for the central market
and the few restaurants in the town.

KOMPONG CHAM

Budget
Mekong Hotel
Overlooking the Mekong.
The rooms on the river afford some
wonderful views.

TAKEO

Budget
Phnom Sonlong Guesthouse
133 Sangkat Rokaknong.
Tel: (32) 931 271.
A marble building near the park.

Where to Eat

What to Eat

Cambodian food draws heavily on the traditions of both its Thai neighbours and its Chinese residents and is often referred to as Thai food but without the spiciness. The main national staple is, of course, rice, but French colonial influence has dictated that the Cambodians eat more bread than any other Southeast Asian country. Because of the country's incredible richness in waterways, freshwater fish and prawns are especially popular. Fresh seafood is also available from the Gulf of Thailand. Beef, pork, chicken, duck and other poultry are widely available. Soup is served as an accompaniment to nearly every meal.

Visitors upcountry will generally find themselves limited to Cambodian cuisine or to the fairly ubiquitous *baguette* and paté. In towns of any size Chinese food will also be available. In the west of the country Thai food is widespread, and in the east, Vietnamese influence is similarly common.

Cambodia overflows with fruit; among the most popular and widespread fruits are mango, coconut, rambutan, durian, mangosteen, starfruit, pineapple, watermelon and a wide variety of bananas.

Drinking Notes

Unlike Laos, Cambodia is not renowned for its beer. There's precious little in the way of draft, and the traveller is often limited to canned "Euro-fizz". International beers to look for are Carlsberg, Heineken, Tiger, ABC, Victoria Bitter, Foster's, San Miguel and Singha; local brands include Angkor, Angkor

Stout and Bayon. Draft Angkor is available in Phnom Penh, Kompong Son and Siem Reap. Imported wine – shades of the French colonial past – is similarly available in major towns, while domestic varieties promising strength and virility are widespread.

It is always best to drink bottled water in Cambodia. The traveller should also beware of ice of unknown origin, particularly up-country or at street stalls. Soft drinks like cola and lemonade manufactured by internationally known companies are available everywhere. Caution should be exercised with fresh fruit juices and sugar-cane juice, but cartons and cans of fruit juice, milk and drinking yoghurt are available in super-markets in the capital and at Kompong Som. Coffee – often very good – and tea are generally available throughout the country.

Restaurant Listings

PHNOM PENH

Khmer

An excellent area for authentic Khmer food can be found by crossing the Sap River at the Japanese Bridge. Here you'll find 5 km (3 miles) of restaurants on both sides of the road. Those on the right are on the banks of the Mekong River. There are many to choose from, but favourites include **Kos Kong**, **Rainbow**, **Heng Lay**, **Heong Neak** and **Monyrath**, all at moderate prices. Other good Khmer restaurants include:

The Crusty Rice Restaurant
Route 2, about 3km (2 miles) south of the Monivong Bridge.
Crusty rice and other Khmer specialities. **$**

Eid
327 Sisowath Quay.
Tel: (23) 367 614.
Serves some very good Khmer dishes as well as special Thai dishes prepared by a Thai cook. **$**

Li Lay Restaurant and Nightclub
321, Street 128 (Kampuchea Krom).
Tel: (23) 428 516.
A popular place with locals for

Chinese and Khmer food and dancing on the first floor. **$$**

Ponlok
319–232 Sisowath Quay.
Tel: (23) 426 051.
Overlooks the Sap River. There are two air-conditioned floors and a terrace. An extensive menu with many Khmer specialities. **$$**

Sorya Restaurant
Street 142,
Sangkat Phsar Thmey.
Tel: (23) 210 638.
Chinese and Khmer cuisine. Also serves Khmer, Chinese and Continental breakfasts. **$$**

Veiryo Tonle
237 Sisowath Quay.
Tel: (012) 847 419.
A selection of Khmer dishes with some international favourites on the menu. Overlooks the Sap River. **$$**

Price Guide

The following price categories are based on a main meal without drinks:
$$$ Expensive: above $20.
$$ Moderate: $4–$20
$ Budget: under $4.

Chinese

Tsui Hang Village Seafood Restaurant
290A Monivong Boulevard.
Tel: (23) 213 328.
Cantonese-style live seafood. **$$**

Hua Nam
753 Monivong Boulevard.
Tel: (23) 364 005,
Fax: (23) 364 454.
Reasonable Chinese fare, but quite expensive. **$$$**

Filipino

San Mig Pub & Restaurant
223 Sisowath Quay (Riverfront).
Tel: (23) 300 218.
Serves authentic Filipino dishes and also some international food. **$**

Thai

Baan Thai
2, Street 306.
Tel: (23) 362 991.
High-quality Thai food: all the well known Thai dishes served. **$$**

Chao Praya
Mao Tse Tung Boulevard (Issarak
Street), near Chinese Embassy.
Tel: (23) 722 754.
Probably the best Thai buffet in
Phnom Penh. **$$**
Chiang Mai
112 Sothearos Boulevard.
Tel: (23) 360 502.
Dinner specials every Friday and
Saturday, also an "all you can eat"
buffet. **$$**
Topaz
102 Sothearos Boulevard, near the
Hong Kong Centre.
Tel: (23) 211 054,
Fax: (23) 212 406.
Popular with Phnom Penh's
international community. Serves
excellent Thai and French food. **$$**
Wang Dome
35, Street 240.
Thai and vegetarian food. **$**

Vietnamese
The Globe
Sisowath Quay.
European and Vietnamese food
served in a beautiful old building
overlooking the Royal Palace and
the Sap River. **$$**
Le Tonkin
Samdech Sothearos Boulevard,
close to the National Assembly.
Fine Vietnamese cuisine in a
comfortable setting. **$$**

Indian/Nepalese/Sri Lankan
Banana Leaf
273 Sisowath Quay (Riverfront).
Tel: (23) 724 508.
Serves a wide variety of sub-
continental cuisine, including
dishes from Sri Lanka and South
India served on banana leaves. **$**
Gurka
130A Sihanouk Boulevard.
Tel: (012) 809 812.
Quality Indian and Nepalese food. **$**

Little India
6, Street 217.
Tel: (23) 217 313.
Excellent chicken tandoori, masalas,
and plenty of vegetarian dishes. **$$**

French
Au Pied de Cochon
No 156, Street 63.
Tel: (23) 219 395.
Traditional French food with French
chef. **$$**
Bayon Hotel and Restaurant
No 2, Street 75, near French
Embassy.
Tel: (23) 427 281.
Some of the best French food in the
town. **$$**
La Croisette
241 Sisowath Quay (Riverfront).
Tel: (012) 876 032.
One of the house specialities is
"Beef Skewers à la Corsaire"; they
also serves good breakfasts. **$$**
Le Deauville
Near Wat Phnom, Street 94.
Tel: (012) 843 204.
Traditional French grill-style cooking;
also has its own bar. **$$**
La Paillote
234, Street 130-53.
Tel: (23) 722 151.
A fine French restaurant with a good
wine list. **$$**
La Taverne de Rio
373–77 Sisowath Quay (Riverfront).
Tel: (23) 725 258.
Near the FCCC. Excellent pancakes
and other French specialities. **$$**
The Palms
36, Street 214.
Tel: (23) 720 273.
Excellent French food in a French-
style house. Monsoon disco on first
floor. **$$**
Café Monivong
Hotel Le Royal, 92 Rukhak Vithei
Daun Penh (off Monwong
Boulevard).
Tel: (23) 981 888.
An elegant brasserie with an
excellent daily buffet. **$$$**

Greek/Turkish
Athena
140 Norodom Boulevard.
Tel: (012) 802 330.
All the usual Greek favourites in
this bar and restaurant **$$**

**Istanbul Turkish Kebab
Restaurant**
315 Sisowath Quay.
Tel: (23) 368 590.
With a Greek restaurant in the
town, why not a Turkish one? Real
kebabs on the riverfront; the waiters
all in traditional Turkish clothing. **$$**

Mexican
The Mex
Corner of Norodom and Sihanouk
boulevards, next to the
Independence Monument.
Tel: (23) 360 535.
Serving reasonable Mexican/US
dishes. Open for breakfasts. **$$**

International/western
Ettamogah Pub
164B Sihanouk Boulevard.
Tel: (23) 211 084,
Fax: (23) 210 633.
A great variety of international
favourites, including the best fish
and chips in the town. **$$**
**Foreign Correspondents Club of
Cambodia**
363 Sisowath Quay (riverfront).
Tel: (23) 210 142,
Fax: (23) 427 758.
Great setting overlooking the
confluence of the rivers. In the early
evenings watch the fishermen on
the Sap River. Draught beer
available, and always an interesting
international menu. **$$**
Happy Herb Bistro
345 Sisowath Quay (Riverfront).
Tel: (23) 362 349.
Excellent pizza, probably the best in
the town. Also good salads. **$$**
Happy P.P. Pizza
157 Sisowath Quay (Riverfront).
Tel: (23) 300 157.
Pizzas, various pastas, vegetarian
lasagne, feta cheese salad, green
salad, steaks, pork chops, prawns
and much more **$$**
Le Rendez-vous
239 Sisowath Quay (Riverfront).
Tel: (015) 831 303.
Has a well-protected pavement area
to sit out on. A pleasant lunchtime
venue with an excellent selection of
soups and other snacks. **$$**
Red
56 Sihanouk Boulevard
Tel: (012) 831 407.

Quality western food in upmarket surroundings. **$$**

The Irish Rover
78 Sihanouk Boulevard, at the corner of Pasteur Street.
Food comprises typical British, Irish and Australian pub grub. The Rover claims to serve the best Irish coffee in Southeast Asia. **$**

Bakeries/Sweets
Apsara Bakery
146, Street 182.
Tel: (23) 364 159.
Comme à la Maison Delicatessen
20, Street 75.
Tel/Fax: (23) 360 801.
The Bakery International
80, Street 128.

SIEM REAP

Bakong Café
Sivutha Street, near Ta Prohm Hotel.
A cool place in the heat of the day. **$**
Banteay Srei
Airport Road, near the hotel of the same name.
A classy restaurant serving both Khmer and European favourites. **$$**
Bayon
Just off Route 6, almost opposite the Chivit Thai Restaurant.
Standard Khmer food and western breakfasts. **$**
Continental
Old French Quarter, by the river.
Tel: (63) 964 036,
Fax: (63) 380 065.
A varied European menu and one of the few places you can get Bayon beer. **$$**
Green House Kitchen
On the Airport road close to the Sivutha Street crossroads.
Thai and western food. **$**
Lotus Restaurant
In front of the Psar Tcha market,
Tel: (63) 964 032. **$**
Marquee
Sivutha Street, by the Swiss Centre.
Serves both Khmer and European food. **$$**
Monorom
Sivutha Street, close to the Zanzybar Pub.
Serves reasonably good Khmer food plus some Chinese dishes. **$**

The Angkor Wat Pub
Street 362,
near Psar Tcha market
Tel: (63) 964 032. **$**

KOMPONG SOM (SIHANOUKVILLE)

Angkor Arms
Ekareach Street.
Tel: (34) 812 695.
A traditional English pub with standard British and Australian bar snacks. **$**
Marlin Bar and Grill
Ekareach Street.
Tel: (34) 320 169.
Regular barbecues. **$**
Mealy Chenda
Near Victory Beach on the northwest side of the town.
Khmer and Thai food served. With its terrace this is a great place to sit and watch the sun go down. **$**

Cat House Tavern
Corner of Streets 118 and 51.
Tel: (23) 360 157.
Open until midnight. Pool tables and darts available. Usually busy.
Club 51
1, Street 51.
Tel: (012) 804 836.
Bar and restaurant.
DMZ Bar
83, Street 240.
Tel: (23) 210 083.
An expat-run bar and restaurant.
Elephant Bar
92 Rukhak Vithei Daun Penh (off Monivong Boulevard).
Tel: (23) 981 888.
A classy bar in the world-famous Le Royal Hotel. Dress accordingly.
Kim's Kiwi Bar
180, Street 130.
Tel: (012) 815 884.
Another bar and restaurant with reasonably priced food and beer.

Phnom Penh
Casa Disco
Hotel Sheraton,
Street 47,
near Wat Phnom.
Live bands feature regularly; gets very popular and crowded at weekends.
Martini
Off Mao Tse Tung Boulevard (Issarak Street), next to the Inter-Continental Hotel.
A large beer garden with snack food available, a very lively disco and open-air movies.
The Manhattan Club,
Holiday International Hotel,
Street 84, Monivong Boulevard.
Tel: (23) 427 402.
A huge disco complex that specialises in techno music and pulsating strobe lights. Phnom Penh's young élite flock here in droves. Open until 5am.
Mega Club
37, Street 282.
One of the longest-lasting and best known of the karaoke bars in town.

Siem Riep
Disco Bakheng
Next to the hotel of the same name.
Can get fairly wild later in the evening, lots of loud music. It is a favourite with the local Khmers.
Martini
At the southern end of the town.
Garden restaurant and bar area with a disco. Quieter than its namesake in Phnom Penh.
Zanzybar
Sivutha Street,
near the Bakheng Hotel.
Opens early evening and closes very late. A good place to finish off a long day.

Sihanoukville
Bobo Disco
Ekareach Street, opposite the Angkor Arms.
Raucous disco situated in the town centre.
Nasa Disco
Just off Golden Lion roundabout.
Apart from the disco there is the occasional live band.

Festivals

January

International New Year's Day
A public holiday celebrated with much the same zest as in other parts of the world.

National Day (7 January)
Celebrates the overthrow of the Khmer Rouge regime by the Vietnamese with Cambodian rebel assistance in 1978–9.

Chinese Lunar New Year and Vietnamese New Year (Tet)
Held in late January or early February. There are large communities of Chinese and Vietnamese in Phnom Penh and other cities. Many shops close for three days. While the exploding of thousands of firecrackers is banned in Vietnam, it is still possible to witness this spectacle in Vietnamese-settled parts of Cambodia.

Magha Bochea
Falls at the time of the January/February full moon; celebrates the gathering of 1,200 disciples to witness the Buddha's last sermon. Candlelit processions take place at temples where devout Buddhists circle the main temple building in a clockwise direction three times.

February

Friendship Day (1 February)
Celebrates the signing of the Friendship Treaty between Vietnam and Cambodia in 1980.

March

International Women's Day (8 March)
Parades with floats are held in many towns around the country.

April

Chaul Chnam or Cambodian New Year (13–15 April)
A three-day festival involving a lot of water-throwing similar to those in Laos, Thailand and Burma (Myanmar); also offerings are made at temples and houses are cleaned. This is a time of year for many overseas Khmers to return home. Children all over the country build miniature sand *stupas* in representation of Mount Meru.

May

International Workers' Day (1 May)

Genocide Day (9 May)
A solemn day commemorating the victims of the Khmer Rouge.

Bon Choat Preah Nengkal or Ploughing of the Holy Furrow
In mid to late May; this marks the beginning of the rice-planting season. It is usually led by the royal family and was originally a Hindu rite. The sacred oxen are offered various foods to eat by the Brahmin priests, and from their choice of beans, maize, rice etc. the bountifulness of the coming harvest can be predicted.

Vesak Buchea (full moon)
Commemorates the Buddha's birth, enlightenment and entry into *nirvana*.

June

Armed Forces Day (19 June)

July

Chol Vassa or Buddhist Lent
Traditionally the most auspicious time for young Cambodian males to join the monkhood. Originally men spent the whole of the rainy season (three months) in the temples, but these days it is more usual to only spend two or three weeks.

September

Bon Kathen or the end of Buddhist Lent
Exact dates are decided by the lunar calendar and can sometimes fall in early October. Offerings are made to ancestors and devout Buddhists, and those wishing to accrue merit give monks new robes and other offerings. This important festival lasts for 29 days.

Bon Dak Ben or "Spirit Commemoration Festival"
In late September; lasts for 15 days and culminates at full moon in Bon Prachum Ben which is the Cambodian equivalent of All Souls' Day. Ancestors are remembered and respects are paid with offerings at temples throughout the country.

October

Bon Om Tuk (Water Festival)
This celebrates the beginning of the dry season. The current in the Sap River reverses at this time of the year and begins to empty back into the Mekong. Boat races are held in Phnom Penh, and monks at many temples around the country will row ceremonial boats. Again this celebration is dependent on the lunar calendar and can sometimes fall in early November.

King Sihanouk's Birthday (31 October)
There is a spectacular show of fireworks by the riverfront at the Royal Palace when the sun has set.

November

Independence Day (9 November)
Marks independence from France in 1953 and Khmer National Day. There are grand parades in front of the Royal Palace with spectacular floats, marching bands and banners highlighting Cambodia's national achievements.

December

National Reconstruction Day (2 December)
International Human Rights Day (10 December)

Shopping

Tel: (23) 211 737,
Fax: (23) 211 738.
**Raksmey Angkor Silver
Handicraft**
11, Street 118,
Phnom Penh.
Tel: (015) 919 511.

Supermarkets

Bayon International Co., Ltd.
133 Monivong Boulevard,
Phnom Penh.
Tel/Fax: (23) 427 066.
Lucky Supermarket
160 Sihanouk Boulevard,
Phnom Penh.
Tel: (23) 362 313.
Ly Heng Thon
69, Street 118,
Phnom Penh.
Tel: (23) 426 764.
Sunrise Superstore
46–48, Street 130,
Phnom Penh.
Tel/Fax: (23) 427 050.
Yom Nam Supermarket
306 Kampuchea Krom Street,
Phnom Penh.
Tel: (23) 723 648.

Antiques

Antica Art & Souvenir Shop
245 Sisowath Quay,
Phnom Penh.
Tel: (23) 428 636.
Bazar
28 Sihanouk Boulevard,
Phnom Penh.
Tel: (012) 866 178,
e-mail: terry@bigpond.com.kh
Run by an interior decorator called
Jean-Pierre. Always has something
interesting on show.
Cambodia Souvenir Shop
36 Mao Tse Tung Boulevard
(Issarak Street),
Phnom Penh.
Tel: (23) 212 887,
Fax: (23) 212 992.
Khamara Souvenir
139 Monivong Boulevard,
Phnom Penh.
Tel: (23) 722 078,
Fax: (015) 914 029.
Nam-Hoa Fine Arts Shop
478, Street 128,
Phnom Penh.
Tel: (23) 366 636.
Rachana Souvenirs
6, Street 118,
Phnom Penh.
Tel: (017) 810 955.

Jewellery/Silverware

Khmer Angkor Silver Handicraft
6, Street 118,
Phnom Penh.
Tel: (017) 810 955.
Lucky Jewellery
9, Street 118,
Phnom Penh.
Tel: (018) 812 229.
Pailin Souvenir
36–38 Mao Tse Tung Boulevard
(Issarak Street),
Phnom Penh.

Sport

Diving

Condor Marine Dive and Survey
Ekareach Street, Kompong Som
(Sihanoukville).
Tel: (34) 320 169, (015) 831 373,
(012) 806 959,
Fax: (34) 933 480,
E-mail:
condor-marlin@cambodia-web.net
Condor can organise a variety of
dives and island cruises.
Naga Dive
Olympic Swimming Pool,
Phnom Penh.
Tel: (23) 365 102,
E-mail: nagadive@cambodia-web.net
A good place to learn to dive before
venturing out at Kompong Som.

Fitness Centres & Swimming

A number of the larger hotels in
Phnom Penh and Siem Riep operate
swimming pools and fitness centres
that are open to public use for a
fee, usually between US$5 and $10
per day.

Phnom Penh
Royal Phnom Penh Hotel
Samdech Sothearos Street.
Tel: (23) 360 026,
Fax: (23) 360 036.
Fitness centre and a large
swimming pool.
The Juliana Hotel
16 Juliana 152 Street,
Sangkat Veal Vong.
Tel/Fax: (23) 366 070–72.
Health club, sauna and a good
swimming pool.
Inter-Continental
Regency Square
296 Mao Tse Tung Boulevard
(Issarak Street).
Tel: (23) 720 888,

Fax: (23) 720 885.
Has a branch of the Clark Hatch
fitness clubs.

Siem Reap
Angkor Hotel
Street 6, Phum Sala Kanseng.
Tel: (63) 964 301,
Fax: (63) 963 302.
Large swimming pool.

Football

You will see people of all ages
playing football around the country,
even in the compounds of the great
temples of Angkor. The national
team now competes in most
international competitions, including
the Southeast Asian Games and the
larger Asian Games. Unfortunately
it has not gained much success;
but it does continue to improve.

Golf

Golf is still in its infancy in
Cambodia, but as in other Southeast Asian nations it appears to be
de rigueur for politicians, businessmen and top military officers to play
as often as possible.
Cambodia Golf and Country Club
35 km (22 miles) south of Phnom
Penh off Route 4, on the way to
Kompong Som.
Tel: (015) 363 666.

Motocross

Surprisingly, motocross has become
quite popular recently, and regular
competitions are held in Phnom
Penh's Olympic Stadium and in the
provinces. There are several training grounds where the young
practise hard for the competitions.

Shooting

**CPSA (Cambodia Practical
Shooting Association)**
35, Street 240/55,
Phnom Penh.
Tel: (012) 813 301,
e-mail: cpsa@cambodia-web.net
Marksmen Club Shooting Range
84 Monivong Boulevard,
Phnom Penh.

Tel: (011) 818 890, (011) 813 830,
e-mail: info@marksmen-club.com
Claims to be the world's best fully
automatic shooting range, and
offers the visitor the opportunity to
fire just about any weapon in the
modern arsenal of warfare, from
AK-47s through M16s to rocket-
propelled grenades and an anti-
aircraft gun. The authorities are
currently talking about closing down
this bizarre attraction.

Snooker

As in Thailand, snooker has
become a very popular pastime.
Many clubs in Phnom Penh offer
excellent facilities. Hourly rates are
very reasonable.
Lucky Snooker Club
405 Monivong Boulevard,
Phnom Penh.
Tel: (23) 722 788.
Mittapheap Hotel
262 Monivong Boulevard,
Phnom Penh.
Tel: (23) 723 331.
**Nanjing Video Games and
Snooker Club**
128, Street 128,
Phnom Penh.
Tel: (23) 428 192.
Sakura
30, Street 242,
Phnom Penh.
Tel: (018) 810 383,
Fax: (23) 427 362.
Sampeov Meas
18, Street 48,
Phnom Penh.
Tel: (23) 428 730.
The Sheraton Hotel
Street 47, near Wat Phnom Penh,
Phnom Penh.
Tel: (23) 360 395,
Fax: (23) 361 199.
Tony Club
99, Street 136,
Phnom Penh.
Tel: (23) 360 696.

Language

Khmer language

The Khmer language, also called
Cambodian, is a Mon–Khmer
language spoken by most of the
people of Cambodia, as well as in
parts of northeastern Thailand and
southern Vietnam. Khmer belongs
to the Austro–Asiatic group of
languages, which is widely spread
throughout mainland Southeast
Asia. Other languages in this group,
which is generally considered to
have been one of the earliest in the
region, include Mon, Vietnamese
and Wa. Cambodian is a non-tonal
language that has borrowed heavily
from Sanskrit, Pali, Thai, Chinese
and Vietnamese. It has been written
since at least the 7th century AD,
using a script derived from India. It
is widely accepted that Thai script
was derived from Khmer in the 12th
century.

Because of the difficulty of
learning Cambodian script, short-
time visitors to the country are
unlikely to achieve any great fluency
in Khmer – though the lack of tones
make it easier for westerners than,
say, Vietnamese or Thai. It is
relatively easy to acquire some
basic vocabulary, however, and any
such effort will be greatly appreciated by the Cambodians. English is
rapidly becoming the second
language, especially in Phnom
Penh, Siem Reap and Kompong
Som. Older people, particularly
among the élite, may speak French.
Some members of the
Sino–Cambodian community speak
Guoyu, or Mandarin Chinese. Thai is
widely understood in Battambang
and the west of the country;
similarly Vietnamese is widely
understood in the east of the

country. Cham, the language of Cambodia's Muslims, is an Austronesian language related to Malay – but virtually all Cambodia's Chams are fluent in Khmer.

Language School

Offering Khmer language classes:
Khmer School of Language
Behind the Chinese Embassy, 13 Street 475 (off Street 183 Mao Tse Tung Boulevard), Phnom Penh. Tel: (23) 360 938.
Ask for either Miss Addheka or Miss Leaksmy.

General

What	ey
Who	niak nah
When	bpehl
Where	eah nah
Why	haeht ey
What is this?	nih ch'muah ey?
Does anyone speak English?	tii nih mian niak jeh piasah ohngkleh teh?
I don't understand	k'nyom men yooul teh

Greetings

Hello	jumreap sooa
How are you?	tau neak sok sapbaiy jea the?
I'm fine	k'nyom sok sapbaiy
Good morning	arun suor sdei
Good afternoon	tiveah suor sdei
Good evening	sayoanh suor sdei
Goodnight	reahtrey suor sdei
My name is ...	k'nyom tch muoh ...
What is your name?	lok tch muoh ey?
Yes	baat
No	dteh
Please	sohm mehta
Thank you	orgoon
Excuse me	sohm dtoh
Goodbye	leah suhn heuy
Where are you from?	niak mao pi patet nah?
I come from ...	k'nyom mao pi ...

Directions/Transport

Where is ...?	noev eah nah ...?
Toilet	bawngkohn
Hotel	sohnthakia
Hospital	mon dtee bpeth
Police station	s'thaanii bpohlis
Turn left	bawt ch'weng
Turn right	bawt s'dum
Go straight on	teuv trawng
Car	laan
Bus	laan ch'noul
Bus station	kuhnlaing laan ch'noul
Boat	dtook
Train	roht plerng
Aeroplane	yohn hawh
Bicycle	kohng
Cyclo	see kloa
Post office	bprai sa nee
Embassy	s'thaantuut

Days & Time

Sunday	t'ngai aadteut
Monday	t'ngai jan
Tuesday	t'ngai onggeea
Wednesday	t'ngai bpoot
Thursday	t'ngai bprahoaa
Friday	t'ngai sok
Saturday	t'ngai sao
Today	t'ngai nih
Tomorrow	t'ngai saaik
Yesterday	m'serl menh
Morning	bpreuk
Afternoon	r'sial
Evening	l'ngiat
Month	khaeh
Year	ch'nam
Last year	ch'nam moon
New Year	ch'nam thmey
Next year	ch'nam groy

Shopping and Restaurants

How much is ...?	t'lay pohnmaan ...?
Money	loey
Change	dow
Cheap	towk
Expensive	t'lay
Market	p'sah
Bank	tho neea kear
Restaurant	haang bai
eat	bpisah
I want a ...	k'nyom jang baan ...
Drinking water	dteuk soht

January	ma ga raa
February	kompheak
March	mee nah
April	meh sah
May	oo sa phea
June	mi thok nah
July	ka kada
August	say haa
September	kan'ya
October	dto laa
November	wech a gaa
December	t'noo

Numbers

One	moo ay
Two	bpee
Three	bey
Four	buon
Five	bpram
Six	bpram moo ay
Seven	bpram bpee
Eight	bpram bey
Nine	bpram buon
Ten	dahp
Eleven	dahp moo ay
Twelve	dahp bpee
Sixteen	dahp bpram moo ay
Twenty	m'phey
Twentyone	m'phey moo ay
Thirty	saam seup
Forty	seah seup
Fifty	haa seup
Sixty	hok seup
Seventy	jeht seup
Eighty	bpait seup
Ninety	gao seup
Hundred	mooay roy
Thousand	mooay bpoan
Ten thousand	mooay meun
One million	mooay leeun

Ice	dteuk kok
Tea	dtae
Coffee	kahfeh
Milk	dteuk daco
Sugar	sko
Rice	bai
Fish	dt'ray
Beef	saich koh
Pork	saich jruk
Chicken	moan
Plate	jahndtiap
Glass	kaehu
Beer	bia

Further Reading

Where to Find Books

A great deal has been written about Cambodia, as a result of both the country's intrinsic interest especially the great civilisation of Angkor – and more recently, its bloody and tragic history in the latter half of the 20th century. Although extensive, the following bibliography is far from complete. Those requiring a more detailed listing and analysis are referred to Helen Jarvis's volume on Cambodia in the World Bibliographical Series (1997) for a more substantial treatment.

General Interest

The Land and People of Cambodia by David F. Chandler (1991). An excellent introduction to Cambodia by the foremost expert.
The Making of Southeast Asia by G. Coedes (London: 1966). A seminal account of the development of Indian cultural influence in Cambodia and elsewhere in Southeast Asia.
The Indianised States of Southeast Asia by G. Coedes (Honolulu: 1968). A more detailed and scholarly version of the above.
Swimming to Cambodia by Spalding Gray (1988). Strange, sometimes moving monologue by an actor and writer involved in the making of the film *The Killing Fields*.
Cambodia: A Portrait by John Hoskin & Tim Hall (1992). Excellent photographic account.
Phnom Penh Then and Now by Michel Igout (1993). As the name implies, photographic record of the Cambodian capital before and after Democratic Kampuchea.
Eternal Phnom Penh by R. Werly & T. Renaut (Hong Kong: Editions d"Indochine, 1995). Well illustrated, with introduction by Jean Lacouture.

Pre-Angkor and Angkor History

Society, Economics and Politics in Pre-Angkor Cambodia by Michael Vickery (Tokyo: Toyo Bunko, 1998). The definitive study of the period. Unlikely to be surpassed.
The Ancient Khmer Empire by Lawrence Palmer Briggs (new edition Bangkok: White Lotus, 1999). Somewhat dated, but well illustrated.
The Customs of Cambodia by Chou Ta-kuan (Zhou Daguan) (Bangkok: The Siam Society, 1987). A must – beautifully illustrated with photographs of contemporary scenes from the Bayon as well as 19th-century French engravings.
Reporting Angkor: Chou Ta-Kuan in Cambodia 1296–97 by Robert Philpotts (1996). The account of the celebrated 13th-century Chinese ambassador seen through contemporary eyes.

Post-Angkor History to the Colonial Period

Facing the Cambodian Past by David P. Chandler (Chiang Mai: Silkworm Books, 1996). Invaluable collection of essays and articles covering a period of Cambodian history which is usually ignored.
A History of Cambodia by David P. Chandler (Chiang Mai: Silkworm Books, 1998). The best introduction available to Cambodian history.
Travels in Siam: Cambodia & Laos 1858-60 by Henri Mouhot (1986). Fascinating 19th-century account by the Frenchman who "discovered" Angkor before going on to die tragically at Luang Prabang in Laos.
Cambodia After Angkor: The Chronicular Evidence for the 14th to 16th Centuries by Michael Vickery (Michigan: 1977). Serious study for the specialist.

Independence and the Vietnam War

Politics and Power in Cambodia: The Sihanouk Years by Milton Osborne (1973). Perceptive account of the mercurial King Sihanouk's role in the making and breaking of independent Cambodia.
My War with the CIA by Norodom Sihanouk (1973). An apologia, but not without merit.
Sideshow: Kissinger, Nixon and the Destruction of Cambodia by William Shawcross (London: André Deutsch, 1979). Seminal – can not really be beaten. This book deeply infuriated Kissinger.
River of Time by Jon Swain (London: William Heinemann, 1996). Magical account of this foreign correspondent's love affair with Vietnam and Cambodia. Swain was one of the journalists menaced by the victorious Khmer Rouge when they entered Phnom Penh – a chilling scene represented in the film *The Killing Fields* which, once seen, can never be forgotten.

Democratic Kampuchea

When the War was Over: The Voices of Cambodia's Revolution and its People by Elizabeth Becker (New York: Simon and Schuster, 1986). Becker was one of only three Westerners in Phnom Penh as the Vietnamese invasion of Democratic Kampuchea began. Contains memorable accounts of her interview with Pol Pot and of the murder of Scottish academic Malcolm Caldwell by unknown assassins.
Brother Enemy: The War after the War, a History of Indochina since the Fall of Saigon by Nayan Chanda (New York: Collier Books, 1986). The best book written about the Third Indochina War by the experienced and knowledgeable editor of *Far Eastern Economic Review*.
Revolution and its Aftermath in Kampuchea: Eight Essays by David P. Chandler & Ben Kiernan (New Haven: Yale University Southeast Asia Studies, 1983). Fascinating study for the specialist.
Pol Pot Plans the Future: Confidential Leadership Documents from Democratic Kampuchea, 1976–1977 by David P. Chandler, Ben Kiernan & Chanthou Boua (New Haven: Yale University Southeast Asia Studies, 1988). An amazing

book – check out the extraordinary Khmer Rouge "plans" to develop tourism ("must build hotels"), and the records of its illicit trade in endangered wildlife.

Brother Number One: A Political Biography of Pol Pot by David P. Chandler (Chiang Mai: Silkworm Books, 1992). Currently the most comprehensive biography of the Khmer Rouge leader.

Voices from S-21: Terror and History in Pol Pot's Secret Prison by David P. Chandler (2000). Accounts from the horrific DK prison of Tuol Sleng.

The Rise and Demise of Democratic Kampuchea by Craig Etcheson (Boulder: Westview Press, 1984). Excellent, balanced account.

Red Brotherhood at War: Indochina since the Fall of Saigon by Grant Evans & Kelvin Rowley (London: Verso Editions, 1984). Analytical study of the Third Indochina War by despairing progressive academics.

Cambodia 1975–1978: Rendezvous with Death edited by Karl D. Jackson (Princeton University Press, 1989). Moving account, well researched.

Genocide & Democracy in Cambodia: The Khmer Rouge, the UN & the International Community edited by Ben Kiernan (1993). Probably the best book yet written on the DK regime by the director of the Cambodia Genocide Programme at Yale University.

Cambodia: Year Zero by F. Ponchaud (New York: Holt, Rinehart and Winston, 1978). By the French priest who first opened the world's eyes to the hideous excesses of the Khmer Rouge regime.

Cambodia 1975–1982 by Michael Vickery (Sydney: George Allen and Unwin, 1984). Meticulously researched study of politics and policies in Democratic Kampuchea.

Personal Accounts

Children of Cambodia's Killing Fields: Memoirs by Survivors by Dith Pran (1997).

Beyond the Horizon: Five Years with the Khmer Rouge by

Laurence Picq (New York: St. Martin's Press, 1989). This is a special book. Picq, a French Communist, was married to a mid ranking Khmer Rouge cadre and voluntarily stayed on in Cambodia after the KR victory. She is the only Westerner to have remained in Phnom Penh throughout the Democratic Kampuchea years; as such her account is unique, though less informative than it might have been as she was never trusted by the top leadership.

The Death & Life of Dith Pran by Sydney Schanberg (1985). The basis for the film *The Killing Fields*.

A Cambodian Prison Portrait: One Year in the Khmer Rouge's S-21 by Vann Nath (Bangkok: White Lotus, 1998). The author was one of the very few prisoners who survived incarceration in Tuol Sleng – saved because he was an artist who could paint and sculpt busts of Pol Pot.

The Vietnamese Period and UNTAC

Land Mines in Cambodia: The Coward's War by Asia Watch Human Rights (1991).

Kampuchea Diary 1983–1986 Selected Articles by Jacques Bekaert (1987). Perceptive record of Cambodia's reconstruction after the DK period. To be read in conjunction with the following work.

The China–Cambodia–Vietnam Triangle by Wilfred Burchett (1981). Political analysis by a veteran Australian Communist.

War of the Mines: Cambodia, Landmines & the Impoverishment of a Nation by Paul Davies & Nic Dunlop (1994). Excellent black-and-white photography.

Heroes by John Pilger (1986).

War and Hope: The Case for Cambodia by Norodom Sihanouk (1980).

The Quality of Mercy: Cambodia, Holocaust and Modern Conscience by William Shawcross (London: André Deutsch, 1984). Critically examines collusion between the defeated Khmer Rouge, China and the west at the expense of Cambodia (and Vietnam).

Contemporary Cambodia

The Tragedy of Cambodian History by David P. Chandler (Chiang Mai: Silkworm Books, 1994). A perceptive and highly readable history seen from the perspective of the late 20th century.

Off the Rails in Phnom Penh: Into the Dark Heart of Guns, Girls and Ganja by Amit Gilboa (Bangkok: Asia Books, 1998). The title says it all – but there is more to Phnom Penh than brothels and marijuana.

Sihanouk: Prince of Light, Prince of Darkness by Milton Osborne (Chiang Mai: Silkworm Books, 1994). A dark portrait of the ruler.

Sympathy for the Devil by Nate Thayer (1999). Thayer is the *Far Eastern Economic Review* correspondent most closely associated with the Khmer Rouge leadership in its final days. He interviewed Pol Pot in the jungle at Anlong Veng before he died, and spoke at length with Ta Mok and other KR leaders.

Minorities & Religion

Islam in Kampuchea (Phnom Penh: NCUFK, 1987). Cambodia's Cham Muslim minority suffered horribly under the Democratic Kampuchean regime, as this book makes clear.

People & Society

The Warrior Heritage: A Psychological Perspective of Cambodian Trauma by Seanglim Bit (El Cerrito: Seanglim Bit, 1991). A fascinating interpretation of the various cultural and historical factors making up the Cambodian psyche from a Khmer scholar.

Cambodian Culture Since 1975: Homeland & Exile edited by May Ebihara, Carol Mortland & Judy Ledgerwood (1994). Useful for its insights into overseas Cambodian communities.

Arts & Culture

Angkor: An Introduction by G. Coedes (1963). Essential reading – insightful, informed and readable.

Angkor Cities and Temples by Claude Jacques & Michael Freeman (1998). Large-format picture book of great beauty and detail.

The Royal Palace of Phnom Penh and Cambodian Royal Life by Julio A. Jeldres (1999). The author is a long-time friend and confidant of King Sihanouk, and so well-placed to write this book.

Angkor: An Introduction to the Temples by Dawn Rooney (1997). The best written and most informative of the guides to Angkor currently available – this will be hard to beat.

Khmer Culture Abroad

Khmer Heritage in Thailand by Etienne Aymonier (1999).

Northeast Thailand from Prehistoric to Modern Times by Peter Rogers (Bangkok: DK Books, 1996). Information on the Suai or ethnic Khmers of the Thai provinces of Surin, Buriram and Sisaket.

Travel

A Dragon Apparent: Travels in Cambodia, Laos and Vietnam by Norman Lewis (London: Eland, 1982). Classic travel writing.

A Pilgrimage to Angkor by Pierre Loti (Chiang Mai: Silkworm, 1996). Reprint of the 19th-century classic.

Silk Roads: The Asian Adventures of Olara and André Malraux by A. Madsen (London: 1990). Malraux planned and executed the theft of several important pieces of sculpture from Banteay Srei in 1923. He was caught and held under house arrest in Phnom Penh until the stolen pieces were returned.

Derailed in Uncle Ho's Victory Garden by Tim Page (1995). Return to Vietnam and Cambodia by the renowned British war photographer, now recording his impressions of Indochina at peace.

Tiger Balm: Travels in Laos, Vietnam and Cambodia by Lucretia Stewart (London: Chatto & Windus, 1998). Excellent contemporary travelogue.

Linguistics

Introduction to Cambodian by Judith M. Jacob (Oxford University Press, 1990).

Seam and Blake's Phonetic English-Khmer Dictionary by Ung Tea Seam & Neil Blake (Bangkok: Asia Books, 1991).

Colloquial Cambodian: A Complete Language Course by David Smyth (London: Routledge, 1997).

The Cambodian System of Writing by Derek Tonkin (1996).

Filmography

Apocalypse Now (1979). Director: Francis Ford Coppola. Starring: Marlon Brando, Martin Sheen, Robert Duvall. Based on the novel *Heart of Darkness* by Joseph Conrad. During the Vietnam War an officer, Captain Willard (Martin Sheen), is sent upriver into Cambodia with orders to find and kill Colonel Kurtz (Marlon Brando). Before reaching Kurtz, Willard embarks on an odyssey of epic and surreal proportions. There are many memorable scenes, not least the helicopter attack on a Vietnamese village to the accompaniment of Wagner''s "Ride of the Valkyries".

Killing Fields (1984). Director: Roland Joffe. Starring: Sam Waterston, Haing S. Ngor, Craig T. Nelson, John Malkovich, Spalding Gray. A *New York Times* journalist and his Cambodian assistant are caught up in the Khmer Rouge revolution of 1975. The film portrays the horrors of the Khmer Rouge period with Dith Pran, played by Haing Ngor, trying to escape the country.

Swimming to Cambodia (1987). Director: Jonathan Demme. Starring: Spalding Gray. A monologue by off-Broadway performance artist Gray. An entertaining but bizarre account of his experiences during the filming of the *The Killing Fields*.

Internet Sites

The Kingdom of Cambodia: The official site of the Ministry of Tourism and probably the best source of information about the country. Has an excellent address listings link. It seems to improve monthly as more and more businesses within the country become aware of the potential of the web. www.cambodia-web.net

General Information on Cambodia: An excellent general site with a comprehensive business directory. www.cambodian-online.com

The Phnom Penh Post: All the latest English-language news on events inside the country. Also has a good address listings link. www.newspapers.com.kh/phnompe nhpost

Beauty and Darkness: Cambodia in Modern History: Documents, essays, oral histories and photos relating to the recent history of Cambodia, with an emphasis on the Khmer Rouge period. http://users.aol.com/cambodia

Phnom Penh Daily: Up-to-date news and information, including links to various tourism related sites. www.phnompenhdaily.com

Cambodian Information Directory Homepage: A news and information directory with a variety of links to all things relating to Cambodia, including history, art, films, songs, books, the economy, culture etc. www.khmernet.com

Khmer Buddhism: Everything you need to know about Cambodian Theravada Buddhism www.khmerbuddhist.org

Specialist books on Cambodia: White Lotus Press based in Bangkok carries new and out-of-print books about Cambodia. www.thailine.com/lotus/linguist

Contemporary Art: A virtual art gallery for contemporary art from Thailand, Vietnam and Burma (Myanmar), and Cambodia. www.thavibu.com

Visiting Cambodia: Two related sites run by Diethelm Travel (a travel agency specialising in tours to all parts of Southeast Asia) are exceptionally informative. www.asiatour.com and www.diethelm-travel.com/cambodia

Cambodian Genocide Progamme: A regularly updated site covering the

political and criminal history of the Khmer Rouge in Democratic Kampuchea and afterwards. Researched by dedicated professionals under the aegis of Professor Ben Kiernan of Yale University.
www.yale.edu/cgp

Cambodian Classical Dance: An interesting introduction to the classical arts of Cambodia. Covers the Cambodian version of the *Ramayana,* known as the *Reamker.*
www.netaxs.com/tskramer/dance

Andy Brouwer's Cambodia Tales: This constantly updated site is the triumph of Andy Brouwer, a very keen Cambodia enthusiast. Personal experiences interspersed with interviews, the latest news and an excellent bibliography.
www.btinternet.com/~andy.brouwer

Other Insight Guides

Celebrating 30 years of travel guide publishing, *Insight Guides* remain the most complete travel guides on the market. Famous for their stunning photography, *Insight Guides* are a great appetite whetter, a practical on-the-spot companion and a superb souvenir.

Insight Guides covering the Southeast Asia region include titles on Bali; Bangkok; Burma (Myanmar); Indonesia; Java; Malaysia; Philippines; Southeast Asia; Southeast Asia Wildlife;

Thailand and Vietnam.
Insight Pocket Guides replace the need for a tour guide – *Pocket Guides* advise on the best and most rewarding things to see. Including up to 20 tailor-made itineraries exploring the main attractions, each guide contains a detailed pull-out map which can be used with the itineraries or independently.

Insight Pocket Guides to Southeast Asia include the following titles: Bali; Bangkok; Chiang Mai; Jakarta; Kuala Lumpur; Phuket; Sabah; Thailand and Vietnam.

Insight Compact Guides are portable and easy-to-use quick reference books – now offering 120 titles. The text, photographs and maps are all carefully cross-referenced, making *Compact Guides* ideal for on-the-spot use. Modestly priced yet comprehensive, *Compact Guide* titles to Southeast Asia include Bali; Bangkok; Cambodia; Chiang Mai; Laos; Manila; Phuket; Thailand and Vietnam.

Insight FlexiMaps are the essential travel map guides – laminated, easy-to-fold, weather and tear proof with an informative easy-to-read approach. They are wipe clean, colour maps which are light to carry and include the top 10 tourist attractions.

There are *FlexiMaps* to Bali; Bangkok; Phuket and Thailand.

ART & PHOTO CREDITS

Picture Spreads

Index

Numbers in italics refer to photographs

> ❝ I was first drawn to the Insight Guides by the excellent "Nepal" volume. I can think of no book which so effectively captures the essence of a country. Out of these pages leaped the Nepal I know – the captivating charm of a people and their culture. I've since discovered and enjoyed the entire Insight Guide series. Each volume deals with a country in the same sensitive depth, which is nowhere more evident than in the superb photography. ❞

Sir Edmund Hillary

☀ INSIGHT GUIDES

The world's largest collection of visual travel guides

Insight Guides – the Classic Series
that puts you in the picture

Alaska	China	Hong Kong	Morocco	Singapore
Alsace	Cologne	Hungary	Moscow	South Africa
Amazon Wildlife	Continental Europe		Munich	South America
American Southwest	Corsica	Iceland		South Tyrol
Amsterdam	Costa Rica	India	Namibia	Southeast Asia
Argentina	Crete	India's Western	Native America	Wildlife
Asia, East	Crossing America	Himalayas	Nepal	Spain
Asia, South	Cuba	India, South	Netherlands	Spain, Northern
Asia, Southeast	Cyprus	Indian Wildlife	New England	Spain, Southern
Athens	Czech & Slovak	Indonesia	New Orleans	Sri Lanka
Atlanta	Republic	Ireland	New York City	Sweden
Australia		Israel	New York State	Switzerland
Austria	Delhi, Jaipur & Agra	Istanbul	New Zealand	Sydney
	Denmark	Italy	Nile	Syria & Lebanon
Bahamas	Dominican Republic	Italy, Northern	Normandy	
Bali	Dresden		Norway	Taiwan
Baltic States	Dublin	Jamaica		Tenerife
Bangkok	Düsseldorf	Japan	Old South	Texas
Barbados		Java	Oman & The UAE	Thailand
Barcelona	East African Wildlife	Jerusalem	Oxford	Tokyo
Bay of Naples	Eastern Europe	Jordan		Trinidad & Tobago
Beijing	Ecuador		Pacific Northwest	Tunisia
Belgium	Edinburgh	Kathmandu	Pakistan	Turkey
Belize	Egypt	Kenya	Paris	Turkish Coast
Berlin	England	Korea	Peru	Tuscany
Bermuda			Philadelphia	
Boston	Finland	Laos & Cambodia	Philippines	Umbria
Brazil	Florence	Lisbon	Poland	USA: Eastern States
Brittany	Florida	Loire Valley	Portugal	USA: Western States
Brussels	France	London	Prague	US National Parks:
Budapest	Frankfurt	Los Angeles	Provence	East
Buenos Aires	French Riviera		Puerto Rico	US National Parks:
Burgundy		Madeira		West
Burma (Myanmar)	Gambia & Senegal	Madrid	Rajasthan	
	Germany	Malaysia	Rhine	Vancouver
Cairo	Glasgow	Mallorca & Ibiza	Rio de Janeiro	Venezuela
Calcutta	Gran Canaria	Malta	Rockies	Venice
California	Great Barrier Reef	Marine Life ot the	Rome	Vienna
California, Northern	Great Britain	South China Sea	Russia	Vietnam
California, Southern	Greece	Mauritius &		
Canada	Greek Islands	Seychelles	St. Petersburg	Wales
Caribbean	Guatemala, Belize &	Melbourne	San Francisco	Washington DC
Catalonia	Yucatán	Mexico City	Sardinia	Waterways of Europe
Channel Islands		Mexico	Scotland	Wild West
Chicago	Hamburg	Miami	Seattle	
Chile	Hawaii	Montreal	Sicily	Yemen

Complementing the above titles are 120 easy-to-carry Insight Compact Guides, 120 Insight Pocket Guides with full-size pull-out maps and more than 60 laminated easy-fold Insight Maps